The Self and Social Relationships

The Self and Social Relationships

Edited by
Joanne V. Wood
Abraham Tesser
John G. Holmes

Routledge
Taylor & Francis Group
LONDON AND NEW YORK

First published in 2008 by Psychology Press

Published 2016 by Routledge
2 Park Square, Milton Park, Abingdon, Oxfordshire OX14 4RN
711 Third Avenue, New York, NY 10017, USA

First issued in paperback 2016

Routledge is an imprint of the Taylor & Francis Group, an informa business

Copyright © 2008 by Taylor & Francis

Typeset by RefineCatch Limited, Bungay, Suffolk, UK
Cover design by Lisa Dynan

Library of Congress Cataloging-in-Publication Data
The self and social relationships / edited by Joanne V. Wood, Abraham Tesser, John G. Holmes.
    p. cm.
    "Sponsored by the International Society for Self and Identity (ISSI)."
    Includes bibliographical references and index.
    ISBN 978-1-84169-488-7 (hardcover : alk. paper)   1. Self—Social aspects.   2. Self.
3. Interpersonal relations.   I. Wood, Joanne V.   II. Tesser, Abraham.   III. Holmes, John G.
(John Grenville), 1945–
    BF697.5.S65S453 2007
    302′.12–dc22   2007021215

ISBN: 978-1-138-00629-4 (pbk)
ISBN: 978-1-84169-488-7 (hbk)

Contents

About the Editors

Joanne V. Wood, since completing her Ph.D. in clinical psychology at the University of California, Los Angeles, has held faculty positions at the State University of New York at Stony Brook and at the University of Waterloo. She has served as an Associate Editor of *Personality and Social Psychology Bulletin* and on the editorial boards for *Journal of Personality and Social Psychology*, *Journal of Experimental Social Psychology*, *Personality and Social Psychology Bulletin*, and *Self and Identity*. Wood's research has been funded by the National Institute of Mental Health in the U.S. and the Social Sciences and Humanities Research Council in Canada. Her recent publications concern emotion regulation, social acceptance, social comparison, and mechanisms underlying the maintenance of self-esteem.

Abraham Tesser completed a Ph.D. in social psychology (Purdue University, 1967) and took a faculty position at the University of Georgia where he is currently Research Professor Emeritus. He has been a visiting Fellow at Yale University, Princeton University, the Center for Advanced Study in the Behavioral Sciences, and The Ohio State University. From 1984 until 1994 he was Director of the University of Georgia's interdisciplinary Institute for Behavioral Research. Tesser was an Associate Editor of *Personality and Social Psychology Bulletin* and an Editor of the *Journal of Personality and Social Psychology*. He chaired the NIMH Social, Personality, and Group Processes Review Committee and is a past President of the Society for Personality and Social Psychology (SPSP).

Tesser has published extensively on self-esteem, attitudes, thought and ruminative processes, interpersonal communication and attraction. This work has earned several awards including a Research Scientist Award (NIMH), the William A. Owens Award (University of Georgia), and the Donald T. Campbell Award (Society for Personality and Social Psychology).

John G. Holmes is University Research Chair in social psychology at the University of Waterloo in Canada. John is a three-time winner of the New Contribution Award for the best new paper in a 2-year period from the International Society for the Study of Personal Relationships, the last two with Sandra Murray. He was invited to write one of six lead review articles for the Millenium Issues of the *European Journal of Social Psychology*. He is past President of the Society for Experimental Social Psychology and past Associate Editor of the *Journal of Personality and Social Psychology*. His enduring interest is in appraisal processes in close relationships, including trust, motivated cognition, and social perception in interpersonal conflict.

Contributors

Susan M. Andersen, New York University, New York, NY, USA

Sarah Angulo, University of Texas at Austin, Austin, TX, USA

Arthur Aron, State University of New York at Stony Brook, Stony Brook, NY, USA

Elaine N. Aron, State University of New York at Stony Brook, Stony Brook, NY, USA

Jodene R. Baccus, McGill University, Montreal, Quebec, Canada

Mark W. Baldwin, McGill University, Montreal, Quebec, Canada

Roy F. Baumeister, Florida State University, Tallahassee, FL, USA

Lane Beckes, University of Minnesota, Twin Cities, Minneapolis, MN, USA

W. Keith Campbell, University of Georgia, Athens, GA, USA

Christine Chang-Schneider, University of Texas at Austin, Austin, TX, USA

Serena Chen, University of California, Berkeley, Berkeley, CA, USA

Stéphane D. Dandeneau, McGill University, Montreal, Quebec, Canada

Joanne Davila, State University of New York at Stony Brook, Stony Brook, NY, USA

Jeffrey D. Green, Virginia Commonwealth University, Richmond, VA, USA

David A. Kenny, University of Connecticut, Storrs, CT, USA

Sarah Ketay, State University of New York at Stony Brook, Stony Brook, NY, USA

Jennifer G. La Guardia, University of Waterloo, Ontario, Canada

Mark R. Leary, Duke University, Durham, NC, USA

Leonard L. Martin, University of Georgia, Athens, GA, USA

Melissa Ramsay Miller, State University of New York at Stony Brook, Stony Brook, NY, USA

Sandra L. Murray, State University of New York at Buffalo, Buffalo, NY, USA

Suzanne Riela, State University of New York at Stony Brook, Stony Brook, NY, USA

Maya Sakellaropoulo, McGill University, Montreal, Quebec, Canada

Steven Shirk, University of Georgia, Athens, GA, USA

Jeffry A. Simpson, University of Minnesota, Twin Cities, Minneapolis, MN, USA

Tyler F. Stillman, Florida State University, Tallahassee, FL, USA

William B. Swann, Jr., University of Texas at Austin, Austin, TX, USA

Yanna J. Weisberg, University of Minnesota, Twin Cities, Minneapolis, MN, USA

Tessa V. West, University of Connecticut, Storrs, CT, USA

Part I

Self-Related Motives Influence Close Relationships

1

Risk Regulation in Relationships: Self-Esteem and the If–Then Contingencies of Interdependent Life

SANDRA L. MURRAY

Romantic relationships pose a unique and unsettling interdependence dilemma. The thoughts and behaviors that are critical for satisfying close connections necessarily increase both the short-term risk and the long-term pain of rejection. Consequently, to risk a sense of connection, people need to feel safe and protected from potential hurts (Murray, Holmes, & Griffin, 2000).

Fortunately, the psychological insurance policy needed to risk connection to a partner—confidence in that partner's acceptance and love—is available within most relationships. People typically see their partner in a more positive and accepting light than their partner sees himself or herself (Murray, Holmes, & Griffin, 1996). Unfortunately, the people most in need of reassurance are least likely to perceive the level of unconditional acceptance they seek (Murray, Griffin, Rose, & Bellavia, 2006). People with low self-esteem underestimate how positively their partner regards their traits (Murray et al., 2000) and they also underestimate how much their partner loves them (Murray, Holmes, Griffin, Bellavia, & Rose, 2001). In contrast, people with high self-esteem correctly perceive their partner's positive regard and unconditional acceptance.

How do such differential expectations of partner acceptance affect the thoughts and behavior and the eventual romantic fates of low and high self-esteem people? This chapter examines this question by utilizing a model of relationship risk regulation (Murray, Holmes, & Collins, 2006). This model assumes that interdependent situations put the goal of promoting connection in conflict with the goal of avoiding painful rejections. By outlining the operation of this risk regulation system, this chapter specifies the imprint that resolving this goal conflict leaves on the relationships of low and high self-esteem people. In particular, it specifies how confidence in a partner's regard prioritizes the pursuit of relationship-promotion goals for people high in self-esteem and how doubts about a partner's regard prioritize the pursuit of self-protection goals for people low in self-esteem.

THE STRUCTURE OF INTERDEPENDENCE DILEMMAS

Situations of dependence are fundamental to romantic life. One partner's actions constrain the other's capacity to satisfy important needs and goals. Such dependence is evident from the lowest to the highest level of generality. At the level of specific situations, couples are interdependent in multiple ways, ranging from deciding whose movie preference to favor on a given weekend to deciding what constitutes a fair allocation of household chores. At a broader level, couples must negotiate different personalities, such as merging one partner's laissez-faire nature with the other's more controlled style (Braiker & Kelley, 1979; Holmes, 2002). At the highest level, the existence of the relationship itself requires both partners' cooperation.

A Recurrent Choice: Self-Protection or Relationship Promotion

Given multiple layers of interdependence, people routinely find themselves in situations where they need to choose how much dependence they can safely risk (Kelley, 1979). Take the simple example of a couple trying to decide whether to go to the current blockbuster action film or a contemplative arts film. Imagine that Sally confides to Harry that she believes that seeing the action film will help distract her from work worries, concerns that she fears the arts film Harry wants to see will only compound. In making this request, Sally is putting her psychological welfare in Harry's hands. Consequently, like most situations where some sacrifice on Harry's part is required, Sally risks discovering that Harry is not willing to be responsive to her needs. The exact nature of such situations may change throughout a relationship's developmental course. However, it is situations as these— situations of dependence where the partner's responsiveness to one's needs is in question—that activate the threat of rejection.

To establish the kind of relationship that can fulfill basic needs for belonging or connectedness, people must choose to risk substantial dependence on a partner in such situations (Murray, Holmes, et al., 2006). They need to behave in ways that give a partner power over their outcomes and think in ways that invest great value and importance in the relationship (Gagné & Lydon, 2004; Murray, 1999). For instance, people in satisfying relationships disclose self-doubts to their partner, seeking social support for personal weaknesses that could elicit rejection (Collins & Feeney, 2000; Simpson, Rholes, & Nelligan, 1992). They also excuse transgressions when a partner has behaved badly, thereby opening the door for future misbehavior (Rusbult, Verette, Whitney, Slovik, & Lipkus, 1991).

Such relationship-promotive choices or transformations are critical for fostering satisfying relationships. However, they also compromise self-protection concerns by increasing the likelihood of rejection in the short term and intensifying how much the ultimate loss of the relationship would hurt (Simpson, 1987).

After all, if Sally relies on Harry for support, she will inevitably expose herself to some less-than-supportive behavior on his part. Therefore, the intense social pain of losing a valued other should increase people's motivation to think and behave in ways that minimize dependence, limiting vulnerability to the partner's actions in the short term and diminishing the long-term potential pain of relationship loss.

OPTIMIZING ASSURANCE: THE RISK REGULATION SYSTEM IN RELATIONSHIPS

The risk regulation model assumes that negotiating interdependent life requires a cognitive, affective, and behavioral regulatory system for resolving the conflict between the goals of self-protection and relationship-promotion (Murray, Holmes, et al., 2006). The goal of this system is to optimize the sense of assurance possible given one's relationship circumstances. This sense of assurance is experienced as a sense of safety in one's level of dependence in the relationship—a feeling of relative invulnerability to hurt. To optimize this sense of assurance, this system must function dynamically, shifting the priority given to the goals of avoiding rejection and seeking closeness so as to accommodate the perceived risks of rejection.

Figure 1.1 illustrates the normative operation of this risk regulation system. It illustrates three "if–then" rule systems people need to gauge the likelihood of a partner's acceptance or rejection and make the *general* situation of being involved in a relationship feel sufficiently safe. Gauging and regulating rejection risk requires appraisal (Path A), signaling or emotion (Path B) and behavioral response (Paths C and D) rules. These rule systems operate in concert to prioritize self-protection goals (and the assurance that comes from maintaining psychological distance) when the perceived risks of rejection are high, or relationship-promotion goals (and the assurance that comes from feeling connected) when the perceived risks of rejection are low.

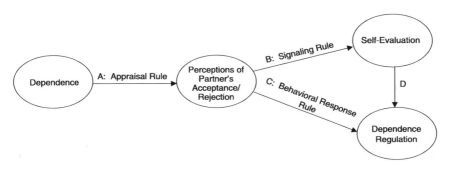

FIGURE 1.1   The risk regulation system in relationships.

The Appraisal System

The link between dependence and perceptions of the partner's regard captures the assumption that situations of dependence increase people's need to gauge a partner's regard (Path A in Figure 1.1). This path captures the operation of an appraisal system. This contingency rule takes the form "if dependent, then gauge acceptance or rejection."

To accurately gauge rejection risk, people need to discern whether a chosen partner is willing to meet their needs. If people are to risk connection, the outcome of this appraisal process needs to give them reason to trust in a partner's responsiveness to needs in situations of dependence (Reis, Clark, & Holmes, 2004; Tooby & Cosmides, 1996). The specific experiences that afford optimistic expectations about responsiveness likely vary across relationships, and perhaps across cultures (Berscheid & Regan, 2005). From the perspective of the risk regulation model, the common diagnostic that affords confidence in a partner's expected responsiveness to needs is the perception that a partner perceives qualities in the self that are worth valuing—qualities that are not readily available in other partners. In more independent cultures, this sense of confidence requires the inference that a partner perceives valued traits in the self (Murray et al., 2000; Swann, Bosson, & Pelham, 2002). In more interdependent cultures, this sense of confidence requires the further inference that a partner's family also values one's qualities (MacDonald & Jessica, 2006).

The Signaling System

The link between perceived regard and self-evaluations (Path B in Figure 1.1) illustrates the operation of a signaling or emotion system that detects discrepancies between current and desired appraisals of a partner's regard and mobilizes action (Berscheid, 1983). The contingency rule governing the signaling system takes the form "if accepted or rejected, then internalize."

This rule reflects a basic assumption of the sociometer model of self-esteem. Leary and his colleagues believe that the need to protect against rejection is so important that people have evolved a system for reacting to rejection threats (Leary & Baumeister, 2000; Leary, Tambor, Terdal, & Downs, 1995; MacDonald & Leary, 2005). They argue that self-esteem is simply a gauge—a "sociometer"— that measures a person's perceived likelihood of being accepted or rejected by others. The sociometer is thought to function such that signs that another's approval is waning diminish self-esteem and motivate compensatory behaviors (Leary et al., 1995). In this sense, the sociometer functions not to preserve self-esteem per se, but to protect people from suffering the serious costs of rejection and not having their needs met.

The need for such a signaling system is amplified in romantic relationships because narrowing social connections to focus on one specific partner raises the personal stakes of rejection. In committing himself to Sally, Harry narrows the number of people he can rely on to satisfy his needs, and in so doing, makes his welfare all the more dependent on Sally's actions. In his routine interactions,

Harry also does not need to seek acceptance from someone he perceives to be rejecting. However, in his relationship with Sally, he is often caught in the position of being hurt by the person whose acceptance he most desires.

Given all that is at stake, the signal that is conveyed by this rule system needs to be sufficiently strong to mobilize action (Berscheid, 1983). Perceiving rejection or drops in a partner's acceptance should hurt and threaten people's general and desired conceptions of themselves as being valuable, efficacious, and worthy of interpersonal connection (Baumeister, 1993; Taylor & Brown, 1988). By making rejection aversive, this signaling system motivates people to avoid situations where relationship partners are likely to be unresponsive and needs for connectedness are likely to be frustrated. In contrast, perceiving acceptance should affirm people's sense of themselves as being good and valuable, mobilizing the desire for greater connection and the likelihood of having one's needs met by a partner.

The Behavioral Response System

The link between perceived regard and dependence-regulating behavior captures the assumption that the threat and social pain of rejection in turn shape people's willingness to think and behave in ways that promote dependence and connectedness (Murray et al., 2000). This path illustrates the operation of a behavioral response system—one that proactively minimizes both the likelihood and the pain of *future* rejection experiences by making increased dependence contingent on the perception of acceptance (Paths C and D in Figure 1.1). As the direct and mediated paths illustrate, this system may be triggered directly, by the experience of acceptance or rejection (Path C in Figure 1.1), and indirectly, through resulting gains or drops in self-esteem (Path D in Figure 1.1). The contingency rule governing this system is "if feeling accepted or rejected, then regulate dependence."

The risk regulation model assumes that the behavioral response system operates to ensure that people only risk as much future dependence as they feel is reasonably safe given recent experience. Suggesting that felt acceptance is a relatively automatic trigger to safety and the possibility of connection, unconsciously primed words that connote security (e.g., accepted) heighten empathy for others (Mikulincer, Gillath, Halevy, Avihou, Avidan, & Eshkoli, 2001), diminish people's tendency to derogate outgroup members (Mikulincer & Shaver, 2001), and increase people's desire to seek support from others in dealing with a personal crisis (Pierce & Lydon, 1998). In contrast, experiencing rejection elicits a social pain akin to physical pain so as to trigger automatic responses, such as aggression, that increase physical or psychological distance between oneself and the source of the pain (MacDonald & Leary, 2005).

Given the general operation of such a dependence regulation system, and the heightened need to protect against romantic rejection, people should implicitly regulate and structure dependence on a specific partner in ways that allow them to minimize the short-term likelihood and long-term potential pain of rejection (Murray et al., 2000). When a partner's general regard is in question, and rejection seems more likely, people should tread cautiously, reserve judgment, and limit future dependence on the partner.

A first line of defense might involve limiting the situations people are willing to enter within their relationships. Efforts to delimit dependence by choosing one's situations carefully might involve conscious decisions to seek support elsewhere, disclose less, or follow exchange norms. These strategies minimize the chance of being in situations where a partner might prove to be unresponsive. A second line of defense might involve shifting the symbolic value attached to the partner and the relationship itself. Such efforts might entail less deliberative shifts in the way people construe their partner's behavior and qualities, such as becoming less willing to excuse specific transgressions (Bradbury & Fincham, 1990), or coming to see a partner's habitual lateness as maddening rather than endearing (Holmes & Rempel, 1989). By diminishing their partner's value as a source of connection, and minimizing the pain of rejection in advance, people can protect a sense of their own worthiness of interpersonal connection against loss.

When confident of a partner's general regard, people can more safely risk increased dependence in the future—entering into situations where the partner has control over their immediate outcomes, forgiving transgressions, attaching greater value to their partner's qualities, and risking a stronger sense of commitment to the partner and relationship.

NEGOTIATING DEPENDENCE DILEMMAS: HOW PERCEIVED REGARD CONTROLS RULE SENSITIVITY

For a relationship risk regulation system to be functional, it needs to adapt itself to suit specific relationship circumstances. If Sally generally perceives Harry to be responsive to her needs, distancing herself from Harry at the first sign of his insensitivity is not likely to be the optimal means of sustaining the needed sense of assurance. If Sally generally perceives Harry to be unresponsive, however, such a response might be Sally's best available means of sustaining some minimal sense of safety from harm. Accordingly, to respond dynamically and adaptively to ongoing events, the regulatory system depicted in Figure 1.1 needs a heuristic means of estimating the level of risk inherent in specific situations.

Figure 1.2 illustrates how this risk calibration occurs. In this individual differences extension of the risk regulation system, people's general or cross-situational sense of confidence in a partner's positive regard and love acts as such an arbiter or barometer—telling people whether it is safe to put self-protection aside and risk thinking and behaving in relationship-promotive ways (Murray, Holmes, et al., 2006). Specifically, feeling more or less positively regarded by a partner interacts with specific event features to control the sensitivity of the appraisal, signaling, and dependence regulation rules people adopt in specific situations.

At the first stage of this process, chronic perceptions of a partner's regard interact with specific event features to control the extent to which people categorize or code specific events as situations of risk. To the extent that Sally is unsure of Harry's regard, even the mundane choice of one movie over another could

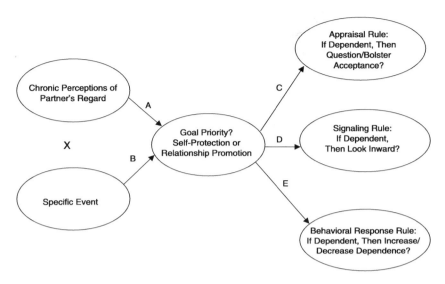

FIGURE 1.2   How perceived regard arbitrates the operation of the risk regulation system.

make concerns about dependence salient. However, to the extent that Sally is more confident of Harry's regard, she might only begin to entertain thoughts about her vulnerability to his actions when they try to negotiate more serious decisions in their relationship, such as deciding whose financial philosophy to follow. Once identified as such, the possibility of rejection inherent in such "dependent" situations activates a situated conflict between self-protection and relationship-promotion goals.

The consequent activation of the need for a sense of assurance then triggers the appraisal, signaling, and behavior response systems, respectively (either individually or in concert). A person's habitual means of optimizing feelings of assurance is revealed in the idiosyncratic or signature ways this person tailors these rules to prioritize self-protection or relationship-promotion goals in specific situations of dependence. From the perspective of the risk regulation model, feeling less positively regarded by a partner generally primes self-protection goals. Questioning a partner's regard activates an "if–then" contingency signature that links situations of dependence to the perception of rejection and hurt feelings and diminished self-esteem to behavioral and psychological tactics meant to diminish dependence. In contrast, feeling more positively regarded generally primes relationship-promotion goals. Confidence in a partner's regard activates an "if–then" contingency signature that links situations of dependence to the perception of acceptance, and behavioral and psychological tactics meant to increase dependence.

However, the specific cognitive, affective, and behavioral strategies that couples adopt to optimize feelings of assurance or safety in the face of risky situations should be tailored to meet the constraints imposed by features of each partner's expectations and the situation they face. For instance, people who generally feel more positively regarded by their partner may differ in their habitual means of increasing closeness in situations where they feel rejected. For some, the activation of rejection concerns may prompt the need to express one's needs more clearly. For others, the activation of rejection concerns may activate care-giving behaviors directed toward the partner. Similarly, people who generally feel less positively regarded may restore feelings of assurance through strategic efforts to reduce dependence. For some, this might involve derogating the partner, a relatively direct strategy. However, for others, such strategies might be ineffective because their partner responds to such behavior in ways that trigger conflicts, and thus further exacerbate rejection anxieties. In such circumstances, dependence reduction strategies might involve limiting conversation to superficialities or turning to friends for support.

THE APPLICATION TO SELF-ESTEEM

How might chronic levels of self-esteem affect the procedural rules people follow in specific risky situations? Figures 1.3 and 1.4 illustrate a potential sequence of cognitive, emotional, and behavioral reactions for low and high self-esteem people, respectively. In developing these arguments, I draw on the literature on global self-esteem, chronic rejection sensitivity (Downey & Feldman, 1996), and attachment anxiety (Collins & Read, 1990) because rejection sensitivity and attachment anxiety are strongly negatively correlated with global self-esteem.

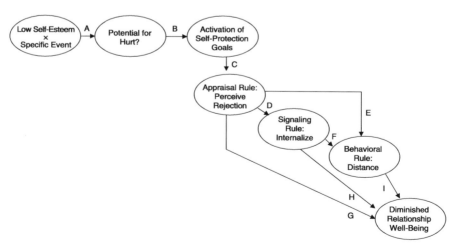

FIGURE 1.3   Low self-esteem and the activation of self-protective contingency rules.

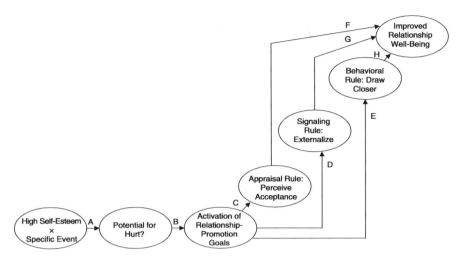

FIGURE 1.4 High self-esteem and the activation of relationship-promotive contingency rules.

Risk Regulation among Low Self-Esteem People

People low in self-esteem underestimate how positively their partner regards their traits (Murray et al., 2000) and they also underestimate how much their partner loves them (Murray et al., 2001). Therefore, for low self-esteem people, the goal of feeling valued and discerning a partner's caring is likely to be chronically activated (Murray, Bellavia, Rose, & Griffin, 2003; Murray, Griffin, Rose, & Bellavia, 2003). The chronic accessibility of this goal should sensitize low self-esteem people to rejection threats, shaping the "if–then" contingencies that are activated in ways that put a premium on self-protection goals. Why would this be the case?[1]

General expectations of rejection, such as those embodied in low self-esteem, make specific rejection experiences all the more painful (Leary & Baumeister, 2000). Such pain is compounded in romantic relationships because low self-esteem people even perceive the person who should be perceived to be most accepting as rejecting (Murray et al., 2001). Accordingly, situated rejections by a romantic partner hurt more because they pose a greater proportional loss to a more precarious, generalized sense of their worthiness of interpersonal connection.

As a result, low self-esteem people are in particular need of a self-protectively weighted or prevention-oriented rule system (Heimpel, Elliot, & Wood, 2006; Higgins, 1996)—one that quickly detects rejection, strongly signals the possibility of further hurt, and motivates them to take defensive action sooner rather than later (Pietrzak, Downey, & Ayduk, 2005). If Harry's low self-esteem causes him to question Sally's general regard for him, such situations remind him that depending on Sally is risky (Path A in Figure 1.3). Harry should maintain some sense of safety in the face of the acute tension between wanting to avoid rejection and wanting to be close by activating procedural rules that put self-protection first (Path B in Figure 1.3). He should perceive rejection in specific episodes (Path C in Figure 1.3, "If dependent situation, then question acceptance"), feel hurt and personally diminished (Path D in Figure 1.3, "If feeling acutely rejected, then internalize"), and respond to such hurts by diminishing his dependence on Sally (Path E in Figure 1.3, "If feeling acutely rejected, then decrease dependence"). Over time, the repeated activation of such contingencies, and the costs they accrue, may then undermine his relationship (Paths G through I in Figure 1.3).

If Dependent, Then Question Acceptance   Two types of prototypic dependent situations are likely to activate appraisal processes for low self-esteem people—self-based situations where one person needs support, and relationship-based situations where a partner behaves badly.

Imagine that Harry is criticized at work for failing to complete a project. Such situations may activate "if–then" contingencies that link his failures to Sally's likely rejection. In fact, people low in self-esteem generally see interpersonal acceptance as conditional in nature (Baldwin & Sinclair, 1996). In dating relationships, people low in self-esteem react to experimentally induced doubts about their intelligence or considerateness by expressing greater concerns about their partner's rejection (Murray, Holmes, MacDonald, & Ellsworth, 1998). Low self-esteem married women also react to day-to-day failures at work by reporting higher levels of anxiety about their husband's acceptance (Murray, Griffin, et al., 2006).

Now imagine that Harry comes home to find Sally in an irritable mood, grumbling about the lack of food in the fridge. Primed to see rejection, a low self-esteem Harry may attribute such grumbling to an interpersonal disposition— Sally's broader displeasure with him. Illustrating this dynamic, dating intimates who are low in self-esteem see their dating partner's negative moods as evidence of ill will toward them (Bellavia & Murray, 2003). Low self-esteem people also react to experimentally induced signs that their partner has a specific complaint about their behavior or personality by forecasting their partner's rejection (Murray, Rose, Bellavia, Holmes, & Kusche, 2002).

Similar effects are also evident for people who are high on attachment-related anxiety or chronic rejection sensitivity (and, thus, are likely to be low in global self-esteem). For instance, dating intimates who are high on attachment-related anxiety about acceptance interpret a partner's hypothetical (Collins, 1996) and actual misdeeds in suspicious ways that are likely to exacerbate hurt feelings (Simpson, Rholes, & Phillips, 1996). People high on attachment-related anxiety even interpret a partner's ambiguous attempts to be supportive as intentionally hurtful (Collins and Feeney, 2004). They also interpret daily conflicts as a sign of their partner's waning commitment (Campbell, Simpson, Boldry, & Kashy, 2005). When gauging their dating partner's thoughts about attractive opposite-sex others, intimates high on attachment-related anxiety are also more empathically accurate, discerning threatening thoughts that are misunderstood by secure intimates (Simpson, Ickes, & Grich, 1999). People who anticipate interpersonal rejection attribute negative intent to a new partner's hypothetical behaviors (Downey & Feldman, 1996).

If Rejected, Then Internalize For low self-esteem people, the signal conveyed by this emotion system needs to be particularly strong because detecting drops in acceptance poses a substantial threat to a limited resource. The need to feel and be more included is so strong for low self-esteem people that their state self-esteem is sensitive to unconsciously activated rejection cues (Sommer & Baumeister, 2002) or signs of a complete stranger's disapproval (Nezlek, Kowalski, Leary, Blevins, & Holgate, 1997). Consequently, a low self-esteem Harry should be more readily hurt by Sally's perceived rejection, questioning his worth in the face of her perceived slights. Consistent with this logic, low self-esteem people respond to induced fears that their dating partner was annoyed by specific aspects of their behavior or personality by reporting diminished state self-esteem (Murray et al., 2002, Experiment 3). Day-to-day anxieties about a spouse's rejection also diminish state self-esteem for people (such as those low in self-esteem) who generally feel less confident of their partner's regard (Murray, Griffin, et al., 2003).

If Rejected, Then Decrease Dependence For a low self-esteem Harry, feeling rejected and personally diminished should then activate the goal of self-protection and the desire to reduce dependence. The existing literature provides multiple examples of such dynamics.

People with low self-esteem respond to induced anxieties about their partner's possible rejection by depending less on their partner as a source of self-esteem and comfort (Murray et al., 1998). They also evaluate their partner's qualities more negatively (Murray et al., 1998; Murray et al., 2002). The need to downplay the value and importance of the partner (the source of the hurt) is sufficiently powerful that derogation effects emerge on the qualities that typically reveal people's positive illusions about their partner (Murray et al., 1996). These devaluing processes also emerge whether these acute rejection anxieties are imagined in response to a newly discovered fault in the self (Murray et al., 1998), or arise in response to the partner's behavior (Murray et al., 2002). Such devaluing efforts appear in part to be automatic as they also surface on implicit measures of partner regard (DeHart, Pelham, & Murray, 2004). Low self-esteem people evaluate their partner's name letters less favorably the more difficulties they currently perceive in their relationships. By diminishing their partner's value, people who feel less valued give their partner less power to hurt them in the future by making the partner a less important source of need satisfaction and a less valued informant on their worthiness of love.[2]

Similar distancing efforts are also evident for people who are likely to be low in self-esteem by virtue of high levels of attachment-related anxiety or chronic rejection sensitivity. Women higher in attachment-related anxiety display greater anger towards their partner in a situation in which their partner may not have been as responsive as they hoped (Rholes, Simpson, & Orina, 1999). After discussing a serious relationship problem, more anxiously attached men and women also reported greater anger and hostility (as compared to controls who discussed a minor problem), and they downplayed their feelings of closeness and commitment (Simpson et al., 1996). To the extent that expressions of anger are a means of trying to control the partner's behavior, such sentiment both directly and indirectly reduces dependence.

Intimates high on attachment-related anxiety also reported feeling less close to their partner in a situation where they accurately inferred the (threatening) content of their partner's thoughts about attractive opposite-sex others (Simpson et al., 1999). People high on attachment-related anxiety also react to higher levels of daily conflict by minimizing their feelings of closeness to their partner (Campbell et al., 2005). Women chronically high on rejection sensitivity respond to a potential partner's indifference by evaluating that partner more negatively (Ayduk, Downey, Testa, Yen, & Shoda, 1999). Rejection-sensitive women are also more likely to initiate conflicts on days after they felt more rejected by their romantic partner, and simply priming rejection-related words automatically activates hostility-related thoughts for these women (Ayduk et al., 1999).

Risk Regulation among High Self-Esteem People

For high self-esteem people, there is little need for a self-protectively calibrated rule system. They generally anticipate and perceive acceptance in most social relationships (Leary & Baumeister, 2000). They also feel positively regarded and valued by their romantic partner (Murray et al., 2001). Because specific rejections pose a smaller proportional loss to a comparably rich resource, high self-esteem people can more safely risk seeking the benefits of connection in situations of dependence. Accordingly, a regulatory system that functions to prioritize relationship-promotion goals best affords people high in self-esteem a continued sense of assurance or safety in the relationship.

Imagine that a high self-esteem Sally faces a conflict with Harry. If the conflict is a serious one, she is likely to code the situation as one involving some level of risk (Path A in Figure 1.4). However, she is likely to resolve any situated tension between avoiding rejection and seeking closeness in favor of relationship-promotion goals (Path B in Figure 1.4). As a primary mechanism of defense, a high self-esteem Sally might perceive evidence of acceptance in such episodes (Path C in Figure 1.4, "If dependent situation, then bolster acceptance"). When Sally does end up feeling rejected, she is not likely to feel personally diminished (Path D in Figure 1.4, "If rejected, then externalize"). Instead, a resilient overall sense of confidence in Harry's acceptance should prompt her to respond to situated rejections by increasing closeness (Path E in Figure 1.4, "If feeling acutely rejected, then increase dependence"). Over time, the repeated activation of such contingencies, and the benefits they provide, may then strengthen the relationship's well-being (Paths F through H in Figure 1.4).

If Dependent, Then Bolster Acceptance   For a high self-esteem Sally, risky situations should activate "if–then" contingencies that link the possibility of Harry's unresponsiveness to ready excuses, or trigger a selective search through memory for those occasions when he was particularly sensitive (Kunda, 1990). Illustrating such compensatory processes, people who are high in self-esteem react to threats to self-esteem by becoming even more convinced of their dating partner's acceptance and love (Murray et al., 1998). For instance, high self-esteem participants reacted to failure on a purported test of intelligence by reminding themselves of their partner's love. High self-esteem people also resist generalizing the meaning of specific episodes where their partner seems upset or annoyed with them. Instead, they actually perceive greater evidence of their partner's acceptance and love in such risk situations (Murray et al., 2002).

If Rejected, Then Externalize   Because Sally's chronic confidence in Harry's regard blunts the sting of specific rejections, she has little need for a strong signaling system. As a result, her situated feelings about her own worth should be reasonably immune to perceived rejections. Consistent with this logic, anxieties about a partner's rejection do not diminish state self-esteem for people who generally feel more valued by their partner (Murray, Griffin, et al., 2003). Moreover, the possibility of a dating partner's annoyance or irritation does not trigger the same acute self-doubts among high self-esteem people as it does among lows (Murray et al., 2002).

If Rejected, Then Increase Dependence   For people high in self-esteem, feeling acutely rejected instead activates "if–then" contingencies that link hurtful situations to the goal of relationship-promotion and increased connectedness. As one example, people high in self-esteem respond to induced concerns about their dating partner's likely annoyance with them by reporting greater feelings of closeness to that same partner (Experiment 2, Murray et al., 2002). Dating intimates high in global self-esteem also react to experimentally induced self-doubts by reporting greater dependence on their partner's reassurance as a source of self-esteem (Murray et al., 1998). Similarly, people low on attachment-related anxiety (and thus higher in self-esteem) come to value their partner more after discussing a serious conflict than a minor conflict (Simpson et al., 1996). Such relationship-promotive tendencies even extend to situations where a partner is attracted to another. Intimates low on attachment-related anxiety feel closer to their partner the more accurate they are in discerning their partner's attraction to others (Simpson et al., 1999).

IMPLICATIONS FOR RELATIONSHIP WELL-BEING

It is one of the enduring ironies of life that people who want something more are often less likely to find it. This same irony riddles romantic life: People low in self-esteem or insecure in attachment style are less likely to find lasting happiness in relationships even though they need this resource the most (Collins & Read, 1990; Hendrick, Hendrick, & Adler, 1988).

The salient explanation for such effects is that people troubled by dispositional insecurities pick worse partners who are less likely to be valuing of them. If that were the case, adopting a self-protective stance would be an adaptive strategy—functioning as a "stop" routine that disrupted fruitless relationship pursuits (Leary & Baumeister, 2000). This seems unlikely. First, low self-esteem people do not necessarily pick worse partners: The association between spouses' self-esteem levels is near zero (Murray et al., 2000). Second, cross-sectional data also reveal that people express just as much love for low self-esteem partners as they do for high self-esteem partners (Murray et al., 2001). People also see low self-esteem partners more positively than they see themselves (Murray et al., 1996). Third, the self-protective tactics of low self-esteem people are still evident when the reality of the partner's actual regard or behavior is controlled (e.g., Murray et al., 2002). What implications does the risk regulation model have for helping clarify exactly why people who are troubled by low self-esteem end up in relationships that *both* partners find less satisfying?

The Self-Fulfilling Effects of Insecurity

The nature of interdependence is such that hurts at the hands of a partner are inevitable. Because people troubled by low self-esteem are likely to doubt their partner's regard (Downey & Feldman, 1996; Murray et al., 2000; Tucker & Anders, 1999), they are not likely to respond to such interdependence dilemmas in ways that promote the relationship. Instead, the slightest offense is likely to be seen as rejection, motivating them to self-protect. Consistent with this logic, perceptions of a partner's regard mediate the link between self-esteem and satisfaction in dating and marital relationships (Murray et al., 2000; Murray et al., 2001).

The desire to reduce dependence and minimize the pain of rejection in the short term then could have the unintended consequence of making partner rejection more likely. For instance, on days after rejection sensitive women felt rejected by their dating partners, their *partners* also reported greater dissatisfaction, even though they had not been upset initially (Downey, Freitas, Michaelis, & Khouri, 1998). In a daily diary study conducted by Murray, Bellavia, et al. (2003), people with partners who felt less valued came to see their partner as being more selfish and unappreciative on days after their partner had felt most rejected, even though they had not been upset with their partner in the first place. In such ways, self-protective attempts to blunt the likelihood and pain of rejection eventually alienate one's partner.

By putting self-protection at a greater premium than relationship promotion, people who feel less positively regarded may create long-term interpersonal realities that defeat their hopes and confirm their fears. Supporting this analysis, a longitudinal daily diary study of married couples suggests that the chronic activation of self-protective appraisal, signaling, and behavioral response rules has a corrosive effect on relationships over time (Murray, Bellavia, et al., 2003; Murray, Griffin, et al., 2003). In this sample, relationship difficulties were more likely to arise when the "if–then" contingencies underlying people's cognition, affect, and behavior mirrored the "if–then" contingencies evident among low self-esteem people.

First, satisfaction declined when people's on-line systems for appraising rejection threats were calibrated in a more self-protective fashion. In particular, when women linked their own personal self-doubts to their husband's lessened acceptance, their *husband* reported relatively greater declines in satisfaction over time (Murray, Griffin, et al., 2003; Murray, Griffin, et al., 2006). Conversely, when women compensated for self-doubts by embellishing their partner's acceptance, their husband reported relatively greater satisfaction (Murray, Griffin, et al., 2003). Second, satisfaction declined when people's signaling systems were more sensitive to rejection. When people reacted to anxieties about rejection by reporting diminished self-esteem the next day, their *partner* reported significantly greater declines in satisfaction. Third, when women's behavioral response to feeling rejected was to self-protect and behave negatively, their husband's satisfaction declined over the year (Murray, Griffin, et al., 2003).

Unfortunately, the potential for negative relationship consequences to ensue is not likely to be part of the consciousness of a person caught in the immediate experience of trying to blunt the short-term pain of a perceived rejection. People respond to experimentally induced fears of lifelong rejection and social isolation by behaving in self-defeating ways, putting short-term pleasures, such as making risky gambles or unhealthy food choices, ahead of the long-term costs of such endeavors (Twenge, Catanese, & Baumeister, 2002). Induced rejection fears also undermine people's scores on intelligence tests (Baumeister, Twenge, & Nuss, 2002), suggesting that coping with rejection impairs the type of executive functioning necessary for effective self-regulation. Unfortunately, for people low on self-esteem, gauging and then responding to perceived rejections may be sufficiently preoccupying that they exhaust the self-regulatory resources needed to anticipate the costs of self-protection (Finkel & Campbell, 2001).

INCORPORATING ALTERNATE THEORETICAL PERSPECTIVES

In helping to elucidate why low self-esteem is a source of relationship difficulties, the risk regulation model offers a means of integrating the assumptions of the sociometer model (Leary & Baumeister, 2000), the relational schemas approach (Andersen & Chen, 2002; Baldwin, 1992), and attachment theory (Mikulincer & Shaver, 2003).

The Sociometer Model

The risk regulation and sociometer perspectives both assume that people are motivated to feel positively regarded and valued by others (Leary & Baumeister, 2000; Leary & MacDonald, 2003; Leary et al., 1995). Both perspectives also assume that social relationships are most likely to be satisfying and stable when people respond to signs of rejection by behaving in ways that put connectedness at a premium. However, the present conceptualization of the inter-relation between self-esteem and connectedness motivations differs from the sociometer model. These motivations are largely isomorphic in the sociometer model. When the threat of rejection is salient, establishing connection represents one principal means of having one's needs for approval met, thereby restoring a sense of esteem in one's relational value.

In the unique context of an adult close relationship, these motivations are more separable, and, consequently, sometimes in conflict. As most people possess one romantic partner at a time, this person has special power in satisfying (or thwarting) people's capacity to meet important needs and goals. Such outcome control makes a romantic partner a uniquely powerful informant on one's worthiness of interpersonal connection. Consequently, people are likely concerned about more than just minimizing the actual potential for rejection (as in the sociometer model). Instead, pre-emptively minimizing the pain of rejection if it were to occur is also an important goal. Accordingly, the risk regulation model assumes that people actively regulate their sense of connection to this *specific* other—letting a partner become a valued and important source of need satisfaction when the potential for rejection seems low. In contrast, minimizing the partner's value may be the best means of discounting the meaning of unresponsive behaviors when people are less sure of another's acceptance. In so doing, people can protect a symbolic sense of connection to others without the cooperation of specific others (in the short term).

The risk regulation and sociometer models provide somewhat different perspectives on why low self-esteem people are involved in less satisfying relationships than high self-esteem people. The sociometer model assumes that seeking connection (a kind of approach motivation) is an unconflicted goal, and that self-esteem reflects people's success or failure in satisfying this goal. The relationship difficulties of low self-esteem people thus reflect problems in interpersonal realities—the inability to establish relationships with accepting others. However, the risk regulation model assumes that dependence activates both approach (or relationship-promotion) and avoidance (or self-protection) goals. Consequently, the relationship difficulties of low self-esteem people stem from the tendency to put greater priority on avoiding rejection than on seeking closeness.

The integration of the sociometer and risk regulation models may rest in the possibility that people possess multiple sociometers, ones that vary in their generality, and thus in their likelihood of being activated in specific contexts (see Kirkpatrick & Ellis, 2001). At the highest level of generality, global self-esteem might operate as a default sociometer. This sociometer might forecast the likelihood of acceptance, and regulate affect and behavior in situations with strangers or casual friends (Leary et al., 1995; Nezlek et al., 1997). Perceptions of a partner's regard might operate as a lower-level sociometer. This gauge might forecast the likelihood of acceptance and regulate behavior within one specific relationship. This lower-level sociometer also might operate in ways that guard against losses to operating level of the general sociometer. In this light, low self-esteem people may distance themselves from a seemingly rejecting partner to protect a more general sense of their own worthiness of interpersonal connection against loss.

Relational Schemas and Relational Selves

The current model shares several points of emphasis with recent social-cognitive analyses of relational schemas (Andersen & Chen, 2002; Baldwin, 1992). Baldwin (1992) argued that people develop relational schemas through past experiences with others that help them navigate their social worlds. These schemas include declarative beliefs about the characteristics of the self in specific contexts, beliefs about the characteristics of others in these same contexts, and "if–then" inter-personal scripts that specify the relation between the self and others (e.g., "If I depend on my spouse for support, he or she will be comforting"). Similarly, Andersen and Chen (2002) argued that accessible ties exist in memory between aspects of people's self-conceptions and representations of specific significant others. Consequently, signs of a significant other's qualities in a new acquaintance can activate the significant other representation through a process of transference. This activation can then shift people's self-concepts to match those self-aspects experienced in the presence of the significant other (e.g., Hinkley & Andersen, 1996).

Both of these theoretical perspectives share points of emphasis with the risk regulation model. These perspectives assume that people are motivated to estab-lish secure ties to others and that people's sense of themselves is shaped by their expectations about the orientation of *specific* significant others toward them. These perspectives also assume that the declarative and procedural aspects of people's working models shape social inference and behavior.

The current model advances thinking about relational schemas because it identifies three "if–then" contingency rules and describes how they develop across situations of dependence. The identification of specific "if–then" contingencies provides a mechanism for understanding why the relationships of low and high self-esteem people function differently.

The risk regulation model also differs in its conceptualization of self-schemas and their relation to schemas of specific others. A relational schemas approach assumes the content of people's working self-concepts shifts to accommodate whatever audience is most salient. For instance, Harry may think of himself as a leader in his dealings with his office subordinates, but as egalitar-ian in his equal status interactions with his wife Sally because the model of other that is activated in each *situation* primes a different aspect of his self-concept. The current model assigns greater causal priority to the reflected aspects of people's self-schemas, such as Harry's perception of how much Sally values his skills. Accordingly, the risk regulation model puts greater emphasis on the importance of individual differences, such as self-esteem, that shape people's appraisals of others' regard for them. In this model, people's reflected image of themselves shapes the goals they adopt in specific situations because such self-schemas afford more or less optimistic inferences about another's likely responsiveness to the self.

Attachment Theory

Risk regulation and attachment perspectives both assume that assessments of an attachment figure's availability and responsiveness determine the strategies people adopt to restore a psychological sense of safety in threatening situations (see Fraley & Shaver, 2000; Mikulincer & Shaver, 2003 for reviews). Both perspectives also assume that understanding people's sensitivity to rejection-related cues and strategic responses to feeling rejected is critical in determining the relationship's current welfare and future stability.

A risk regulation perspective on the nature of the relation between expectations of self and other presents a different twist on attachment theory. Attachment theorists generally argue that the systems that detect rejection threats operate largely independently of the systems that respond to such threats (Bartholomew, 1990; Griffin & Bartholomew, 1994; but see Mikulincer & Shaver, 2003 for a recent exception). Fraley and Shaver (2000) argued that attachment-related anxiety governs the threat detection system, whereas attachment-related avoidance governs the system regulating behavioral responses to threat. As these systems are thought to be independent in principle, people can express strong fears of rejection and strong desires for closeness (i.e., preoccupied), or few anxieties about rejection and strong desires for distance (i.e., dismissing).

Accordingly, attachment theorists might localize the relationship difficulties of low self-esteem people in the content or structure of their working models of self. They might also assume that the relationship difficulties low self-esteem people encounter will be differentiated or moderated by general expectations about the responsiveness of others. People with low self-esteem who nonetheless desire connection (i.e., preoccupied) should have substantially different relationship experiences than people with low self-esteem who avoid closeness (i.e., fearful).

The risk regulation model assumes that models of self and specific others are inextricably linked. It contends that the "if–then" rules that sensitize people to perceiving and internalizing a partner's rejection must be connected to the "if–then" rules that dull the impact of such threats if people are to sustain feelings of assurance. In other words, people are not likely to see qualities in a specific other that would elicit proximity-seeking unless they can first find reason to trust in that specific other's regard. Consequently, the relationship experiences of low self-esteem people may be more uniform than attachment researchers predict, because generalized expectations about one's worthiness of love and the trust-worthiness of others have common effects, mediated through the specific beliefs about a partner's regard they foster.

An integration of the attachment and risk regulation approaches may depend on the recognition that the ultimate effect of people's general expectations about themselves and others may be modified by people's partner-specific beliefs (see Collins, Guichard, Ford, & Feeney, 2004). If that is the case, people who are troubled by dispositional vulnerabilities, such as low self-esteem, may respond adaptively to threat if they believe their partner sees qualities in them that merit attention, nurturance, and care. Consistent with this logic, women high in attachment anxiety who nonetheless believe that their partner will be responsive during the transition to parenthood remain satisfied in their marriages during this stressful time (Rholes, Simpson, Campbell, & Grich, 2001). People high in attachment anxiety who nonetheless feel confident in a partner's acceptance also report better quality interactions in daily life than people who possess pessimistic general and specific expectations (Pierce & Lydon, 1998).

CONCLUSION

Ironically, relationships that have the most potential to satisfy adult needs for interpersonal connection are the very relationships that activate the most anxiety about rejection (Baumeister, Wotman, & Stillwell, 1993). Given the personal stakes associated with narrowing social connections to focus on one partner, some level of caution is required. However, to be happy over the longer term, people need to set rejection concerns aside and risk substantial dependence (Murray, Holmes, et al., 2006). An application of the risk regulation model suggests that low self-esteem people are less likely to experience a relationship as satisfying and fulfilling because they put the desire to avoid rejection ahead of the need to seek connection.

ACKNOWLEDGMENT

The preparation of this chapter was supported by a grant from the National Institute of Mental Health (MH 060105).

NOTES

1. Although people with low self-esteem generally feel less valued than people with high self-esteem, the correlation is not a perfect one (Murray et al., 2001). Consequently, some low self-esteem people may feel sufficiently valued by their partner to risk relationship promotion in most circumstances. In fact, the risk regulation model assumes that specific expectations of acceptance regulate the operation of the system. This raises the possibility that low self-esteem people who nonetheless feel valued by their partner may behave and think more like high self-esteem people. In contrast, high self-esteem people who nonetheless feel devalued by their partner may behave and think more like low self-esteem people (Murray et al., 2005).

2. The risk regulation model assumes that thoughts and behaviors, such as derogating a partner, reflect people's attempt to diminish dependence (and thus the perceived likelihood and pain of future rejections). Readers might wonder instead whether such behaviors simply reflect learned responses to the actual behavioral contingencies that exist in the relationship. However, the distancing efforts of people who feel less valued arise in the complete absence of any actual provoking threat or behavior from the partner (Murray, Griffin, et al., 2003).

REFERENCES

Andersen, S. M., & Chen, S. (2002). The relational self: An interpersonal social-cognitive theory. *Psychological Review, 109,* 619–645.

Ayduk, O., Downey, G., Testa, A., Yen, Y., & Shoda, Y. (1999). Does rejection elicit hostility in rejection sensitive women? *Social Cognition, 17,* 245–271.

Baldwin, M. W. (1992). Relational schemas and the processing of social information. *Psychological Bulletin, 112,* 461–484.

Baldwin, M. W., & Sinclair, L. (1996). Self-esteem and "if . . . then" contingencies of interpersonal acceptance. *Journal of Personality and Social Psychology, 71*, 1130–1141.

Bartholomew, K. (1990). Avoidance of intimacy: An attachment perspective. *Journal of Social and Personal Relationships, 7*, 147–178.

Baumeister, R. F. (1993). *Self-esteem: The puzzle of low self-regard.* New York: Plenum Press.

Baumeister, R. F., Twenge, J. M., & Nuss, C. K. (2002). Effects of social exclusion on cognitive processes: Anticipated aloneness reduces intelligent thought. *Journal of Personality and Social Psychology, 83*, 817–827.

Baumeister, R. F., Wotman, S. R., Stillwell, A. M. (1993). Unrequited love: On heartbreak, anger, guilt, scriptlessness, and humiliation. *Journal of Personality and Social Psychology, 64*, 377–394.

Bellavia, G., & Murray, S. L. (2003). Did I do that? Self-esteem related differences in reactions to romantic partners' moods. *Personal Relationships, 10*, 77–96.

Berscheid, E. (1983). Emotion. In H. H. Kelley, E. Berscheid, A. Christensen, J. H. Harvey, T. L. Huston, G. Levinger, et al. (Eds.), *Close relationships* (pp. 110–168). New York: W. H. Freeman.

Berscheid, E., & Regan, P. (2005). *The psychology of interpersonal relationships.* Upper Saddle River, NJ: Prentice Hall.

Bradbury, T. N., & Fincham, F. D. (1990). Attributions in marriage: Review and critique. *Psychological Bulletin, 107*, 3–23.

Braiker, H. B., & Kelley, H. H. (1979). Conflict in the development of close relationship. In R. L. Burgess & T. L. Huston (Eds.), *Social exchange in developing relationship* (pp. 135–168). New York: Academic Press.

Campbell, L., Simpson, J. A., Boldry, J., & Kashy, D. A. (2005). Perceptions of conflict and support in romantic relationships: The role of attachment anxiety. *Journal of Personality and Social Psychology, 88*, 510–531.

Collins, N. L. (1996). Working models of attachment: Implications for explanation, emotion and behavior. *Journal of Personality and Social Psychology, 71*, 810–832.

Collins, N. L., & Feeney, B. C. (2000). A safe haven: An attachment theory perspective on support seeking and caregiving in intimate relationships. *Journal of Personality and Social Psychology, 78*, 1053–1073.

Collins, N. L., & Feeney, B. C. (2004) Working models of attachment shape perceptions of social support: Evidence from experimental and observational studies. *Journal of Personality and Social Psychology, 87*, 363–383.

Collins, N. L., Guichard, A. C., Ford, M. B., & Feeney, B. C. (2004). Working models of attachment: New developments and emerging themes. In W. S. Rholes & J. A. Simpson (Eds.), *Adult attachment: Theory, research, and clinical implication* (pp. 196–239). New York: Guilford Press.

Collins, N. L., & Read, S. J. (1990). Adult attachment, working models, and relationship quality in dating couples. *Journal of Personality and Social Psychology, 58*, 644–663.

DeHart, T., Pelham, B., Murray, S. L. (2004). Regulating dependency in close relationships: Implicit evaluations of significant others. *Social Cognition, 22*, 126–146.

Downey, G., & Feldman, S. I. (1996). Implications of rejection sensitivity for intimate relationships. *Journal of Personality and Social Psychology, 70*, 1327–1343.

Downey, G., Freitas, A. L., Michaelis, B., & Khouri, H. (1998). The self-fulfilling prophecy in close relationships: Rejection sensitivity and rejection by romantic partners. *Journal of Personality and Social Psychology, 75*, 545–560.

Finkel, E. J., & Campbell, W. K. (2001). Self-control and accommodation in close relationships: An interdependence analysis. *Journal of Personality and Social Psychology*, *81*, 263–277.

Fraley, R. C., & Shaver, P. R. (2000). Adult romantic attachment: Theoretical developments, emerging controversies, and unanswered questions. *Review of General Psychology*, *4*, 132–154.

Gagné, F. M., & Lydon, J. E. (2004). Bias and accuracy in close relationships: An integrative review. *Personality and Social Psychology Review*, *8*, 322–338.

Griffin, D. W., & Bartholomew, K. (1994). Models of the self and other: Fundamental dimensions underlying measures of adult attachment. *Journal of Personality and Social Psychology*, *67*, 430–445.

Heimpel, S. A., Elliot, A. J., & Wood, J. V. (2006). Basic personality dispositions, self-esteem, and personal goals: An approach-avoidance analysis. *Journal of Personality*, *74*, 1293–1319.

Hendrick, S. S., Hendrick, C., & Adler, N. L. (1988). Romantic relationships: Love, satisfaction, and staying together. *Journal of Personality and Social Psychology*, *54*, 980–988.

Higgins, E. T. (1996). The "self digest": Self-knowledge serving self-regulatory functions. *Journal of Personality and Social Psychology*, *71*, 1062–1083.

Hinkley, K., & Andersen, S. M. (1996). The working of self-concept in transference: Significant-other activation and self-change. *Journal of Personality and Social Psychology*, *71*, 1279–1295.

Holmes, J. G. (2002). Interpersonal expectations as the building blocks of social cognition: An interdependence theory perspective. *Personal Relationship*, *9*, 1–26.

Holmes, J. G., & Rempel, J. K. (1989). Trust in close relationships. In C. Hendrick (Ed.), *Review of personality and social psychology: Close relationships* (Vol. 10, pp. 187–219). Newbury Park, CA: Sage.

Kelley, H. H. (1979). *Personal relationships: Their structures and processes*. Hillsdale, NJ: Lawrence Erlbaum Associates, Inc.

Kirkpatrick, L. A., & Ellis, B. J. (2001). An evolutionary-psychological approach to self-esteem: Multiple domains and multiple functions. In G. J. O. Fletcher & M. S. Clark (Eds.), *Blackwell handbook of social psychology: Interpersonal processes* (pp. 411–436). Oxford: Blackwell Publishers.

Kunda, Z. (1990). The case for motivated reasoning. *Psychological Bulletin*, *108*, 480–498.

Leary, M. R., & Baumeister, R. F. (2000). The nature and function of self-esteem: Sociometer theory. In M. P. Zanna (Ed.), *Advances in experimental social psychology* (Vol. 32, pp. 2–51). San Diego, CA: Academic Press.

Leary, M. R., & MacDonald, G. (2003). Individual differences in self-esteem: A review and theoretical integration. In M. R. Leary & J. P. Tangney (Eds.), *Handbook of self and identity* (pp. 401–450). New York: Guilford Press.

Leary, M. R., Tambor, E. S., Terdal, S. K., & Downs, D. L. (1995). Self-esteem as an interpersonal monitor: The sociometer hypothesis. *Journal of Personality and Social Psychology*, *68*, 518–530.

MacDonald, G., & Jessica, M. (2006). Family approval as a constraint in dependency regulation: Evidence from Australia and Indonesia. *Personal Relationships*, *13*, 183–194.

MacDonald, G., & Leary, M. R. (2005). Why does social exclusion hurt? The relationship between social and physical pain. *Psychological Bulletin*, *131*, 202–223.

Mikulincer, M., Gillath, O., Halevy, V., Avihou, N., Avidan, S., & Eshkoli, N. (2001). Attachment theory and reactions to others' needs: Evidence that activation of the sense of attachment security promotes empathic responses. *Journal of Personality and Social Psychology, 81*, 1205–1224.

Mikulincer, M., & Shaver, P. R. (2001). Attachment theory and intergroup bias: Evidence that priming the secure base schema attenuates negative reactions to outgroups. *Journal of Personality and Social Psychology, 81*, 97–115.

Mikulincer, M., & Shaver, P. R. (2003). The attachment behavioral system in adulthood: Activation, psychodynamics, and interpersonal processes. In M. Zanna (Ed.), *Advances in experimental social psychology* (Vol. 35, pp. 52–153). New York: Academic Press.

Murray, S. L. (1999). The quest for conviction: Motivated cognition in romantic relationship. *Psychological Inquiry, 10*, 23–34.

Murray, S. L., Bellavia, G., Rose, P., & Griffin, D. (2003). Once hurt, twice hurtful: How perceived regard regulates daily marital interaction. *Journal of Personality and Social Psychology, 84*, 126–147.

Murray, S. L., Griffin, D. W., Rose, P., & Bellavia, G. (2003). Calibrating the sociometer: The relational contingencies of self-esteem. *Journal of Personality and Social Psychology, 85*, 63–84.

Murray, S. L., Griffin, D. W., Rose, P., & Bellavia, G. (2006). For better or worse? Self-esteem and the contingencies of acceptance in marriage. *Personality and Social Psychology Bulletin, 32*, 866–882.

Murray, S. L., Holmes, J. G., & Collins, N. L. (2006). Optimizing assurance: The risk regulation system in relationships. *Psychological Bulletin, 132*, 641–666.

Murray, S. L., Holmes, J. G., & Griffin, D. (1996). The benefits of positive illusions: Idealization and the construction of satisfaction in close relationships. *Journal of Personality and Social Psychology, 70*, 79–98.

Murray, S. L., Holmes, J. G., & Griffin, D. W. (2000). Self-esteem and the quest for felt security: How perceived regard regulates attachment processes. *Journal of Personality and Social Psychology, 78*, 478–498.

Murray, S. L., Holmes, J. G., Griffin, D. W., Bellavia, G., & Rose, P. (2001). The mismeasure of love: How self-doubt contaminates relationship beliefs. *Personality and Social Psychology Bulletin, 27*, 423–436.

Murray, S. L., Holmes, J. G., MacDonald, G., & Ellsworth, P. (1998). Through the looking glass darkly? When self-doubts turn into relationship insecurities. *Journal of Personality and Social Psychology, 75*, 1459–1480.

Murray, S. L., Rose, P., Bellavia, G., Holmes, J., & Kusche, A. (2002). When rejection stings: How self-esteem constrains relationship-enhancement processes. *Journal of Personality and Social Psychology, 83*, 556–573.

Murray, S. L., Rose, P., Holmes, J. G., Derrick, J., Podchaski, E., Bellavia, G., et al. (2005). Putting the partner within reach: A dyadic perspective on felt security in close relationships. *Journal of Personality and Social Psychology, 88*, 327–347.

Nezlek, J. B., Kowalski, R. M., Leary, M. R., Blevins, T., & Holgate, S. (1997). Personality moderators of reactions to interpersonal rejection: Depression and trait self-esteem. *Personality and Social Psychology Bulletin, 23*, 1235–1244.

Pierce, T., & Lydon, J. (1998). Priming relational schemas: Effects of contextually activated and chronically accessible interpersonal expectations on responses to a stressful event. *Journal of Personality and Social Psychology, 75*, 1441–1448.

Pietrzak, J., Downey, G., & Ayduk, O. (2005). Rejection sensitivity as an interpersonal vulnerability. In M. Baldwin (Ed.), *Interpersonal cognition* (pp. 62–84). New York: Guilford Press.

Reis, H. T., Clark, M. S., & Holmes, J. G. (2004). Perceived partner responsiveness as an organizing construct in the study of intimacy and closeness. In D. Mashek & A. P. Aron (Eds.), *Handbook of closeness and intimacy* (pp. 201–225). Mahwah, NJ: Lawrence Erlbaum Associates, Inc.

Rholes, S. W., Simpson, J. A., Campbell, L., & Grich, J. (2001). Adult attachment and the transition to parenthood. *Journal of Personality and Social Psychology, 81,* 421–435.

Rholes, W. S., Simpson, J. A., & Orina, M. M. (1999). Attachment and anger in an anxiety-provoking situation. *Journal of Personality and Social Psychology, 76,* 940–957.

Rusbult, C. E., Verette, J., Whitney, G. A., Slovik, L. F., & Lipkus, I. (1991). Accommodation processes in close relationship: Theory and preliminary research evidence. *Journal of Personality and Social Psychology, 60,* 53–78.

Simpson, J. A. (1987). The dissolution of romantic relationships: Factors involved in relationship stability and emotional distress. *Journal of Personality and Social Psychology, 53,* 683–692.

Simpson, J. A., Ickes, W., & Grich, J. (1999). When accuracy hurts: Reactions of anxious-ambivalent dating partners to a relationship-threatening situation. *Journal of Personality and Social Psychology, 76,* 754–769.

Simpson, J. A., Rholes, W. S., & Nelligan, J. S. (1992). Support seeking and support giving within couples in an anxiety-provoking situation: The role of attachment styles. *Journal of Personality and Social Psychology, 62,* 434–446.

Simpson, J. A., Rholes, W. S., & Phillips, D. (1996). Conflict in close relationships: An attachment perspective. *Journal of Personality and Social Psychology, 71,* 899–914.

Sommer, K. L., & Baumeister, R. F. (2002). Self-evaluation, persistence, and performance following implicit rejection: The role of trait self-esteem. *Psychological Bulletin, 28,* 926–938.

Swann, W. B., Bosson, J. K., & Pelham, B. W. (2002). Different partners, different selves: Strategic verification of circumscribed identities. *Personality and Social Psychology Bulletin, 28,* 1215–1228.

Taylor, S. E., & Brown, J. D. (1988). Illusion and well-being: A social psychological perspective on mental health. *Psychological Bulletin, 103,* 193–210.

Tooby, J., & Cosmides, L. (1996). Friendship and the banker's paradox: Other pathways to the evolution of adaptations for altruism. *Proceedings of the British Academy, 88,* 119–143.

Tucker, J. S., & Anders, S. L. (1999). Attachment style, interpersonal perception accuracy, and relationship satisfaction in dating couples. *Personality and Social Psychology Bulletin, 25,* 403–412.

Twenge, J. M., Catanese, K. R., & Baumeister, R. F. (2002). Social exclusion causes self-defeating behavior. *Journal of Personality and Social Psychology, 83,* 606–615.

2

On the Role of Psychological Needs in Healthy Functioning: Integrating a Self-Determination Theory Perspective with Traditional Relationship Theories

JENNIFER G. LA GUARDIA

*R*elationships serve as sources of the most gratifying experiences as well as provide a foundation for working though those experiences that are challenging. Healthy functioning is anchored in good quality social relationships (Deci & Ryan, 1985; Reis, Collins, & Bersheid, 2000; Ryan & Deci, 2000a, 2000c; Ryff, 1995; Uchino, Cacioppo, & Kiecolt-Glaser, 1996). Yet, while much of the good that emerges in our lives comes from our important relationships, much psychopathology and physical health risk also has its origin in and is further perpetuated by dysfunctional interpersonal exchanges or less than optimal relationships (House, Landis, & Umberson, 1988; Ryan, Deci, Grolnick, & La Guardia, 2006).

Self-determination theory (SDT; Deci & Ryan, 2000; Ryan & Deci, 2000a, 2000c) provides an important framework for understanding how relationships influence personal growth and development. From an SDT perspective, humans are active, growth oriented organisms that are naturally inclined to engage in interesting activities, exercise their capacities and skills, and pursue connections with others. Over the course of development, humans must also integrate diverse social-interpersonal experiences as well as cultural norms into a coherent self-structure to guide further interactions and goal directed behaviors. SDT suggests that what fuels humans toward greater self-differentiation, integration of social norms and behavior, identity formation, and growth across contexts and throughout the lifespan are the psychological needs for autonomy, competence, and relatedness (La Guardia & Ryan, 2000; Ryan & La Guardia, 2000). Further, it is the relational environments that support these needs that provide the backdrop for optimal human functioning. That is, although tendencies toward growth and integration operate naturally, the social environment acts to support or thwart this innate trajectory, thereby affecting personal well-being and relational functioning. Thus, SDT in its essence is a theory of relationships, as the need framework provides an understanding of core motivational processes and the necessary social conditions to support optimal growth and development.

In this chapter I review evidence for the way the concept of needs frames the development of self, and how need-supportive relationships facilitate people's overall well-being and functioning within their relationships, across time and across cultures. Then I draw on three established areas within the relationship research tradition—attachment, intimacy, and interdependence theories—to illustrate how the concept of needs may coalesce with each of these frameworks and provide a glimpse of future avenues of collaborative theory and research.

As I discuss in this chapter, traditional relational theories tend to focus on defining how connectedness is formed or maintained through interpersonal exchange. While SDT has much to say about this as well, it also defines how relationships function to stimulate or impede other important growth processes that occur in the context of close relationships over the lifespan. First, I review the major tenets of self-determination theory, beginning with the concept of basic psychological needs.

SELF-DETERMINATION THEORY AND BASIC PSYCHOLOGICAL NEEDS

The central organizing concept within SDT that provides a framework for understanding the facilitation of intrinsic motivation, social development, and well-being is that of basic psychological needs. SDT suggests that there are three basic psychological needs—autonomy, competence, and relatedness (Deci & Ryan, 2000; Ryan & Deci, 2000a, 2000c). *Autonomy* literally means "self-rule" and refers to actions that are self-initiated, willingly endorsed, and experienced as wholeheartedly engaged and volitional (deCharms, 1968, Deci, 1975). The opposite experience of autonomy is heteronomy, which concerns feeling compelled or controlled in one's behavior. *Competence*, introduced by White (1959) as effectance motivation, refers to the propensity to have influence on the environment, and is experienced as mastery and challenge in activity. Expressions of competence are witnessed in curiosity, exploration, and challenge seeking, and fulfillment of this need relies on the act of engaging in activity to stretch one's capacities, regardless of the separable rewards, material benefits, or success experiences that competent behavior might result in. Finally, the "need to belong" or *relatedness* refers to the human tendency to form strong, stable interpersonal bonds (Baumeister & Leary, 1995; Ryan & Deci, 2000a). Relatedness is experienced when one feels significant in the eyes of others, or is deeply connected to others. This connectedness is not derived simply from lauding the outcomes of a person's behavior, their appearance or status, or their possessions, but occurs instead when the "true" self has been regarded. Notably, how one achieves relatedness is the key focus of most traditional relational theories.

Evidence from daily diary studies attests to the importance of need fulfillment for overall well-being. For example, Sheldon, Ryan, and Reis (1996) found that satisfaction of autonomy and competence needs related to well-being (as indexed by measures of positive and negative mood, vitality, and physical symptoms) both at trait level and in day-to-day fluctuations. Reis, Sheldon, Gable, Roscoe, and Ryan (2000) also found that daily variation in emotional well-being may be understood in terms of the degree to which all three needs are satisfied in daily activity, such that each of the needs showed independent contributions to daily well-being.

As mentioned previously, the social environment is key toward understanding whether needs are facilitated or enhanced or whether optimal functioning will be impeded (Ryan & Deci, 2000c). Need-supportive partners actively attempt to understand the person's interests, preferences, and perspectives; they get involved with, show interest in, and direct energy towards the person; and they convey that that person is significant, cared for, and loved wholeheartedly. Need-supportive partners are those with whom a person can share their interests and activities and capitalize on positive experiences, and they provide the supportive backdrop for the person to face challenges optimally, so the person is not overwhelmed but is guided toward mobilizing and organizing his or her thoughts, feelings, and behaviors. With this supportive foundation in place, the person is able to explore, challenge themselves, try new experiences, and take interpersonal risks toward forming deeper, more intimate connections with others. In contrast, when social environments are excessively controlling, overchallenging, or rejecting, optimal functioning will suffer (Ryan & Deci, 2000c, 2001). Social partners that are not need supportive may place contingencies on, or restrict and limit choice in, the person's behavior, emphasizing obedience and compliance to the partner's own wants or interests rather than taking the person's needs into account. Partners that are not need supportive may subtly or explicitly pit needs against each other, as when a person is asked to constrict her feelings or limit her activities and interests in order to preserve affiliation. They may also convey that the person's worth is dependent on success in a given domain or activity, thereby making activity pressured or high stakes. In any case, there are interpersonal and health consequences as a result of the lack of support from the social context (Ryan et al., 2006).

Given that much of what we do throughout our lives is embedded in the context of our relationships, it is important to understand the developmental processes and behaviors that may be affected by the social context. Further, using the SDT framework, we can understand how these processes or behaviours may be fuelled by needs, as well as come to predict the functional consequences of need support on these processes or behaviors. I now turn to a discussion of intrinsic motivation and the integration of extrinsic behaviors, and present a very brief review of evidence from the SDT literature implicating the role of needs and the social context's support of these needs in optimal functioning (Deci & Ryan, 2000; Ryan & Deci, 2000b, 2000c).

INTRINSIC MOTIVATION, EXTRINSIC MOTIVATION, AND INTEGRATION

The contemporary conceptualization of intrinsic motivation reflects the innate propensity to seek out novelty and challenges, to extend and exercise one's capacities, to explore and learn (White, 1959), with activity experienced as volitional and willingly engaged (deCharms, 1968). As such, intrinsically motivated behavior is performed for the inherent satisfaction or enjoyment in its doing.

Intrinsic motivation is fundamentally implicated in the development of self and identity, as many activities that later promote deeply held identities begin as intrinsically motivated behaviors (La Guardia, 2007; Ryan & Deci, 2003). Children's first activities center around play—the prototypical expression of intrinsic motivation—and as play is honed and refined into more complex behaviors, many children find their interests, special talents, and skills. Indeed, intrinsic motivation underlies many learning pursuits and much exploration in school, work, and leisure activities throughout life.

In SDT terms, intrinsic motivation is based in people's needs to feel competent and autonomous. Notably, while relatedness is not essential for intrinsic motivation per se, as many intrinsically motivated activities may be solitary pursuits or at least do not require direct involvement of others to engage in activity, the encouragement by close others contributes to these interests being solidified as part of identity. Thus relatedness provides a key backdrop to make engagement in intrinsically motivated activity more readily energized and maintained.

Early experiences with parents and teachers contribute significantly to the activities that are of first focus, and throughout the lifespan, important others, such as friends and romantic partners, shape the extent to which intrinsic activities are given energy. Within SDT, several decades of research have shown that parents and teachers intimately influence intrinsic motivation processes in children (see La Guardia & Ryan, 2002; Ryan & La Guardia, 1999 for reviews). For example, parental support and encouragement of children's initiations and autonomy during play has been shown to be associated with greater mastery motivation and persistence in tasks by children (e.g., Grolnick, Bridges, & Frodi, 1984; Deci, Driver, Hotchkiss, Robbins, & Wilson, 1993). Further, teachers who are more warm and autonomy supportive (considering the students' perspectives, facilitating students to tackle challenges and find solutions) have students that show greater curiosity, desire for challenge, and independence toward learning tasks in school, while teachers who are more cold or controlling (using more rewards and punishments, social comparisons, and external contingencies or pressure) have students who show less curiosity and interest in mastery, feel less confident doing schoolwork, and have lower feelings of self-worth (Deci, Schwartz, Sheinman, & Ryan, 1981; Ryan & Grolnick, 1986). Because intrinsic motivation has been linked to greater interest in taking on cognitive challenges (Danner & Lonky, 1981), more creative (Amabile, 1996) and deep conceptual processing (Utman, 1997), better cognitive performance at complex tasks (Grolnick & Ryan, 1987; Utman, 1997), and greater resilience in the face of challenges and failures (Boggiano & Katz, 1991), the importance of a supportive relational context on optimal early development becomes apparent.

Intrinsic motivation also remains critically important into adulthood. That is, even with increased external demands in adulthood, people continue to exercise intrinsic capacities in the time they have available, developing passions for different activities such as sport or artistic creation (Vallerand et al., 2003), turning work challenges into play (Sansone, Weir, Harpster, & Morgan, 1992), and developing new interests and avocations outside of normative family and work responsibilities (Ryan & La Guardia, 2000). Further, need support has been implicated in energizing and maintaining these pursuits (Ryan & Deci, 2000a, 2000c).

While intrinsically motivated activity has great importance, many of the behaviors people engage in in everyday life are not in themselves inherently interesting, and thus are not intrinsically motivated but instead are extrinsically motivated—performed in order to accomplish some outcome separable from the activity per se. Extrinsic motivation was traditionally viewed as a unitary construct, however behaviors can vary considerably in their relative level of engagement. SDT suggests four dimensions of extrinsically regulated behaviors—external, introjected, identified, and integrated—that vary on a continuum of autonomy (Ryan & Connell, 1989). *External regulation* refers to the traditional view of extrinsic motivation, such that a person engages in behavior simply to gain rewards or avoid punishments. Externally regulated activity is directly controlled or compelled by others, and these behaviors are poorly maintained when reward or punishment contingencies are removed. *Introjected regulation* refers to behaviors that are initiated and regulated by internally controlling imperatives, such as "I should" and other internally self-pressuring mechanisms (e.g., guilt, anxiety, or want for approval). Unlike externally regulated behaviors, introjects are contingencies that are not directly administered by someone else, but instead are often experienced as the internal voice that a person has "swallowed whole" from others without digesting it and making it his or her own. *Identified regulation* refers to behaviors that are self-endorsed and carried out because they are valued, or the person deeply identifies with their purpose. Finally, *integrated regulation* is the most autonomous form of extrinsic motivation in that behaviors are in line with other self-endorsed behaviors and thus do not create a sense of conflict in their pursuit. In sum, this continuum of extrinsic behaviors reflects the extent to which the behaviors are willingly engaged in, or in SDT terms, autonomously engaged in or self-determined, with those extrinsically motivated behaviors that are clearly pressured or compelled by outside forces (external, introjected) reflecting a low degree of autonomy, and those that reflect personally endorsed and integrated behaviors (identified, integrated) reflecting a high degree of autonomy.

Assimilation of activities and pursuits that are extrinsic and valued by others (e.g., doing your homework or chores, settling into a career) is regarded as a basic process in development (Piaget, 1952, 1981; Bruner, 1962). Socializing agents such as parents and teachers, and later spouses, friends, and colleagues, can be more or less encouraging in helping assimilate various behaviors and values, and the consequences of how social partners support the internalization and regulation of behaviors is significant for development and ongoing functioning.

Research has shown that early in life, parents and teachers are a powerful influence on children adopting important values and behaviors regarding schooling, peer relations, and career development (Grolnick, Deci, & Ryan, 1997). For example, the more parents are controlling around doing homework and chores, the less deeply their children value and show initiative for these tasks (Grolnick & Ryan, 1989). Further, when parents are less involved (a proxy for relatedness), and have more inconsistent structure for their children (a scaffolding for competence), their children have a poorer sense of personal control of their outcomes (e.g., grades), as well as poorer adjustment and lower school achievement. Finally, parents' autonomy support also helps adolescents build their peer relations on the basis of more well-integrated motives, and this in turn is related to greater feelings of competence and satisfaction in these peer relationships (Soenens & Vansteenkiste, 2005). Teachers' autonomy support has been shown to influence students' engagement and sense of competence in school, and this in turn engenders greater internalization for school activities and greater academic performance in school (Guay & Vallerand, 1996). Overall, more internalized forms of academic motivation have been associated with better student outcomes, such as greater interest, confidence, and less anxiety in school (Black & Deci, 2000; Ryan and Connell, 1989), higher self-esteem and life satisfaction (Chirkov and Ryan, 2001), and better school performance (Black & Deci, 2000; Fortier, Vallerand, & Guay, 1995; Grolnick & Ryan, 1989). Further, this has also been shown cross-culturally (Chirkov & Ryan, 2001; Hayamizu, 1997; Yamauchi & Tanaka, 1998).

Parallel to findings in children and adolescents, the need supportiveness of the social contexts in which adults operate has important consequences for the relative internalization of work (Deci, Ryan, Gagné, Leone, Usunov, & Kornazheva, 2001; Gagné & Deci, 2005), parenting (Grolnick, 2003), health (Ryan, Plant, & O'Malley, 1993; Williams, Grow, Ryan, Friedman, & Deci, 1996), and other behaviors central to identity, such as religious commitment (O'Connor & Vallerand, 1990; Ryan, Rigby, & King, 1993). Across each of these domains, greater need support is associated with more internalized forms of regulation (Ryan & Deci, 2000c), and goal attainments associated with more internalized regulations predict more positive adjustment and well-being outcomes (Sheldon & Elliot, 1998; Sheldon & Kasser, 1998).

In sum, the work reviewed points to the importance of need-supportive environments for the engagement of innate and socially prescribed tasks. Relational partners can have a profound impact in early initiation, exploration, and engagement in important developmental tasks, as well as in ongoing behaviors throughout the lifecourse. While traditional relational theories do not largely focus on these processes, there is another function—emotion regulation—that has been the focus of many relational theories, and for which needs have essential influence. I now briefly turn to a discussion of the role of needs and their implications for healthy emotion regulation.

RELATION OF PSYCHOLOGICAL NEEDS TO EMOTION REGULATION

The capacity to regulate and integrate emotional experiences is central to the definition of well-being and healthy interpersonal functioning (La Guardia & Ryff, 2003; Ryan & Deci, 2001). From an SDT perspective, emotions can be seen as powerful indicators of the ways in which people are being need supported (or not) in their relationships. People are naturally energized by their needs to engage emotions fully, incorporating *both* positive and negative emotional experiences as they arise. However, relationship partners can enhance or constrain these basic tendencies by welcoming emotional experiences and expressions and facilitating the person's processing of emotions or alternatively (subtly or directly) restricting or placing constraints on the experience or expression of emotion. The person can actively respond to these relational affordances by then adhering to his or her needs—engaging more fully to process emotions within the relationship when supportive, or withdrawing energy from the relationship when non-supportive— or instead sacrificing his or her needs in the service of "preserving" the relationship. Across time, this dynamic exchange shapes the development and maintenance of the person's emotion regulation capacities, as well as the depth, connection, and functioning of the relationship. Thus, emotion regulation is an interplay of both intrapersonal *and* interpersonal processes, and the concept of needs can inform both. Understanding the context of need support helps to determine how relational partners activate emotional responses, exacerbate or facilitate a person's efforts to regulate emotions, and may sustain these dynamics over time (La Guardia, 2006; La Guardia & Ryff, 2003), with the key to health defined by the ways in which people engage their emotional experiences in accord with their needs in the context of their relationships.

Research in the SDT tradition attests to the importance of need fulfillment in emotion regulation. Greater need fulfillment within relationships has been linked to greater attachment security (e.g., La Guardia, Ryan, Couchman, & Deci, 2000), willingness to garner emotional support from the partner (Ryan, La Guardia, Solky-Butzel, Chirkov, & Kim, 2005) and give support to one's partner (Deci, La Guardia, Moller, Sheiner, & Ryan, 2006), and demonstrate more understanding and less defensive responses to conflict (Knee, Lonsbary, Canevello, & Patrick, 2005). As these processes of attachment, utilization of social support, and conflict resolution are essentially emotion regulation functions, need support has important implications for proximal functioning within relationships. Further, current work in SDT examines the emotional dynamics of partners at single points in time and across time. Research focuses on how need support facilitates emotional awareness and intrapersonal processing of emotional experience, *choiceful* disclosure of emotions to others, and orientations around specific regulatory strategies over time. A more in-depth discussion of this work and the implication of needs for emotion regulation processes follows in the upcoming sections.

SUMMARY OF SDT

In sum, SDT in its essence is a theory of relationships. That is, core needs operate largely in the context of interpersonal exchanges and their fulfillment is enhanced or forestalled by relational supports. The need framework provides an understanding of motivational processes and the necessary social conditions for optimal growth and development. Less than optimal support leaves the person ill-equipped for developmental challenges such as identity formation and interpersonal regulatory challenges posed in relationships with others, and may set the stage for more profound disturbances in personal well-being and relational functioning.

In the next section, I review the core aspects of three traditional relational theories—those of attachment, intimacy, and interdependence—and show how research within the SDT tradition dovetails with these traditions. I will also suggest how the SDT need framework might complement these three traditions in creating a parsimonious conceptualization of interpersonal behavior.

SDT AND TRADITIONAL RELATIONAL THEORIES

Attachment Theory

One of the earliest and well-articulated relational theories is that of attachment theory (Bowlby, 1969). Bowlby suggested that the attachment system is an innate regulatory system that is activated when under threat from the environment, with its primary function being to reduce arousal or anxiety and promote safety and survival. Thus, when the attachment system is activated, behaviors thereby stimulated (e.g., crying, proximity seeking) recruit important others such as caregivers or other close relational partners in the service of providing regulatory functions which that person cannot do alone (Sroufe & Waters, 1977). Further, when the person is not activated by threat, the relationship serves as a base from which exploration, risk, and stretching of skills emerge.

In its optimal form—a secure attachment—the child turns toward the caregiver to obtain comfort, care, and confidence and the caregiver attends to and is responsive to his or her child's needs. As a responsive base, the caregiver is available and ready to respond when called on, to encourage, assist, and actively intervene when needed (Bowlby, 1969, 1988; Bretherton, 1985; Sroufe, 1990). Certainly, not all caregivers are appropriately responsive, and thus children may develop alternative, less optimal ways to cope with their distress. These insecure forms of attachment have been labeled avoidant, anxious-ambivalent, and disorganized styles, and reflect characteristic ways in which a child may cope with rejecting, emotionally unavailable, inconsistent, or chaotic and frightening caregivers. According to attachment theory, sensitivity of early caregivers contributes to the child's development of self and later relational functioning.

While behaviors in infancy and early childhood are aimed at actual proximity, protection, soothing, or a secure base from which to explore the environment, as the child develops cognitively the system is an internalized, ever-present foundation for regulation and exploration. Thus the internal working model developed through early childhood experiences provides the cognitive, motivational, and affective lens through which expectations about current relational partners, and behaviors towards these partners, are influenced. Similar to childhood, adult attachment is generally classified by a characteristic style in accord with continuous-variable ratings of different attachment styles (e.g., Scharfe & Bartholomew, 1994) or different attachment dimensions such as the anxiety and avoidance dimensions (e.g., Brennan, Clark, & Shaver, 1998). These styles or dimensions reflect characteristic patterns of how people view themselves as love- or care-worthy and whether they believe their partners to be available, consistent, and responsive. New experiences with partners contribute to proximal felt security— the confidence in one's partner's love and commitment, and the expectation that one's partner is available, reliable, and responsive to one's needs—and may also contribute to changes in attachment over time. In adults, romantic partners are regarded as the primary attachment relationships (Hazan & Zeifman, 1994) and some of the most important sources of emotional and instrumental support (Hazan & Shaver, 1994). Indeed, in cross-sectional, daily diary, and laboratory studies, greater partner responsiveness and supportiveness is associated with feeling more cared for and valued by their partner (a proxy for security), and with greater satisfaction and happiness within the relationship (see Collins & Feeney, 2004 for a review). Thus, in adulthood, partners' actual responsivity continues to be an important foundation for attachment.

A long and rich research tradition attests to the importance of attachment security for well-being across the lifespan. Further, those with greater attachment security also show more optimal relational functioning, as indicated by greater willingness to seek support when needed, greater relationship longevity, greater relational stability, as well as greater trust, commitment, satisfaction, and interdependence in relationships (see Cassidy & Shaver, 1999 and Simpson & Rholes, 2004 volumes for reviews).

SDT and attachment perspectives have many qualities in common. Both theories outline processes that are assumed to be innate, have developmental relevance, and rely on support from important others across the lifespan for optimal functioning. Using the need framework, recent research in the SDT tradition offers some insights into the definition of responsivity, as well as an understanding of the importance of the immediate social context (rather than individual differences) in the proximal causes of security.

From the SDT perspective, the concept of responsivity or sensitivity can be differentiated with respect to the three needs (La Guardia et al., 2000). Indeed, definitions of sensitivity emphasize the support of others' sense of self-initiation and agentic action (autonomy), support for their sense of effectance and self-confidence (competence), and provision of a warm, loving, and nurturing environment (relatedness) (e.g., Bretherton, 1987; Sroufe and Waters, 1977). Thus sensitive others who respond to initiatives, encourage exploration, and provide non-contingent positive regard for their partner are supporting their intrinsic needs.

Furthermore, SDT would suggest that without *all three needs* being satisfied, optimal health, development, and relational functioning will not be evidenced. For example, Steinberg and Silverberg (1986) argued that adolescents individuate by becoming "emotionally autonomous"—detaching or distancing from parents, being less trusting of their guidance, and being more reluctant to follow their lead. In essence, they suggested that healthy development requires giving up related-ness in order to gain autonomy. Ryan and Lynch (1989) argued that "emotional autonomy" neither represents autonomy as volition nor healthy individuation, and as expected found that "emotional autonomy" was negatively related to parental support of their teenager's autonomy (as volition or willing engagement), felt connectedness to the family, and well-being. Also, in a recent study by Assor, Roth, and Deci (2004), university students were asked about their mothers' and fathers' use of conditional regard with them while they were growing up. Conditional regard conveys that the child will only be loved or shown care if he or she behaves in ways or adheres to social practices that are acceptable to the parent. Results indicated that parents' use of conditional regard was associated with children's reports of fluctuating self-esteem (contingent on their parents' approval), greater sense of rejection, and resentment towards their parents. Thus, having to give up one's autonomy in order to gain relatedness to others can be quite costly to developing a close, secure relationship and stable sense of self. The need construct thus helps to define more specifically what must be provided by partners to be "responsive," and as such predicts healthy relational outcomes.

Although attachment is theorized as a dynamic process between partners, attachment researchers (with some exceptions) still largely examine attachment as an individual difference in working models or styles. Clearly, attachment styles that develop with primary caretakers have a significant degree of stability over time and across relationships (Bowlby, 1980), and early attachment relationships influence the way people regulate their subsequent interpersonal behaviors and emotions (Ainsworth, Blehar, Waters, & Wall, 1978). However, attachments also vary over time and across important relationships (e.g., Baldwin, Keelan, Fehr, Enns, & Koh-Rangarajoo, 1996; Cook, 2000; Davila, Burge, & Hammen, 1997; Fox, Kimmerly, & Schafer, 1991, Fraley & Shaver, 2000; La Guardia et al., 2000; Lewis, 1994; Shaver, Collins, & Clark, 1996), such that people do not always enact the same relational style and do not experience the same sense of security with each partner, even across close relationships within the family, or across family, best friends, and romantic partners.

From an SDT perspective, emphasis is placed on the immediate social context, or more specifically the relationship, as the central means by which attachment is influenced. In a recent study, my colleagues and I demonstrated the importance of measuring attachment not simply as an individual difference but as specific to the relational context (La Guardia et al., 2000). Specifically, we showed that attachment security was systematic, such that security was greater in relation-ships that supported basic psychological needs for autonomy, competence, and relatedness. Further, we also showed that attaching differently to relational partners (getting closer to those who meet one's needs and creating more distance from those who do not) is adaptive and may represent *selectivity* of health promoting partners. While attachment security, both at mean levels and in specific relationships, was predictive of greater well-being, this association between attachment security and well-being was substantially mediated by need satisfaction. Thus, among the principal reasons for which attachment security relates to well-being is that secure attachments provide an arena in which people are able to satisfy their basic psychological needs.

The idea of selective engagement dovetails nicely with a recent diary study examining the dynamics of perceived regard in spousal interactions over several weeks (Murray, Bellavia, Rose, & Griffin, 2003). Results showed that those who generally felt more valued by their partner tended to draw closer to their partner on days when they felt most vulnerable and in need of support, and were less reactive after days when they experienced hurts or slights from the partner. In contrast, those who generally felt less valued by their partner tended to distance themselves from their partner on days when they felt most vulnerable or in need of support, and were quicker to show protective behaviors (e.g., distancing) or to retaliate against the partner following days when they felt hurt by their partner. From an SDT perspective, perceived regard is derived from experiences of need support, and thus the adaptive regulation in accord with partners' support shown in this study suggests further evidence for the SDT model.

In sum, the SDT concept of needs may help to organize an understanding of variation in attachment that has been evidenced, defining the necessary nutriments of supportive partners and thereby predicting likely attachment responses on the part of the person. One question for future research is to understand how prior attachment orientations—the rich developmental history of need exchanges with others—affects how partners enter into a given relationship and shape expectations for acceptance and responsiveness of the partner over time. La Guardia et al. (2000) would suggest that despite general trait attachment styles, significant variation still seems to be in line with *relationship specific* need fulfillment experiences. Thus, the frequency of negative and positive exchanges, and thereby the stability versus variability of need support over time, become key variables of interest in understanding these personal health trajectories, as well as the quality and longevity of people's relationships. With a context-specific focus, these theories may be prescriptive, informing interventions that teach partners to be responsive to each other's emotional needs, and help people make better choices in selecting and attaching to partners who are capable of adequate need support.

Intimacy Theory

Intimacy processes are closely related to concepts within attachment theory, as both describe emotion regulation through interpersonal exchanges (Reis & Patrick, 1996). The interpersonal process model of intimacy (Reis & Shaver, 1988) defines a transactional process between partners involving self-disclosure and partner responsiveness. Intimacy requires that one person communicates personally relevant information (verbally and/or non-verbally), revealing thoughts and feelings to the other. For intimacy to develop, the partner must respond to the disclosures by conveying acceptance, validation, and care for the discloser, and the partner must "receive" this to occur. Responsiveness—defined as the extent to which people perceive that their partner pays attention to and responds perceptively to the individual's central defining features of the self—encompasses diverse phenomena including reflected appraisal (e.g., believing that a partner respects one's personal qualities), emotional understanding (e.g., feeling an emotional bond with others), and responsiveness to needs (e.g., believing that a partner will respond with concern to expressions of need) (Reis, Clark, & Holmes, 2004). The reciprocal emotional exchange process occurs over time between the partners, and as the interplay of disclosure and responsiveness unfolds, partners perform each of these functions more deeply to form stronger, more intimate connections (Laurenceau, Rivera, Schaffer, & Pietromonaco, 2004).

Research has demonstrated that the quality of disclosures and responsiveness specifically informs the intimacy process. Disclosures that are more emotional and reveal more personal information (in contrast to factual disclosures) are regarded as stimulating greater intimacy (Laurenceau, Feldman Barrett, & Pietromonaco, 1998). Across several daily diary studies, (Laurenceau, Feldman Barrett, & Rovine, 2005; Laurenceau et al., 1998) examining participants' interactions across a variety of social relationships over a week or several weeks, Laurenceau and colleagues showed that greater self-disclosure and greater partner disclosure predict greater intimacy. Further, these effects were mediated by partner responsiveness, such that disclosure was associated with greater intimacy in part because of the responsivity of one's partner to one's disclosures. Laurenceau et al. (2005) also replicated these findings in a sample of married couples over the course of nearly 2 months.

Both SDT and intimacy theories highlight the dynamics between partners, grounding interpersonal behavior in emotionally supportive exchanges, and defining specifiable outcomes as a product of these exchanges. Within the SDT tradition, recent research has demonstrated that need fulfillment impacts emotional experience, people's willingness to express their emotions and the relative authenticity of these expressions, subsequent orientations toward emotional exchanges with partners, and the consequences of this regulation for personal and relational functioning.

La Guardia (2001) demonstrated that differences in emotional experience and expression across people's relationships are associated with the differential relational affordances for psychological needs. The more need-fulfilled people were within each of their relationships with their mother, father, romantic partner, best friend, and roommate, the more they were able to experience positive affect and less negative affect, as well as to express both when they emerged. Further, within relationships, the more people felt they could experience positive affect and less negative affect, as well as express both positive and negative affect when they emerged, the more they felt vital and satisfied within their relationships.

Further, Ryan et al. (2005) also showed systematic variation in emotional reliance (defined as the willingness to turn toward significant others for emotional support) in concert with need support, such that greater need satisfaction within relationships was associated with greater willingness to rely on relational partners.

Additionally, although mean level differences in emotion reliance were found across culturally distinct groups (U.S., Russia, South Korea, Turkey) and gender, suggesting that cultural context and gender may impact both the level of emotional reliance and to whom it is directed, emotional reliance still showed significant benefit to well-being. As such, this work provided evidence that emotional reliance may be implicated by need fulfillment and may be universally important, as the benefits for health and well-being remain despite differences in gender and cultural contexts.

Finally, new work examines how need support informs healthy emotion regulation between partners (La Guardia, 2006). In a sample of heterosexual dating couples, partners completed measures assessing their overall emotional engagement with their partner (awareness, openness in internal processing, and disclosure), their relational functioning, and their personal well-being, as well as daily diaries of emotional interactions and relational functioning with their partner over a 2-week period. Overall within the relationship, greater need fulfillment was associated with greater emotional awareness, openness to internally process emotions, and emotional disclosure to one's partner. Further, using actor-partner modeling to assess the simultaneous contribution of members of the dyad, greater emotional awareness, openness, and disclosure on the part of both the person and his or her partner was associated with greater intimacy, attachment security, and relational vitality for the person. Moreover, greater awareness and disclosure by the person and his or her partner was associated with greater feelings of positive affect and life satisfaction, while less openness and disclosure both by the person and his or her partner was associated with greater risk for depression, anxiety, physical symptoms, and negative affect in the person. Thus how one's partner regulates his or her emotions has consequences for one's personal health and relational functioning, above and beyond one's own regulation. Also, emotional engagement and its consequences is in part a function of need support in the relationship. Additionally, using diary measures, daily need fulfillment was used to predict how partners would orient around their residual affect from positive or negative experiences with their partner during the day, and thereby affect the extent to which they emotionally engaged with their partner at the day's end. In line with SDT, people were more self-protective when perceiving that their partner was not need supportive, and were more emotionally engaging and open with their partner when perceiving that their partner was need supportive during the day. Specifically, when a negative event was "sticking with" a partner at the day's end, less perceived need support from the partner was associated with a greater tendency to close off from their partner for men, and for women a greater tendency to "perseverate on the event and punish the partner" and lower likelihood to orient toward reconnecting with him. When a positive event was left over, greater perceived need satisfaction was associated with less likelihood to contain emotions for men, and for women was associated with less likelihood to contain their emotions as well as greater efforts to capitalize on positive emotions. Further, regulating around need fulfillment evidenced consequences for daily health. Specifically, when coping with leftover negative events, men experienced more negative affect when they closed off from their partner, while women experienced more negative affect when they "perseverated and punished" their partner. When a positive event was left over, both men and women experienced more vitality and positive affect when they capitalized on positive feelings, and less vitality and more negative affect when they contained their positive feelings.

In sum, this research suggests a potential role of need support in further informing ideas about disclosure and responsivity addressed by intimacy theory. Specifically, SDT's concept of basic psychological needs helps to define patterns of disclosure, the quality of emotional disclosures (authentic vs. non-genuine; open vs. restricted, closed), as well as informing us about what it functionally means to be responsive in relationships. As these theories highlight recursive models, it will be vital in the future to further examine how patterns of disclosure and support unfold and influence subsequent exchange, thereby more accurately predicting whether close intimate bonds are formed, or distance and dissolution are more likely.

INTERDEPENDENCE FRAMEWORK

While the attachment and intimacy literatures both speak specifically to affective interpersonal processes that unfold between relational partners, interdependence theory provides a broader model for studying interpersonal exchange. According to the interdependence framework, partners in close relationships exert mutual influence on each other in meaningful ways, across varied occasions, contexts, and time (Kelley & Thibaut, 1978). Interactions between partners are viewed as a function of each person's attitudes, motives, and goals in relation to each other, as well as their relevance within any given situation (Holmes & Cameron, 2005; Kelley, Holmes, Kerr, Reis, Rusbult, & Van Lange, 2003).

Research in the interdependence tradition has demonstrated how reciprocal exchanges within partnerships impact and shape various relationship processes over time. For example, Drigotas, Rusbult, Wieselquist, and Whitton (1999) examined the extent to which the self is shaped by one's partner's perceptions and behaviors. Coined the "Michelangelo phenomenon," the self is expected to develop as a consequence of repeated interactions between the person and his or her partner, with selective development of some behavioral tendencies and elimination of others resulting in a more stable, long-term foundation of personal motives and dispositions. While partners may shape each other in ways that are more or less healthy, the model suggests that relational well-being is dependent on the ability of partners to "bring out the best" in each other, and as such move the person closer to their ideal self. Across various studies, research has demonstrated that partners' affirming expectations and behaviors of each other sculpt movement toward more idealized selves, and this in turn is associated with greater couple well-being.

Murray, Griffin, Rose, and Bellavia (2003) have also modeled interdependence examining the concept of the sociometer in romantic relationships. The sociometer is suggested to be a dedicated psychological system that monitors social events for cues relevant to a person's "relational value" or importance to partners, evaluates the risk for interpersonal rejection, and activates behaviors to either enhance relational value (e.g., seek approval or connection) or withdraw from social interaction if the relationship is expected to be rejecting (see Leary & Baumeister, 2000 for a review). Self-esteem is assumed to be the internal representation of social acceptance and rejection, such that the individual's sense of self-worth reflects whether he or she is being included versus excluded by others. Testing a relationship specific sociometer, Murray et al. (2003) assessed how chronic perceptions of a partner's regard—the sense of felt security in being valued, accepted, and loved by one's partner—influence how married and cohabiting partners function to protect self-esteem within their relationship over time. Results showed that those who generally experienced more positive regard from their partner felt more accepted and loved on days after they felt bad about themselves (or in other words, on days they experienced low self-esteem). In contrast, those who generally experienced less positive regard from their partner felt bad about themselves (low self-esteem) on days after they experienced more anxiety about their partner's acceptance than was typical. In sum, a person's self-regard is viewed as a function of how one has been regarded chronically in the relationship, and this chronic regard also impacts how the person orients toward the partner proximally.

Clearly, work from SDT on attachment and intimacy processes previously cited in this chapter attests to the importance of understanding the dynamics of interdependence in relationships, and the consequences for optimal development and functioning. Other work has also specifically examined mutuality in motivational orientations toward relationships as well as mutuality in need support between partners. For example, in a study of married couples, Blais, Sabourin, Boucher, and Vallerand (1990) found that partners who are more autonomously oriented toward their relationship are more likely to have relationships of greater quality than those who display less autonomous forms of motivation, feeling more satisfied and seeing relationship problems as challenges in contrast to experiencing more conflict, tension, and anxiety in the relationship. Also, Deci et al. (2006) examined the impact of mutuality of autonomy support on personal health and relational functioning within close friendships dyads. *Receiving* autonomy support from a friend predicted greater emotional reliance, attachment security, and adjustment, as well as more positive psychological health in the recipient. Further, *giving* autonomy support to a friend conferred benefits to the giver's functioning in the relationship, over and above the effects of receiving autonomy support from his or her friend. Finally, in a study examining mutuality of need support in dating and married couples, Patrick, Knee, Canavello, and Lonsbary (2006) found that lower perceived need fulfillment in the person is associated with more defensive responses and greater perceived conflict in the partnership, and this was more pronounced when the partner also experienced lower need fulfillment (particularly lower relatedness) in the relationship. Further, greater satisfaction in the relationship was also evidenced when the person experienced need support, and again this was more pronounced when the partner also felt supported in his or her needs (particularly relatedness). In sum, as this body of research suggests, relational partners show interdependence in need functions, with mutuality conferring the most positive personal and relational outcomes.

The continued challenge for researchers in both SDT and interdependence traditions is to effectively model dynamic exchange between the person and his or her relational environment, both in the moment and as it unfolds across time. With advances in sophisticated methodologies (e.g., diary studies) and statistical modeling techniques, greater precision in understanding how dynamics unfold over time, across different developmental epochs and cultural contexts is more readily attainable. Also, recently Kelley et al. (2003) introduced a taxonomy of interpersonal situations to help define the nature of key social interchanges encountered in everyday life, and to provide a platform for understanding how each partner contributes to a given relational exchange. While Kelley and colleagues do not utilize the concept of needs, the dynamics of need support can be readily seen in the interpersonal exchanges described in the atlas. Further, as the situations described may call for different types of interactions or skills employed, the need framework may continue to inform the dynamics described by providing the foundation for predicting what aspects of the interpersonal exchange will promote personal and relational flourishing. Indeed, SDT has shown the power of needs in predicting social exchange in diverse settings, relationships (including those differentiated by authority or expertise as well as peer or mutual relations), and cultural contexts. In future work, it would be useful to understand the extent to which the need framework and dimensions used to structure the atlas converge, and alternatively what each may uniquely contribute to the understanding of relational processes.

SUMMARY AND FUTURE DIRECTIONS

In this chapter I sought to highlight how the SDT perspective may complement a rich body of work in attachment, intimacy, and interdependence theories, and create a dialogue about some potential avenues of future collaboration. I have suggested that the SDT framework, and specifically the concept of basic psychological needs, might help to understand a broader swath of motivated behavior within the context of relationships, and thus create a parsimonious understanding of the impact of social exchange within relationships on developmental tasks, growth, and well-being. Specifically, from an SDT perspective, needs centrally underlie the processes of intrinsic motivation, internalization, and emotion regulation, and relationship partners may either enhance or thwart these processes. As such, the development of a person's interests, the identities he or she develops, and the capacities for emotionally navigating life's ups and downs will be directly impacted by the social environment. As inevitably even the best partners will not always be need supportive, understanding the regulation of needs—both their fulfillment and their sacrifice in the service of the relationship—will be vital to predicting personal and relational health outcomes in the short and long term.

REFERENCES

Ainsworth, M. D. S., Blehar, M. C., Waters, E., & Wall, S. (1978). *Patterns of attachment*. Hillsdale, NJ: Lawrence Erlbaum Associates, Inc.

Amabile, T. M. (1996). *Creativity in context*. New York: Westview Press.

Assor, A., Roth, G., & Deci, E. L. (2004). The emotional costs of parents' conditional regard: A self-determination theory analysis. *Journal of Personality, 72*, 47–88.

Baldwin, M. W., Keelan, J. P. R., Fehr, B., Enns, V., & Koh-Rangarajoo, E. (1996). Social-cognitive conceptualization of attachment working models: Availability and accessibility effect. *Journal of Personality and Social Psychology, 71*, 94–109.

Baumeister, R., & Leary, M. R. (1995). The need to belong: Desire for interpersonal attachments as a fundamental human motivation. *Psychological Bulletin, 117*, 497–529.

Black, A. E., & Deci, E. L. (2000). The effects of instructors' autonomy support and students' autonomous motivation on learning organic chemistry: A self-determination theory perspective. *Science Education, 84*, 740–756.

Blais, M. R., Sabourin, S., Boucher, C., & Vallerand, R. (1990). Toward a motivational model of couple happiness. *Journal of Personality and Social Psychology, 59*, 1021–1031.

Boggiano, A. K., & Katz, P. A. (1991). Mastery motivation in boys and girls: The role of intrinsic versus extrinsic motivation. *Sex Roles, 25*, 511–520.

Bowlby, J. (1969). *Attachment and loss: Vol. 1: Attachment*. New York: Basic Books.

Bowlby, J. (1980). *Attachment and loss: Vol. 3: Loss*. New York: Basic Books.

Bowlby, J. (1988). *A secure base*. New York: Basic Books.

Brennan, K. A., Clark, C. L., & Shaver, P. R. (1998). Self-report measure of adult attachment: An integrative overview. In J. A. Simpson & W. S. Rholes (Eds.), *Attachment theory and close relationships* (pp. 46–76). New York: Guilford Press.

Bretherton, I. (1985). Attachment theory: Retrospect and prospect. In I. Bretherton & E. Waters (Eds.), Growing points in attachment theory and research. *Monographs of the Society for Research in Child Development, 50* (1–2, Serial No. 209).

Bretherton, I. (1987). New perspectives on attachment relations: Security, communication and internal working models. In J. Osofsky (Ed.), *Handbook of infant development* (pp. 1061–1100). New York: Wiley.

Bruner, J. (1962). *On knowing: Essays for the left hand*. Cambridge, MA: Harvard University Press.

Cassidy, J., & Shaver, P. R. (Eds.) (1999). *Handbook of attachment: Theory, research, and clinical applications*. New York: Guilford Press.

Chirkov, V. I., & Ryan, R. M. (2001). Parent and teacher autonomy-support in Russian and U.S. adolescents: Common effects on well-being and academic motivation. *Journal of Cross Cultural Psychology, 32*, 618–635.

Collins, N. L., & Feeney, B. C. (2004). An attachment theory perspective on closeness and intimacy. In D. Mashek & A. Aron (Eds.), *Handbook of closeness and intimacy* (pp. 163–187). Mahwah, NJ: Lawrence Erlbaum Associates, Inc.

Cook, W. L. (2000). Understanding attachment security in family context. *Journal of Personality and Social Psychology, 78*, 285–294.

Danner, E. W., & Lonky, E. (1981). A cognitive-developmental approach to the effects of rewards on intrinsic motivation. *Child Development, 52*, 1043–1052.

Davila, J., Burge, D., & Hammen, C. (1997). Why does attachment style change? *Journal of Personality and Social Psychology, 73*, 826–838.

deCharms, R. (1968). *Personal causation: The internal affective determinants of behavior.* New York: Academic Press.

Deci, E. L. (1975). *Intrinsic motivation.* New York: Plenum.

Deci, E. L., Driver, R. E., Hotchkiss, L., Robbins, R. J., & Wilson, I. M. (1993). The relation of mothers' controlling vocalizations to children's intrinsic motivation. *Journal of Experimental Child Psychology, 55*, 151–162.

Deci, E. L., La Guardia, J. G., Moller, A. C., Scheiner, M. J., & Ryan, R. M. (2006). On the benefits of giving as well as receiving autonomy support: Mutuality in close friendships. *Personality and Social Psychology Bulletin, 32*, 313–327.

Deci, E. L., & Ryan, R. M. (1985). *Intrinsic motivation and self-determination in human behavior.* New York: Plenum.

Deci, E. L., & Ryan, R. M. (2000). The "what" and "why" of goal pursuits: Human needs and the self-determination of behavior. *Psychological Inquiry, 11*, 227–268.

Deci, E. L., Ryan, R. M., Gagné, M., Leone, D. R., Usunov, J., & Kornazheva, B. P. (2001). Need satisfaction, motivation, and well-being in the work organizations of a former Eastern Bloc country. *Personality and Social Psychology Bulletin, 27*, 930–942.

Deci, E. L., Schwartz, A. J., Sheinman, L., & Ryan, R. M. (1981). An instrument to assess adults' orientations toward control versus autonomy with children: Reflections on intrinsic motivation and perceived competence. *Journal of Educational Psychology, 73*, 642–650.

Drigotas, S. M., Rusbult, C. E., Wieselquist, J., & Whitton, S. W. (1999). Close partner as sculptor of the ideal self: Behavioral affirmation and the Michelangelo phenomenon. *Journal of Personality and Social Psychology, 77*, 293–323.

Fortier, M. S., Vallerand, R. J., & Guay, F. (1995). Academic motivation and school performance: Toward a structural model. *Contemporary Educational Psychology, 20*, 257–274.

Fox, N. A., Kimmerly, N. L., & Schafer, W. D. (1991). Attachment to mother/attachment to father: A meta-analysis. *Child Development, 62*, 210–225.

Fraley, R. C., & Shaver, P. R. (2000). Adult romantic attachments: Theoretical developments, emerging controversies, and unanswered questions. *Review of General Psychology, 4*, 132–154.

Gagné, M., & Deci, E. L. (2005). Self-determination theory and work motivation. *Journal of Organizational Behavior, 26*, 331–362.

Grolnick, W. S. (2003). *The psychology of parental control: How well-meant parenting backfires.* Mahwah, NJ: Lawrence Erlbaum Associates, Inc.

Grolnick, W. S., Bridges, L., & Frodi, A. (1984). Maternal control style and the mastery motivation of one-year-olds. *Infant Mental Health Journal, 5*, 72–82.

Grolnick, W. S., Deci, E. L., & Ryan, R. M. (1997). Internalization within the family. In J. E. Grusec & L. Kuczynski (Eds.), *Parenting and children's internalization of values: A handbook of contemporary theory* (pp. 135–161). New York: Wiley.

Grolnick, W. S., & Ryan, R. M. (1987). Autonomy in children's learning: An experimental and individual difference investigation. *Journal of Personality and Social Psychology, 52*, 890–898.

Grolnick, W. S., & Ryan, R. M. (1989). Parent styles associated with children's self-regulation and competence in school. *Journal of Educational Psychology, 81*, 143–154.

Guay, F., & Vallerand, R. J. (1996). Social context, students' motivation, and academic achievement: Toward a process model. *Social Psychology of Education, 1*, 211–233.

Hayamizu, T. (1997). Between intrinsic and extrinsic motivation: Examination of reasons for academic study based on the theory of internalization. *Japanese Psychological Research*, 39, 98–108.

Hazan, C., & Shaver, P. R. (1994). Attachment as an organizational framework for research on close relationships. *Psychological Inquiry*, 5, 1–22.

Hazan, C., & Zeifman, D. (1994). Sex and the psychological tether. In K. Bartholomew & D. Perlman (Eds.), *Attachment processes in adulthood. Advances in personal relationships* (pp. 151–178). London: Jessica Kingsley.

Holmes, J. G., & Cameron, J. (2005). An integrated review of theories of interpersonal cognition: An interdependence theory perspective. In M. Baldwin (Ed.), *Interpersonal cognition* (pp. 415–447). New York: Guilford Press.

House, J. S., Landis, K. R., & Umberson, D. (1988). Social relationships and health. *Science*, 241, 540–545.

Kelley, H. H., Holmes, J. G., Kerr, N., Reis, H., Rusbult, C. E., & Van Lange, P. A. (2003). *An atlas of interpersonal situations*. Cambridge: Cambridge University Press.

Kelley, H. H., & Thibaut, J. W. (1978). *Interpersonal relations: A theory of interdependence*. New York: Wiley.

Knee, C. R., Lonsbary, C., Canevello, A., & Patrick, H. (2005). Self-determination and conflict in romantic relationships. *Journal of Personality and Social Psychology*, 89, 997–1009.

La Guardia, J. G. (2001). *Interpersonal compartmentalization: An examination of self-concept variation, need satisfaction, and psychological vitality*. Unpublished doctoral dissertation, University of Rochester, NY.

La Guardia, J. G. (2006). *Emotional engagement within couples: Impact on personal and relationship functioning*. Paper for the Symposium: The Us in You and Me: Modeling the Dyad in Relational Processes, presented at the Annual Meeting of the Society for Personality and Social Psychology, Palm Springs, CA.

La Guardia, J. G. (2007). Developing who I am: A self-determination theory approach to the establishment of healthy identities. To appear in Special Issue on Motivation and Identity, *Educational Psychologist*.

La Guardia, J. G., & Ryan, R. M. (2000). Personal goals, fundamental psychological needs, and well-being: Self-determination theory and its applications. *Revue Quebecoise de Psychologie*, 21, 283–306.

La Guardia, J. G., & Ryan, R. M. (2002). What adolescents need: A self-determination theory perspective on development within families, school, and society. In F. Pajares & T. Urdan (Eds.), *Adolescence and education* (Vol. 2, pp. 193–219). Greenwich, CT: Information Age Publishing.

La Guardia, J. G., Ryan, R. M., Couchman, C. E., & Deci, E. L. (2000). Within-person variation in security of attachment: A self-determination theory perspective on attachment, need fulfillment, and well-being. *Journal of Personality and Social Psychology*, 79, 367–384.

La Guardia, J. G., & Ryff, C. (2003). Self-esteem challenges. *Psychological Inquiry*, 14, 48–51.

Laurenceau, J.-P., Feldman Barrett, L. A., & Pietromonaco, P. R. (1998). Intimacy as an interpersonal process: The importance of self-disclosure and perceived partner responsiveness in interpersonal exchanges. *Journal of Personality and Social Psychology*, 74, 1238–1251.

Laurenceau, J.-P., Feldman Barrett, L., & Rovine, M. J. (2005). The interpersonal process model of intimacy in marriage: A daily-diary and multilevel modeling approach. *Journal of Family Psychology* 19, 314–323.

Laurenceau, J.-P., Rivera, L. M., Schaffer, A., & Pietromonaco, P. R. (2004). Intimacy as an interpersonal process: Current status and future directions. In D. Mashek & A. Aron (Eds.), *Handbook of closeness and intimacy* (pp. 61–78). Mahwah, NJ: Lawrence Erlbaum Associates, Inc.

Leary, M. R., & Baumeister, R. F. (2000). The nature and function of self-esteem: Sociometer theory. In M. P. Zanna (Ed.), *Advances in experimental social psychology* (Vol. 32, pp. 1–62). San Diego, CA: Academic Press.

Lewis, M. E. (1994). Does attachment imply a relationship or multiple relationships? *Psychological Inquiry, 5,* 47–51.

Murray, S. L., Bellavia, G., Rose, P., & Griffin, D. (2003). Once hurt, twice hurtful: How perceived regard regulates daily marital interaction. *Journal of Personality and Social Psychology, 84,* 126–147.

Murray, S. L., Griffin, D. W., Rose, P., & Bellavia, G. (2003). Calibrating the sociometer: The relational contingencies of self-esteem. *Journal of Personality and Social Psychology, 85,* 63–84.

O'Connor, B. P., & Vallerand, R. J. (1990). Religious motivation in the elderly: A French-Canadian replication and an extension. *Journal of Social Psychology. 130* (1), 53–59.

Patrick, H., Knee, C. R., Canevello, A., & Lonsbary, C. (2006). *The role of need fulfillment in relationship functioning and well-being: A self-determination theory perspective.* Unpublished manuscript, Baylor College of Medicine, Houston, TX.

Piaget, J. (1952). *The origins of intelligence in children.* New York: International Universities Press.

Piaget, J. (1981). *Intelligence and affectivity: Their relationship during child development.* Palo Alto, CA: Annual Reviews.

Reis, H. T., Clark, M. S., & Holmes, J. G. (2004). Perceived partner responsiveness as an organizing construct in the study of intimacy and closeness. In D. Mashek & A. Aron (Eds.), *Handbook of closeness and intimacy.* Mahwah, NJ: Lawrence Erlbaum Associates, Inc.

Reis, H. T., Collins, W. A., & Berscheid, E. (2000). The relationship context of human behavior and development. *Psychological Bulletin, 126,* 844–872.

Reis, H. T., & Patrick, B. C. (1996). Attachment and intimacy: Component processes. In E. T. Higgins & A. W. Kruglanski (Eds.), *Social psychology: Handbook of basic principles* (pp. 523–563). New York: Guilford Press.

Reis, H. T., & Shaver, P. (1988). Intimacy as an interpersonal process. In S. Duck (Ed.), *Handbook of personal relationships* (pp. 367–389). Chichester, UK: John Wiley and Sons.

Reis, H. T., Sheldon, K. M., Gable, S. L., Roscoe, J., & Ryan, R. M. (2000). Daily well-being: The role of autonomy, competence, and relatedness. *Personality and Social Psychology Bulletin, 26,* 419–435.

Ryan, R. M., & Connell, J. P. (1989). Perceived locus of causality and internalization: Examining reasons for acting in two domains. *Journal of Personality and Social Psychology, 57,* 749–761.

Ryan, R. M., & Deci, E. L. (2000a). The darker and brighter sides of human existence: Basic psychological needs as a unifying concept. *Psychological Inquiry, 11,* 319–338.

Ryan, R. M., & Deci, E. L. (2000b). Intrinsic and extrinsic motivations: Classic definitions and new directions. *Contemporary Educational Psychology, 5,* 54–67.

Ryan, R. M., & Deci, E. L. (2000c). Self-determination theory and the facilitation of intrinsic motivation, social development, and well-being. *American Psychologist, 55,* 68–78.

Ryan, R. M., & Deci, E. L. (2001). On happiness and human potentials: A review of research on hedonic and eudaimonic well-being. *Annual Review of Psychology*, 52, 141–166.

Ryan, R. M., & Deci, E. L. (2003). On assimilating identities to the self: A self-determination theory perspective on internalization and integrity within cultures. In M. R. Leary & J. P. Tangney (Eds.), *Handbook of self and identity* (pp. 253–272). New York: Guilford Press.

Ryan, R. M., Deci, E. L., Grolnick, W. S., & La Guardia, J. G. (2006). Autonomy, relatedness, and the self: Their relation to development and psychopathology. In D. Cicchetti and D. J. Cohen (Eds.), *Developmental psychopathology: Vol. 1. Theory and methods* (pp. 618–655). New York: John Wiley & Sons, Inc.

Ryan, R. M., & Grolnick, W. S. (1986). Origins and pawns in the classroom: Self-report and projective assessments of individual differences in children's perceptions. *Journal of Personality and Social Psychology*, 50, 550–558.

Ryan, R. M., & La Guardia, J. G. (1999). Achievement motivation within a pressured society: Intrinsic and extrinsic motivations to learn and the politics of school reform. In T. Urdan (Ed.), *Advances in motivation and achievement* (Vol. 11, pp. 45–85). Greenwich, CT: JAI Press.

Ryan, R. M., & La Guardia, J. G. (2000). What is being optimized? Self-determination theory and basic psychological needs. In S. Qualls & R. Abeles (Eds.), *Psychology and the aging revolution: How we adapt to longer life* (pp. 145–172). Washington, DC: APA Books.

Ryan, R. M., La Guardia, J. G., Solky-Butzel, J. S., Chirkov, V., & Kim, Y. (2005). On the interpersonal regulation of emotions: Emotional reliance across gender, relationships and cultures. *Personal Relationships*, 12, 146–163.

Ryan, R. M., & Lynch, J. H. (1989). Emotional autonomy versus detachment: Revisiting the vicissitudes of adolescence and young adulthood. *Child Development*, 60, 340–356.

Ryan, R. M., Plant, R. W., & O'Malley, S. (1993). Initial motivations for alcohol treatment: Relations with patient characteristics, treatment involvement and dropout. *Addictive Behaviors*, 20, 279–297.

Ryan, R. M., Rigby, S., & King, K. (1993). Two types of religious internalization and their relations to religious orientations and mental health. *Journal of Personality and Social Psychology*, 65, 586–596.

Ryff, C. D. (1995). Psychological well-being in adult life. *Current Directions in Psychological Science*, 4, 99–104.

Sansone, B. R., Weir, C., Harpster, L., & Morgan, C. (1992). Once a boring task always a boring task? Interest as a self-regulatory mechanism. *Journal of Personality and Social Psychology*, 63, 379–390.

Scharfe, E., & Bartholomew, K. (1994). Reliability and stability of adult attachment patterns. *Personal Relationships*, 1, 23–43.

Shaver, P. R., Collins, N. J., & Clark, C. L. (1996). Attachment styles and internal working models of self and relationship partners. In G. J. O. Fletcher & J. Fitness (Eds.), *Knowledge structures in close relationships: A social psychological approach*. Mahwah, NJ: Lawrence Erlbaum Associates, Inc.

Sheldon, K. M., & Elliot, A. J. (1998). Not all personal goals are "personal": Comparing autonomous and controlling goals on effort and attainment. *Personality and Social Psychology Bulletin*, 24, 546–557.

Sheldon, K. M., & Kasser, T. (1998). Pursuing personal goals: Skills enable progress but not all progress is beneficial. *Personality and Social Psychology Bulletin*, 24, 1319–1331.

Sheldon, K. M., Ryan, R. M., & Reis, H. T. (1996). What makes for a good day? Competence and autonomy in the day and in the person. *Personality and Social Psychology Bulletin, 22,* 1270–1279.

Simpson, J. A., & Rholes, W. S. (Eds.) (2004). *Adult attachment: Theory, research, and clinical implications.* New York: Guilford Press.

Soenens, B., & Vansteenkiste, M. (2005). Antecedents and outcomes of self-determination in three life domains: The role of parents' and teachers' autonomy support. *Journal of Youth and Adolescence, 34,* 589–604.

Sroufe, L. A. (1990). An organizational perspective on the self. In D. Cicchetti & M. Beeghly (Eds.), *The self in transition: Infancy to childhood.* Chicago: University of Chicago Press.

Sroufe, L. A., & Waters, E. (1977). Attachment as an organizational construct. *Child Development, 48,* 1184–1199.

Steinberg, L., & Silverberg, S. (1986). The vicissitudes of autonomy in adolescence. *Child Development, 57,* 841–851.

Uchino, B. N., Cacioppo, J. T., & Kiecolt-Glaser, J. K. (1996). The relationship between social support and physiological processes: A review with emphasis on underlying mechanisms and implications for health. *Psychological Bulletin, 119,* 488–531.

Utman, C. H. (1997). Performance effects of motivational state: A meta-analysis. *Personality and Social Psychological Review, 1,* 170–182.

Vallerand, R. J., Blanchard, C. M., Mageau, G. A., Koestner, R., Ratelle, C., Léonard, M., et al. (2003). Les passions de l'âme: On obsessive and harmonious passion. *Journal of Personality and Social Psychology, 85,* 756–767.

White, R. W. (1959). Motivation reconsidered: The concept of competence. *Psychological Review, 66,* 297–333.

Williams, G. C., Grow, V. M., Ryan, R. M., Friedman, Z., & Deci, E. L. (1996). Motivational predictors of weight loss and weight-loss maintenance. *Journal of Personality and Social Psychology, 70,* 115–126

Yamauchi, H., & Tanaka, K. (1998). Relations of autonomy, self-referenced beliefs and self-regulated learning among Japanese children. *Psychological Reports, 82,* 803–816.

3

Self-Verification in Relationships as an Adaptive Process

WILLIAM B. SWANN, JR., CHRISTINE CHANG-SCHNEIDER, and SARAH ANGULO

O nce people form their self-views, they work to verify and preserve them. This is the core contention of self-verification theory (Swann, 1983). The theory has wide-ranging implications for understanding close relationships. That is, it not only predicts the partners people select, but also how happy they are with those partners, and whether they remain with them or divorce them. What makes the theory interesting is that it challenges the widely accepted notion that relationship quality is optimized when partners entertain and communicate exalted evaluations of one another. Rather, the theory predicts that people prefer partners who validate their *negative* as well as positive self-views. Moreover, because self-views have the same functional properties regardless of their degree of specificity, the theory applies whether self-views pertain to global qualities (e.g., personal value) or highly specific ones (e.g., athleticism). Furthermore, the theory holds that self-verification is an adaptive process that, paradoxically, promotes health and well-being.

Let us begin by describing a study that provides a glimpse of the phenomenon we have in mind. The goal of this study, which we will call the "Mr. Nice–Mr. Nasty study," was to assess how much people with positive self-views and negative self-views wanted to interact with partners who held positive or negative evaluations of them (Swann, Stein-Seroussi, & Giesler, 1992). To this end, we invited college students to a laboratory experiment. Shortly after participants arrived, they learned that two evaluators had formed an impression of them based on their responses to a personality test they had completed earlier. The experimenter then showed participants some comments that each of the "evaluators" (who were actually fictitious) had ostensibly written about them. One evaluator (whom we will call "Mr. Nice") was favorably impressed with the participant, noting that he or she seemed self-confident, well-adjusted, and happy. The other evaluator ("Mr. Nasty") was distinctly unimpressed, commenting that the participant was unhappy, unconfident, and anxious around people. The results revealed a clear preference for self-verifying partners. As shown in Figure 3.1, participants with positive self-views tended to choose Mr. Nice but those with negative self-views tended to choose Mr. Nasty.

These findings inspired considerable incredulity among advocates of positivity strivings. Many simply questioned the reliability of the phenomenon, asserting that "It won't happen again!" Researchers at the University of Texas and elsewhere responded by attempting to replicate the effect using diverse methodologies. Seventeen replications later it was clear that the tendency for people to prefer self-verifying evaluations and interaction partners was robust, even if the self-views of participants happened to be negative (e.g., Hixon & Swann, 1993; Robinson & Smith-Lovin, 1992; Swann, Hixon, Stein-Seroussi, & Gilbert, 1990; Swann, Pelham, & Krull, 1989; Swann, Wenzlaff, Krull, & Pelham, 1992; Swann, Wenzlaff, & Tafarodi, 1992). Further, people with negative self-views seem to be truly drawn to self-verifying interaction partners rather than simply avoiding non-verifying ones—when given the option of being in a different experiment, people with negative self-views chose to interact with the negative evaluator over participating in another experiment, and they chose being in a different experiment over interacting with a positive evaluator (Swann, Wenzlaff, & Tafarodi, 1992).

Both men and women displayed this propensity, whether or not the self-views were easily changed and whether the self-views were associated with qualities that were specific (intelligence, sociability, dominance) or global (self-esteem, depression). People were particularly likely to seek self-verifying evaluations if their self-views were confidently held (e.g., Pelham & Swann, 1994; Swann & Ely, 1984; Swann, Pelham, & Chidester, 1988) and important (Swann & Pelham, 2002), or extreme (Giesler, Josephs, & Swann, 1996). Finally, in recent years researchers have shown that people also strive to verify negative (and positive) self-views associated with group membership. Such strivings emerge for both collective self-views (personal self-views people associate with group membership, such as "sensitivity" for many women; Chen, Chen, & Shaw, 2004) or group identities (convictions about the characteristics of the groups of which they are members,

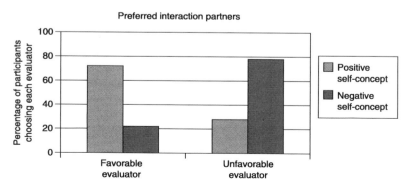

FIGURE 3.1 Preferred interaction partners. Adapted from Swann, Stein-Seroussi, and Giesler (1992).

such as "chronically late" for most Spaniards; Gómez, Seyle, Morales, Huici, Gaviria, & Swann, 2006; Lemay & Ashmore, 2004).

But is it appropriate to suggest that the behavior of people with negative self-views is "paradoxical?" If the frame of reference is contemporary social psychology, we think so. After all, the notion that people possess a fundamental, pervasive desire for positive evaluations may be *the* bedrock assumption of the social psychological discipline. And perhaps it should be, as there are sound reasons to believe that the desire for self-enhancement is truly fundamental. First, there is the apparent ubiquity of this desire. Whether one examines people's social judgments, attributions, or overt behaviors, there appears to be a widespread tendency for them to favor themselves over others (for reviews, see Jones, 1973; Taylor & Brown, 1988). Indeed, some (Greenwald & Ronis, 1978) have argued that self-enhancement was a hidden assumption underlying many variations of consistency theories, including dissonance theory (Brehm & Cohen, 1962).

Second, traces of a preference for positivity emerge extremely early in life. Within mere weeks of developing the ability to discriminate facial characteristics, for example, 5-month-olds attend more to smiling faces than to non-smiling ones (Shapiro, Eppler, Haith, & Reis, 1987). Similarly, as early as 4½ months of age, children orient preferentially to voices that have the melodic contours of acceptance as compared to non-acceptance (Fernald, 1993). Third, when people react to evaluations, a preference for positive evaluations emerges before other preferences (Swann et al., 1990). Thus, for example, when participants who viewed themselves negatively chose between an evaluator who appraised them either negatively or positively, those forced to choose quickly preferred the positive evaluator; only those who had some time to reflect chose the negative (self-verifying) partner (more on the mechanism underlying this phenomenon later).

Yet as potent as the desire for positivity may be, the results of the Mr. Nice–Mr. Nasty study suggest that it may sometimes be trumped by a desire for self-verification. Most strikingly, among people with negative self-views, the desire for self-stability leads people to embrace negative rather than positive partners.

But, one might protest, what relevance do a bevy of laboratory investigations have for readers of a volume on close relationships? Quite a bit, if one takes seriously the implications of a parallel line of research on people involved in ongoing relationships. The first study in this series, dubbed the "marital bliss study" was designed to compare how people with positive self-views and those with negative self-views reacted to positive versus negative marital partners (Swann, Hixon, & De La Ronde, 1992). The investigators recruited married couples who were either shopping at a local mall or enjoying an afternoon's horseback riding at a ranch in central Texas, and invited them to complete a series of questionnaires. They began with the Self-Attributes Questionnaire (SAQ; Pelham & Swann, 1989), a measure that focused on five attributes that most Americans regard as important: intelligence, social skills, physical attractiveness, athletic ability, and artistic ability. On completion, participants went through the SAQ again, this time rating their spouse. Finally, participants filled out a measure of their commitment to the relationship. While each person completed these questionnaires, his or her spouse completed the same ones. The researchers thus had indices of what everyone thought of themselves, what their spouses thought of them, and how committed they were to the relationship.

How did people react to positive or negative evaluations from their spouses? As shown in Figure 3.2, people with positive self-views responded in the intuitively obvious way—the more favorable their spouses were, the more committed they were. By contrast, people with negative self-views displayed the opposite reaction; the more favorable their spouses were, the *less* committed they were. Those with moderate self-views were most committed to spouses who appraised them moderately.

Subsequent researchers attempted to replicate this effect (e.g., Cast & Burke, 2002; De La Ronde & Swann, 1998; Murray, Holmes, Dolderman, & Griffin, 2000; Ritts & Stein, 1995; Schafer, Wickrama, & Keith, 1996; Swann, De La Ronde, & Hixon, 1994). Although the strength of the effect varied, each study reported that some evidence of a preference for self-verifying partners emerged among married participants (for a discussion of an error in the Murray et al. report, see the last section of this chapter). Furthermore, both men and women displayed this preference whether they had positive or negative self-views and whether they resided in any of several cities across the United States. Similarly, it did not matter whether the research participants were volunteers from the community or university students; again and again, a preference for self-verifying marital partners emerged.

The major goal of this chapter is to explain why people display self-verification strivings, with special emphasis on how these strivings are adaptive for people trying to maintain enduring relationships. We begin by discussing the nature and boundary conditions of self-verification processes, with special attention to the relationship of self-verification strivings to positivity strivings.

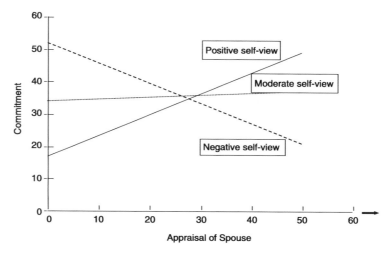

FIGURE 3.2   Commitment in marital relationships. Adapted from Swann, Hixon, and De La Ronde (1992).

SELF-VERIFICATION THEORY

Prescott Lecky (1945) was the first to propose the notion that people are motivated to maintain their self-views. The core ideas surfaced again in various self-consistency theories (e.g., Aronson, 1968; Festinger, 1957; Secord & Backman, 1965). Self-verification theory (Swann, 1983; Swann, Rentfrow, & Guinn, 2003) elaborated these approaches by shifting away from the notion that people desired psychological *consistency* to an emphasis on the desire for psychological *coherence*. Self-verification theory is thus less interested in the mental gymnastics through which people create consistency between their behaviors and their transient self-images. Although such gymnastics could contribute to coherence, the concept of coherence is broader and deeper because it refers to the unity, integrity, and continuity of the entire knowledge system. This knowledge system transcends the here and now and embraces all of individuals' experiences. Because self-views summarize and organize these experiences, they are a vital source of coherence.

Ultimately, self-verification theory can be traced to the assumption that children initially form their self-views by observing how others treat them (e.g., Cooley, 1902; Mead, 1934). As children mature, the more their self-views are confirmed, and the more certain they become in the accuracy of these self-views. Such certainty, in turn, encourages people to rely on their self-views more in making predictions about their worlds, guiding behavior, and maintaining a sense of coherence, place, and continuity. As a result, by mid-childhood there emerges a preference for evaluations that confirm self-views (e.g., Cassidy, Ziv, Mehta, & Feeney, 2003).

The theory's most provocative prediction is that a preference for self-verifying evaluations should emerge even if the self-view happens to be negative. In some cases, it is obvious how the desire to maintain negative self-views can be adaptive. After all, all people possess flaws and weaknesses, and it makes sense for them to cultivate and maintain appropriately negative self-views to reflect these flaws and weaknesses. For example, to avoid confusion and disappointment, just as those who are musical should want others to see them as musical, so too will tone-deaf people benefit from having others see them as tone-deaf. Nevertheless, the adaptiveness of self-verifying strivings is more difficult to see when people develop globally negative self-views (e.g., "I am worthless") that have no compelling object-ive basis. Active efforts to maintain such negative self-views by, for example, gravitating toward harsh or abusive partners, seem maladaptive.

Which raises a question: What's so important about stable self-views that people will endure hardship to maintain them? The psychological significance of stable self-views can be better appreciated by considering what happens to individuals whose self-views have been stripped away. Consider the case study of William Thompson, a man whose chronic alcohol abuse led him to develop memory loss so profound that he could no longer remember who he was (Sacks, 1985). Able to remember only scattered fragments from his past, Thompson lapsed into a state of incoherence and psychological anarchy. Desperately striving to recover the self that eluded his grasp, he frantically developed hypotheses about who he was and then tested these hypotheses on whomever happened to be present ("You must be Hymie, the Kosher butcher next door . . . But why are there no blood-stains on your coat? . . ."). Tragically, Thompson could never remember the results of the latest test for more than a few seconds and so he was doomed to repeat his experiments once again. Thompson's case not only shows that stable self-views are essential to the feelings of coherence that give meaning to our worlds, it also shows how critically important self-views are to guiding action. Thompson did not know how to act toward people because his sense of self kept disappearing like a Cheshire cat. No wonder, then, that people will fight like tigers to preserve their self-views.

How Self-Verification Strivings Shape Actual and Perceived Social Reality

People may use three distinct processes to create—either in actuality or in their own minds—self-verifying social worlds. First, people may construct self-verifying "opportunity structures" (i.e., social environments that satisfy people's needs; McCall & Simmons, 1966) by seeking and entering into relationships in which they are apt to enjoy confirmation of their self-views. We believe that this is a particularly important and influential process, which is why we introduced it above. Thus, whereas the Mr. Nice–Mr. Nasty study suggests that people seek self-verifying interaction partners, the marital bliss study suggests that if they fail to find a self-verifying spouse, they will leave the relationship.

A second self-verification strategy includes the processes through which people systematically communicate their self-views to others. One way they may do this is by judiciously displaying identity cues—highly visible signs and symbols of who they are. Physical appearances represent a particularly salient class of identity cues. The clothes one wears, for instance, can advertise numerous social self-views, including one's political leanings, income level, religious convictions, and so on. Pratt and Rafaeli (1997) found that dress, style, and fabric revealed a great deal about individuals' jobs, roles, and self-concepts. Even body posture and demeanor communicate identities to others.

People may also communicate their identities to others by the way they interact with them. Evidence suggests, for example, that mildly depressed college students were more likely to solicit unfavorable feedback from their roommates than were non-depressed students (Swann, Wenzlaff, et al., 1992). Such efforts to acquire unfavorable feedback apparently bore fruit; the more unfavorable feedback they solicited in the middle of the semester, the more their roommates derogated them and planned to find another roommate at the semester's end. Furthermore, if people recognize that they have failed to evoke self-verifying reactions, they will redouble their efforts. For example, in one study participants who perceived themselves as either likable or dislikable learned that they would be interacting with someone who probably found them likable or dislikable. Participants displayed increased efforts to elicit self-verifying evaluations when they suspected that evaluators' appraisals challenged their self-views (e.g., Swann & Read, 1981a, Study 2).

And what if people's efforts to acquire self-verifying evaluations run aground?

Even then, people may still cling to their self-views through the third strategy of self-verification: "seeing" evidence that does not objectively exist. That is, there is considerable evidence that expectancies (including self-conceptions) channel information processing (e.g., Higgins & Bargh, 1987; Shrauger & Lund, 1975). Self-views may guide at least three distinct aspects of information processing. For example, an investigation of selective attention revealed that participants with positive self-views spent longer scrutinizing evaluations when they anticipated that the evaluations would be positive, and people with negative self-views spent longer scrutinizing evaluations when they anticipated that the evaluations would be negative (Swann & Read, 1981a, Study 1). Participants in a follow-up study displayed signs of selective recall. In particular, participants who perceived themselves positively remembered more positive than negative statements, and those who perceived themselves negatively remembered more negative than positive statements. Finally, numerous investigators have shown that people tend to interpret information in ways that reinforce their self-views. For example, Murray et al. (2000) reported that people with low self-esteem systematically distort their impressions of their partners' feelings as being more negative than they actually are. Together, such attentional, encoding, retrieval, and interpretational processes may stabilize people's self-views by allowing them to "see" self-confirming evaluations where they do not exist (for a more detailed discussion of various strategies of self-verification, see Swann et al., 2003).

One distinctive feature of the above findings was the nearly symmetrical preferences of participants with positive and negative self-views. That is, just as participants with positive self-views displayed a preference for positive evaluations, participants with negative self-views displayed a preference for negative evaluations, regardless of the particular strategy of self-verification the researchers examined. To those mired in the assumption that self-enhancement is the most basic of human motives, such activities seem bizarre and pointless. In the next section, we point to evidence that neither of these characterizations applies to self-verification strivings.

Why People Self-Verify

If examples such as William Thompson leave little doubt that stable self-views are essential to survival, they do not fully explain *why* this should be so. One can pose the "why" question at several different levels of analysis. At the most distal level, consider an evolutionary perspective. Most evolutionary biologists assume that humans spent most of their evolutionary history in small hunter-gatherer groups. Stable self-views would be advantageous in such groups, as they would stabilize behavior, which in turn would make the individual more predictable to other group members (e.g., Goffman, 1959). Mutual predictability would, in turn, facilitate division of labor, making the group more effective in accomplishing its objectives and promoting the survival of its members.

In a similar vein, Leary's "sociometer theory" (Leary & Baumeister, 2000) suggests that self-knowledge helps regulate group relationships. In particular, self-esteem presumably acts as an "interpersonal monitor" (Leary, Tambor, Terdal, &

Downs, 1995), informing people about their degree of inclusion or exclusion in the social group. Support for this idea comes from evidence that state self-esteem ratings are associated with how included people feel in their relationships (Leary et al., 1995). Whereas sociometer theory emphasizes how low self-esteem may warn people that they are at risk for being excluded from the group, low self-esteem might also serve the adaptive function of bringing people's expectations about their status in the group into line with the actual appraisals of other group members. From this vantage point, a key function of self-views is to ensure that people do not develop expectations that are disjunctive with their actual qualities, as to do so might promote behaviors that result in being excluded from the group. By enabling people to avoid such disjunctions, self-views and the quest for self-verifying evaluations they guide may help ward off situations that would threaten their ability to enjoy the benefits of group membership (see Fletcher, Simpson, & Boyes, in press; Kirkpatrick and Ellis, 2006). From this perspective, self-views serve the pragmatic function of fostering harmonious group relations.

At a psychological level, stable self-views and the self-verifying evaluations that sustain them are desirable because, as noted above, they bolster feelings of psychological coherence. Self-verifying evaluations may foster feelings of coherence for purely epistemic reasons—because self-verifying evaluations affirm people's sense that things are as they should be. In addition, self-verifying evaluations may foster feelings of coherence for pragmatic reasons—by reassuring people that their interaction partners understand them and that their interactions are thus likely to proceed smoothly. For both epistemic and pragmatic reasons, then, people may find self-verifying evaluations reassuring and emotionally comforting, even if such evaluations happen to be negative. In contrast, non-verifying evaluations may precipitate psychological anarchy.

Finally, people may even be attuned to self-verifying evaluations at the neurological level. Theoretically, predictable, familiar stimuli should be more perceptually fluent and more easily processed than unfamiliar stimuli. Because self-verifying evaluations are more predictable than non-verifying evaluations, they should also be similarly fluent and easily processed. The heightened fluency of self-verifying evaluations could explain why people see them as more diagnostic than non-verifying evaluations (Swann & Read, 1981b, Study 3). Elevated perceptions of diagnosticity might, in turn, help explain why people come to prefer and seek self-verifying evaluations. For these and related reasons, people should develop a preference for evaluations that validate and confirm their self-views.

Are Self-Verification Strivings Something Other Than What They Appear To Be?

Advocates of positivity strivings have questioned the foregoing explanations of the mechanisms underlying self-verification strivings. They have protested that even if the desire for negative self-verifying evaluations is robust, it is limited to a very small segment of the population who suffer from a personality flaw such as masochism or self-destructive tendencies. From this vantage point, it was the personality flaw, rather than the negative self-view, that caused people with negative self-views to embrace negative evaluations and evaluators.

One counter to such claims is offered by an interesting twist in the results of the marital bliss study described above. That is, it was not just persons with negative self-views who eschewed overly positive evaluations; even people with positive self-views displayed less commitment to spouses whose evaluations were *extremely* favorable (Swann et al., 1994). Thus the self-verification effect was not restricted to people with negative self-views; anyone who felt that a spouse appraised them in an unduly favorable manner tended to withdraw from the relationship.

Although these data support a self-verification explanation, they do not explicitly show that it was the self-views of people who thought poorly of themselves that caused them to choose negative evaluators. In search of such evidence, Swann et al. (1990) proposed that there were likely differences in the cognitive operations that gave rise to positivity strivings versus self-verification strivings. Positivity strivings seemed to require only one step: on classifying the evaluation, embrace positive evaluations and avoid negative evaluations. In contrast, self-verification strivings logically required at least two steps. Not only did the evaluation need to be classified, it also needed to be compared to the self-view; only then could the person decide to embrace verifying evaluations and avoid non-verifying ones. This reasoning led them to hypothesize that if they were to deprive people of cognitive resources while they were choosing a positive or negative evaluation, it would interfere with their ability to access their self-concept. The result would be that people who might ordinarily self-verify would self-enhance instead.

To test these ideas, while choosing an evaluation to scrutinize, some participants were deprived of cognitive resources by having them rehearse a phone number. While they were struggling to keep the phone number in memory, they were asked to choose between a positive or a negative evaluation. So deprived, people with negative self-views suddenly behaved like their positive self-view compatriots—they chose positive evaluations over negative ones. Nevertheless, when these same participants were later given several moments to access their self-views, they chose the negative, self-verifying evaluation. Later studies replicated this effect using other manipulations of resource deprivation, such as having participants choose partners hurriedly (Hixon & Swann, 1993). The resource deprivation studies thus suggested that it was the accessibility of negative self-views that caused some people to choose negative evaluators, and thus diminished the plausibility of the "flawed personalities" hypothesis.

Another way of testing the flawed personalities hypothesis was to seek insight into what people were thinking as they chose an interaction partner. To this end, Swann, Stein-Seroussi, et al. (1992) conducted a "think aloud" study. The procedure paralleled the one used in the Mr. Nice–Mr. Nasty study, except that participants thought out loud into a tape recorder as they chose an evaluator to interact with. As in the Mr. Nice–Mr. Nasty study, people with positive self-views tended to choose the positive evaluator, and people with negative self-views tended to choose the negative evaluator. Of greatest relevance here, subsequent analyses of the tape recordings revealed no evidence that masochism or self-destructive tendencies drove the self-verifying choices of participants.[1] If anything, people with negative self-views seemed torn and ambivalent as they chose negative partners. One person with negative self-views, for example, noted that:

> I like the [favorable] evaluation but I am not sure that it is, ah, correct, maybe. It *sounds* good, but [the negative evaluator] . . . seems to know more about me. So, I'll choose [the negative evaluator].

Examination of the protocols from the think aloud study also provided evidence that offered direct support for self-verification theory. There was evidence, for example, that self-verifiers—both those with negative self-views who chose negative partners and those with positive self-views who chose favorable partners—preferred partners who made them feel that they knew themselves. That is, consistent with self-verification theory, the overriding concern seemed to be the degree of coherence between the partner's evaluation and what they knew to be true of themselves:

> Yeah, I think that's pretty close to the way I am. [The negative evaluator] better reflects my own view of myself, from experience.
> That's just a very good way to talk about me. Well, I mean, after examining all of this I think [the negative evaluator] pretty much has me pegged.

Consistent with the notion that pragmatic considerations contribute to self-verification strivings, self-verifiers voiced concern about getting along with the evaluators during the forthcoming interaction. Participants wanted their interactions to unfold in a predictable, orderly manner:

> Since [the negative evaluator] seems to know my position and how I feel sometimes, maybe I'll be able to get along with him.
> Seeing as he knows what he's dealing with we might get along better . . . so I think I'll have an easier time getting along with [the negative evaluator].

The foregoing results support the assumptions underlying self-verification theory. That is, people choose self-verifying partners with an eye to how well their evaluations fit with their self-views, as well as how well they will get along with the evaluator in the forthcoming interaction. The results of the think aloud study were also useful in addressing several "ironic" explanations of self-verification strivings. These explanations were based on the assumption that evidence that people seek negative evaluations actually reflects a desire for praise and adulation that, ironically, goes awry. At the most general level, this ironic perspective assumes that many seemingly counter-productive behaviors are actually positivity strivings run amuck (for other examples, see Berglas & Jones, 1978; Wachtel & Wachtel, 1986). To determine if such ironic processes could explain why people prefer self-verifying relationship partners, we revisited the think aloud and marital bliss studies and tested the viability of several ironic reasons why people with negative self-views might choose negative partners.

Perceptiveness of the Evaluator   There is a subtle but important distinction between desiring an evaluator who seems perceptive versus one who bolsters one's feelings of coherence, parallel to the difference between choosing a wife because she makes a good salary versus choosing her because she makes you feel fortunate. In the think aloud study, people who mentioned a concern with perceptiveness focused on qualities of the evaluator, such as being "on the ball" or "insightful." In contrast, people who emphasized coherence stressed that the evaluator made them feel they knew themselves. Those who mentioned being concerned with the perceptiveness of the evaluator were not the same ones who expressed coherence-related concerns, indicating that the two sets of concerns were independent. In addition, evidence from the marital bliss study indicated that it was the extent to which the spouse was self-confirming rather than perceptive that determined relationship quality. In particular, commitment to relationships was related to people's conviction that their spouses' appraisals would make them "feel that they really knew themselves" rather than "confused them," but was independent of estimates of the perceptiveness of spouses.

Self-Improvement   People with negative self-views might choose interaction partners who think poorly of them because they believe such partners will give them critical feedback that will help them improve themselves. There was no evidence from the think aloud study that this was the goal of self-verifiers. The results of the marital bliss study also argued against self-improvement: When asked if they thought their spouse would provide them with information that would enable them to improve themselves, people with negative self-views were decidedly pessimistic, thus suggesting it was not the hope of improving themselves that led them to remain in self-verifying relationships.

Perceived Similarity   The research literature indicates that people prefer those who have similar values and beliefs as themselves over those who have dissimilar values and beliefs. For example, people typically prefer their friends and associates who share their political beliefs, tastes in music, and the like (Byrne, 1971). If people believe that those who judge them in ways that confirm their self-views also have similar attitudes, then they may find self-verifying partners appealing because they suspect that such partners will agree with them on topics and issues that are unrelated to who they are. There was no evidence of this, however; participants in the think aloud study scarcely mentioned the partners' likely attitudes. The results of the marital bliss study also provided no evidence that people's affinity for self-verifying partners could be understood as an effort to align themselves with spouses with similar attitudes.

Winning Converts   Were people with negative self-views interested in negative evaluators because they hoped to "win over" exceptionally harsh critics? After all, converting an enemy into a friend is no mean feat, so pulling off such a stunt ought to be especially gratifying. Several participants in the think aloud study did indeed allude to a desire to win over a partner ("I kind of think that [the negative evaluator] is . . . the kind of guy or girl I'd like to meet and I would like to show them that I'm really not that uncomfortable [around people]"). Nevertheless, it was only people with *positive* self-views who mentioned this concern; people with negative self-views never brought it up. This makes sense, as people with negative self-views have little confidence that they can turn an enemy into a friend, so it might not occur to them as readily.

The marital bliss study provided even more compelling evidence against the "winning converts" hypothesis. If people with negative self-views wished to "convert" a spouse who was initially critical, it follows that they would be most interested in partners whose evaluations of them seemed likely to grow more favorable over the course of the relationship. In reality, people with negative self-views displayed a slight tendency to commit themselves more to spouses whose evaluations they expected to grow increasingly negative over time. The evidence suggests, then, that people with positive self-views choose rejecting interaction partners for very different reasons than people with low self-views do.

Self-Verification or Accuracy

There is one final ironic explanation of self-verification strivings: Perhaps people with negative self-views seek negative evaluations because such people actually are deficient in some way. That is, perhaps they seal their own fate because an objective assessment of them indicates that they *deserve* to be viewed in a negative manner, and they are better off seeking such evaluations than having others discover their inadequacies for themselves.

Let us begin by acknowledging that many people with negative self-views surely possess negative qualities. Nevertheless, we suggest that it is people's *conviction* that they are flawed rather than the actual flaws themselves that underlie self-verification strivings. From this vantage point, at times people with negative self-views may seek negative evaluations even though they do not "deserve" such evaluations. Support for this idea comes from research in which the researchers compared the feedback-seeking activities of people who were depressed or non-depressed (Giesler et al., 1996). They discovered that depressed people regarded negative evaluations to be especially accurate and were more apt to seek them (similarly, it is difficult to imagine an "objective" justification for the conviction of low self-esteem persons that they are worthless and undeserving of love). Moreover, if depressed persons truly were as deficient as their negative self-views would suggest, one would expect that their negative self-views would remain negative on a more-or-less permanent basis. In fact, once the depression clears, their self-views bounce back to normal.

In short, the research literature offers little support for various ironic explanations of self-verification strivings. Instead, it appears that a desire for self-stability and associated feelings of coherence motivate people to strive for self-verification. If so, then it should be possible to provide direct evidence that receiving self-verifying evaluations is adaptive.

Are Self-Verification Strivings Functional?

Earlier we noted that during human evolutionary history, self-verification strivings may have increased inclusive fitness by making successful self-verifiers more predictable to other group members. Self-verification strivings may be similarly adaptive for modern humans. For example, insofar as people gravitate toward self-verifying partners, their relationships will be more predictable and thus manageable. Such predictability and manageability may not only improve the likelihood that people can achieve their relationship goals (e.g., raising children), it may also be psychologically comforting. Such psychological comfort may, in turn, reap physiological dividends in the form of reduced anxiety. From this vantage point, self-verification processes serve to regulate affect.

Several studies support the notion that receiving non-verifying evaluations may be more stressful than verifying evaluations. For instance, Wood, Heimpel, Newby-Clark, and Ross (2005) compared how high and low self-esteem participants reacted to success experiences. Whereas high self-esteem persons reacted quite favorably to success, low self-esteem participants reported being anxious and concerned, apparently because success was surprising and unsettling for them (see Lundgren & Schwab, 1977). Similarly, Mendes and Akinola (2006) observed participants' cardiovascular responses to positive and negative evaluations that either did or did not verify their self-views. When they received positive feedback, those with negative self-views were physiologically "threatened" (distressed and avoidant). In contrast, when they received negative feedback, participants with negative self-views were physiologically "challenged" or "galvanized" (i.e., cardiovascularly aroused, but in a positive manner associated with approach motivation). People with positive self-views displayed the opposite pattern.

This evidence that people with negative self-views are stressed by positive information raises an intriguing possibility: If positive but non-verifying experiences are stressful for people with negative self-views, then over an extended period such experiences might prove to be physically debilitating. Several independent investigations support this proposition. An initial pair of prospective studies (Brown & McGill, 1989) examined the impact of positive life events on the health outcomes of people with low and high self-esteem. Among high self-esteem participants, positive life events (e.g., improvement in living conditions, getting a very good grade or grades) predicted increases in health; among people low in self-esteem, positive life events predicted *decreases* in health. A recent study (Shimizu & Pelham, 2004) replicated and extended these results, including the most intriguing finding that positive life events predicted increased illness among people low in self-esteem. Furthermore, this finding emerged even while controlling for negative affectivity, thereby undercutting the rival hypothesis that negative affect influenced both self-reported health and reports of symptoms. Here again, for people with negative self-views, the disjunction between positive life events and their chronic beliefs about themselves appears to have been so psychologically threatening that it undermined physical health.

The results of the foregoing studies clearly suggest that it may be psychologically and physiologically adaptive for people with negative self-views to seek and embrace negative feedback. Having said this, we add two caveats. First, although we are suggesting that self-verification strivings are adaptive, this does not necessarily apply to negative self-views themselves. Instead, negative self-views are adaptive only when they accurately reflect an intransigent personal limitation (e.g., thinking that you are tone-deaf when you truly are); *inappropriately* negative self-views—that is, negative self-views that exaggerate or misrepresent the person's limitations—are *mal*adaptive (e.g., thinking you are too fat when in reality you are anorexically thin). Second, although striving for negative but self-verifying evaluations can be functional in some respects (e.g., it may foster a sense of coherence), it may be dysfunctional in other respects (e.g., it may imperil relationships). For this reason, when they have the option of seeking feedback about their strengths or weaknesses, people with low global self-esteem try to evade the anguished antinomy between positivity and truth by seeking verification for their positive self-views (Swann, Pelham, & Krull, 1989).

SEEKING PARTNERS WHO WILL PROVIDE SELF-VERIFICATION FOR THE LONG HAUL: THE ADAPTIVE CONTEXT OF SELF-VERIFICATION FOR PEOPLE WITH NEGATIVE SELF-VIEWS

When it comes to choosing relationship partners, people with negative self-views are in an unenviable position. On the one hand, if they choose a non-verifying partner who sees them in an overly positive manner, their desire for coherence will be frustrated and anxiety will result. On the other hand, if they choose a negative, self-verifying partner, the partner's negativity may prove problematic. In the marital bliss study (Swann, Hixon, et al., 1992), for example, the more negatively their partners evaluated each other on the specific self-views measured by the SAQ (Pelham & Swann, 1989), the more apt their partners were to label them "bad persons." By embracing partners who view them as "bad persons," then, people with negative self-views may be putting themselves at risk of being treated poorly, or being abandoned altogether.

To be sure, the fact that the self-verification strivings of people with negative self-views may place them at risk of rejection should not be misunderstood to mean that rejection is the *goal* of the self-verification process. For example, Murray, Rose, Holmes, Derrick, Podchaski, and Bellavia (2005) have credited self-verification theory with assuming that "low self-esteem people want to feel unloved" (p. 327). Such mischaracterizations of self-verification theory appear to presume that if people with negative self-views gravitate toward unloving or rejecting partners, they must be uninterested in love. There are three problems with this claim. First, the fact that self-verifying partners are sometimes unloving does not mean that unlovingness was the specific quality that self-verifiers sought in their partner. More likely, self-verifiers with negative self-views gravitated toward self-verifying partners whose halo biases encouraged them to generalize from negative specific appraisals (e.g., "unsociable") to globally negative (e.g., "unworthy") appraisals. Second, self-verifiers want to secure a *steady* supply of self-confirming feedback, a goal that requires finding partners who feel sufficiently accepting about them to remain in the relationship. Because unloving partners may be tempted to cut off their supply of self-verification by terminating the relationship, the logic of self-verification requires people with self-negative views to avoid such partners.

Moreover, direct tests of the hypothesis that people with negative self-views desire rejection have not supported it. For example, Murray, Holmes, and Griffin (1996) reported that when spousal evaluations involved likability of their partners (e.g., perceptions of the partners' virtues, faults, and social commodities; fondness), people preferred positive over self-verifying evaluations. Similarly, Rudich and Vallacher (1999) have provided evidence suggesting that people with low self-esteem may actually be more concerned with being accepted than people with positive self-views. Research by Davila and Bradbury (2001) suggests this may be particularly true of avoidantly attached people; when such individuals encounter conflict, they leave the relationship to avoid intimacy.

Therefore, when people with negative self-views are in the early, formative stages of their relationships, they withdraw from partners who harbor negative perceptions of them, because negative perceptions at this stage in the relationship may signal an impending loss of the relationship, and as we noted earlier, one can only self-verify if one has a relationship in which to do so.[2] As this is particularly true in highly evaluative relationships such as when dating, it is only after people with negative self-views are in committed relationships that they feel safe to indulge their desire for self-verification because at this point the perpetuation of the relationship is more certain. Indeed, in marriage relationships, the dominant pragmatic concern is to negotiate identities that can be sustained over the long haul (i.e., realistic identities). Self-verification strivings will also gain force from epistemic concerns, as the partners' evaluations will be more credible as intimacy increases. The result is a phenomenon that Swann et al. (1994) dubbed the "marital shift," a tendency for self-verification strivings to replace positivity strivings as the dominant force in the relationship once the relationship transitions from dating to married status.

Davila and Bradbury's (2001) research on the effects of adult attachment classification may add further insight into the marital shift phenomenon. These authors reported that spouses with negative self-views who remained in unhappy marriages had exceptionally high levels of anxiety of abandonment, a quality that is the hallmark of a preoccupied (or ambivalent) attachment pattern. In contrast, those who fled unhappy marriages tended to be have attachment classifications that were high in avoidance of intimacy (Hazan & Shaver, 1987). Such evidence suggests that different people may comprise the samples of dating and married people in the marital shift study (Swann et al., 1994). That is, if avoidantly attached people flee from relationships in which they are evaluated negatively (as is typically the case in unhappy relationships), then they would be under-represented in married couples in self-verification studies (e.g., Swann et al., 1994, De La Ronde & Swann, 1998). Instead, the only people with negative self-views left in the married couple sample and thus seeking self-verification would be ones who are ambivalently attached, and who remain in unhappy relationships because of their fear of abandonment. In shorter term dating relationships, however, people with avoidant attachments styles would be well represented, but they would display a preference for self-enhancing partners over self-verirfying ones, as the former would be more compatible with their desire to avoid intimacy. In short, among people with negative self-views, avoidants may be primarily responsible for the positivity strivings of dating couples, and ambivalents may be primarily responsible for the self-verification strivings of married couples. This hypothesis is readily testable.

Whatever the links between attachment classification and self-verification strivings ultimately wind up being, these adjacent literatures raise a more general issue regarding how people reconcile their desire for self-verification with their other motivational states. One recent hypothesis along these lines is that people with negative self-views simultaneously seek global acceptance together with verification of specific characteristics.

The Specific Verification, Global Acceptance Hypothesis

Neff and Karney (2003; 2005) have provided some evidence that people with negative self-views may desire partners who recognize their specific shortcomings but are still globally accepting of them. Such partners would be appealing because they would not only be self-verifying (at a specific level) but they would also be likely to be a *continued* source of self-verification because their global acceptance would shore up their commitment to the relationship.

Although we agree with Neff and Karney's (2003) contention that people are motivated to satisfy both enhancement and verification motives simultaneously, we have reservations about the specific verification, global acceptance hypothesis. Conceptually, because global self-views presumably serve all the same functions as specific self-views (e.g., coherence, prediction, and control), the *desire* for self-verification should be just as strong at the global level as it is at the specific level. As such, it seems unlikely that people would suspend their desire for global verification, as doing so would presumably impose psychological costs in the form of a diminished sense of coherence. Empirically, several findings are inconsistent with the specific verification, global acceptance hypothesis. For example, several studies indicate that depressed and low self-esteem people prefer evaluations and interaction partners that are globally negative (Giesler et al., 1996; Little et al., 2005; Swann, Wenzlaff, et al., 1992; Swann, Wenzlaff, & Tafarodi, 1992), even when the evaluator is a good friend (Swann, Wenzlaff, et al., 1992). Moreover, because ratings of specific qualities tend to spill over onto global perceptions (Neff & Karney, 2003; Swann et al., 1994), partners who verify specific negative qualities also tend to harbor negative global evaluations. This means that even if people wanted specific verification, global acceptance, they would have trouble finding it because of the inability of their partners to separate their specific and global evaluations.

But if people really prefer global as well as specific verification, how should one interpret Neff and Karney's evidence that global acceptance contributes to relationship quality in the presence of specific verification? We believe that this finding reflects a tendency for ratings of global acceptance to covary with something that people really do want, which is their partners' interest in remaining in the relationship (Boyes & Fletcher, 2006). That is, the global evaluations Neff and Karney studied (e.g., personal warmth, estimated worth as a human being) are closely related to their willingness to remain with the partner. Given that relationships must survive if they are to provide self-verification, global positive evaluations represent a practical necessity. This phenomenon has been discussed under the rubric of relationship relevance.

The Relationship-Relevance Hypothesis

People appear to be highly motivated to bring their relationship partners to see them positively with regard to qualities that are important to the survival of the relationship. Consider the uniquely important dimension of physical attractiveness. Perhaps not surprisingly, there is evidence that people take steps to ensure that their close relationship partners see them as physically attractive. Swann, Bosson, and Pelham (2002), for example, found that participants not only wanted their dating partners to see them as much more attractive than they saw themselves, they actually took steps to ensure their partners viewed them this way. Moreover, such steps were effective: their partners actually came to see them in ways that verified their more-attractive-than-usual selves. Apparently, people with negative self-views recognize that for their relationships to "work," they must be perceived in a relatively positive manner on relationship-relevant dimensions. They accordingly arrange it so that their partners actually develop such positive evaluations.

The Swann et al. (2002) findings provide an empirical foundation for understanding how people with negative self-views navigate the treacherous interpersonal waters created by their self-views. On the one hand, they prefer and seek negative evaluations regarding characteristics that are low in relationship-relevance, presumably because evaluations are self-verifying and will not threaten the survival of the relationship. At the same time, on dimensions that are critical to the survival of the relationship, they strive to acquire evaluations that are more positive than those they typically receive, but that *do* verify the self they have presented to their partners. In this way, participants may enjoy the relationship stability that is presumably cultivated by receiving favorable evaluations on relationship-relevant dimensions, yet still feel that the evaluations were supported by the identity they had negotiated with their partner. In this instance, people appeared to be seeking verification of circumscribed, highly positive selves rather than of their "typical" selves—a phenomenon that Swann and Schroeder (1995) dubbed "strategic self-verification." Such strategic self-verification is a clear cousin to Drigotas, Rusbult, Wieselquist, and Whitton's (1999) "Michelangelo phenomenon," in which a partner views the target in a manner that is congruent with the target's ideal self, and to Murray, Holmes, and Griffin's (2003) notion that mutual idealization contributes to the quality of relationships. It is also related to recent evidence that relationship partners not only trade exceptionally positive mutual evaluations, but that they are aware of this process and such awareness is actually beneficial to the relationship (Boyes & Fletcher, 2006).

At first blush, the Swann et al. (2002) findings may seem to support Murray and her colleagues' (Murray, Holmes, & Griffin, 1996) assertion that people want to create positive illusions in their relationships. Although our argument is similar in some respects, we believe that it is inappropriate to use the word "illusions" here. That is, although our participants received verification for circumscribed selves that outstripped their chronic selves, these circumscribed selves were *not* illusory. Rather, they were relationship-specific selves that they successfully negotiated with their partners. Therefore, our participants did not create illusions, they created idiosyncratically skewed social realities that were validated by their partners.

If evidence for the relationship-relevance hypothesis is consistent with self-verification theory's notion that people strive for convergence between their self-views and the social realities that maintain them, it is inconsistent with the original theory's assumption that people strive to negotiate identities that match their *characteristic* self-views (Swann, 1983). Apparently, people will seek verification of their negative self-views only if doing so does not lead to a risk of being abandoned, which would completely cut off the supply of potential verification. This evidence of strategic self-verification shows that self-verification strivings do not exist in a social psychological vacuum but are instead woven into the fabric of everyday life. Note, however, that when self-verifiers pragmatically enacted positive relationship-specific selves, they created micro-social environments that supported the relationship-specific self. Thus, while this relationship-specific selves argument departs from the assumptions of classical trait and self theory, it is quite consistent with Mischel and Shoda's (1999) notion that people strive for intra-individual consistency and to Swann's (1984) suggestion that people strive for circumscribed accuracy (e.g., Gill & Swann, 2004).

CODA: DOES SELF-VERIFICATION IN RELATIONSHIPS MATTER?

In recent years several authors have questioned the importance and social significance of self-verification research. One argument has been that self-verification strivings are rare relative to self-enhancement strivings (Baumeister, 1998; Murray et al., 2000; Sedikides, Skowronski, & Gaertner, 2004). Careful examination, however, of the evidentiary basis of such assertions reveals serious shortcomings. For example, although there are scores of studies whose results are relevant to the relative strength of the two motives, Baumeister (1998) arbitrarily focused his review on the results of six laboratory investigations by Sedikides (1993). This is an astonishing choice because five of the six studies Sedikides (1993) reported are irrelevant to the debate because he failed to measure chronic self-views, a necessary condition for testing self-verification theory. Furthermore, the only study that provided a fair test of the two theories showed equally strong verification and enhancement effects. Despite the inconclusive nature of Sedikides' (1993) studies, Baumeister (1998) followed Sedikides' lead in concluding that they provided definitive evidence that self-enhancement regularly prevails over self-verification.

More recent efforts by Sedikides to champion self-enhancement strivings are similarly problematic. For example, Sedikides and Green (2004, p. 23) dismiss the significance of evidence that verification strivings trump self-enhancement strivings in studies of memory (Swann & Read, 1981a) by arguing that self-verification research generally focuses on peripheral traits, such as extraversion. This assertion is factually incorrect because the two studies of self-verification and memory of which we are aware—Story (1998) and Swann and Read (1981a)—showed that people with negative self-views preferentially recalled information indicating that they were low in self-esteem or dislikable—neither of which are peripheral traits.

Even more relevant to this volume on close relationships, Murray and her colleagues have reported considerable evidence of self-enhancement strivings in their work and no evidence of self-verification. Some of this discrepancy can be attributed to the fact that most of this work has focused on dating couples, perceived rather than actual appraisals, and their use of a measure of self-views (Interpersonal Qualities Scale, IQS; Murray et al., 1996) that is quite high in relationship relevance. All of these features tend to diminish or eliminate self-verification effects. In one study, however, Murray et al. (2000) report (in footnote 15) that they found evidence of self-enhancement but not self-verification in a sample of married participants using the SAQ. Nevertheless, this alleged failure to replicate is misleading because Murray (2005, personal communication, August 22) subsequently acknowledged that a substantial number of the "married" participants were actually cohabiting. This is important because when cohabitating couples were eliminated from Murray et al.'s sample, a marginally reliable self-verification effect emerged among male participants (Murray, 2005, personal communication).

In short, at present there is no persuasive evidence that self-enhancement strivings are more common than self-verification strivings. There is, however, growing evidence that self-verification strivings are predictive of a host of important social outcomes, such as marital satisfaction and divorce (Cast & Burke, 2002; for a review, see Swann, Chang-Schneider, & McClarty, 2007), desire to remain with college roommates (Swann & Pelham, 2002), identification with and performance in small groups (Swann, Milton, & Polzer, 2000), reactions to diversity in the workplace (Polzer, Milton, & Swann, 2002; Swann, Polzer, Seyle, & Ko, 2004), reactions to procedural fairness in the workplace (Wiesenfeld, Swann, Brockner, & Bartel, in press) and worker job retention (Schroeder, Josephs, & Swann, 2006).

It thus appears that self-verification strivings influence a wide array of important social behaviors. The ubiquity of such strivings offers further testimony to their adaptiveness—after all, were they completely dysfunctional, people would presumably stop enacting them. From this vantage point, when it comes to information about the self, people will often seek the truth, even when there is a sense in which the truth hurts.

AUTHOR NOTE

Address correspondence to William B. Swann, Jr., Department of Psychology, University of Texas at Austin, Austin, Texas 78712. Email: swann@mail.utexas.edu.

NOTES

1. Also, although we recognize that think aloud techniques have something of a checkered reputation in psychology, the most cogent critiques have been directed at *retrospective* think aloud methodologies (e.g., Nisbett & Wilson, 1977). More recently, researchers have shown that when people think aloud *as they are making their decisions*, as Swann, Stein-Seroussi, and Giesler (1992) did, think aloud procedures yield useful insights into psychological processes (e.g., Ericsson & Simon, 1980).
2. The pseudo relationships formed with strangers in the laboratory offer an interesting exception to this rule, as the decontextualized nature of such relationships strips them of the evaluative concerns that are often present outside the laboratory, while sparing epistemic considerations.

REFERENCES

Aronson, E. (1968). A theory of cognitive dissonance: A current perspective. In L. Berkowitz (Ed.), *Advances in experimental social psychology* (Vol 4, pp. 1–34). New York: Academic Press.

Baumeister, R. F. (1998). The self. In D. Gilbert & S. Fiske (Eds.), *Handbook of social psychology* (pp. 680–740). Boston: McGraw-Hill.

Berglas, S., & Jones, E. E. (1978). Drug choice as a self-handicapping strategy in response to non-contingent success. *Journal of Personality and Social Psychology, 36,* 405–417.

Boyes, A. D., & Fletcher, G. J. O. (2006). *Meta-perceptions of bias in intimate relationships.* Unpublished manuscript, University of Canterbury, New Zealand.

Brehm, J. W., & Cohen, A. R. (1962). *Explorations in cognitive dissonance.* New York: Wiley.

Brown, J. D., & McGill, K. J. (1989). The cost of good fortune: When positive life events produce negative health consequences. *Journal of Personality and Social Psychology, 55,* 1103–1110.

Byrne, D. (1971). *The attraction paradigm.* New York: Academic Press.

Cassidy, J., Ziv, Y., Mehta, T. G., & Feeney, B. C. (2003). Feedback seeking in children and adolescents: Associations with self-perceptions, representations, and depression. *Child Development, 74,* 612–628.

Cast, A. D., & Burke, P. J. (2002). A theory of self-esteem. *Social Forces, 80,* 1041–1068.

Chen, S., Chen, K. Y., & Shaw, L. (2004). Self-verification motives at the collective level of self-definition. *Journal of Personality and Social Psychology, 86,* 77–94.

Cooley, C. H. (1902). *Human nature and the social order.* New York: Scribner's.

Davila, J., & Bradbury, T. N. (2001). Attachment insecurity and the distinction between unhappy spouses who do and do not divorce. *Journal of Family Psychology, 15,* 371–393.

De La Ronde, C., & Swann, W. B., Jr. (1998). Partner verification: Restoring shattered images of our intimates. *Journal of Personality and Social Psychology, 75,* 374–382.

Drigotas, S. M., Rusbult, C. E., Wieselquist, J., & Whitton, S. W. (1999). Close partner as sculptor of the ideal self: Behavioral affirmation and the Michelangelo phenomenon. *Journal of Personality and Social Psychology, 77*, 293–323.

Ericsson, K. A., & Simon, H. A. (1980). Verbal reports as data. *Psychological Review, 87*, 215–251.

Fernald, A. (1993). Approval and disapproval: Infant responsiveness to verbal affect in familiar and unfamiliar languages. *Child Development, 64*, 657–674.

Festinger, L. (1957). *A theory of cognitive dissonance*, Evanston, IL: Row, Peterson.

Fletcher, G. J. O., Simpson, J. A., & Boyes. A. D. (in press). Accuracy and bias in romantic relationships: An evolutionary and social psychological analysis. In M. Schaller, J. A. Simpson, & D. T. Kenrick (Eds.), *Evolution and social psychology*. New York: Psychology Press.

Giesler, R. B., Josephs, R. A., & Swann, W. B., Jr. (1996). Self-verification in clinical depression: The desire for negative evaluation. *Journal of Abnormal Psychology, 105*, 358–368.

Gill, M. J., & Swann, W. B., Jr. (2004) On what it means to know someone: A matter of pragmatics. *Journal of Personality and Social Psychology, 86*, 405–418.

Goffman, E. (1959). *The presentation of self in everyday life*. Garden City, NY: Doubleday/ Anchor.

Gómez, Á., Seyle, C. D., Morales, J. F., Huici, C., Gaviria, E. & Swann, W. B., Jr. (2006) *Seeking verification of one's group identity*. Unpublished manuscript.

Greenwald, A. G., & Ronis, D. L. (1978). Twenty years of cognitive dissonance: Case study of the evolution of a theory. *Psychological Review, 85*, 53–57.

Hazan, C., & Shaver, P. R. (1987). Romantic love conceptualized as an attachment process. *Journal of Personality and Social Psychology, 52*, 511–524.

Higgins, E. T., & Bargh, J. A. (1987). Social cognition and social perception. In M. R. Rosenzweig & L. W. Porter (Eds.), *Annual review of psychology* (Vol. 38, pp. 369–425). Palo Alto, CA: Annual Reviews.

Hixon, J. G., & Swann, W. B., Jr. (1993). When does introspection bear fruit? Self-reflection, self-insight, and interpersonal choices. *Journal of Personality and Social Psychology, 64*, 35–43.

Jones, S. C. (1973). Self and interpersonal evaluations: Esteem theories versus consistency theories. *Psychological Bulletin, 79*, 185–199.

Kirkpatrick, L. A., & Ellis, B. J. (2006). What is the evolutionary significance of self-esteem? In M. H. Kernis (Ed.), *Self-esteem issues and answers: A source book of current perspectives* (pp. 334–339). New York: Psychology Press.

Leary, M. R., & Baumeister, R. F. (2000). The nature and function of self-esteem: Socio-meter theory. In M. P. Zanna (Ed.), *Advances in experimental social psychology* (Vol. 32, pp. 2–51). San Diego, CA: Academic Press.

Leary, M. R., Tambor, E. S., Terdal, S. K., & Downs, D. L. (1995). Self-esteem as an interpersonal monitor: The sociometer hypothesis. *Journal of Personality and Social Psychology, 68*, 518–530.

Lecky, P. (1945). *Self-consistency: A theory of personality*. New York: Island Press.

Lemay, E. P., & Ashmore, R. D. (2004). Reactions to perceived categorization by others during the transition to college: Internalization of self-verification processes. *Group Processes and Interpersonal Relations, 7*, 173–187.

Little, K. J., Amidon, A., Garroway-Chrisman, J., Baum, E., Durham, J., Rude, S. S., et al. (2005). *Predicting relationship intimacy through partner self-verification*. Poster presented at the annual meeting of the American Psychological Association, Washington, DC, August 2005.

Lundgren, D. C., & Schwab, M. R. (1977). Perceived appraisals by others, self-esteem, and anxiety. *The Journal of Psychology, 97,* 205–213.

McCall, G. J., & Simmons, J. L. (1966). *Identities and interactions: An examination of human associations in everyday life.* New York: Free Press.

Mead, G. H. (1934). *Mind, self and society.* Chicago: University of Chicago Press.

Mendes, W. B., & Akinola, M. (2006). *Getting what you expected: How self-verifying information reduces autonomic and hormonal responses related to threat.* Manuscript in preparation.

Mischel, W., & Shoda, Y. (1999). Integrating dispositions and processing dynamics within a unified theory of personality: The Cognitive Affective Personality System (CAPS). In L. A. Pervin & O. John (Eds.), *Handbook of personality: Theory and research 2* (pp. 197–218). New York: Guilford Press.

Murray, S. L., Holmes, J. G., Dolderman, D., & Griffin, D. W. (2000). What the motivated mind sees: Comparing friends' perspectives to married partners' views of each other. *Journal of Experimental Social Psychology, 36,* 600–620.

Murray, S. L., Holmes, J. G., & Griffin, D. W. (1996). The benefits of positive illusions: Idealization and the construction of satisfaction in close relationships. *Journal of Personality and Social Psychology, 70,* 79–98.

Murray, S. L., Holmes, J. G., & Griffin, D. W. (2003). Reflections on the self-fulfilling effects of positive illusions. *Psychological Inquiry, 14,* 289–295.

Murray, S. L., Rose, P., Holmes, J. G., Derrick, J., Podchaski, E., & Bellavia, G. (2005). Putting the partner within reach: A dyadic perspective on felt security in close relationships. *Journal of Personality and Social Psychology, 88,* 327–347.

Neff, L. A., & Karney, B. R. (2003). Judgments of a relationship partner: Specific accuracy but global enhancement. *Journal of Personality, 70,* 1079–1112.

Neff, L. A., & Karney, B. R. (2005). To know you is to love you: The implications of global adoration and specific accuracy for marital relationships. *Journal of Personality and Social Psychology, 88,* 480–497.

Nisbett, R., & Wilson, T. (1977). Telling more than we can know. Verbal reports on mental processes. *Psychological Review, 84,* 231–259.

Pelham, B. W., & Swann, W. B., Jr. (1989). From self-conceptions to self-worth: The sources and structure of self-esteem. *Journal of Personality and Social Psychology, 57,* 672–680.

Pelham, B. W., & Swann, W. B., Jr. (1994). The juncture of intrapersonal and interpersonal knowledge: Self-certainty and interpersonal congruence. *Personality and Social Psychology Bulletin, 20,* 349–357.

Polzer, J. T., Milton, L. P., & Swann, W. B., Jr. (2002). Capitalizing on diversity: Interpersonal congruence in small work groups. *Administrative Science Quarterly, 47,* 296–324.

Pratt, M. G., & Rafaeli, A. (1997). Organizational dress as a symbol of multilayered social identities. *Academy of Management Journal, 40* (4), 862–898.

Ritts, V., & Stein, J. R. (1995). Verification and commitment in marital relationships: An exploration of self-verification theory in community college students. *Psychological Reports, 76,* 383–386.

Robinson, D. T., & Smith-Lovin, L. (1992). Selective interaction as a strategy for identity maintenance: An affect control model. *Social Psychology Quarterly, 55,* 12–28.

Rudich, E. A., & Vallacher, R. R. (1999). To belong or to self-enhance? Motivational bases for choosing interaction partners. *Personality and Social Psychology Bulletin, 11,* 1387–1404.

Sacks, O. (1985). *The man who mistook his wife for a hat and other clinical tales*. New York: Simon & Schuster.

Schafer, R. B., Wickrama, K. A. S., & Keith, P. M. (1996). Self-concept disconfirmation, psychological distress, and marital happiness. *Journal of Marriage and the Family*, *58*, 167–177.

Schroeder, D. G., Josephs, R. A., & Swann, W. B., Jr. (2006). *Forgoing lucrative employment to preserve low selfesteem*. Working paper, University of Texas, Austin.

Secord, P. F., & Backman, C. W. (1965). An interpersonal approach to personality. In B. Maher (Ed.), *Progress in experimental personality research* (Vol. 2, pp. 91–125). New York: Academic Press.

Sedikides, C. (1993). Assessment, enhancement, and verification determinants of the self-evaluation process. *Journal of Personality and Social Psychology*, *65*, 317–338.

Sedikides, C., & Green, J. D. (2004). What I don't recall can't hurt me: Information negativity versus information inconsistency as determinants of memorial self-defense. *Social Cognition*, *22*, 4–29.

Sedikides, C., Skowronski, J. J., & Gaertner, L. (2004). Self-enhancement and self-protection motivation: From the laboratory to an evolutionary context. *Journal of Cultural and Evolutionary Psychology*, *2*, 61–79.

Shapiro, B., Eppler, M., Haith, M., & Reis, H. (1987). *An event analysis of facial attractiveness and expressiveness*. Paper presented at the Society for Research in Child Development, Baltimore, MD.

Shimizu, M., & Pelham, B. W. (2004). The unconscious cost of good fortune: Implicit and positive life events, and health. *Health Psychology*, *23*, 101–105.

Shrauger, J. S., & Lund, A. (1975). Self-evaluation and reactions to evaluations from others. *Journal of Personality*, *43*, 94–108.

Story, A. L. (1998). Self-esteem and memory for favorable and unfavorable personality feedback. *Personality and Social Psychology Bulletin*, *24*, 51–64.

Swann, W. B., Jr. (1983). Self-verification: Bringing social reality into harmony with the self. In J. Suls & A. G. Greenwald (Eds.), *Psychological perspectives on the self* (Vol. 2, pp. 33–66). Hillsdale, NJ: Lawrence Erlbaum Associates, Inc.

Swann, W. B., Jr. (1984). Quest for accuracy in person perception: A matter of pragmatics. *Psychological Review*, *91*, 457–477.

Swann, W. B., Jr., Bosson, J. K., & Pelham, B. W. (2002). Different partners, different selves: The verification of circumscribed identities. *Personality and Social Psychology Bulletin*, *28*, 1215–1228.

Swann, W. B., Jr., Chang-Schneider, C. S., & McClarty, K. L. (2007). Do our self-views matter? Self-concept and self-esteem in everyday life. *American Psychologist*, *62*, 84–94.

Swann, W. B., Jr., De La Ronde, C., & Hixon, J. G. (1994). Authenticity and positivity strivings in marriage and courtship. *Journal of Personality and Social Psychology*, *66*, 857–869.

Swann, W. B., Jr., & Ely, R. J. (1984). A battle of wills: Self-verification versus behavioral confirmation. *Journal of Personality and Social Psychology*, *46*, 1287–1302.

Swann, W. B., Jr., Hixon, J. G., & De La Ronde, C. (1992). Embracing the bitter "truth": Negative self-concepts and marital commitment. *Psychological Science*, *3*, 118–121.

Swann, W. B., Jr., Hixon, J. G., Stein-Seroussi, A., & Gilbert, D. T. (1990). The fleeting gleam of praise: Behavioral reactions to self-relevant feedback. *Journal of Personality and Social Psychology*, *59*, 17–26.

Swann, W. B., Jr., Milton, L. P., & Polzer, J. T. (2000). Should we create a niche or fall in line? Identity negotiation and small group effectiveness. *Journal of Personality and Social Psychology*, 79, 238–250.

Swann, W. B., Jr., & Pelham, B. W. (2002). Who wants out when the going gets good? Psychological investment and preference for self-verifying college roommates. *Journal of Self and Identity*, 1, 219–233.

Swann, W. B., Jr., Pelham, B. W., & Chidester, T. (1988). Change through paradox: Using self-verification to alter beliefs. *Journal of Personality and Social Psychology*, 54, 268–273.

Swann, W. B., Jr., Pelham, B. W., & Krull, D. S. (1989). Agreeable fancy or disagreeable truth? Reconciling self-enhancement and self-verification. *Journal of Personality and Social Psychology*, 57, 782–791.

Swann, W. B. Jr., Polzer, J. T., Seyle, C. & Ko, S. (2004). Finding value in diversity: Verification of personal and social self-views in diverse groups. *Academy of Management Review*, 29, 9–27.

Swann, W. B., Jr., & Read, S. J. (1981a). Self-verification processes: How we sustain our self-conceptions. *Journal of Experimental Social Psychology*, 17, 351–372.

Swann, W. B., Jr., & Read, S. J. (1981b). Acquiring self-knowledge: The search for feedback that fits. *Journal of Personality and Social Psychology*, 41, 1119–1128.

Swann, W. B., Jr., Rentfrow, P. J., & Guinn, J. (2003). Self-verification: The search for coherence. In M. Leary and J. Tagney, *Handbook of self and identity* (pp. 367–383). New York: Guilford Press.

Swann, W. B., Jr., & Schroeder, D. G. (1995). The search for beauty and truth: A framework for understanding reactions to evaluations. *Personality and Social Psychology Bulletin*, 21, 1307–1318.

Swann, W. B., Jr., Stein-Seroussi, A., & Giesler, B. (1992). Why people self-verify. *Journal of Personality and Social Psychology*, 62, 392–401.

Swann, W. B., Jr., Wenzlaff, R. M., Krull, D. S., & Pelham, B. W. (1992). The allure of negative feedback: Self-verification strivings among depressed persons. *Journal of Abnormal Psychology*, 101, 293–306.

Swann, W. B., Jr., Wenzlaff, R. M., & Tafarodi, R. W. (1992). Depression and the search for negative evaluations: More evidence of the role of self-verification strivings. *Journal of Abnormal Psychology*, 101, 314–371.

Taylor, S. E., & Brown, J. D. (1988). Illusion and well being: Some social psychological contributions to a theory of mental health. *Psychological Bulletin*, 103, 193–210.

Wachtel, E. F., & Wachtel, P. L. (1986). *Family dynamics in individual psychotherapy: A guide to clinical strategies*. New York: Guilford Press.

Wiesenfeld, B. M., Swann, W. B., Jr., Brockner, J., & Bartel, C. (in press). Is more fairness always preferred? Self-esteem moderates reactions to procedural justice. *Academy of Management Journal*.

Wood, J. V., Heimpel, S. A., Newby-Clark, I., & Ross, M. (2005). Snatching defeat from the jaws of victory: Self-esteem differences in the experience and anticipation of success. *Journal of Personality and Social Psychology*, 89, 764–780.

4

Narcissism and Interpersonal Self-Regulation

W. KEITH CAMPBELL and JEFFREY D. GREEN

At the icy heart of narcissism is the conviction that one is better than others; higher in status, more attractive, smarter, more influential. Ironically, the narcissist's ability to stand alone and above others is highly dependent on the behavior of those others. One cannot be admired without someone doing the admiring; one cannot associate with the rich and famous without close proximity to those rich and famous. Without social relationships, a narcissist would have to engage in more isolated forms of self-regulation—living in a cabin and struggling to engage with others by writing manifestos, perhaps.

In psychological terms, narcissists' use of others to enhance the positivity of the self can be thought of as interpersonal self-regulation. Relationships for narcissists are largely instrumental in that they serve the purpose of maintaining or increasing the positivity of the narcissistic self. For example, a man might start dating an attractive woman because her beauty will serve as an enhancing fashion accessory for him. He buys the woman designer clothing and suggests that she wear a particular outfit to a company party, which might be interpreted as an act of affection. After the grand entrance to the party, however, he starts flirting with another woman and later makes jokes at his significant other's expense to the amusement of his co-workers at the bar. This unfortunate sequence of events might occur repeatedly. (Please note: throughout this chapter we try to use both male and female examples and pronouns rather than he/she in each example. This is an effort to increase readability. The greater use of male examples is an effort to reflect the naturally occurring higher levels of narcissism in males (estimated 50–75% clinically, *Diagnostic and Statistical Manual* (DSM-IV), American Psychiatric Association, 1994; $r = .12$ in a large Internet sample, Foster, Campbell, & Twenge, 2003).)

In this example, the narcissist's behavior is part of a broad campaign of self-regulation. He drapes his girlfriend in designer clothing so he looks impressive. He flirts with another woman so he feels attractive and important. He makes jokes at his girlfriend's expense so he is viewed positively by the crowd at the bar. The other individuals are conscripted in order to make this whole system work.

Importantly, the perception that others have of him varies greatly. His girlfriend really likes him initially, but then grows to hate him. The woman with whom he is flirting thinks he is charming. The folks at the bar find him the life of the party.

There is a downside as well, however, from this pattern of self-regulation. He does not have a stable, long-term romantic relationship; he might develop a reputation as a player; he might run out of people to date and to impress. Those in relationships with the narcissist have mixed outcomes as well. Some will find him a great new boyfriend or entertaining party guest. Others will think he is an arrogant, manipulative, two-faced weasel. Overall, then, narcissistic self-regulation involves trade-offs both for the narcissist and for those interacting with him or her.

In the present chapter, we focus on narcissists' interpersonal self-regulation. Although we discuss briefly some of the literature on narcissistic personality disorder (NPD), we focus primarily on the personality trait of narcissism or normal narcissism: that is, narcissism that does not contain the degree of pathology found in NPD. We begin with a brief definition and background of narcissism. We present an interpersonal agency model of narcissistic self-regulation. We then focus on some of the trade-offs that are associated with narcissistic self-regulation across a range of relationships. Finally, we examine the links between our approach to narcissism and several other self and self-in-relationship models.

BACKGROUND

Freud

Narcissism has both the blessing and the curse of a long history in psychology and related disciplines. It began as a construct from myth: a youth, Narcissus, who fell in love with his own image in a pool of water and died. The often-forgotten interpersonal dynamics in this myth supply its power and timelessness. Narcissus set out on a mission to find a mate, but was not satisfied with anyone. He met the beautiful Echo, who repeated everything he said, but he rejected her and she faded away. Thus the original narcissist was unable to love because he could not lower himself to connect with others, and another person suffered because of this narcissism. A similar interpersonal dynamic can be seen in many relationships with narcissists today.

The name of Narcissus was initially adopted by Havelock Ellis (1898), a British sexologist. It was Freud (1914/1957), however, who made the construct of narcissism central to psychological theorizing. Freud described narcissism in many different domains, including a normal developmental stage and a potentially pathological state. However, Freud's view of narcissism as central to interpersonal self-regulation holds the most interest for us. Freud made a very early case for two basic approaches to love, a *narcissistic* type and an *anaclitic* type. The former was focused on a form of self-enhancement in love and the latter on a form of intimate connection. This approach has presaged much of the work on the interpersonal circumplex (e.g., Leary, 1957) and is central to how we think about the operation of narcissistic self-regulation in relationships. Freud later wrote about narcissism as an adult personality construct or individual difference (1931/1950). The narcissistic libidinal type was aggressive, self-sufficient, independent, and energetic. Although Freud identified benefits to narcissism, there were psychological costs as well. Notably, the libido invested in the self could not be invested in others; the narcissist would thus suffer from a lack of love and concomitant long-term psychological problems (Freud, 1914/1957).

Whatever criticisms may be leveled at Freud and his ideas, it is safe to say that he thought more deeply about self-regulation and the role of internalized others, or "objects" in this process than anyone before him. Without Freud, we might not have some of the great interpersonal theories in social/personality psychology, like attachment theory, or even some of the social cognitive work on relationships. Freud also was a pioneer at building bridges from clinical constructs to psychodynamics, child development and family life, normal personality, dyadic social relationships, group processes, and social, cultural and religious history. This effort to span levels of analysis can be seen in more recent work, in which narcissism has been conceptualized as both a psychological disorder and a normal personality variable. We briefly discuss each of these.

Narcissistic Personality Disorder

Probably the biggest confusion in the study of narcissism is a result of the difference between narcissistic personality disorder (NPD) and what might be called narcissistic personality or normal narcissism. According to the DSM-IV, the diagnosis of NPD requires the presence of five of nine specific criteria. Briefly, these include: (a) grandiose self-importance, (b) preoccupation with grandiose fantasies, (c) a sense of specialness and uniqueness, (d) a need for excessive admiration, (e) entitlement, (f) exploitativeness, (g) a lack of empathy, (h) envy of others or belief that others envy him or her, and (i) arrogant behaviors. While this might sound like many a boss, co-worker or ex-spouse, according the APA, the prevalence rate of NPD is less than 1% of the population—about the same as schizophrenia (American Psychiatric Association, 1994). It is unclear why the estimated base rates for NPD are so low. One possibility is that the criteria for NPD are quite stringent. For example, while we might argue that most people need some degree of admiration, there is a point at which the need might become pathologically excessive. Another possibility is that an NPD diagnosis also requires significant impairment. However, most individuals with these symptoms might be able to navigate happily and successfully through the world—perhaps even ending up with their own reality TV shows or Fortune 500 companies. A third and related possibility is that clinicians simply encounter only a small sample of narcissists in psychiatric settings (Campbell, 2001). Most individuals who see themselves as profoundly special and unique do not cross paths with clinicians. Finally, the diagnostic criteria for NPD seem to assess a fair amount of vulnerability or neediness. In the DSM-IV, those with NPD "require" admiration, are "preoccupied" with fantasies of success, and are envious of others. These criteria separate in a subtle but powerful way those with NPD from those with high levels of narcissistic personality. Individuals with normal narcissism like admiration and seek it out, but do not "require" it (Campbell, 1999). Likewise, they fantasize about power, but are not "preoccupied" with these fantasies (Raskin & Novacek, 1991). This choice of language in the DSM-IV is likely a result of the conceptualizations of narcissism by Kernberg (1974, 1975) and Kohut (1977), both of whom saw narcissism as primarily defensive.

Given the current confusion about the link between NPD and normal narcissism, we think it is safest to consider NPD as both an extreme form of normal narcissism and a variant of normal narcissism that is associated with some form of pathology and vulnerability. Pathology is likely to be primarily interpersonal (e.g., those with NPD will experience troubled work or romantic relationships). As we will describe, individuals scoring high on the personality dimension of narcissism report many problems similar to those experienced by individuals with NPD, but these problems typically are counterbalanced by many benefits.

Narcissistic Personality

As noted, Freud's description of narcissism as a personality type did not include pathology (Freud, 1931/1950). Rather, narcissists were described as active, assertive, and natural leaders. Henry Murray also took a personality approach to narcissism, which he termed narcism or egophilia. He developed what we believe was the first self-report measure of narcissism, and he published the first correlation of narcissism with an outcome variable (Murray, 1938).

Even though narcissism has been considered as a normal personality variable over three quarters of a century (significantly longer than it has been considered a personality disorder), research into the personality variable of narcissism did not begin in earnest until the 1980s after Raskin and Hall created the *narcissistic personality inventory* (NPI, Raskin & Hall, 1979). Furthermore, the publication of two short versions of the scale by Emmons (1984) and Raskin and Terry (1988) shifted narcissism research into high gear.

The NPI was based largely on the clinical definition of NPD, but designed specifically for use in normal populations. As such, it does not pick up significant pathology. Rather, the NPI captures many of the features of NPD as well as many features of narcissistic personality described by Freud (1931/1950) such as extraversion, energy, and leadership. Narcissism as measured by the NPI is also a continuous variable. Indeed, there is no latent taxon for narcissism as measured by the NPI (Foster & Campbell, 2007).

The vast majority of research findings described throughout this chapter rely on the NPI. Furthermore, when we use the term "narcissists" and "nonnarcissists" in our discussion, we are using this terminology as shorthand for "individuals scoring high on the NPI." There is no discrete typology for normal narcissism; we use the clinical terminology (i.e., NPD) to describe narcissistic personality disorder. We turn next to elaborating our definition of narcissism.

DEFINING NARCISSISM

Although narcissism might appear to be a confusing construct, at its core are three components: a positive and inflated self, a relative lack of intimacy or closeness (or the absence of a need for intimacy), and an arsenal of self-regulatory strategies that maintain and enhance the self. These three components cover the DSM-IV's nine criteria ((a)–(i)) discussed previously. A positive self is seen in (a) grandiose self-importance, (c) a sense of specialness and uniqueness, and (e) entitlement; the relative lack of intimacy can be seen in (g) a lack of empathy; and the self-regulatory strategies can be seen in (b) a preoccupation with grandiose fantasies, (d) a need for excessive admiration, (f) exploitativeness, (h) envy of others or belief that others envy him or her, and (i) arrogant behaviors. These same three components also cover most of what is known about narcissism in the social-personality literature. We now briefly review these findings.

Narcissists' self-concept positivity is not indiscriminate in focus; rather it is centered on domains about which narcissists care the most. These are largely in the category of *agency* (e.g., status, power, intelligence, creativity, uniqueness, physical attractiveness). For example, narcissists report that they are better than the average other—and even their current romantic partner—on agentic traits, but not communal traits (e.g., caring, warmth, morality; Campbell, Rudich, & Sedikides, 2002). Indeed, narcissists feel closer to their ideal self than do nonnarcissists on many attributes (Rhodewalt & Morf, 1995). This self-concept positivity is especially evident when comparing self-views to objective criteria. Narcissists overestimate their intellectual abilities and intelligence (e.g., Gabriel, Critelli, & Ee, 1994) and physical appearance (Gabriel et al., 1994) relative to more objective criteria. They even overclaim knowledge about bogus general knowledge items (Paulhus, Harms, Bruce, & Lysy, 2004).

The qualities of narcissists' self-concepts are also evident when comparing NPI scores to scores on a range of measures. Narcissists, for example, self-report high agency (Bradlee & Emmons, 1992). They also report high extraversion on the Big Five, which is a marker of agency (Bradlee & Emmons, 1992). Other data confirm these self-report differences: Narcissists show high nPower and nAchievement on the Thematic Apperception Test (TAT) (Carroll, 1987). Likewise, narcissism is related to the self-reported need for uniqueness (Emmons, 1984) and entitlement (Campbell, Bonacci, Shelton, Exline, & Bushman, 2004). Finally, narcissism is linked to approach orientation (Rose & Campbell, 2004) and sensation-seeking (Emmons, 1991), which can be seen experimentally in gambling studies (Campbell, Goodie, & Foster, 2004).

Narcissists' relative lack of interest in communal relationships can be viewed in several ways. (We use the term "relative" because, depending on the measure, narcissists generally report either negative or neutral interest in communal relationships, but the interest in communal relationships will invariably be less than the interest in agentic concerns.) Narcissists, for example, self-report communion scores at the scale midpoint and low agreeableness scores on the Big Five (Bradlee & Emmons, 1992). On the TAT, narcissists report low nIntimacy (Carroll, 1987).

As mentioned above, narcissists do not report being better-than-average on communal traits (Campbell, Rudich, et al., 2002).

If the narcissist thinks that he is better than others (and better than he actually is), he needs to self-regulate. If he seeks social validation for his inflated beliefs (as opposed to spending his time alone writing manifestos and cursing the small-minded fools who misunderstand him), he must have others play an important part in these regulation efforts. That is, he must adopt some interpersonal self-regulation strategies. If he possesses many agentic qualities (dominance seeking, extraversion, approach orientation) and has little interest in forming close, warm connections with others, his self-regulation will be directed in apparently paradoxical ways. For example, he can use his extraversion and confidence to pull individuals into his orbit, but then rely on his low need for intimacy to exploit these individuals for self-promotion. What looks on the surface like communal behavior on the narcissists' part (starting romantic relationships, going to parties) is actually agentic behavior that results in narcissistic self-regulation.

There is an almost unlimited range of potential self-regulation techniques that can be adopted by narcissists. Several of these self-regulation strategies have been reported in the literature. Narcissists seek attention, brag, and show-off (Buss & Chiodo, 1991). In conversation, they redirect the dialogue to their own positive qualities or simply let their eyes glaze over in an effort to establish status (Vangelisti, Knapp, & Daly, 1990). In an unstructured environment, narcissists will simply talk about themselves (Raskin & Shaw, 1988). More generally, narcissists are more likely to take on "colorful" personalities (Hogan & Hogan, 2001) and be entertaining (Paulhus, 1998). Donald Trump, whose reputation has risen and fallen more than a tech stock as marriages and bankruptcies have added up, still managed to become a billionaire reality TV star, with his eponymous buildings prominently featured. The Donald's vast popularity is largely a tribute to his larger-than-life persona: Who wouldn't want to spend time with someone as colorful and entertaining as The Donald?

An effective strategy for interpersonal self-regulation regarding agency is to compete and win, thus working one's way up the social dominance hierarchy. Narcissists report being highly competitive (Bradlee & Emmons, 1992; Emmons, 1984). This is even reflected in their performance. Wallace and Baumeister (2002), for example, found that narcissists outperformed nonnarcissists on a skills-based task when they thought the results of the task were going to be made public. Self-regulation can also take the form of self-serving attributional biases, particularly when they do not perform as well as they desired. This might include placing the blame for failure on teammates or co-workers, or stealing credit from these others in the case of success (Campbell, Reeder, Sedikides, & Elliot, 2000; Gosling, John, Craik, & Robins, 1998). In a related vein (Stucke, 2003), narcissists also show a willingness to attack the source of feedback that threatens the positivity of the self (ego threat), or social standing (disrespect) (e.g., Bushman & Baumeister, 1998; Twenge & Campbell, 2003, respectively).

Finally, it is worth noting that narcissists' self-regulation strategies can occur intrapsychically. For example, narcissists are more likely than nonnarcissists to fantasize about having high agency (e.g., power and glory; Raskin & Novacek,

1991). Likewise, narcissists display a self-serving bias on individual tasks, where they blame external factors for failure (e.g., Campbell et al., 2000; Rhodewalt & Morf, 1995).

THE AGENCY MODEL OF NARCISSISM

Self-Regulatory Models of Narcissism

Self-regulation is clearly central to the conceptualization of narcissism, so most social-personality theories of narcissism have included some self-regulatory component. In general, there is a link between narcissistic self-beliefs, affect/emotions and behaviors. Typically, this link is either explicitly or implicitly self-reinforcing. For example, the narcissist will have a positive self-view, act confidently, and gain attention and this, in turn, will reinforce or further inflate the narcissist's positive self-view. We will describe several of the existing models of narcissistic self-regulation shortly.

What makes narcissists' interpersonal self-regulation of particular interest is that the self-regulatory strategies that keep narcissists looking and feeling good often require: (a) replacing others in the social environment when they are no longer useful, or (b) constantly increasing narcissistic behavior to capture the attention and admiration of others. For example, a narcissist might gain esteem from a trophy spouse, but will eventually need to trade up for a younger and more attractive trophy spouse to maintain the esteem benefits. Of course, the other might leave the narcissist because of shoddy treatment. Likewise, a narcissist can gain esteem from vanquishing an opponent, but this self-regulation strategy will require the addition of new, possibly tougher opponents to be vanquished. If you are the Harlem Globetrotters basketball team and you beat the Washington Generals every night, the self-enhancement benefits start to diminish. In terms of maintaining the attention and admiration of others, narcissists will need to keep elevating their performance. A narcissist can keep telling the story of how he was a star on the 2005 season of the TV show *Survivor*, but that tale will lose its luster after his associates hear it for the 80th time. The reasonable alternative, of course, is for the narcissist to keep joining new groups of people or bringing new people into his or her circle. The version of the agency model that we present below has been modified to include this interpersonal component.

One of the first self-regulatory models in the social-personality literature was proposed by Raskin and colleagues (Raskin, Novacek, & Hogan, 1991). In this model, narcissists' grandiose behaviors, beliefs, and fantasies serve the role of enhancing and maintaining narcissists' self-esteem. Campbell's (1999) self-orientation model focused directly on narcissists' interpersonal self-regulation, specifically their use of romantic relationships to bolster their social status, esteem, and importance. The self-orientation model focused on two specific mechanisms of self-regulation: associating or identifying with high status others, and being admired by others. Indeed, narcissists reported a relative preference for a romantic partner who had both high status and high admiration for them. Morf and

Rhodewalt's (2001) dynamic self-regulatory processing model emphasizes increasing and maintaining positive self-views and identifies four elements of narcissism—self-knowledge, intrapersonal self-regulatory processes, interpersonal behaviors, and social relationships—that interact and mutually reinforce each other. Importantly, these authors note that narcissists tend to apply their self-regulatory strategies in a coarse manner that will harm social relationships, which, of course, necessitates forming new social relationships in which the process repeats itself.

Three additional models of narcissistic self-regulation focus primarily on the affective and emotional outcomes of narcissistic self-regulation. First, Baumeister and Vohs (2001) proposed that efforts at narcissistic self-regulation can be experienced as an emotional "rush" or "high." If this is indeed the case, narcissistic self-regulation will take on aspects of an addiction. (The authors note that narcissism and narcotic share a similar etymology.) The experience of public success, glory, admiration, or attention will lead to a rapid and very positive emotional state. This will lead to the desire to repeat this behavior, and, if habituation occurs, increase this or similar behaviors. The narcissist, for example, might get a rush sailing around the harbor in her new boat. Eventually, however, she will need a bigger boat to get the same rush.

Second, Tracy and Robins (2004) have focused directly on the emotion regulation that underlies narcissism. They report direct evidence that narcissism is associated with two forms of pride, both the more socially acceptable form of achievement-oriented pride, and the more egotistic and arrogant form of hubristic pride (e.g., winning a contest and then rubbing the opponent's nose in it). In a sense, then, narcissism is useful for regulating the generally pleasurable experience of pride.

Third, both Sedikides and colleagues (Sedikides, Rudich, Gregg, Kumashiro, & Rusbult, 2004) and Rose (2002) have developed models of narcissism and psychological health. In a wide range of studies, narcissists report feeling relatively happy and untroubled. The key mechanism in these models is self-esteem. Narcissists will feel good to the extent that they generate or experience self-esteem.

A final model of narcissism worth noting is Paulhus' "minimalist model." Paulhus (1998) focuses on the underlying structure of narcissism: high egotism (which corresponds to what we are referring to as agency) and low morality (which we are referring to as communion).

The Agency Model

We label our approach to narcissism the agency model (Campbell, Brunell, & Finkel, 2006; Campbell & Foster, in press). In this chapter, we extend the agency model to focus more directly on the interpersonal aspects of narcissistic self-regulation. Specifically, we extend the agency model to incorporate others who are attracted into relationships with the narcissist. Before adding this element, however, we briefly review the previous version of the agency model.

The agency model borrows heavily from the models previously mentioned, but differs in several important ways. First, we add narcissists' skills as an essential component of their interpersonal self-regulation. We argue that to be a successful narcissist, one needs to possess particular social skills. Without the ability to manipulate, cajole, attract, or exploit others, narcissists would have to rely increasingly on intrapersonal self-regulation. They would still remain narcissists if this intrapersonal self-regulation were effective, but as Festinger's classic dissonance work has shown, distorted beliefs are hard to maintain without social proof (Festinger, Riecken & Schacter, 1956). Second, we conceptualize self-esteem in the model as "narcissistic esteem." We address this point below.

The agency model is presented in Figure 4.1. The model begins with four mutually interacting and self-sustaining components of narcissistic self-regulation: basic qualities, interpersonal strategies, interpersonal skills, and narcissistic esteem. Basic qualities include high agency and relatively low communion, high approach orientation, desire for self-enhancement, a sense of entitlement, and inflated self-views. Narcissists also use a wide variety of strategies for interpersonal self-regulation, such as acquiring trophy romantic partners, public self-promotion, winning in competition, and materialistic displays of status. These strategies are enhanced by narcissists' social skills. For example, narcissists are socially confident, charming, extraverted, and charismatic. Finally, narcissism is associated with what we call narcissistic esteem. This is a variant of self-esteem that is associated with (1) social dominance (Brown & Zeigler-Hill, 2004), (2) the emotional experience of pride (Tracy & Robins, 2004), and (3) the experience of a rush or high (Baumeister & Vohs, 2001).

These components are mutually interactive (i.e., activation in one component will increase activation in the other components). For example, a narcissist might

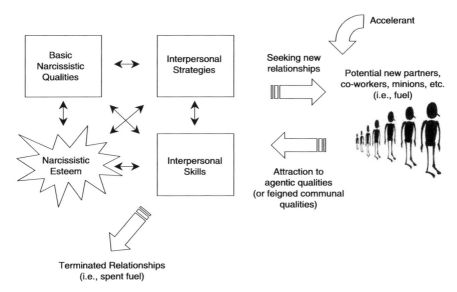

FIGURE 4.1   The agency model with an interpersonal component.

be highly approach-oriented (i.e., he is cued into success but ignores failures). The narcissist might go to a bar and try to form a relationship with every attractive woman there, which, after enough efforts, results in finding a romantic partner. This process gives the narcissist a sense of esteem, and also helps him hone his social skills. Two months later, he returns to the bar and tries to find a more attractive partner. He is successful, feels a short-term burst of esteem, and a longer-term increase in the positivity of his self-concept. He then decides that he deserves to belong to a higher status social group, so he frequents a higher-end social club, and so on. These components are also self-sustaining: the existence of each component reinforces the existence of the other components. In other words, the narcissist's social skills allow her to successfully use interpersonal self-regulation strategies. These strategies allow the narcissist's basic qualities (e.g., entitlement, agentic concerns) to stay intact and her esteem to stay high.

Extending the Agency Model with an Interpersonal Component

Most natural systems need to take in aspects of the world around them to continue to operate. In many cases, these aspects of the outside world serve as fuel. Forest fires need dry brush and timber, hurricanes need warm seas, cows need grass and feed. Likewise, narcissistic interpersonal self-regulation relies on fuel to operate effectively. (We modify this fuel notion from the psychodynamic literature for use in a social-personality model.) What is this narcissistic fuel? It is individuals who reinforce narcissists' basic qualities, narcissistic esteem, skills, and strategies. Note that we are limiting the discussion to human "fuel" because this chapter primarily addresses interpersonal self-regulation; a material good like a Maserati could serve a similar purpose. Individuals who directly increase narcissists' esteem may be considered the human fuel that helps a narcissist function at top speed. This would include those that give narcissists esteem via admiration, association, competition, blame, or direct status elevation. There are also individuals in the narcissist's environment who make the consumption of this fuel more rapid or efficient. This "accelerant" would include, for example, the person who introduces the narcissist to the high status crowd, the CEO's daughter who provides the narcissist access to her father, or the person who pays the narcissist's clothing bills.

If we accept the metaphor of narcissism as a self-regulating system that needs fuel from the outside, we must assume that (1) narcissists seek fuel, and (2) the fuel does what it is supposed to do. Evidence for the first is clear in the narcissism literature. Narcissists, for example, pay high attention to alternatives (i.e., potential future partners) in their dating relationships (Campbell, Foster, & Finkel, 2002). Narcissists also seek out opportunities to win the admiration of peers in a performance setting (Wallace & Baumeister, 2002), or of partners in a dating context (Campbell, 1999). Less studied is the issue of how narcissists make sure the fuel does what it should. (It is trickier using people as fuel than it is using dry grass.) Nevertheless, there is evidence that narcissists use a variety of strategies for attracting people. Narcissists act in an entertaining and colorful manner, which leads to their being liked in the short-term (Paulhus, 1998). Narcissists' social extraversion also allows them to emerge as leaders in unacquainted groups

(Brunell, Gentry, Campbell, & Kuhnert, 2006). In romantic relationships, narcissists are charming and present a sense of confidence and status (Brunell, Campbell, Smith, & Krusemark, 2004). Narcissists also use material goods to convey a sense of status (Vohs & Campbell, 2006), and brag and draw attention to themselves (Buss & Chiodo, 1991).

We should also note two other relevant processes that might make themselves known when the "fuel" is particularly uncooperative. The first is aggression. Narcissists are prone to aggress in response to both negative evaluative feedback and social disrespect or exclusion (Bushman & Baumeister, 1998; Twenge & Campbell, 2003). Second, there is the possibility that the reflected appraisals will be distorted such that the narcissist sees admiration from others where none actually exists.

Narcissists actively seek out opportunities that allow their self-regulation strategies to work. Narcissists are able to attract this fuel with largely agentic qualities (extraversion, charm, status displays) although some anecdotal evidence exists that narcissists feign communal qualities to attract others as well (Campbell, 2005). One issue still to be addressed is: What kind of fuel is sought? Five types of fuel readily come to mind (though others certainly exist). These are admiration, association, competition, blame, or direct status elevation. Narcissists seek out people who admire them and this admiration increases narcissists' esteem and self-conceptions (Campbell, 1999). Narcissists also may find fuel in the form of high-status people with whom to associate (Campbell, 1999). For example, joining an exclusive club aids in the narcissistic self-regulation process. Competition is sought by narcissists because it offers the opportunity for glory and status (Wallace & Baumeister, 2002). Indeed, there is evidence that narcissists particularly enjoy competitive contexts (Morf, Weir, & Davidov, 2000). Finding someone to blame when things go poorly is useful for narcissists' self-regulation. We are not aware of any scientific evidence that narcissists actually seek out individuals who are potential scapegoats for their failings. Research does support the idea that the narcissist will blame whoever is most readily available, whether it is a work partner (e.g., Campbell et al., 2000) or an experimenter (Kernis & Sun, 1994). Finally, narcissists can find fuel in the form of individuals who directly increase their social status. For example, a narcissist might act in a sycophantic way toward a boss in order to gain a promotion. There is no direct empirical evidence for this process, although it is easy to think of real-world examples (e.g., the reality TV show *The Apprentice*).

In sum, we can think of narcissism as a self-regulating system that operates within a broader social context. Like the angler fish that uses a colorful lighted appendage to lure small fish to play the role of lunch, narcissists will lure others into their world to provide valuable self-regulatory functions. These functions range from providing esteem from association or simple admiration to being a scapegoat for blame. Still to be addressed in this model is: What becomes of the fuel that propels narcissistic self-regulation? Fuel use generally implies some change in state of the fuel; as the energy is extracted from the fuel, the fuel becomes less valuable. The dry grass consumed by a forest fire, for example, turns into cinders. The same arguably holds true for the fuel in narcissists' relationships.

To give a real-world example that one of us (Campbell) heard recently, a woman stated that her unfaithful, narcissistic husband "took her youth" and then took up with another woman. This experienced of being "used" in relationships is commonly reported by those in romantic relationships with narcissists (Campbell, 2005), which partly explains the large drop in satisfaction reported during relationships with narcissists (Foster, Shrira, & Campbell, 2003). Individuals who become involved with narcissists even use the term "burned" to describe their scarring experience. Unfortunately, there have been few empirical investigations of the long-term effects of interactions with narcissists. However, there is evidence of a cost born by others even in the short term, with the most extreme examples being sexual assault (Bushman, Bonacci, Van Dijk, & Baumeister, 2003) and aggression (Bushman & Baumeister, 1998).

THE INHERENT TRADE-OFFS IN NARCISSISTS' INTERPERSONAL SELF-REGULATION

Tesser (2000) has argued that individual differences (and theoretical ideas in psychology in general) can be either "sensual" or "boring." Individual differences are boring to the extent that they predict simple consistency outcomes. If, for example, we proposed that narcissism is invariably bad, and only predicts poor outcomes for both the self and other, the topic would be boring. Even if narcissism predicted positive outcomes for the self, but negative outcomes for others, it would only be moderately interesting. Fortunately, the approach that we are taking to narcissism assumes that narcissism can be considered either good or bad to the extent that it predicts both (1) positive and negative outcomes for self and (2) positive and negative outcomes for the other. Furthermore, these outcomes will vary as a function of context and time. (Although this does not make narcissism research overwhelmingly sensual, it is not boring to us!)

Narcissism, then, is better considered as a trade-off (e.g., Morf & Rhodewalt, 2001) or a mixed blessing (Paulhus, 1998). One vivid example of the trade-offs involved in narcissism can be seen in an experimental test of the classic resource dilemma paradigm (Campbell, Bush, Brunell, & Shelton, 2005). Narcissists' performance was better than others in the short term. Narcissists also outperformed their competitors in the long term, but because they destroyed the common resource (overharvested timber), everyone became worse off. The trade-off of this increased early success was the cost borne by the competitors, the forest, and, after the initial rounds, the narcissists themselves.

A slightly different pattern of trade-offs can be seen in narcissistic relationships. Across a variety of relationships, narcissists initially are liked and judged exciting or entertaining (Brunell et al., 2004; Paulhus, 1998). This is a short-term benefit *both* to the narcissists and to the other. In the longer term, however, narcissists take advantage of the other (a plus for the narcissist, a minus to the other). In romantic relationships, for example, narcissists display infidelity, game-playing, and controlling behavior (Campbell, 2006). Finally, the relationship usually ends because the narcissist is dumped or fired (a minus to the narcissist, neutral to the other) or the narcissist moves on to another relationship (a plus to the narcissists, an ambivalent neutral to the other). What separates this relationship pattern from the pattern in the competitive commons dilemma is that the other in this example derives a short-term benefit from the relationship with the narcissist. Indeed, this short-term rush of excitement could plausibly explain why people repeatedly get involved in relationships with narcissists. In a sense, a romantic relationship with a narcissist is like eating chocolate cake: there is a very positive short-term benefit, but the prospect of a longer-term cost (Campbell, 2005).

A third pattern of trade-offs in narcissism can be seen in individual judgment and decision making. A classic example of this is the case of the individual self-serving bias, where narcissists take individual credit for success but blame situational factors for failure (e.g., Rhodewalt & Morf, 1996). This behavior suggests a short-term esteem benefit for the narcissist, but both short- and long-term costs may take the form of not learning from mistakes. One study looked at this self-view versus performance trade-off through the lens of overconfidence. When a penalty existed for making overconfident judgments, narcissists were more likely to be penalized and score lower than nonnarcissists, though they still believed that they outperformed others (Campbell, Goodie, & Foster, 2004). This long-term performance failure is illustrated most clearly in longitudinal research on university grades. Narcissists report that they are smarter than others in their early years at university, but their grades decline over time (Robins & Beer, 2001).

In sum, narcissistic self-regulation results in a complex series of trade-offs for the narcissist and the others interacting with him or her. Narcissism generally involves a trade-off of short-term benefits (particularly self-esteem or egoistic benefits) for longer-term costs. Narcissists' benefits often come at the expense of the others, who suffer short- and long-term losses from their involvement with narcissists.

LINKING NARCISSISM TO OTHER SELF AND RELATIONSHIP MODELS

Our approach to narcissism and interpersonal self-regulation has some important similarities and differences with a range of self and relationship models in the social-personality psychology literature. We discuss some intriguing links between models below. This list is certainly not exhaustive, but it does include a range of models from the more relational to the more cognitive.

"Win/Win" Models of the Self in Relationships

Like the agency model, several well-studied models in the social-personality literature explain positive changes in the self from close relationships. Whereas the agency model predicts that the relationship partner typically loses in the process of the relationship with the narcissist (a win/lose model), these models typically predict long-term self-concept growth and enhancement by both partners (win/win models).

Murray and colleagues (e.g., Murray, Holmes, & Griffin, 1996) have proposed and empirically verified a process by which an individual with positive self-views will see her partner as having positive qualities, and this will, in turn, lead her partner to have positive self-views. The partner, at the same time, reciprocates by seeing his partner as having positive qualities, which leads the partner to have positive self-views. These researchers argue convincingly that such "rose-colored glasses" are associated with positive relational outcomes.

Why do narcissists tend to derogate their partners (Campbell, Rudich, & Sedikides, 2002), whereas Murray et al.'s participants with positive self-views enhance their partners? One possibility is that the positive self-conceptions in Murray et al.'s research cover both agentic and communal traits. If this is the case, their participants might be more similar to the prototypical high self-esteem individual than narcissistic individual (Campbell, Rudich, et al., 2002). It is also possible that a win/win model does work in narcissists' relationships during the very early stages when those involved with the narcissist actually report great satisfaction (Campbell, 2006). These are interesting questions for future research.

A second, related win/win model is the Michelangelo phenomenon (Drigotas, Rusbult, Wieselquist, & Whitton, 1999). According to the Michelangelo phenomenon, if an individual sees her partner as close to his ideal self, she will behaviorally confirm his behaviors that are consistent with his ideal self. Over time, he will actually become his ideal self. Does this Michelangelo phenomenon occur in a narcissist's relationships? It is likely that the progression toward the ideal self is not mutual but unilateral—only for the narcissist. That is, the narcissist could become his ideal self as a result of his partner's behavioral confirmation, but he might not engage in behavioral confirmation of his partner or even be very aware of the contents of his partner's ideal self.

Sociometer

Leary and colleagues (e.g., Leary & Baumeister, 2000) proposed that self-esteem acts as a sociometer: the extent to which an individual feels accepted by a social group. The agency model suggests (as does work on narcissism and even the interpersonal circumplex) the possibility of extending the sociometer to include two primary gauges: a gauge of social belongingness and a gauge of social dominance. (The assumption we are making is that belongingness corresponds more strongly with communal concerns than with agentic concerns; if belongingness underlies both, however, our logic is not correct.) Theoretically, self-esteem could result from both of these processes. If this is indeed the case, research suggests that narcissists would pay much more attention to the dominance sociometer than the belongingness sociometer, or even that their belongingness sociometer is mis-calibrated (Brown & Zeigler-Hill, 2004; Campbell, Rudich, et al., 2002). Indeed, a more complex multi-sociometer has been proposed (Kirkpatrick, Waugh, Valencia, & Webster, 2002). In this model, self-beliefs in a specific evolutionary domain (e.g., social belongingness, mating competition) will be the best predictor of aggression following threat in one of those domains. In this research, the specific self-belief measures were better predictors than was narcissism. In sum, there is the possibility for self-esteem to be a "master" sociometer, narcissism to function generally with two sociometers (agency and communion), and more specific self-views to act as sociometers for far more specific social contexts.

Attachment Theory

Attachment theory provides a model of self and other that does seem to align reasonably well with the interpersonal circumplex, which suggests some correspondence between attachment and narcissism. A dismissing attachment style reflects a positive view of self and a negative view of others, which is consistent with findings regarding narcissism. Indeed, there is some evidence for a connection between narcissism and attachment. Narcissism, and particularly the entitlement subscale, correlates primarily with dismissing attachment (Campbell, Bonacci, et al., 2004; Campbell & Foster, 2002; Neumann & Bierhoff, 2004). We note, however, that we have not found the link between narcissism and attachment in some unpublished data sets, so we do not want to make too strong a case for the association with dismissing attachment.

The best developmental data that we have on narcissism are self-reports of parenting collected from high school and college samples (Horton, Bleau, & Drwecki, 2006). Narcissism was associated with high school reports of parenting that stressed permissiveness. In a sense, to the extent that parents did not generally keep track of their children's behavior, the children were more likely to be narcissistic.

The Self-Zoo

Tesser and colleagues (Tesser, Crepaz, Collins, Cornell, & Beach, 2000; Tesser, Martin, & Cornell, 1996) proposed that the multiplicity and diversity of self-esteem enhancement strategies be corralled into the term "self-zoo," and that one mechanism is substitutable for another. For example, self-affirmation following a task might result in reduced use of a self-serving bias, and vice versa. According to these findings, individuals apparently do not need to engage in several self-esteem enhancement mechanisms simultaneously or subsequently. Individuals appear to be satisficers of self-esteem rather than maximizers. Although narcissists' pervasive self-regulation is very consistent with the zoo model, we doubt that narcissists would satisfice, particularly in agency domains. For example, in one study (Campbell et al., 2000), participants were given randomly determined success or failure feedback on a dyadic "creativity" task and then given two opportunities to self-enhance/protect. Narcissists used both opportunities to self-enhance, whereas nonnarcissists only enhanced on one measure. This evidence suggests that narcissists may be self-esteem maximizers more than satisficers, and may be willing to use the entire zoo of enhancement mechanisms if available.

Mnemic Neglect and Other Memory Distortion Models

The mnemic neglect model (Sedikides, Green, & Pinter, 2004) attempts to account for the ways in which individuals process threatening self-referent information. Techniques from the person memory literature were appropriated to compare processing of and memory for self-referent versus other-referent information. In several experiments, recall of negative self-referent information pertaining to central traits was poor relative to recall of positive central self-referent information or negative central other-referent information (Green & Sedikides, 2004; Sedikides & Green, 2000). This mnemic neglect was found in a hypothetical feedback setting as well as a more realistic feedback setting, in which the behavioral information was presented as feedback from a highly reliable computer-administered personality inventory (Sedikides & Green, 2000).

One interesting question to ask is: How does narcissism link to mnemic neglect? In one investigation, greater mnemic neglect was shown by individuals high in narcissism than for individuals low in narcissism (i.e., a greater disparity between recall of positive versus negative self-referent behaviors), but this effect was not replicated in a subsequent experiment (Green & Sedikides, 2006). This unreliable result possibly reflects the fact that the traits used in these studies were communal (i.e., trustworthy and kind). Future research will examine these processes with agentic traits.

Narcissism should also plausibly predict memory distortion in a self-enhancing direction (see Wilson & Ross, 2001). In one study, for example, Rhodewalt and Eddings (2002) investigated memory distortion by narcissists in response to romantic rejection. High and low narcissistic men reported their impressions of an interaction with a potential dating partner, were informed 1 week later that they had been accepted or rejected as a date, and then again reported their impressions of the initial interaction. Contrary to the pattern of low narcissists, narcissists who had been rejected reported more positive dating histories. These self-serving memory distortions by narcissists served the process of self-regulation. Future research could further investigate the self-regulatory role of mnemic neglect and memory distortion in narcissists.

CONCLUSIONS

What Can Work on Narcissism Gain from Other Self and Relationships Research?

Theoretical insights into narcissistic self-regulation are only possible because of the extensive research that has already gone into understanding basic self and relational processes. Narcissistic self-regulation is made apparent by plugging narcissism into a classic model of self or relationships (e.g., the better-than-average effect; Alicke, Klotz, Breitenbecher, Yurak, & Vredenberg, 1995, or self-serving bias; Campbell & Sedikides, 1999).

We might even go as far as to argue that the understanding of narcissism in a field is only as good as the basic models it builds on. Narcissism started primarily as a psychoanalytic or psychodynamic construct. Despite our fondness for Freud, the basic psychodynamic models of human behavior are sufficiently intractable that very little clear insight into narcissism has resulted. In contrast, narcissism's relatively brief 25 years in social-personality psychology has resulted in an explosion of understanding of the construct. This reflects the strength of the basic models of the personality, self-regulation and relationships in social-personality psychology as well as, more broadly, the benefits of scientific inquiry.

What Can the Study of Narcissism Add to Self Research?

The study of narcissism adds a good deal to the larger area of self research. First, research on narcissism, and the agency model in particular, highlights the importance of looking at self-enhancement and self-regulation in terms of both agency and communion. It is possible that for certain individuals, enhancement will occur primarily in one domain or the other.

Second, work on narcissism is a good example of the utility of individual difference variables for understanding general self-regulation processes. Indeed, because individuals are likely to use different and often contradictory self-regulation strategies, self-regulation will at times only be seen accurately with the inclusion of the relevant individual difference variable. For example, research has found that individual displays of the self-serving bias are constrained in close relationships (Sedikides, Campbell, Reeder, & Elliot, 1998). Further research, however, found that this "general" process actually reflected two processes: non-narcissists actually other-enhanced in these contexts, but narcissists self-enhanced (Campbell et al., 2000)

Third, work on narcissism is a nice example of a research program that bridges multiple levels of analyses. Narcissism can serve as a bridge between cultural factors, personality, self-concept, self-regulation, cognitive processing, interpersonal relationships, and more. Narcissism is not alone in serving this bridging function (self-variables, in general, are very useful for this purpose) but has proven to be very helpful in this context.

Finally, we think that narcissism provides a vivid example of *radically pervasive* self-regulation. Narcissists are adept at using a multiplicity of behaviors to self-regulate. One of us (Campbell) frequently receives emails from strangers describing narcissistic self-regulation efforts. The diversity of these efforts is unbelievable. One recent email, for example, described an individual who commented that his birthday was only a few days before Christmas, so he must be similar to Jesus. Of course, when one hears stories like this it is easy to say: These ridiculous narcissists are playing such an obvious game of self-regulation. Slightly more self-reflective individuals, however, might also ask: Wow, am I playing just as hard but at a different game?

REFERENCES

Alicke, M. D., Klotz, M. L., Breitenbecher, D. L., Yurak, T. J., & Vredenberg, D. S. (1995). Personal contact, individuation, and the better-than-average effect. *Journal of Personality and Social Psychology, 68,* 804–825.

American Psychiatric Association (1994). *Diagnostic and statistical manual of mental disorders* (4th ed., revised). Washington, DC: Author.

Baumeister, R. F., & Vohs, K. D. (2001). Narcissism as addiction to esteem. *Psychological Inquiry, 12,* 206–210.

Bradlee, P. M., & Emmons, R. A. (1992). Locating narcissism within the interpersonal circumplex and the five-factor model. *Personality and Individual Differences, 13,* 821–830.

Brown, R. P., & Zeigler-Hill, V. (2004). Narcissism and the non-equivalence of self-esteem measures: A matter of dominance? *Journal of Research in Personality, 38,* 585–592.

Brunell, A. B., Campbell, W. K., Smith, L., & Krusemark, E. A. (2004). *Why do people date narcissists? A narrative study.* Poster presented at the annual meeting of the Society for Personality and Social Psychology, Austin, TX, February 2004.

Brunell, A. B. Gentry, W., Campbell, W. K., & Kuhnert, K. (2006). *Narcissism and emergent leadership.* Poster presented at the annual meeting of the Society for Personality and Social Psychology, Palm Springs, CA, January 2006.

Bushman, B. J., & Baumeister, R. F. (1998). Threatened egotism, narcissism, self-esteem, and direct and displaced aggression: Does self-love or self-hate lead to violence? *Journal of Personality and Social Psychology, 75,* 219–229.

Bushman, B. J., Bonacci, A. M., Van Dijk, M., & Baumeister, R. F. (2003). Narcissism, sexual refusal, and aggression: Testing a narcissistic reactance model of sexual coercion. *Journal of Personality and Social Psychology, 84,* 1027–1040.

Buss, D. M., & Chiodo, L. M. (1991). Narcissistic acts in everyday life. *Journal of Personality, 59,* 179–215.

Campbell, W. K. (1999). Narcissism and romantic attraction. *Journal of Personality and Social Psychology, 77,* 1254–1270.

Campbell, W. K. (2001). Is narcissism really so bad? *Psychological Inquiry, 12,* 214–216.

Campbell, W. K. (2005). *When you love a man who loves himself: How to deal with a one-way relationship.* Chicago: Sourcebooks Casablanca.

Campbell, W. K. (2006). *Narcissism and romantic relationships.* Paper presented at Relationships Preconference at the annual meeting of the Society for Personality and Social Psychology, Palm Springs, CA, January 2006.

Campbell, W. K., Bonacci, A. M., Shelton, J., Exline, J. J., & Bushman, B. J. (2004). Psychological entitlement: Interpersonal consequences and validation of a new self-report measure. *Journal of Personality Assessment, 83,* 29–45.

Campbell, W. K., Brunell, A. B., & Finkel, E. J. (2006). Narcissism, interpersonal self-regulation, and romantic relationships: An agency model approach. In E. J. Finkel & K. D. Vohs (Eds.), *Self and relationships: Connecting intrapersonal and interpersonal processes.* New York: Guilford Press.

Campbell, W. K., Bush, C. P., Brunell, A. B., & Shelton, J. (2005). Understanding the social costs of narcissism: The case of tragedy of the commons. *Personality and Social Psychology Bulletin, 31,* 1358–1368.

Campbell, W. K., & Foster, C. A. (2002). Narcissism and commitment in romantic relationships: An investment model analysis. *Personality and Social Psychology Bulletin, 28,* 484–495.

Campbell, W. K., & Foster, J. D. (in press). The narcissistic self: Background, an extended agency model, and ongoing controversies. In C. Sedikides & S. Spencer (Eds.), *Frontiers in social psychology: The self*. Philadelphia: Psychology Press.

Campbell, W. K., Foster, C. A., & Finkel, E. J. (2002). Does self-love lead to love for others? A story of narcissistic game playing. *Journal of Personality and Social Psychology, 83*, 340–354.

Campbell, W. K., Goodie, A. S., & Foster, J. D. (2004). Narcissism, overconfidence, and risk attitude. *Journal of Behavioral Decision Making 17*, 297–311.

Campbell, W. K., Reeder, G. D., Sedikides, C., & Elliot, A. J. (2000). Narcissism and comparative self-enhancement strategies. *Journal of Research in Personality, 34*, 329–347.

Campbell, W. K., Rudich, E., & Sedikides, C. (2002). Narcissism, self-esteem, and the positivity of self-views: Two portraits of self-love. *Personality and Social Psychology Bulletin, 28*, 358–368.

Campbell, W. K., & Sedikides, C. (1999). Self-threat magnifies the self-serving bias: A meta-analytic integration. *Review of General Psychology, 3*, 23–43.

Carroll, L. (1987). A study of narcissism, affiliation, intimacy, and power motives among students in business administration. *Psychological Reports, 61*, 355–358.

Drigotas, S. M., Rusbult, C. E., Wieselquist, J., & Whitton, S. W. (1999). Close partner as sculptor of the ideal self: Behavioral confirmation and the Michelangelo phenomenon. *Journal of Personality and Social Psychology, 77*, 293–323.

Ellis, H. (1898). Auto-erotism: A psychological study. *The Alienist and Neurologist, 19*, 260–299.

Emmons, R. A. (1984). Factor analysis and construct validity of the Narcissistic Personality Inventory. *Journal of Personality Assessment, 48*, 291–300.

Emmons, R. A. (1991). Relationship between narcissism and sensation seeking. *Journal of Social Behavior and Personality, 6*, 943–954.

Festinger, L., Riecken, H. W., & Schacter, S. (1956). *When prophecy fails: A social and psychological study of a modern group that predicted the destruction of the world*. New York: Harper & Row.

Foster, J. D., & Campbell, W. K. (2007). *The taxometrics of narcissism*. Unpublished manuscript, University of Georgia.

Foster, J. D., Campbell, W. K., & Twenge, J. M. (2003). Individual differences in narcissism: Inflated self-views across the lifespan and around the world. *Journal of Research in Personality, 37*, 469–486.

Foster, J. D., Shrira, I., & Campbell, W. K. (2003). *The trajectory of relationships involving narcissists and non-narcissists*. Poster presented at the annual meeting of the American Psychological Society, Atlanta, GA, June 2003.

Freud, S. (1914/1957). On narcissism: An introduction. In J. Strachey (Ed. and Trans.), *The standard edition of the complete psychological works of Sigmund Freud* (Vol. 14, pp. 67–104). London: Hogarth Press.

Freud, S. (1931/1950). Libidinal types. In J. Strachey (Ed. and Trans.), *The standard edition of the complete psychological works of Sigmund Freud* (Vol. 21, pp. 217–220). London: Hogarth Press.

Gabriel, M. T., Critelli, J. W., & Ee, J. S. (1994). Narcissistic illusions in self-evaluations of intelligence and attractiveness. *Journal of Personality, 62*, 143–155.

Gosling, S. D., John, O. P., Craik, K. H., & Robins, R. W. (1998). Do people know how they behave? Self-reported act frequencies compared with on-line coding by observers. *Journal of Personality and Social Psychology, 74*, 1337–1349.

Green, J. D., & Sedikides, C. (2004). Retrieval selectivity in the processing of self-referent information: Testing the boundaries of self-protection. *Self and Identity*, 3, 69–80.

Green, J. D., & Sedikides, C. (2006). *The mnemic neglect model: Recall and recognition in self- versus other-perception*. Unpublished manuscript.

Hogan, R., & Hogan, J. (2001). Assessing leadership: A view from the dark side. *International Journal of Selection and Assessment*, 9, 40–51.

Horton, R. S., Bleau G., & Drwecki, B. (2006). Parenting narcissus: Does parenting contribute to the development of narcissism? *Journal of Personality*, 74, 345–376.

Kernberg, O. (1974). Barriers to falling and remaining in love. *Journal of the American Psychoanalytic Association*, 22, 486–511.

Kernberg, O. (1975). *Borderline conditions and pathological narcissism*. New York: Jason Aronson.

Kernis, M. H., & Sun. C. (1994). Narcissism and reactions to interpersonal feedback. *Journal of Research in Personality*, 28, 4–13.

Kirkpatrick, L. A., Waugh, C. E., Valencia, A., & Webster, G. D. (2002). The functional domain-specificity of self-esteem and the differential prediction of aggression. *Journal of Personality and Social Psychology*, 82, 756–767.

Kohut, H. (1977). *The restoration of the self*. New York: International Universities Press.

Leary, M. R., & Baumeister, R. F. (2000). The nature and function of self-esteem: Sociometer theory. In M. P. Zanna (Ed.), *Advances in experimental social psychology* (Vol. 32, pp. 1–62). San Diego, CA: Academic Press.

Leary, T. (1957). *Interpersonal diagnosis of personality: A functional theory and methodology for personality evaluation*. New York: Ronald Press.

Morf, C. C., & Rhodewalt, F. (2001). Unraveling the paradoxes of narcissism: A dynamic self-regulatory processing model. *Psychological Inquiry*, 12, 177–196.

Morf, C. C., Weir, C., & Davidov, M. (2000). Narcissism and intrinsic motivation: The role of goal congruence. *Journal of Experimental Social Psychology*, 15, 424–438.

Murray, H. A. (1938). *Explorations in personality: A clinical and experimental study of fifty men of college age*. New York: Oxford University Press.

Murray, S. L., Holmes, J. G., & Griffin, D. W. (1996). The benefit of positive illusions: Idealization and the construction of satisfaction in close relationships. *Journal of Personality and Social Psychology*, 70, 79–98.

Neumann, E., & Bierhoff, H. W. (2004). Narzissmus im Zusammenhang mit Bindung und Liebesstilen [Egotism versus love in romantic relationships: Narcissism related to attachment and love styles]. *Zeitschrift für Sozialpsychologie*, 35, 33–44.

Paulhus, D. L. (1998). Interpersonal and intrapsychic adaptiveness of trait self-enhancement: A mixed blessing? *Journal of Personality and Social Psychology*, 74, 1197–1208.

Paulhus, D. L., Harms, P. D., Bruce, M. N., & Lysy, D. C. (2004). The over-claiming technique: Measuring self-enhancement independent of ability. *Journal of Personality and Social Psychology*, 84, 890–904.

Raskin, R. N., & Hall, C. S. (1979) A narcissistic personality inventory. *Psychological Reports*, 45, 590.

Raskin, R. N., & Novacek, J. (1991). Narcissism and the use of fantasy. *Journal of Clinical Psychology*, 47, 490–499.

Raskin, R. N., Novacek, J., & Hogan, R. (1991). Narcissistic self-esteem management. *Journal of Personality and Social Psychology*, 60, 911–918.

Raskin, R. N., & Shaw, R. (1988). Narcissism and the use of personal pronouns. *Journal of Personality*, 56, 393–404.

Raskin, R. N., & Terry, H. (1988). A principal components analysis of the Narcissistic Personality Inventory and further evidence of its construct validity. *Journal of Personality and Social Psychology, 54*, 890–902.

Rhodewalt, F., & Eddings, S. K. (2002). Narcissus reflects: Memory distortion in response to ego relevant feedback in high and low narcissistic men. *Journal of Research in Personality, 36*, 97–116.

Rhodewalt, F., & Morf, C. C. (1995). Self and interpersonal correlates of the Narcissistic Personality Inventory. *Journal of Research in Personality, 29*, 1–23.

Rhodewalt, F., & Morf, C. C. (1996). On self-aggrandizement and anger: A temporal analysis of narcissism and affective reactions. *Journal of Personality and Social Psychology, 74*, 672–685.

Robins, R. W., & Beer, J. S. (2001). Positive illusions about the self: Short-term benefits and long-term costs. *Journal of Personality and Social Psychology, 80*, 340–352.

Rose, P. (2002). The happy and unhappy faces of narcissism. *Personality and Individual Differences, 33*, 379–392.

Rose, P., & Campbell, K. (2004). Greatness feels good: A telic model of narcissism and subjective well-being. In F. Columbus (Ed.), *Advances in psychology research* (Vol. 31, pp. 1–25). Huntington, NY: Nova Science Publishers.

Sedikides, C., Campbell, W. K., Reeder, G. D., & Elliot, A. J. (1998). The self-serving bias in relational context. *Journal of Personality and Social Psychology, 74*, 378–386.

Sedikides, C., & Green, J. D. (2000). On the self-protective nature of inconsistency/negativity management: Using the person memory paradigm to examine self-referent memory. *Journal of Personality and Social Psychology, 79*, 906–922.

Sedikides, C., Green, J. D., & Pinter, B. T. (2004). Self-protective memory. In D. Beike, J. Lampinen, & D. Behrend (Eds.), *The self and memory* (pp. 161–179). Philadelphia: Psychology Press.

Sedikides, C., Rudich, E. A., Gregg, A. P., Kumashiro, M., & Rusbult, C. (2004). Are normal narcissists psychologically healthy? Self-esteem matters. *Journal of Personality and Social Psychology, 87*, 400–416.

Stucke, T. S. (2003). Who's to blame? Narcissism and self-serving attributions following feedback. *European Journal of Personality, 17*, 465–478.

Tesser, A. (2000). Theories and hypotheses. In R. Sternberg (Ed.), *Guide to publishing in psychology journals* (pp. 58–80). Cambridge, UK: Cambridge University Press.

Tesser, A., Crepaz, N., Collins, J. C., Cornell, D., & Beach, S. R. H. (2000). Confluence of self-esteem mechanisms: On integrating the self-zoo. *Personality and Social Psychology Bulletin, 26*, 1476–1489.

Tesser, A., Martin, L., & Cornell, D. (1996). On the substitutability of self-protective mechanisms. In P. M. Gollwitzer & J. A. Bargh (Eds.), *The psychology of action: Linking motivation and cognition to behavior* (pp. 400–432). New York: Guilford Press.

Tracy, J. L., & Robins, R. W. (2004). Putting the self into self-conscious emotions: A theoretical model, *Psychological Inquiry, 15*, 103–125.

Twenge, J., & Campbell, W. K. (2003). "Isn't it fun to get the respect that we're going to deserve?" Narcissism, social rejection, and aggression. *Personality and Social Psychology Bulletin, 29*, 261–272.

Vangelisti, A., Knapp, M. L., & Daly, J. A. (1990). Conversational narcissism. *Communication Monographs, 57*, 251–274.

Vohs, K. D., & Campbell, W. K. (2006). *Narcissism and materialism.* Unpublished data, University of British Columbia.

Wallace, H. M., & Baumeister, R. F. (2002). The performance of narcissists rises and falls with perceived opportunity for glory. *Journal of Personality and Social Psychology, 82,* 819–834.

Wilson, A. E., & Ross, M. (2001). From chump to champ: People's appraisals of their earlier and present selves. *Journal of Personality and Social Psychology, 80,* 572–584.

5

Functions of the Self in Interpersonal Relationships: What Does the Self Actually Do?

MARK R. LEARY

S cholarly interest in personal relationships and in the self has been accompanied by a great deal of attention to connections between these two topics. Many researchers who identify themselves as relationship researchers have incorporated self-processes into their study of relationships, and many researchers who identify themselves as self researchers have plied their wares in the relationship domain. For example, theories of self-enhancement have been applied to the question of how people regulate their dependency on romantic partners, self-verification processes have been examined in the context of romantic and roommate relationships, work on self-construal has explored how people incorporate others into their self-concepts, and research has examined the link between self-esteem and relationship behaviors.

Much of this work is based on the assumption that people's behavior in interpersonal contexts is strongly influenced by three basic self-motives—self-enhancement, self-verification, and self-expansion. Although differing in specifics, these perspectives assume that certain interpersonal behaviors are motivated by intrapsychic processes that operate primarily to serve self-relevant goals—to maintain self-esteem, verify one's self-concept, or expand one's self, for example. The goal of this chapter is to challenge this fundamental assumption. I argue that the notion that behavior is strongly influenced by motives to manage one's personal self-image is questionable, and that what have been viewed as self-motives actually operate in the service of interpersonal rather than intrapsychic outcomes.

To begin, I discuss the nature of the self, then describe three self-motives that have received the greatest attention from relationship researchers—self-enhancement, self-verification, and self-expansion.[1] After laying out a case for why these so-called self-motives are not likely to be the basis of the interpersonal phenomena that have been attributed to them, I discuss each motive and its supporting literature in detail.

THE FUNCTIONS OF THE SELF

Progress in understanding self-processes has been impeded by inconsistency in use of the term, "self." Various writers have used "self" to refer to the entire person, all or part of personality, the seat of consciousness, mental self-representations or self-beliefs, the cognitive ability that underlies self-reflection, and the executive control center that is responsible for self-regulation and decision-making (Leary & Tangney, 2003). In the long run, we may wish to abolish the word "self" from scholarly writing altogether, substituting terms that more clearly specify their referents, but in the meantime, my preference is to regard the self as the cognitive system that underlies self-awareness, self-referential thought, and self-regulation. As such, the self is not a monolithic entity but rather a complex cognitive system that comprises a number of distinct processes. In our analysis of how the human self may have evolved, Nicole Buttermore and I suggested that the self seems to involve at least three distinct cognitive abilities, each of which may have evolved at different times for different purposes (Leary & Buttermore, 2003).

The first component of the self, the extended-self ability, underlies people's ability to think about themselves over time. Whereas most other animals appear to live perpetually in the present moment (Gallup, 1997), human beings can think about themselves back in the past and ahead in the future. The extended-self ability is involved any time people transcend the present situation in their own mind and, thus, is essential for planning, reminiscing, and deliberate self-regulation.

The second ability—the private-self ability—involves the capacity to think about internal, subjective information such as one's emotions, thoughts, physical sensations, goals, and other private states. Although all mammals presumably experience some of these internal states, they seem unable to introspect on them. In contrast, human beings can think about their inner experiences, use subjective information to make decisions, and recognize that these states are not observable by others. In addition, theorists have suggested that the ability to contemplate one's own private states may underlie people's ability to draw inferences about other people's private states (Gallup, 1997; Humphrey, 1982). The only way to infer another person's thoughts, emotions, or intentions is for people to imagine how they themselves would react, with adjustments made based on their knowledge of the other individual.

A third component of the self—the conceptual-self ability—involves people's capacity to think about themselves in abstract and symbolic ways (as being a conservative, a Marxist, or a fashion maven, for example), and to evaluate themselves using arbitrary criteria (such as being a good piano player, or a bad loser). The conceptual-self ability allows people to represent and think about their abstract characteristics and is necessary for the symbolic self-concept, self-evaluation, and self-presentation.

To say it differently, the self has at least three primary functions that involve thinking about oneself over time (the extended-self ability), introspection (the private-self ability), and self-representation and -evaluation (the conceptual-self ability). Although one could conceivably propose additional self-reflective capacities, most of the self-processes that have been studied by social and personality psychologists appear to rely on one or more of these three abilities, sometimes working in tandem. It is difficult to think of self-related phenomena that do not rely on thinking about oneself in a temporal fashion, introspection (and inferring other people's thoughts and feelings), or symbolic self-thought and self-evaluation.

The adaptive advantages of each of these abilities are obvious, so it is not too much of a stretch to imagine that each evolved because it facilitated survival and reproduction during human evolution (Gallup, 1997; Leary & Buttermore, 2003; Sedikides & Skowronski, 1997). Being able to analyze the past and imagine the future, utilize subjective information and infer others' inner states, and construe oneself in abstract ways likely increased people's success in dealing with their physical and social environments. In fact, the evolution of these three self-relevant abilities may have been partly responsible for setting human beings on a different trajectory from all other species (Leary, 2004; Leary & Buttermore, 2003).

THE (SO-CALLED) SELF-MOTIVES

A good deal of research has been based on the idea that the self is motivated to protect, if not enhance, self-esteem (self-enhancement), maintain a consistent self-image (self-verification), and expand itself (self-expansion). Yet, nothing in the conceptualization of the self as a set of cognitive self-referential abilities suggests that the self possesses any motivational features with respect to itself. What does it mean to say that the self is motivated to enhance, verify, and expand itself? Is the "self" that motivates the person to enhance, verify, and expand the self the same as the "self" that is being enhanced, verified, or expanded? If we regard the self as a set of cognitive abilities, as described earlier, it is unclear where the motivation originates, and if we regard the self as a set of self-representations, it is difficult to explain how a cognitive representation is motivated to enhance, verify, or expand itself. Common ways of talking about self-motives imply that some other self (or feature of the self) must motivate the self toward self-enhancement, -verification, and -expansion, but, if so, what would that be?

This conceptual quagmire might be resolved if we assume that the motivational impetus behind self-enhancing, -verifying, and -expanding patterns of thought and behavior do not operate to serve the psychological self. If the self evolved because it conferred advantages in meeting life's challenges and opportunities (Leary & Buttermore, 2003; Sedikides & Skowronski, 1997), then the activities of the self must be fundamentally aimed toward eliciting beneficial external outcomes rather than maintaining certain intrapsychic states. The ability to conceptualize oneself in a temporal fashion allowed people to plan for the future and learn from the past, the ability to introspect allowed people to use subjective information to make decisions and to think about others' inner states, and the ability to think conceptually about oneself allowed people to contemplate and evaluate themselves. It does not seem likely that these self-abilities evolved primarily to manage people's perceptions and evaluations of themselves—for example to make them feel better about themselves than they objectively should, to distort feedback to make it consistent with their self-concepts, or to promote an expanded self-concept.

Thus it is not clear that self-enhancement, self-verification, and self-expansion are fundamental motives in their own right. Whereas some theorists regard self-enhancement, self-verification, and self-expansion as inherent properties of the self, it may be more parsimonious to consider these phenomena to be things that an organism with extended-, private-, and conceptual-self abilities sometimes does rather than as inherent properties of the self per se. These patterns of behavior operate to satisfy other motives that facilitate adjustment to one's external environment, including other people, rather than to maintain certain states or conditions of the self (for a similar view, see Holmes, 2004). It is surprising that social psychologists, who typically trace the antecedents of behavior to interpersonal motives and processes, have placed so much emphasis on purely intrapsychic motives.

To be clear, I am not suggesting that people do not engage in behaviors that are self-enhancing, self-verifying, and self-expanding. However, the data are less clear that these patterns arise from motives to enhance, verify, or expand one's self-concept. But, if these patterns do not serve the self by maintaining certain self-views and self-evaluations, what function do these "self-motives" serve? I argue here that these so-called self-motives are, at heart, interpersonal processes that are involved in facilitating people's social effectiveness in relationships and groups, particularly their efforts to be valued and accepted by others. As many theorists have noted, human beings have a strong and pervasive desire to be accepted and to avoid rejection (Baumeister & Leary, 1995). Many of the phenomena that have been attributed to the motives to self-enhance, self-verify, and self-expand may be traced to this basic need to belong.

SELF-ENHANCEMENT

Self-enhancement is the tendency for people to behave in ways that promote positive self-views (and avoid negative self-views) or, alternatively, to protect and enhance their self-esteem. Since the earliest days of psychology, many writers have regarded the need for self-esteem as a fundamental human motive (James, 1890; Maslow, 1954; Rogers, 1959), and self-enhancement has been invoked as an explanation for a wide range of thought, emotion, and behavior. Among other things, self-enhancement has been used to explain why people think they are better than most other people (Alicke & Govorun, 2005), overvalue people, places, and things with which they are associated (Pelham, Mirenberg, & Jones, 2002), make self-serving attributions for success and failure (Blaine & Crocker, 1993), derogate other people in order to feel good about themselves (Fein & Spencer, 1997), distance themselves from other people who are more successful than they are (Tesser, 1988), perceive other people in ways that reflect well on them personally (Dunning & Hayes, 1996), compare themselves with others who are worse off than they are (Wood, Giordano-Beech, & Ducharme, 1999), and, despite falling victim to all of these self-enhancing biases, claim that they are not biased (Pronin, Lin, & Ross, 2002).

Furthermore, theorists have suggested that positive self-views and high self-esteem provide important benefits, thereby explaining why people might possess a motive to self-enhance (Taylor & Brown, 1988, 1994). High self-esteem is associated with certain indices of psychological well-being, including lower anxiety, depression, and stress; greater self-confidence, resilience, and persistence; and a lower likelihood of drug abuse, delinquency, and membership in deviant groups (see Baumeister, Campbell, Krueger, & Vohs, 2003; Bonanno, Rennicke, & Dekel, 2005; Mecca, Smelser, & Vasconcellos, 1989; Taylor & Brown, 1988, 1994; Taylor, Lerner, Sherman, Sage, & McDowell, 2003a, 2003b). If high self-esteem offers these psychological and practical benefits, perhaps the self-enhancement motive is rooted in the quest for these beneficial outcomes.

However, questions have been raised about whether self-esteem is as beneficial as has been assumed. Critics have observed that the relationships between self-esteem and positive outcomes are rather weak, and that high self-esteem and self-enhancement have several notable personal and interpersonal drawbacks as well (Baumeister, Heatherton, & Tice, 1993; Baumeister, Smart, & Boden, 1996; Baumeister, Wotman, & Stillwell, 2003; Block & Colvin, 1994; Bonanno et al., 2005; Colvin, Block, & Funder, 1995; Heatherton & Vohs, 2000; Paulhus, 1998; Robins & John, 1997). In addition, positive life outcomes often appear to be the cause rather than the result of high self-esteem (Baumeister et al., 2003).

The debate between those who see self-enhancement in a positive vs. negative light is complicated by a failure to distinguish self-enhancement from high self-esteem. Many studies have operationalized self-enhancement in terms of the positivity of people's self-ratings, their level of self-esteem, or a positive difference between their ratings of themselves and their ratings of others (e.g., Alicke, 1985; Taylor et al., 2003a), none of which necessarily reflects whether the individual's perceptions are self-enhancing as opposed to accurately favorable (Kwan, John, Kenny, Bond, & Robins, 2004). Studies that assess self-enhancement independently of the positivity of people's self-evaluations have revealed mixed relationships between self-enhancement and well-being (Kwan et al., 2004; Paulhus, Harms, Bruce, & Lysy, 2003). Overall, self-enhancement may make people feel good about themselves and have other short-term benefits but, in the long run, it may undermine their well-being and interpersonal relationships (Colvin et al., 1995; Crocker & Park, 2004; Leary, Bednarski, Hammon, & Duncan, 1997; Paulhus, 1998; Robins & Beer, 2001). These considerations make it difficult to conclude that people are inherently motivated to self-enhance because self-enhancement promotes well-being. But if people do not possess a basic motive to self-enhance, what underlies self-enhancing patterns of thought and behavior?

Why Do People Self-Enhance?

Recently, theorists have offered explanations that root self-enhancement in fundamental, potentially adaptive motives involving the maintenance of social dominance (Barkow, 1980), the pursuit of social acceptance (Leary & Downs, 1995), and the avoidance of existential terror (Solomon, Greenberg, & Pyszczynski, 1991). Each of these theories suggests that people do not seek self-esteem for its own sake, but rather because it is associated with some commodity that improves personal or interpersonal well-being. Space does not permit a detailed critique of these approaches, so I will focus on only one possible interpersonal function of self-enhancement (for reviews, see Barkow, 1980; Leary, 2002; Solomon, Greenberg, & Pyszczynski, 2004).

As noted, human beings are motivated to be accepted by other people, and much of their behavior is oriented toward fostering acceptance or avoiding rejection (Baumeister & Leary, 1995). Given that people who possess socially desirable attributes are more likely to be accepted than those with less desirable characteristics, people generally want to maintain a positive image in other people's eyes (Leary, 1995). Thus people tend to self-enhance because it is better to be seen positively rather than negatively on virtually every attribute that one can imagine. In fact, given the importance of being viewed favorably, people's automatic, default orientation is toward public self-enhancement (Paulhus & Levitt, 1987). Furthermore, because different images promote acceptance by different individuals, people self-enhance selectively on dimensions that they think others will favor (Leary, 1995; Sedikides, Gaertner, & Toguchi, 2003; Swann, Bosson, & Pelham, 2002).

Sociometer theory suggests that self-esteem is part of a psychological monitoring system—a sociometer—that keeps tabs on people's relational value in other people's eyes (Leary & Baumeister, 2000; Leary & Downs, 1995). When the sociometer detects cues indicating that other people may devalue or reject them, people are alerted by an aversive loss of self-esteem. Thus events that lower people's self-esteem—such as failure, rejection, humiliating events, and immoral actions—do so because these events might result in devaluation or rejection (Leary, Tambor, Terdal, & Downs, 1995). According to the theory, people do not seek self-esteem for its own sake, but rather seek to avoid rejection. When people show self-enhancing biases, they are usually trying to increase their value and acceptance in others' eyes.

In support of sociometer theory, experimental manipulations that convey low relational value (e.g., rejection, disapproval, disinterest) consistently lower participants' state self-esteem (Leary, Cottrell, & Phillips, 2001; Leary, Haupt, Strausser, & Chokel, 1998; Leary et al., 1995; Nezlek, Kowalski, Leary, Blevins, & Holgate, 1997). Even people who claim to be unconcerned with other people's approval and acceptance show declines in self-esteem when they are rejected (Leary et al., 2003). Similarly, rejecting events in everyday life are associated with negative self-feelings (Baumeister, Wotman, & Stillwell, 1993), the effects of performing certain actions on people's self-esteem closely mirror how they believe those behaviors will affect the degree to which others accept them (Leary et al., 1995; MacDonald,

Saltzman, & Leary, 2003), and perceived relational value prospectively predicts changes in self-esteem (Murray, Griffin, Rose, & Bellavia, 2003; Srivastava & Beer, 2005). These findings suggest that the basic impetus behind self-enhancement may lie in the desire for social connections and not in a motive to merely feel good about oneself or to have a favorable self-image.

Self-Enhancement and Relationship Commitment

Much of the work on the relational implications of self-esteem and self-enhancement has emerged from Murray and Holmes' ideas about how people regulate their dependency on romantic partners (Murray & Holmes, 1997; Murray, Holmes, & Griffin, 1996, 2000; Murray, Rose, Bellavia, Holmes, & Kusche, 2002). This work is based on the assumption that people are willing to commit themselves to a relationship only to the extent to which they feel reasonably sure their feelings will be reciprocated (Berscheid & Fei, 1977; Holmes & Rempel, 1989). To do otherwise would put the individual at risk of investing in a doomed or inequitable relationship and suffering the hurt of eventual rejection.

Because people's perceptions of their partners' regard for them are influenced by their own self-perceptions, people with lower self-esteem generally feel less highly regarded by their partners than people with higher self-esteem (Leary & MacDonald, 2003; Murray, Holmes, & Griffin, 2000). And, because these feelings of insecurity affect perceptions of and commitment to the partner, people with lower self-esteem perceive their partners less favorably and have less commitment to their relationships than people with higher self-esteem. Murray and Holmes (2000) conceptualized this process as driven partly by the self-enhancement motive. In their words,

> enhancing the value of the relationship is likely to be seen as a viable or safe strategy of self-enhancement only by individuals who trust in the continued stability of their relationships. . . . We believe that the resulting motive to protect the self from the possibility of loss typically interferes with processes of attachment and relationship-valuing for low self-esteem individuals. (p. 179)

Put simply, people are willing to commit to partners and relationships only when the potential threat to their self-esteem is low.

Not only do people with low trait self-esteem view their partners and relationships less favorably than those with high self-esteem, but failures, relational insecurities, and other events that promote self-doubt lead people with low self-esteem to have less confidence in their partner's positive regard and to value their relationships less (Murray et al., 2000; Murray, Holmes, Griffin, Bellavia, & Rose, 2001; Murray, Holmes, MacDonald, & Ellsworth, 1998; Murray et al., 2002). And, this process can create a self-fulfilling cycle in which people with low self-esteem pull back from relationships in which they feel insecure, thereby undermining the quality of the relationship (Murray et al., 1998; Murray et al., 2002).

Clearly, people generally desire to feel good rather than bad about themselves, and often respond in ways that promote positive self-feelings. Furthermore, as noted, people hesitate to commit to relationships in which they are unsure about their partner's regard (Murray & Holmes, 2000). The question is whether people's reluctance or willingness to commit themselves involves a motive to maintain or enhance self-esteem.

Careful reading of the studies cited above suggests that a parsimonious explanation of these effects does not require reference to a motive to self-enhance. Let me posit four, relatively uncontroversial assumptions: (1) People perceive the practical and emotional risks to be lower in relationships in which the partner accepts and loves them at least as much as they accept and love the partner than in relationships in which people's acceptance and love for the partner are not reciprocated (Berscheid & Fei, 1977; Holmes & Rempel, 1989; Murray & Holmes, 2000); (2) people's commitment to a partner and relationship is affected by the degree to which the partner appears to accept and love them (Holmes & Rempel, 1989); (3) people with low trait self-esteem perceive that others value, accept, and love them less than people with high self-esteem (Leary & MacDonald, 2003); and (4) failures and relational threats lower people's self-esteem and make them feel less acceptable.

Together, these assumptions explain why people prefer not to commit to those who are not committed to them, and why people with low self-esteem become particularly nervous about commitment in the face of events that lower their feelings of acceptability. And, importantly, these assumptions explain these effects without reference to a motive to self-enhance. Put differently, people's reactions to these kinds of relationship events reflect primarily their desire to obtain a dependable relationship that provides acceptance, affection, and support, rather than their desire to maintain their self-esteem. People's feelings of self-esteem are relevant to this process because self-esteem provides people with a guide to how they are faring in their relationships (Leary & Baumeister, 2000), but people are fundamentally concerned with what their relationships provide rather than with intrapsychic self-enhancement for its own sake.

A similar process may operate in instances in which people distance themselves from close others who outperform them on important dimensions, which has typically been explained in terms of self-evaluation maintenance (Tesser, 1988). Although this phenomenon may appear contrary to the notion that people are motivated to be accepted, it may emerge from the implicit realization that being outperformed in important domains may undermine one's social acceptance in other people's eyes. As a result, people may distance themselves from those in their social circles who, by virtue of their superiority, undermine their own basis for acceptance.

Self-Affirmation

More broadly, researchers have suggested that threats to self-worth induce a motive to self-enhance that affects how people behave toward others. For example, self-affirmation theory suggests that people have a need to maintain an image of self-integrity (i.e., moral and adaptive adequacy) (Steele, 1988). As a result, threats to people's self-images motivate them to affirm the global integrity of the self.

In an early demonstration of this effect, Steele (1975) threatened women's self-images by telling them that, as members of their community, it was common knowledge that they either were cooperative with community projects, uncoopera- tive with community projects, or not concerned about driving safely. (A fourth, control group received no information relevant to their self-images.) Two days later, a confederate called each woman, asking her to list every food item in her kitchen to help a food co-op. Women who had been told they were uncooperative people or careless drivers two days earlier helped the confederate almost twice as much as women in the other groups. Self-affirmation theory explains this effect in terms of the women's motive to restore cognitive consistency with their self-concepts as cooperative people:

> The simplest explanation seems to be that women in the negative name conditions helped more in order to reaffirm their general goodness and worth after their goodness had been threatened. Whereas helping with a food co-op could not disprove the bad driver label, it could go some way in proving that they were good, worthy people. (Steele, 1988, pp. 265–266)

Note that self-affirmation theory traces the reaction to intrapsychic concerns with consistency, self-integrity, and self-worth rather than to the real or imagined inter- personal implications of the researcher's derogatory comments about participants' cooperativeness or driving.

Many studies have examined the effects of self-threats on other self- enhancement tactics, such as self-serving attributions (Dunning, Leuenberger, & Sherman, 1995), derogating minority group members (Fein & Spencer, 1997), and exaggerating one's self-ratings (Brown & Smart, 1991). Furthermore, allowing people to affirm their self-integrity, for example by prompting them to think about important personal values, reduces defensive reactions to self-threats (e.g., Schimel, Arndt, Banko, & Cook, 2004; Siegel, Scillitoe, & Parks-Yancy, 2005; Steele & Liu, 1983; Tesser & Cornell, 1991). Thus threats to self-worth increase self-enhancing actions, which are lowered by opportunities to self-affirm. But, again, the question is whether these effects arise from a motive to reaffirm one's goodness and worth to oneself.

A person who behaves in an ethically questionable fashion, fails at a task, or is criticized by others experiences an implied threat to social acceptance. (Even when others are not aware that the person has behaved in an undesirable or questionable manner, the individual may nonetheless feel less acceptable than he or she did beforehand.) Perceiving oneself as a less socially acceptable person should generally induce processes that address one's interpersonal shortcomings and render oneself more acceptable to others. Reflecting on evidence of one's goodness or worth (i.e., engaging in self-affirmation) short-circuits this effect by restoring the sense that one is acceptable to other people. Although these judg- ments may occur in one's own mind (and involve the extended-, private-, and conceptual-self abilities discussed earlier), they nonetheless involve thoughts that are relevant to one's social acceptability rather than merely efforts to restore one's private self-worth or self-esteem (see Baldwin & Holmes, 1987).

Private Self-Enhancement

Of course, people sometimes self-enhance in their own minds even when no interpersonal outcomes are at stake and no one else is privy to either their mis-behaviors or self-enhancing thoughts. However, these examples of "private" self-enhancement are parsimoniously regarded as a secondary use of self-reflection that makes people feel good in the absence of outcomes that would normally raise self-esteem. Animals without a self can feel good only by creating actual situations that evoke positive feelings (by finding food, a mate, or safety, for example). However, once human beings developed the conceptual-self ability, they could induce emotions in themselves by deliberately thinking in certain ways (Leary, in press). As a result, people can feel good and reduce anxiety by telling themselves that they are desirable, competent people, that their problems are not their fault, or that other people are worse off than they are. These self-enhancing thoughts are simply cognitive ways of regulating emotions under conditions in which people might otherwise feel bad, but they do not indicate the existence of a motive to self-enhance. People talk themselves into a variety of emotional states in their own minds in order to experience particular feelings and not because they possess a fundamental motive to do so.

SELF-VERIFICATION

Self-verification theory (Swann, 1983, 1990) proposes that people are motivated to verify, validate, and sustain their existing self-concepts. The theory does not deny that people enjoy positive evaluations or occasionally self-enhance, but rather asserts that they also seek self-verifying information because it satisfies their need for psychological coherence. Swann has suggested that self-verification emerges from both epistemic concerns (a stable, certain view of oneself promotes the experience of a coherent world in which one's actions and outcomes are meaningful and predictable) and pragmatic concerns (a stable self-concept facilitates behavioral stability and smooth social interactions) (Swann, 1983, 1990).

According to the theory, the self-verification motive leads people to seek feedback, environments, and interpersonal relationships that validate their self-views. In support of the theory, experiments have documented that people often prefer to interact with those who see them as they see themselves, and this preference for self-verifying interactions may override the preference for self-enhancing interactions (Hixon & Swann, 1993; Swann & Pelham, 2002; Swann, Pelham, & Krull, 1989; Swann & Read, 1981; Swann, Stein-Seroussi, & Giesler, 1992). Overall, people with favorable self-views prefer to interact with those who have positive impressions of them, whereas people with unfavorable self-views prefer to interact with those who hold unfavorable impressions of them (Swann, Stein-Seroussi, & Giesler, 1992). People also tend to solicit feedback from others that supports their self-images, even if those self-images are negative (Swann, Wenzlaff, Krull, & Pelham, 1992).

Studies of existing relationships show similar patterns. People whose spouses perceive them differently from the way they see themselves—in either a positive or a negative direction—become more distant from them over time than people whose spouses see them similarly to how they see themselves (Burke & Stets, 1999; Swann, De Le Ronde, & Hixon, 1994). Likewise, students whose self-views coincide with group members' appraisals of them feel more connected to their groups and perform more successfully in them than students who see themselves differently from the way other group members do (Swann, Milton, & Polzer, 2000). In a study of college roommates, Swann and Pelham (2002) found that, among students who were invested in their self-views, those with a negative self-view expressed a stronger preference for living with roommates who appraised them unfavorably. Although exceptions to the self-verifying pattern have been found, studies suggest that people find it unsettling to confront information that contradicts their self-views, and gravitate toward interactions and relationships that verify them.

However, the source of self-verification effects is less certain. Without dismissing the epistemic and pragmatic sources of self-verification suggested by others, it seems that self-verification may also serve the desire for social acceptance. Many of the empirical findings may be explained by assuming that people want others to perceive them in ways that maximize the quality, strength, and stability of their relationships. This interpersonal explanation is easy to see in the case of verifying positive self-views. We want others to verify our positive self-views because positive impressions increase the probability of acceptance, thereby fulfilling our desire to be valued, accepted, or loved.

Ironically, the same logic applies when people hold negative self-views, because being regarded more favorably than we see ourselves presents a serious risk to social acceptance, at least in the long run. Acceptance, liking, or love that is based on an erroneously positive impression is tenuous at best. Interactions and relationships may be derailed at any time by information showing the person to be less than others imagined. Having one's partner later learn the ugly truth—that one is not as competent, nice, ethical, or whatever as they once thought—will invariably result in disillusionment and disappointment. Thus, to the extent that people seek security in their relationships, they will want those with whom they establish important relationships to see them reasonably accurately, even if those impressions are not highly positive. The extended-self ability allows people to ruminate on the worrisome possibility of being "found out" and leads them to prefer partners who see them approximately as they see themselves. Of course, making a favorable or even overly positive impression is sometimes desirable, particularly early in a relationship when people may view self-aggrandizement as a necessary risk in order to attract another's attention. But once affection and commitment develop, being perceived too favorably poses a greater risk, so people should prefer their partners to see them as they see themselves.

To take this point one step further, people may feel more loved and accepted by a partner who sees them less positively (but, in their mind, accurately) than by one who has an inflated view of them. Being loved by someone who accurately sees one's flaws connotes a stronger, more abiding connection than being loved by someone who regards us more favorably than we believe we deserve. Knowing that one is accepted or loved in spite of one's deficiencies and weaknesses is a particularly secure and gratifying form of validation. People may feel closer to a romantic partner, friend, or roommate who likes them for who and what they are compared to one who adores them based on mistaken impressions.

Swann et al. (2002) showed that people are selective regarding the dimensions on which they self-enhance vs. self-verify; enhancing on dimensions that are critical to the formation of relationships, but verifying on dimensions that are less so. Furthermore, self-verification appears to operate primarily within a particular relationship, in that people want to be viewed consistently by a particular partner but are less concerned with being seen in the same manner by different people. These findings alone attest to the important role that concerns with acceptance play in self-enhancement and self-verification, and show that self-consistency per se is not as important as being accepted.

Working under the assumption that people have both a motive to self-enhance and a motive to self-verify, researchers have examined how people resolve conflicts between these motives (Swann et al., 1989). However, if we assume that both patterns serve the quest for social acceptance, we need not regard the two tendencies as in conflict. Rather, we can conclude that people who desire to make favorable impressions and be accepted are concerned with appearing both positive and consistent (Schlenker, 1975), and will weigh these tactics differently depending on the interpersonal context. Overall, people seek self-enhancement and self-verification simultaneously (Swann et al., 1989), trying to be seen as positively as reasonably possible, while being sure that they are not perceived too much more favorably than they deserve.

Together, these considerations suggest that people prefer interacting with those who see them as they see themselves in order to establish secure, fulfilling relationships rather than to serve some intrapsychic need for self-verification or coherence. As before, I am not suggesting that people do not sometimes seek self-verifying information because obtaining feedback consistent with one's self-views is inherently gratifying, but, I think we have overlooked the fundamental interpersonal processes that underlie the effect.

SELF-EXPANSION

Aron and his colleagues have proposed that another central motivation is the desire to "expand the self"—to obtain resources, perspectives, and identities that enhance a person's ability to accomplish goals (Aron & Aron, 1996, 1997; Aron, Norman, & Aron, 1998). Self-expansion theory goes beyond earlier theories that stress the reward value of behaving competently (see White, 1959) to suggest that people derive satisfaction merely from expanding the self. Key to the theory is the idea that people may pursue relationships and memberships in groups partly due to this drive for self-expansion (Aron & Aron, 1996, 1997; Wright, Aron, & Tropp, 2002), but these phenomena may arise from a desire to foster certain kinds of relationships rather than a motive to expand the self.

Self-expansion theory is based on the assumption that people incorporate other individuals into their sense of self (James, 1890), a feature of the conceptual-self ability. Essentially, the self-concept "expands" with the development of new relationships and group memberships because connections with other people provide new roles, perspectives, identities, knowledge, and other resources. New people may perceive and validate aspects of the person that were previously ignored by others, bring out facets of the person that he or she never knew were there, or lead the person to develop new competencies. Or, the person may try out new or suppressed identities, thereby expanding his or her behavioral repertoire. Merely being in a new relationship or group provides new elements to a person's self-concept.

Consistent with the notion that relationships expand the self, Aron, Paris, and Aron (1995) found that entering into new love relationships led people to describe themselves in more diverse ways and to an increased sense of self-efficacy. Students who reported falling in love over a 10-week period showed greater diversity in the characteristics they used to describe themselves. Essentially, their self-concept had "expanded." Furthermore, students who fell in love during the study showed greater increases in self-efficacy and self-esteem than students who did not fall in love. The changes in self-esteem could be due to an increased sense of being accepted (Leary & Baumeister, 2000), but increased self-efficacy suggests that participants may have incorporated the new partner's resources into their own sense of self.

The concept of "including others in the self" is more than a metaphor. When people incorporate others into their sense of self, their cognitive representations of themselves and the other literally overlap. For example, people take longer to make "me–not me" decisions when rating traits that are true of themselves but not of their spouses, as if knowledge about oneself is confounded with knowledge about close others (Aron, Aron, Tudor, & Nelson, 1991; Aron & Fraley, 1999). Similarly, people who have incorporated an in-group into their sense of self conflate judgments of themselves and the group (Smith & Henry, 1996; Tropp & Wright, 2001). Furthermore, people make less egotistical social comparisons when they have included the comparison others as part of the self (Gardner, Gabriel, & Hochschild, 2002).

Self-expansion theory proposes not only that relationships expand people's sense of self, but also that part of the impetus for pursuing relationships and group memberships is to experience self-expansion (Wright et al., 2002). Furthermore, people's choices of which relationships and groups to pursue are partly influenced by the potential of those relationships to expand the self. Interacting with others who are just like oneself—with precisely the same personality, skills, interests, and experiences—does not expand one's own self-view as much as interacting with others who are different from oneself. This consideration raises the possibility that, although people seek out others who share basic similarities, they may also be attracted to those whose interests, abilities, and perspectives differ from their own (Aron, Steele, & Kashdan, 2002). Along these lines, Amodio and Showers (2005) found that, for people in less committed relationships, greater perceived dissimilarity predicted liking, possibly because dissimilarity provides a greater potential for self-expansion.

Self-expansion seems to promote positive affect and relationship quality (Aron, Norman, Aron, McKenna, & Heyman, 2000; Reissmann, Aron, & Bergen, 1993). However, the positive emotions associated with self-expansion early in a relationship may wane as the process of self-expansion slows over time, which may account for the plateau or decline in closeness and satisfaction in long-term relationships. If so, giving couples new opportunities for self-expansion might reignite positive feelings. In support of this hypothesis, laboratory and field experiments show that couples who participated in self-expanding activities reported increases in relationship satisfaction (Aron et al., 2000; Reissman et al., 1993).

Evaluating the merits of the self-expansion perspective is complicated by the fact that discussions of self-expansion theory use the word "self" in two ways. In one usage, the self expands in the sense that the person's beliefs about him- or herself broaden to include not only the other person but also new identities, roles, and abilities. Thus, when Aron et al. discuss "including others in the self," they are referring to the process of incorporating another person (or, perhaps, one's relationship with another person) as part of one's own self-definition.

The second usage of self-expansion employs "self" as a synonym for the "person," suggesting that self-expansion involves increasing the person's psychological and material resources in ways that promote efficacy in dealing with life's opportunities and challenges. This use of "self-expansion" seems to involve a natural movement toward acquiring resources and increasing effectance (White, 1959). Exploration, curiosity, desire for novelty, and social bonding in pursuit of resources are widespread in the animal kingdom (Toates, 1980), so it is not surprising that people are motivated to enter groups and relationships for the benefits they offer. The more interesting claim, from the standpoint of understanding the self, is that the motivation to expand the self is a motivation in its own right. People presumably enter relationships primarily for what those relationships have to offer and, in that sense, self-expansion theory's claim that people are motivated to obtain resources, perspectives, and identities that enhance their ability to accomplish their goals is correct (Aron & Aron, 1997; Aron, Aron, & Norman, 2001; Aron et al., 1998). But in what sense is this process motivated by a motive to expand the psychological self?

Although people seek to be accepted, they do not indiscriminately try to form relationships with everyone (Baumeister & Leary, 1995). People have a limited amount of time and a limited number of relationship niches, and efforts to form additional relationships ultimately backfire by lowering the quality of the relationships one already has (Tooby & Cosmides, 1996). Given these limitations, people must be selective in their choices of friends, romantic partners, and group memberships. Many considerations enter into these selections, but one consideration is the potential of the relationship or membership to facilitate goal achievement. Thus, among their options of possible relationships, people will be drawn to those that enhance their ability to accomplish important goals. However, the process would seem to be driven primarily by the desire for certain kind of relationships rather than by a motive to "expand the self."

The effects of self-expansion on positive affect, closeness, and relationship satisfaction can also be explained without reference to a self-expansion motive.

Presumably, the kinds of shared relational experiences that expand the self, such as those used in studies of marital satisfaction (e.g., Aron et al., 2000; Reissman et al., 1993), are precisely the kinds of activities that bring a couple closer together, strengthen their relationship, and satisfy their need for acceptance. An activity that expanded the self yet undermined the relationship would presumably not increase feelings of closeness, indicating that people are pursuing accepting, supportive relationships rather than self-expansion.

CONCLUSION

Many theorists have suggested that self-enhancement, self-verification, and self-expansion are fundamental or core motives. For example, writing about self-enhancement, Markus (1980) asserted that "the notion that we will go to great lengths to protect our ego or preserve our self-esteem is . . . probably one of the great psychological truths" (p. 127). Similarly, Swann et al. (1989) referred to self-verification as a "fundamental social motive" (p. 788), and Aron et al. (2001) proposed that self-expansion is "a central human motivation" (p. 478).

In this chapter, I have questioned whether these are inherent motives of the self and, indeed, whether the self has any motives at all. If we stand back from these phenomena and ask ourselves what people are really trying to do when they enhance, verify, or expand themselves, the answer typically is that they are trying to navigate their interpersonal interactions and relationships in ways that are beneficial to them. Granted, sometimes they are just trying to allay anxiety or evoke positive affect by thinking about themselves in particular ways, but even then, there is no reason to think that there are special "self-motives" that are dedicated to generating pleasing thoughts. It is surprising that contemporary behavioral scientists, who have roundly criticized Freud and others for anchoring human motivation in intrapsychic processes, should also fall victim to the notion that human behavior is strongly directed by psychological processes that are designed to keep one's inner psyche in working order. Let me reiterate that I am not denying that people engage in patterns of behavior that are self-enhancing, self-verifying, or self-expanding. I simply think that attributing these patterns to inherent self-enhancement, self-verification, or self-expansion motives misses their underlying interpersonal causes.

NOTE

1. Other self-motives have been proposed—including motives for self-assessment, self-improvement, and self-actualization—but these have not been widely studied in the context of interpersonal relationships and, thus, will not be discussed here (see Sedikides, 1993).

REFERENCES

Alicke, M. D. (1985). Global self-evaluation as determined by the desirability and controllability of trait adjectives. *Journal of Personality and Social Psychology*, 49, 1621–1630.

Alicke, M. D., & Govorun, O. (2005). The better-than-average effect. In M. D. Alicke, M. L. Klotz, D. A. Dunning, & J. I. Krueger (Eds.), *The self in social judgment* (pp. 85–106). Philadelphia: Psychology Press.

Amodio, D. M., & Showers, C. J. (2005). "Similarity breeds liking" revisited: The moderating role of commitment. *Journal of Social and Personal Relationships*, 22, 817–836.

Aron, A., & Aron, E. N. (1996). Self- and self-expansion in relationships. In G. J. O. Fletcher & J. Fitness (Eds.), *Knowledge structures in close relationships: A social psychological approach* (pp. 325–344). Mahwah, NJ: Lawrence Erlbaum Associates, Inc.

Aron, A., & Aron, E. N. (1997). Self-expansion motivation and including others in the self. In S. Duck (Ed.), *Handbook of personal relationships* (2nd ed., Vol. 1, pp. 251–270). London: Wiley.

Aron, A., Aron, E. N., & Norman, C. (2001). Self-expansion model of motivation and cognition in close relationships and beyond. In G. J. O. Fletcher & M. S. Clark (Eds.), *Blackwell handbook of social psychology: Interpersonal processes* (pp. 478–501). Malden, MA: Blackwell.

Aron, A., Aron, E., Tudor, M., & Nelson, G. (1991). Close relationships as including others in the self. *Journal of Personality and Social Psychology*, 60, 241–253.

Aron, A., & Fraley, B. (1999). Relationship closeness as including others in the self: Cognitive underpinnings and measures. *Social Cognition*, 17, 140–160.

Aron, A., Norman, C. C., & Aron, E. (1998). The self-expansion model and motivation. *Representative Research in Social Psychology*, 22, 1–13.

Aron, A., Norman, C. C., Aron, E. N., McKenna, C., & Heyman, R. (2000). Couple's shared participation in novel and arousing activities and experienced relationship quality. *Journal of Personality and Social Psychology*, 78, 273–284.

Aron, A., Paris, M., & Aron, E. N. (1995). Falling in love: Prospective studies of self-concept change. *Journal of Personality and Social Psychology*, 69, 1102–1112.

Aron, A., Steele, J., & Kashdan, T. (2002). *Attraction to others with similar interests as moderated by perceived opportunity for a relationship*. Unpublished manuscript, SUNY-Stony Brook, NY.

Baldwin, M. W., & Holmes, J. G. (1987). Salient private audiences and awareness of the self. *Journal of Personality and Social Psychology*, 52, 1087–1098.

Barkow, J. H. (1980). Prestige and self-esteem: A biosocial interpretation. In D. R. Omark, F. F. Strayer, & D. G. Freedman (Eds.), *Dominance relations: An ethological view of human conflict and social interaction* (pp. 319–332). New York: Garland STPM.

Baumeister, R. D., Campbell, J. D., Krueger, J. I., & Vohs, K. D. (2003). Does high self-esteem cause better performance, interpersonal success, happiness, or healthier lifestyles? *Psychological Science in the Public Interest*, 4, 1–44.

Baumeister, R. F., Heatherton, T. F., & Tice, D. M. (1993). When ego threats lead to self-regulation failure: Negative consequences of high self-esteem. *Journal of Personality and Social Psychology*, 64, 141–156.

Baumeister, R. F., & Leary, M. R. (1995). The need to belong: Desire for interpersonal attachments as a fundamental human motivation. *Psychological Bulletin*, 117, 497–529.

Baumeister, R. F., Smart, L., & Boden, J. M. (1996). Relation of threatened egotism to violence and aggression: The dark side of high self-esteem. *Psychological Review*, *103*, 5–33.

Baumeister, R. F., Wotman, S. R., & Stillwell, A. M. (1993). Unrequited love: On heartbreak, anger, guilt, scriptlessness, and humiliation. *Journal of Personality and Social Psychology*, *64*, 377–394.

Berscheid, E., & Fei, J. (1977). Romantic love and sexual jealousy. In G. Clanton & L. G. Smith (Eds.), *Jealousy* (pp. 101–109). Englewood Cliffs, NJ: Prentice Hall.

Blaine, B., & Crocker, J. (1993). Self-esteem and self-serving biases in reactions to positive and negative events: An integrative review. In R. F. Baumeister (Ed.), *Self-esteem: The puzzle of low self-regard* (pp. 55–85). New York: Plenum Press.

Block, J., & Colvin, C. R. (1994). Positive illusion and well-being revisited: Separating fiction from fact. *Psychological Bulletin*, *116*, 28.

Bonanno, G. A., Rennicke, C., & Dekel, S. (2005). Self-enhancement among high-exposure survivors of the September 11th terrorist attack: Resilience or social maladjustment? *Journal of Personality and Social Psychology*, *88*, 984–998.

Brown, J. D., & Smart, S. A. (1991). The self and social conduct: Linking self-representations to prosocial behavior. *Journal of Personality and Social Psychology*, *60*, 368–375.

Burke, P. J., & Stets, J. E. (1999). Trust and commitment through self-verification. *Social Psychology Quarterly*, *62*, 347–397.

Colvin, C. R., Block, J., & Funder, D. C. (1995). Overly positive self evaluations and personality: Negative implications for mental health. *Journal of Personality and Social Psychology*, *68*, 1152–1162.

Crocker, J., & Park, L. E. (2004). The costly pursuit of self-esteem. *Psychological Bulletin*, *130*, 392–414.

Dunning, D., & Hayes, A. F. (1996). Evidence for egocentric comparison in social judgment. *Journal of Personality and Social Psychology*, *71*, 213–229.

Dunning, D., Leuenberger, A., & Sherman, D. A. (1995). A new look at motivated inference: Are self-serving theories of success a product of motivational forces? *Journal of Personality and Social Psychology*, *59*, 58–68.

Fein, S., & Spencer, S. J. (1997). Prejudice as self-image maintenance: Affirming the self through derogating others. *Journal of Personality and Social Psychology*, *73*, 31–44.

Gallup, G. G., Jr. (1997). On the rise and fall of self-conception in primates. In J. G. Snodgrass & R. L. Thompson (Eds), *The self across psychology* (pp. 73–82). New York: New York Academy of Sciences.

Gardner, W. L., Gabriel, S., & Hochschild, L. (2002). When you and I are "we," you are not threatening: The role of self-expansion in social comparison. *Journal of Personality and Social Psychology*, *82*, 239–251.

Heatherton, T. F., & Vohs, K. D. (2000). Interpersonal evaluations following threats to self: Role of self-esteem. *Journal of Personality and Social Psychology*, *78*, 725–736.

Hixon, J. G., & Swann, W. B., Jr. (1993). When does introspection bear fruit? Self-reflection, self-insight, and interpersonal choices. *Journal of Personality and Social Psychology*, *64*, 35–43.

Holmes, J. G. (2004). The benefits of abstract functional analysis in theory construction: The case of interdependence theory. *Personality and Social Psychology Review*, *8*, 146–155.

Holmes, J. G., & Rempel, J. K. (1989). Trust in close relationships. In C. Hendrick (Ed.), *Review of personality and social psychology: Close relationships* (Vol. 10, pp. 187–219). Newbury Park, CA: Sage.

Humphrey, N. (1982, August 19). Consciousness: A just-so story. *New Scientist*, 474–477.

James, W. (1890). *The principles of psychology*. New York: Dover.

Kwan, V. S. Y., John, O. P., Kenny, D. A., Bond, M. H., & Robins, R. W. (2004). Reconceptualizing individual differences in self-enhancement bias: An interpersonal approach. *Psychological Review, 111*, 94–111.

Leary, M. R. (1995). *Self-presentation: Impression management and interpersonal behavior*. Boulder, CO: Westview Press.

Leary, M. R. (2002). The interpersonal basis of self-esteem: Death, devaluation, or deference? In J. Forgas & K. D. Williams (Eds.), *The social self: Cognitive, interpersonal, and intergroup perspectives*. New York: Psychology Press.

Leary, M. R. (2004). *The curse of the self: Self-awareness, egotism, and the quality of human life*. New York: Oxford University Press.

Leary, M. R. (in press). How the self became involved in affective experience: Three sources of self-reflective emotions. In J. Tracy, R. Robins, & J. P. Tangney (Eds.), *Handbook of self-conscious emotions*. New York: Guilford Press.

Leary, M. R., & Baumeister, R. F. (2000). The nature and function of self-esteem: Sociometer theory. In M. P. Zanna (Ed.), *Advances in experimental social psychology* (Vol. 32, pp. 1–62). San Diego, CA: Academic Press.

Leary, M. R., Bednarski, R., Hammon, D., & Duncan, T. (1997). Blowhards, snobs, and narcissists: Interpersonal reactions to excessive egotism. In R. M. Kowalski (Ed.), *Aversive interpersonal behaviors*. New York: Plenum Press.

Leary, M. R., & Buttermore, N. (2003). The evolution of the human self: Tracing the natural history of self-awareness. *Journal for the Theory of Social Behaviour, 33*, 366–404.

Leary, M. R., Cottrell, C. A., & Phillips, M. (2001). Deconfounding the effects of dominance and social acceptance on self-esteem. *Journal of Personality and Social Psychology, 81*, 898–909.

Leary, M. R., & Downs, D. L. (1995). Interpersonal functions of the self-esteem motive: The self-esteem system as a sociometer. In M. Kernis (Ed.), *Efficacy, agency, and self-esteem* (pp. 123–144). New York: Plenum Press.

Leary, M. R., Gallagher, B., Fors, E. H., Buttermore, N., Baldwin, E., Lane, K. K., et al. (2003). The invalidity of disclaimers about the effects of social feedback on self-esteem. *Personality and Social Psychology Bulletin, 29*, 623–636.

Leary, M. R., Haupt, A., Strausser, K., & Chokel, J. (1998). Calibrating the sociometer: The relationship between interpersonal appraisals and state self-esteem. *Journal of Personality and Social Psychology, 74*, 1290–1299.

Leary, M. R., & MacDonald, G. (2003). Individual differences in self-esteem: A review and theoretical integration. In M. R. Leary & J. P. Tangney (Eds.), *Handbook of self and identity* (pp. 401–418). New York: Guilford Press.

Leary, M. R., Tambor, E. S., Terdal, S. K., & Downs, D. L. (1995). Self-esteem as an interpersonal monitor: The sociometer hypothesis. *Journal of Personality and Social Psychology, 68*, 518–530.

Leary, M. R., & Tangney, J. P. (2003). The self as an organizing construct in the self and behavioral sciences. In M. R. Leary & J. P. Tangney (Eds.), *Handbook of self and identity* (pp. 3–14). New York: Guilford Press.

MacDonald, G., Saltzman, J. L., & Leary, M. R. (2003). Social approval and trait self-esteem. *Journal of Research in Personality, 37*, 23–40.

Markus, H. (1980). The self in thought and memory. In D. M. Wegner & R. R. Vallacher (Eds.), *The self in social psychology* (pp. 102–130). New York: Oxford University Press.

Maslow, A. (1954). *Motivation and behavior*. New York: Harper & Row.

Mecca, A. M., Smelser, N. J., & Vasconcellos, J. (Eds.). (1989). *The social importance of self-esteem*. Berkeley, CA: University of California Press.

Murray, S. L., Griffin, D. W., Rose, P., & Bellavia, G. (2003). Calibrating the sociometer: The relational contingencies of self-esteem. *Journal of Personality and Social Psychology, 85*, 63–84.

Murray, S. L., & Holmes, J. G. (1997). A leap of faith? Positive illusions in romantic relationships. *Personality and Social Psychology Bulletin, 23*, 586–804.

Murray, S. L., & Holmes, J. G. (2000). Seeing the self through a partner's eyes: Why self-doubts turn into relationship insecurities. In A. Tesser, R. B. Felson, & J. M. Suls (Eds.), *Psychological perspectives on self and identity* (pp. 173–197). Washington, DC: American Psychological Association.

Murray, S. L., Holmes, J. G., & Griffin, D. W. (1996). The benefits of positive illusions: Idealization and the construction of satisfaction in close relationships. *Journal of Personality and Social Psychology Bulletin, 70*, 79–98.

Murray, S. L., Holmes, J. G., & Griffin, D. W. (2000). Self-esteem and the quest for felt security: How perceived regard regulates attachment processes. *Journal of Personality and Social Psychology, 78*, 478–498.

Murray, S. L., Holmes, J. G., Griffin, D. W., Bellavia, G., & Rose, P. (2001). The mismeasure of love: How self-doubt contaminates relationship beliefs. *Personality and Social Psychology Bulletin, 27*, 423–436.

Murray, S. L., Holmes, J. G., MacDonald, G., & Ellsworth, P. (1998). Through the looking glass darkly? When self-doubt turns into relationship insecurities. *Journal of Personality and Social Psychology, 75*, 1459–1480.

Murray, S. L., Rose, P., Bellavia, G., Holmes, J. G., & Kusche, A. (2002). When rejection stings: How self-esteem constrains relationship-enhancement processes. *Journal of Personality and Social Psychology, 83*, 556–573.

Nezlek, J. B., Kowalski, R. M., Leary, M. R., Blevins, T., & Holgate, S. (1997). Personality moderators of reactions to interpersonal rejection: Depression and trait self-esteem. *Personality and Social Psychology Bulletin, 23*, 1235–1244.

Paulhus, D. L. (1998). Interpersonal and intrapsychic adaptiveness of trait self-enhancement: A mixed blessing? *Journal of Personality and Social Psychology, 74*, 1197–1208.

Paulhus, D. L., Harms, P. D., Bruce, M. N., & Lysy, D. C. (2003). The over-claiming technique: Measuring self-enhancement independent of ability. *Journal of Personality and Social Psychology, 84*, 890–904.

Paulhus, D. L., & Levitt, K. (1987). Desirable responding triggered by affect: Automatic egotism? *Journal of Personality and Social Psychology, 52*, 245–259.

Pelham, B. W., Mirenberg, M. C., & Jones, J. T. (2002). Why Susie sells seashells by the seashore: Implicit egoism and major life decisions. *Journal of Personality and Social Psychology, 82*, 469–487.

Pronin, E., Lin, D. Y., & Ross, L. (2002). The bias blind spot: Perceptions of bias in self versus others. *Personality and Social Psychology Bulletin, 28*, 369–381.

Reissman, C., Aron, A., & Bergen, M. R. (1993). Shared activities and marital satisfaction: Causal direction and self-expansion versus boredom. *Journal of Social and Personal Relationships, 10*, 243–254.

Robins, R. W., & Beer, J. S. (2001). Positive illusions about the self: Short-term benefits and long-term costs. *Journal of Personality and Social Psychology, 80*, 340–352.

Robins, R. W., & John, O. P. (1997). The quest for self-insight: Theory and research on accuracy and bias in self-perception. In R. Hogan, J. A. Johnson, & S. R. Briggs

(Eds.), *Handbook of personality psychology* (pp. 649–679). New York: Academic Press.

Rogers, C. (1959). A theory of therapy, personality, and interpersonal relationships, as developed in the client-centered framework. In S. Koch (Ed.), *Psychology: A study of a science* (Vol. 3, pp. 184–256). New York: McGraw-Hill.

Schimel, J., Arndt, J., Banko, K. M., & Cook, A. (2004). Not all self-affirmations were created equal: The cognitive and social benefits of affirming the intrinsic (vs. extrinsic) self. *Social Cognition, 22,* 75–99.

Schlenker, B. R. (1975). Self-presentation: Managing the impression of consistency when reality interferes with self-enhancement. *Journal of Personality and Social Psychology, 32,* 1030–1037.

Sedikides, C. (1993). Assessment, evaluation, and verification determinants of the self-evaluation process. *Journal of Personality and Social Psychology, 65,* 317–338.

Sedikides, C., Gaertner, L., & Toguchi, Y. (2003). Pancultural self-enhancement. *Journal of Personality and Social Psychology, 84,* 60–79.

Sedikides, C., & Skowronski, J. J. (1997). The symbolic self in evolutionary context. *Personality and Social Psychology Review, 1,* 80–102.

Siegel, P. A., Scillitoe, J., & Parks-Yancy, R. (2005). Reducing the tendency to self-handicap: The effect of self-affirmation. *Journal of Experimental Social Psychology, 41,* 589–597.

Solomon, S., Greenberg, J., & Pyszczynski, T. (1991). A terror management theory of social behavior: The psychological functions of self-esteem and cultural worldviews. In M. Zanna (Ed.), *Advances in experimental social psychology* (Vol. 24, pp. 91–159). Orlando, FL: Academic Press.

Solomon, S., Greenberg, J., & Pyszczynski, T. (2004). The cultural animal: Twenty years of terror management theory and research. In J. Greenberg, S. L. Koole, & T. Pyszczynski (Eds.), *Handbook of experimental existential psychology* (pp. 13–34). New York: Guilford Press.

Smith, E. R., & Henry, S. (1996). An in-group becomes part of the self: Response time evidence. *Personality and Social Psychology Bulletin, 22,* 635–642.

Srivastava, S., & Beer, J. S. (2005). How self-evaluations relate to being liked by others: Integrating sociometer and attachment perspectives. *Journal of Personality and Social Psychology, 89,* 966–977.

Steele, C. M. (1975). Name-calling and compliance. *Journal of Personality and Social Psychology, 31* (2), 361–370.

Steele, C. M. (1988). The psychology of self-affirmation: Sustaining the integrity of the self. *Advances in Experimental Social Psychology, 21,* 261–302.

Steele, C. M., & Liu, T. J. (1983). Dissonance process as self-affirmation. *Journal of Personality and Social Psychology, 45,* 5–19.

Swann, W. B., Jr. (1983). Self-verification: Bringing social reality into harmony with the self. In J. Suls & A. G. Greenwald (Eds.), *Psychological perspectives on the self* (Vol. 2, pp. 33–66). Hillsdale, NJ: Lawrence Erlbaum Associates, Inc.

Swann, W. B., Jr. (1990). To be adored or to be known: The interplay of self-enhancement and self-verification. In R. M. Sorrentino & E. T. Higgins (Eds.), *Handbook of motivation and cognition* (Vol. 2, pp. 408–448). New York: Guilford Press.

Swann, W. B., Jr., Bosson, J., & Pelham, B. W. (2002). Different partners, different selves: Strategic verification of circumscribed identities. *Personality and Social Psychology Bulletin, 28,* 1215–1228.

Swann, W. B., Jr., De La Ronde, C., & Hixon, J. G. (1994). Authenticity and positivity strivings in marriage and courtship. *Journal of Personality and Social Psychology*, 66, 857–869.

Swann, W. B., Milton, L., & Polzer, J. (2000). Creating a niche or falling in line: Identity negotiation and small group effectiveness. *Journal of Personality and Social Psychology*, 79, 238–250.

Swann, W. B., Jr., & Pelham, B. (2002). Who wants out when the going gets good? Psychological investment and preference for self-verifying college roommates. *Self and Identity*, 1, 219–233.

Swann, W. B., Jr., Pelham, B. W., & Krull, D. S. (1989). Agreeable fancy or disagreeable truth? Reconciling self-enhancement and self-verification. *Journal of Personality and Social Psychology*, 57, 782–791.

Swann, W. B., Jr., & Read, S. J. (1981). Self-verification processes: How we sustain our self-conceptions. *Journal of Experimental Social Psychology*, 17, 351–372.

Swann, W. B., Jr., Stein-Seroussi, A., & Giesler, R. B. (1992). Why people self-verify. *Journal of Personality and Social Psychology*, 62, 392–401.

Swann, W. B., Jr., Wenzlaff, R. M., Krull, D. S., & Pelham, B. W. (1992). The allure of negative feedback: Self-verification strivings among depressed persons. *Journal of Abnormal Psychology*, 101, 293–306.

Taylor, S. E., & Brown, J. D. (1988). Illusion and well-being: A social psychological perspective on mental health. *Psychological Bulletin*, 103, 193–210.

Taylor, S. E., & Brown, J. D. (1994). Positive illusions and well-being revisited: Separating fact from fiction. *Psychological Bulletin*, 116, 21–27.

Taylor, S. E., Lerner, J. S., Sherman, D. K., Sage, R. M., & McDowell, N. K. (2003a). Are self-enhancing cognitions associated with healthy or unhealthy biological profiles? *Journal of Personality and Social Psychology*, 85, 605–615.

Taylor, S. E., Lerner, J. S., Sherman, D. K., Sage, R. M., & McDowell, N. K. (2003b). Portrait of the self-enhancer: Well adjusted and well liked or maladjusted and friendless? *Journal of Personality and Social Psychology*, 84, 165–176.

Tesser, A. (1988). Toward a self-evaluation model of social behavior. *Advances in Experimental Social Psychology*, 21, 181–227.

Tesser, A., & Cornell, D. P. (1991). On the confluence of self processes. *Journal of Experimental Social Psychology*, 27, 501–526.

Toates, F. M. (1980). *Animal behavior: A systems approach*. Chichester, UK: Wiley.

Tooby, J. & Cosmides, L. (1996). Friendship and the Banker's Paradox: Other pathways to the evolution of adaptations for altruism. In W. G. Runciman, J. Maynard Smith, & R. I. M. Dunbar (Eds.), *Evolution of social behaviour patterns in primates and man: Proceedings of the British Academy*, 88, 119–143.

Tropp, L. R., & Wright, S. C. (2001). Ingroup identification and inclusion of ingroup in the self. *Personality and Social Psychology Bulletin*, 27, 585–600.

White, R. W. (1959). Motivation reconsidered: The concept of confidence. *Psychological Review*, 66, 297–333.

Wood, J. V., Giordano-Beech, M., & Ducharme, M. J. (1999). Compensating for failure through social comparison. *Personality and Social Psychology Bulletin*, 25, 1370–1386.

Wright, S. C., Aron, A., & Tropp, L. R. (2002). Including others (and groups) in the self: Self-expansion and intergroup relations. In J. P. Forgas & K. D. Williams (Eds.), *The social self: Cognitive, interpersonal, and intergroup perspectives* (pp. 343–363). New York: Psychology Press.

Part II

Reciprocal Influences of Self and Other, I: Self-Perception and Self-Regulation

6

Self-Perception as Interpersonal Perception

DAVID A. KENNY and TESSA V. WEST

A self-perception is a perception of someone who is also the perceiver. In this sense, self-perceptions are a very special type of person perception and several insights can be had by viewing them as such. In this chapter, we consider how self-perceptions are related to perceptions made of individuals by other people, how they are related to the perception of others, and how they are related to perceptions that individuals have of how they believe they are perceived by others.

To assist in the understanding of the interplay between different types of perceptions, the social relations model (SRM; Kenny & La Voie, 1984) is used in this chapter as a methodological framework. The SRM permits a detailed examination of interpersonal perceptions that can be theoretically rich. Because the SRM may be unfamiliar to researchers, and likely even more so to self-researchers, we briefly describe the model.

Consider the perception that Doug has of Tara's level of competence. Imagine that Doug and Tara are members of a workgroup within an organization. The SRM implies a decomposition of Doug's perception of Tara into the following five different components:

Group mean:	How competent do members of the work group think other members of the group are?
Actor effect:	How competent does Doug see others in the work group?
Partner effect:	How competent is Tara seen by other members in the work group?
Relationship effect:	How competent does Doug particularly see Tara?
Error:	How much noise is there in Doug's perception of Tara's level of competence?

In order to partition a dyadic judgment into these five components, we need to have at least four members in each group, and all group members must perceive the competence of all other group members; such a design is commonly called a *round robin.* To be able to separate error variance from relationship variance, there must be multiple replications; that is, competence must be measured at multiple times or by multiple measures. Note also that variance due to group is typically not estimated in trait rating studies because it is often negligible (i.e., less than 5 percent of the total variance).

The remainder of the chapter addresses four questions that examine self-perception from an interpersonal perspective. First, we ask whether self-perception varies as a function of interaction partner. If Doug views himself as competent when he interacts with Tara, does he also view himself as competent when he interacts with Sara? Second, we consider possible discrepancies between the perception of self and the perception of others, or self-enhancement. Kwan, John, Kenny, Bond, and Robins (2004) developed an index of self-enhancement that combines two aspects of the perceptions of others: how the person sees others and how others see the person. We review a recent study that uses Kwan et al.'s index of self-enhancement. Third, we consider the perceptions that individuals have of how others view them, termed metaperceptions. We review the finding that how people think others generally view them correlates strongly with how they view themselves. Fourth, we consider the methodological issue of idiographic analysis. Such analyses enable researchers to examine moderators of the relationships between perceptions of the self and perceptions of others.

THE RELATIONAL SELF

Following James (1890), the self is often viewed as fundamentally interpersonal, composed of a repertoire of relational selves. The self therefore is thought to vary across social roles that individuals play in their daily interactions (e.g., Donahue, Robins, Roberts, & John, 1993), by group membership (Brewer, 1991; Tajfel & Turner, 1986; Turner, Hogg, Oakes, Reicher, & Wetherell, 1987), and interaction partner (Kenny & Malloy, 1988; Kenny, Mohr, & Levesque, 2001). We discuss all three ways in which self-perceptions are relational.

Researchers examining how the self varies as a function of role are often interested in the degree to which self-perceptions are consistent across roles, but they may also be interested in the degree to which consistency in self-perceptions predicts individual or interpersonal outcomes. An individual may have several social roles, such as friend, co-worker, and parent, and her or his self-perceptions may differ as a function of that role. Donahue et al. (1993) assessed self-concept differentiation; that is, the degree to which an individual's self-perceptions are consistent across five social roles: student, friend, romantic partner, son or daughter, and worker. Participants were asked to rate themselves on 60 traits for each of the five roles. The authors found individual variability in the degree to which people see themselves consistently across social roles. Self-concept differentiation also predicted mental health outcomes: Individuals who saw themselves very differently across roles were more depressed and neurotic and had lower self-esteem than individuals who saw themselves as similar across roles.

In addition to defining oneself in terms of social role, self-perceptions can change as a function of group membership or social category (Tajfel & Turner, 1986; Turner et al., 1987). One focus in this theory is the interplay between ingroup identification and individuality. For example, research on optimal distinctiveness theory (Snyder & Fromkin, 1980) has examined how the balance between collective identity (i.e., identity derived from group membership), and personal identity function to form self-perceptions. Research on the theory has found that individuals strive to find some middle ground between group identity and individuality (Brewer, 1991).

Besides social role and group, an individual's relational partner provides a context in which self-judgments are made (Kenny & Malloy, 1988; Kenny et al., 2001). For example, research on social comparison theory (Festinger, 1954) has demonstrated that self-perceptions change as a function of the comparison other; specifically, the comparison other aids in determining the degree to which an individual sees him or herself positively (Gibbons, Benbow, & Gerrard, 1994). Additionally, Andersen and Chen (2002) examined how self-perceptions are related to perceptions of significant others in particular. The authors propose a model where self-perceptions are linked to representations of significant others, and these linkages form specific relational selves for each significant other. Individuals have many relational selves. Thus self-perceptions are not independent from other-perceptions.

We now review several studies that test the degree of consistency in self-perceptions across different interaction partners. In most of the studies, persons who were previously unacquainted interacted for a brief time with several different interaction partners, and after each interaction, made self-judgments. For each partner, the person rated how he or she behaved in the interaction on one or more trait measures. For instance, Frank interacts with Sam and Harry, and we ask Frank how agreeable he was in each of the interactions. All of the studies used the social relations model to partition judgments into the three sources of variance previously described: actor, partner, and relationship. We present an overview of the procedure for each of these studies, followed by a discussion of overall trends in the SRM variance partitioning.

In Oliver (1988), 56 persons were broken into 14 sets of two males and two females. Each of the two males interacted one-on-one with each of the two females in a simulated date. The interactions lasted approximately 15 minutes. After each interaction, both partners made ratings of how positive (e.g., mature and friendly) and how active (e.g., outgoing and confident) they were during the interaction. The analyses were done separately for the two measures and for men and women and then averaged. We present in Table 6.1 the average of the four analyses. The results for this study, as well as the others, are discussed after the methodological details of the remaining studies are presented.

In Christensen, Stein, and Means-Christensen (2003), 124 previously unacquainted persons were placed in four-person groups. In a round-robin design, each person took turns engaging in three separate getting-acquainted conversations in dyads. The conversations were each 5 minutes. After each interaction, persons rated their own personality on 15 traits. Among the traits used

TABLE 6.1   Social Relations Variance Partitioning of Dyadic Self-Ratings

Study	Actor	Partner	Relationship	Error
Oliver (1988)	.540	.054	.416	° ° °
Christensen et al. (2003)	.555	.001	.439	° ° °
Yingling (1980)	.472	.000	.528	° ° °
Albright & Malloy (2006)	.442	.029	.528	° ° °
Robins et al. (2004)	.407	.067	.526	° ° °
Strack (2004)	.217	.027	.110	.646

° ° ° Relationship variance cannot be separated from error variance.

were sociable, dependable, and related. The results are averaged across the 15 traits.

In Yingling (1980), 24 women were placed into six groups of four persons. Each woman interacted one-on-one with each other in a round-robin design. After each interaction, the woman completed a measure of her social competence (Spitzberg & Cupach, 1984) with the interaction partner. The results are presented for that single measure.

Albright and Malloy (2006) studied 17 four-person groups, 9 of which were previously acquainted and 8 previously unacquainted. Individuals in the groups engaged in 5-minute one-on-one interactions with other group members. The participants rated themselves on nine measures of personality. The results did not vary much due to acquaintance, and so we have pooled them and averaged over the nine measures.

In Robins, Mendelsohn, Connell, and Kwan (2004), 70 four-person, mixed gender groups were instructed to get acquainted. Thirty of the groups were face-to-face interactions, 20 were by phone, and 20 were computer mediated. The interactions lasted between 5 and 10 minutes. After each interaction, both partners made ratings of talkative, warm, and nervous for both themselves and their partners. The self-rating results are averaged over the three measures and the three conditions.

Finally, Strack (2004) investigated self-perceptions in weekly student work groups. There were 98 groups with between four and eight members, resulting in a total of 604 people. Groups interacted in sessions of 100 minutes and ratings were obtained after the second or third meeting. Participants rated themselves on the three SYMLOG dimensions (Bales & Cohen, 1979) of positive–negative, forward–backward, and upward–downward. We averaged results across the three variables.

One benefit of examining self-perceptions using the SRM is that self-judgments are dyadic variables, and the variance can be partitioned into SRM components. The SRM components of actor, partner, and relationship have the following interpretations:

Actor:	How does a person see her or himself across all interactions?
Partner:	How does a person "make" others view themselves when they interact with him or her?
Relationship:	How does a person differently perceive her or himself depending on interaction partner?

To illustrate the variance partitioning for self-judgments, consider self-ratings of friendliness. A large amount of actor variance would reflect the tendency for some individuals to believe that they are friendly across all of their interactions and for others to believe that they are not friendly across all of their interactions (i.e., there is variability in the extent to which people report being friendly across all inter-action partners). A large amount of partner variance reflects that some individuals elicit self-ratings of friendliness from others and others do not elicit friendliness. Specifically, people in general who interact with one individual tend to see them-selves as friendly, and people in general who interact with another individual see themselves as unfriendly. Finally, a large amount of relationship variance reflects that individuals see themselves as friendly with particular interaction partners, and as unfriendly with other particular interaction partners.

The view that self-perceptions do not differ as a function of interaction part-ner or social context implies a substantial amount of actor variance and relatively little partner and relationship variance. That is, people see themselves the same way across the context of interaction partner. The presence of substantial partner and relationship variance would suggest that self-ratings vary by interaction partner.

Table 6.1 presents the results from the six studies reviewed here. We see from these studies that the bulk of the variance, about 44 percent, is at the level of the actor: People see themselves in essentially the same way across different interaction partners. Partner variance is very weak, averaging only 3 percent. Thus we do not find that some people elicit the same self-perceptions across partners. Only Strack (2004) separated error variance from relationship variance. Therefore, we can only examine relationship variance for this study. She found non-trivial levels of relationship variance, 11 percent: Self-perceptions did change with interaction partner. Note that most of the relationship variance came from the positive–negative dimension, for which relationship explains 22 percent of the total variance, whereas the other two dimensions averaged only 6 percent of variance.

The overall results for the variance partitioning might seem surprising given prior work on the self as relational. There are several possible explanations as to why our results do not demonstrate variability in self-perceptions by interaction partner. First, the studies we have reviewed have focused on traits judgments, which people generally believe to be a stable. If emotions (e.g., feelings of happi-ness and sadness) were measured, we would likely find relationship variance and perhaps even partner variance. The finding in the Strack (2004) study of relational variance for the positive–negative dimension supports this view. Second, partici-pants in these studies engaged in similar tasks with their interaction partners before making self-judgments. If a variety of interaction tasks were studied, there might have been less consistency. Third, the roles of the partner were essentially the same. If very different types of interaction partners (e.g., romantic partner, casual acquaintance, parent, and boss) were studied, we might have found differ-ing self-perceptions. Andersen and Chen's (2002) research on relational selves has demonstrated that self-perceptions and perceptions of close others are tightly intertwined. It is unlikely that the same holds true for acquaintances and especially for strangers. Consistency of self-perceptions should be studied using close others as well as strangers and acquaintances. Fourth, it should also be noted that because members of non-Western cultures may have a more collective sense of self (Markus & Kitayama, 1991), they might show greater amounts of relationship and perhaps even partner variance as well. In sum, consistency in self-perceptions may be moderated by several variables.

SELF-ENHANCEMENT BIAS

Thus far, we have used the social relations model as a framework for understanding how self-perceptions change as a function of interaction partner, and what might moderate consistency of self-perceptions from partner to partner. In this section, we elaborate on the SRM to examine a ubiquitous bias found in self-perception: self-enhancement. A classic question in both personality and social psychology is the extent to which people self-enhance, and what the antecedents and consequences of self-enhancement are. One major source of interest in this question is due to the important article by Taylor and Brown (1988) on positive illusions. They made the highly controversial argument that people benefited psychologically by seeing themselves as better than others. Another source of interest is in the area of cross-cultural comparisons. Researchers have debated whether people from Western cultures tend to self-enhance and whether those from Eastern cultures self-efface (e.g., see Sedikides, Gaertner, & Toguchi, 2003).

There has also been debate about the measurement of self-enhancement. Kwan et al. (2004) note that self-enhancement has been conceptualized in two very different ways. The first uses the comparison between an individual's self-perceptions and the perceptions *of* others in order to determine the extent to which an individual self-enhances, and is based on social comparison theory (Festinger, 1954). The second is Gordon Allport's (1937) notion of self-insight, which compares an individual's self-perception to perceptions of that individual *by* others.

Thus there are two different senses of self-enhancement: People can see themselves as better than they see others, or they can see themselves as better than others see them. Kwan et al. (2004) argue that self-enhancement is properly examined by combining both theoretical approaches. To successfully assess both questions in one analysis, a componential analysis needs to be undertaken.

Kwan et al. (2004) proposed that three components are needed for a complete account of self-enhancement: (1) self-perception, (2) perception of others, and (3) perception made by others. The authors extended the SRM to conceptualize self-perception as an interpersonal perception in which the perceiver and the target are the very same person. The relationship effect or an individual's idiosyncratic self-view reflects individual differences in self-enhancement. Kwan et al. (2004) examined self-enhancement across 32 personality traits, and found that the self-insight index, the social comparison index, and the SRM index are not empirically equivalent. They also found that self-esteem correlates positively with the SRM index of self-enhancement, indicating illusory self-esteem.

Recent research has extended the study of self-enhancement beyond individual difference variables to group-relevant variables. Anderson, Srivastava, Beer, Spataro, and Chatman (2006) used the Kwan et al. (2004) self-enhancement index to examine self-enhancement of group status. They were interested in the extent to which individuals are accurate about their status in groups, and how self-enhancement and accuracy of group status affect social acceptance. Groups ranging in size from four to six members engaged in four work sessions. Self-perceptions and other-perceptions of group status were collected using a round-robin design where everyone rated everyone else and themselves. Anderson et al. (2007) found that people showed a self-enhancement bias in perceiving their acceptance, but they showed a self-effacement bias in perceiving their status. Additionally, they found that self-enhancement of status resulted in lower levels of acceptance by others over time.

There is a complication in the computation of the self-enhancement index. Kwan et al. (2004) suggested adjusting how a person sees him or herself by how the person sees others in general (the actor effect) as well as how the person is seen by others in general (the partner effect). This strategy presumes that actor and partner effects affect self-perceptions as strongly as they affect the perceptions of others; an assumption that may not be true. Following, Kenny (1994), Kenny and West (2007) have developed a more general strategy for the measurement of self-enhancement.

SELF AND METAPERCEPTION

The focus of this section is the relation between self-perceptions and what people think others think of them. These perceptions of perceptions have been called *reflected appraisals* (Felson, 1981) or *metaperceptions* (Laing, Phillipson, & Lee, 1966), the term we shall use. Theorists have related metaperceptions to self-perceptions in two different ways. First, Leary and Downs' (1995) sociometer theory proposes that self-esteem is a reflection of individuals' meta-perceptions of social inclusion and exclusion. Second, symbolic interactionists have proposed that metaperception plays a key role in the formation of the self-concept (Kinch, 1963). Recent work has suggested that self-perceptions may affect metaperceptions more than vice versa (Kenny & DePaulo, 1993). In this section of the chapter, we examine this relationship between self-perceptions and metaperceptions.

Recall that within the social relations model or SRM, a judgment made by a perceiver can be partitioned into three sources of variance: actor, partner, and relationship. The same partitioning can be undertaken for a metaperception, but the components have different meanings. Consider the metaperception that Tara has of Doug's perception of Tara's level of competence (i.e., how competent does Tara think that Doug sees her). Assume again that Tara and Doug are both members of a group, and all group members make perceptions and meta-perceptions of other group members' level of competence. Within the SRM, Tara's metaperception has five different components:

Group mean: How competent do members of the group think that other members of the group see them?

Actor effect: How competent does Tara think that other group members see her?

Partner effect: How competent do other group members think that Doug sees them?

Relationship effect: How competent does Tara think that Doug particularly sees her, above and beyond other group members?

Error: How much noise is in Tara's metaperception of Doug's perception of her level of competence?

We can take metaperceptions in a group and partition the total variance into these five components. Particularly relevant in this chapter is the correlation of the actor effect in metaperception with a self-judgment. For example, if Tara sees herself as competent, does Tara also think others see her as competent?

The correlation between self and metaperception is relevant to the question of meta-accuracy: To what extent do people know what others think of them? With the SRM, there are two types of meta-accuracy: *generalized meta-accuracy,* and *dyadic meta-accuracy.* We can examine generalized meta-accuracy, or how accurate Tara's metaperceptions are in general, by correlating the partner effect in perceptions of Tara's level of competence (i.e., how competent do others in general perceive Tara to be) with the actor effect in Tara's metaperception. The degree to which Tara's metaperception of Doug's perception of her in particular is accurate is termed dyadic meta-accuracy.

If metaperceptions are accurate, what is driving their accuracy? Self-judgments appear to play a key role in the process of forming metaperceptions, and in predicting their accuracy. Kenny and DePaulo (1993; see also Chapter 8 in Kenny, 1994) review eight SRM studies that examine the correlation between metaperceptions and self-ratings. The authors were interested in the degree to which individuals use their own self-perceptions in making judgments of what they think others think of them, and how accurate these perceptions are, both at the level of the dyad, and in general. Across the studies that examine meta-perceptions of traits, a large portion of the variance in metaperceptions was at the level of the actor (on average, 55% of the variance). This finding indicates that individuals tend to believe that others view them in consistent ways, and is consistent across all levels of acquaintance. For example, Tara thinks every-one sees her as competent (or not competent). In addition, individuals' meta-perceptions for specific others are not very distinguishable; relationship variance in metaperceptions is small. Thus Tara does not distinguish between how competent she thinks Doug thinks she is from how competent she thinks other group members see her to be.

We know that individuals are not good at distinguishing what specific others think of them, and they generally believe that people perceive them consistently. In terms of how accurate perceivers' metaperceptions are, results are consistent. Kenny and DePaulo's (1993) review indicates that people are fairly accurate in general, but are not particularly apt at distinguishing between what specific others think of them; dyadic meta-accuracy was weak across the reviewed studies. What then, is driving meta-accuracy?

Kenny and DePaulo (1993) claimed that metaperceptions are largely driven by self-perceptions. Consistently across the affect and trait studies, the average correlation between self-perceptions and the actor effect in metaperceptions is .87. At the generalized level, there is a strong correlation between how individuals view themselves, and how they believe others view them. Evidence from across several studies indicates that self-perceptions and metaperceptions are generally very highly correlated.

Researchers have debated the direction of causation for self-perception to metaperception. Symbolic interactionists have argued that the causation goes from metaperception (of significant others) to self-perceptions: We perceive what significant others think of us, and then we form impressions of ourselves based on these perceptions. However, Kenny and DePaulo (1993) argue that individuals probably do not use feedback from others in forming their self-perceptions, but rather, use their self-perceptions to form metaperceptions. If individuals did use feedback from others in forming self-perceptions, targets would be more accurate at knowing what specific others thought of them, indicated by larger dyadic meta-accuracy than the authors found.

Alternatively, people may base their self-perceptions on their interpersonal behavior, and then assume that others will similarly interpret their behavior, and therefore judge them consistently with how they judge themselves. Thus metaperception is based on self-perception, and self-perception is based on behavior. Gilovich, Savitsky, and Medvec (1998) have theorized that people believe, quite mistakenly, that who they are is readily transparent to others. Despite conflicting theories on the origin of metaperceptions, there is strong empirical evidence that self-perceptions are strongly related to metaperceptions, even more so than other perceptions. The strong relationship between self-perception and metaperception has been replicated studying a variety of variables, and across non-Western cultures (e.g., Shechtman & Kenny, 1994).

Moderators of the Self-Perception–Metaperception Relationship

Given the strong correlations found by Kenny and DePaulo (1993), several researchers have attempted to examine factors that might lower that correlation. Some researchers have focused on the process of metaperception, others on acquaintance, and still others on group membership. In this section, we review research that examines these possible moderators.

Albright, Forest, and Reiseter (2001) examined whether the correlation between self-perception and metaperception is the result of people using their self-perceptions to form metaperceptions, or the result of people using their actual behavior to form metaperceptions. By instructing participants to engage in a self-presenting role (i.e., either optimists or pessimists), they created a situation where self-perception would not be correlated with interpersonal behavior. The authors theorized that successful self-presentation would lead to accurate metaperception. Results indicated that actors predicted with a high degree of accuracy how they were judged; all correlations between the actor effect in metaperception with the partner effect in other-perception were in the .90s. Metaperceptions were not based on self-perceptions of optimism; the correlations between self-perceptions and metaperceptions were not statistically reliable and were all very weak. Interestingly, self-perceptions also correlated weakly with behavioral measures; thus individuals were not inferring their self-perceptions from their behaviors. When participants were not instructed to act out roles, the correlation between self-perceptions and metaperceptions was high, consistent with the findings of Kenny and DePaulo (1993) that focused on dispositional judgments. These results indicate that when individuals are instructed to do so, they can focus on the perceptual salience of their behaviors rather than on their self-concepts, which enables them to use the same cues that perceivers use.

Albright and Malloy (1999) hypothesized that perhaps metaperceptions are not based on perceptions made by others because individuals make the actor–observer bias in attribution. Originally articulated by Jones and Nisbett (1972), the bias may be particularly relevant to the development of metaperceptions because the environment is more salient to the actor, and the actor is more salient to the observer. Differences in perceptual salience between actors and observers may lead to inaccurate metaperceptions. Albright and Malloy investigated how the opportunity to observe oneself from a visual perspective affects the relationship between self-perception and metaperceptions, and meta-accuracy. In three studies, individuals in groups interacted with each other while being videotaped, and then made self-judgments, other-judgments, and metaperceptions of anxiety. Meta-accuracy was the greatest among groups where individuals were allowed to view the videotaped interactions (with a visual and auditory focus on themselves) before making metaperceptions. Results from Albright and Malloy (1999) suggest that self-observation increases meta-accuracy because of differences in stimulus information. The authors argue that perceivers and targets have shared meaning systems for visual and verbal data, and when targets are given the same information as perceivers, the process of determining what behavioral information is available to others is no longer inferential. Thus perceivers and targets have the same information on which to base judgments. This finding is consistent with Albright et al. (2001), who manipulated how salient individuals' self-concept was by instructing them to self-present. When individuals are forced to take the perspective of the perceiver, they appear to be using the same behavioral cues as other perceivers, rather than their self-perceptions on which to base metaperceptions.

Christensen et al. (2003) were interested in how an individual difference variable, social anxiety, explains the correlation between self-perception and metaperception. The authors were particularly interested in the negative biases that social anxiety has on both self-perceptions and metaperceptions of trait ratings. The authors found that social anxiety explained some, but not all, of the relationship between self-perceptions and metaperceptions. Socially anxious individuals saw themselves negatively and in turn perceived that others saw them negatively as well. This study illustrates how an individual difference variable, social anxiety, shapes self-perceptions, and ultimately, metaperceptions.

Thus far, all of the studies reviewed used unacquainted or newly acquainted perceivers and targets. Levesque (1997) investigated the hypothesis that acquaintance might moderate the correlation between self-perceptions and metaperceptions for personality traits and affective judgments (i.e., liking). He found that consistent with studies reviewed by Kenny and DePaulo, variance in metaperceptions is largely at the level of the actor and the relationship, and correlations between the actor effect in metaperceptions and self-perceptions were quite large and near 1, indicating that at the generalized level, individuals perceived themselves as they thought others perceived them. At the dyadic level, the correlations were weaker, but still substantial, although Levesque's (1997) findings were consistent with Kenny and DePaulo's (1993) review that meta-accuracy is much greater at the generalized level than at the dyadic level, Levesque is cautious to interpret his findings as an indication that individuals do not use feedback in making self-perceptions. It may not be particularly beneficial to know, for example, that a particular person views the self as extroverted. Rather, it is more useful for individuals to know what others think of them in general. He argued that this is especially the case among acquainted individuals, who are better able to gauge the consistency of a target's behavior than strangers, and behavioral consistency is correlated with self-perceptions (Levesque & Kenny, 1993). Although the process by which other-perceptions are incorporated in the self-view may change as a function of acquaintance, individuals' self-judgments are strongly related to their metaperceptions among both acquainted and unacquainted individuals.

Malloy, Albright, Kenny, Agatstein, and Winquist (1997) examined metaperceptions for non-overlapping social groups. Target individuals made metaperceptions for three friends, three family members, and three co-workers. The authors found that individuals believe that they are seen similarly, but not exactly the same, across the three social groups; the average correlation between the social groups is .735. Generalized meta-accuracy was the largest for family members, and the smallest for co-workers, but the differences were small.

In a study examining gender as a moderator of the self-perception–metaperception relationship, Marcus and Miller (2003) examined self-perceptions, metaperceptions, and other-perceptions of physical attractiveness among strangers. Groups of strangers in a round-robin design made self-judgments, judgments of other group members, and metaperceptions of physical attractiveness. Results indicated that metaperceptions of attractiveness highly correlated with self-perceptions of attractiveness, and these results differed slightly for men and women. Women who rated themselves as attractive believed that both men and women perceived them as attractive. Thus the correlation between self-perceptions and metaperceptions for women was positive both for metaperceptions of what men and for metaperceptions of what women thought of them. However, men who rated themselves as attractive only believed that women perceived them as attractive, not other men. Thus there was not a self-perception–metaperception correlation for metaperceptions of what men thought of them. Consistent with Kenny and DePaulo (1993), there was a considerable degree of generalized meta-accuracy for both men and women.

Finally, Frey and Tropp (2006) speculated that the strong correlation between self-perceptions and metaperceptions exists for metaperceptions of ingroup members but not for outgroup members. Directly relevant to this hypothesis, Santuzzi (in press) studied group interactions. Within those interactions, persons stated whether they smoked cigarettes or not and then later made perceptions of personality. In this study, ingroup perceptions are perceptions of smokers made by smokers as well as perceptions of non-smokers made by non-smokers; outgroup perceptions are those of smokers made by non-smokers and vice versa. Interestingly, Santuzzi (in press) found stronger self-metaperception correlations for ingroup than for outgroup members. Work by Vorauer and Kumhyr (2001) on meta-stereotypes also suggests that self-perceptions may not be related to metaperceptions of outgroup members.

Self-Perceptions and Metaperceptions across Cultures

Researchers may question the generalizability of the strong correlation between metaperceptions and self-judgments. Particularly, metaperceptions made by individuals in cultures that use more direct communication styles may be more accurate and correlate more highly with other perceptions if individuals are more candid communicators within these cultures. Shechtman and Kenny (1994) examined generalized and dyadic meta-accuracy using a sample of Israelis. They measured meta-accuracy in a population with a more straightforward communication style and proposed that directness would lead individuals to be more accurate metaperceivers than Americans. Israeli participants who were previously unacquainted interacted with each other in a context that encouraged feedback. Shechtman and Kenny (1994) found ample evidence for generalized meta-accuracy, and little evidence for dyadic meta-accuracy. Consistent with Kenny and DePaulo (1993), self-perceptions correlated highly with metaperceptions. Results did not support the hypothesis that within a culture with more direct communication style, individuals would be more meta-accurate perceivers.

Along these same lines, we examined data gathered by Jung (2006), who examined self-, other-, and metaperceptions of personality traits in South Korea. Perhaps it is the case that because the collective self is used more in Asian cultures than in Western cultures (Markus & Kitayama, 1991), and that in some Asian cultures people are less likely to enhance the individual self than in Western cultures (e.g., Heine & Lehman, 1997), individuals in collectivist cultures will be more accurate metaperceivers, and the individual level self will less likely to be used in forming metaperceptions.

Jung (2006) examined metaperception on several traits in groups of persons who were acquainted for 1 and 3 years. He found that consistent with findings in Western cultures, self-perceptions correlate very strongly with the actor effect in metaperceptions, the average correlation being .70. This finding was consistent across length of acquaintance; individuals who were acquainted for 1 year used self-perceptions in making metaperceptions to the same extent as those who were acquainted for 3 years. In sum, research has consistently demonstrated cross-culturally that individuals largely incorporate their self-judgments into their metaperceptions.

Summary of Metaperception Research

We reviewed a growing body of research that examines the relationship between self-perception and metaperception. Strong evidence indicates that individuals use their self-perceptions in forming perceptions of what they believe others think of them, and this process is consistent across Eastern and Western cultures. In addition, individuals believe they are seen consistently by others; however, individuals are less able to predict how particular others view them, even when these others are acquaintances and not strangers.

Research focusing on the process of forming metaperceptions has demonstrated that when individuals focus on their behaviors rather than on their self-concepts, the strong relationship between self-perception and metaperception declines (Albright et al., 2001). In a similar vein, when individuals are given the same information about their own behavior as other perceivers are given, the correlation between self-perceptions and metaperceptions is reduced. In general, inducing individuals to draw on their behaviors rather than their self-concepts in forming metaperceptions leads them to become more accurate metaperceivers.

It appears that acquaintance does not moderate the strong self-metaperception correlation, however, group membership does. Santuzzi (in press) found that individuals are more likely to use self-judgments of ingroup members than of outgroup members. Also, Marcus and Miller (2003) found evidence for stronger self-metaperception correlations for opposite-sex judgments than same-sex judgments for males.

IDIOGRAPHIC ANALYSES

In the final section of this chapter, we consider a methodological issue in interpersonal perception studies. A long-standing question in person perception in particular, and social perception in general, is the extent to which social judgments are accurate or biased. Self-judgments have often been used in this debate. In terms of bias in the perception of others, one major area of study has been the study of assumed similarity or false consensus: To what extent do perceivers use self-perceptions to determine how it is that they see others? Self-judgments are also often used as the standard for accuracy (Funder, 1995). That is, to determine if judgments about a target are correct or not, the researcher asks the target for self-judgments, presumes that the target is correct, and examines the relationship between self-judgments and judgments of the target by other perceivers. In this case, the researcher is interested in *self–other agreement.*

Let us carefully consider the question of self–other agreement. This agreement is usually measured by correlating across *persons*; that is, how a person sees him or herself on a given trait with how others see him or her on that trait. Alternatively, we can compute this correlation within person and across *variables*; for example, we can have a person rate him or herself and another on a set of variables (e.g., sociable, intelligent, and honest). We then compute a correlation for that person between the person's self-ratings and the rating of the other person. For this correlation, the variable is the unit of analysis and there is a different correlation for each person. Such a within-person analysis has many names—*q* analysis, ipsative analysis—but we prefer the term *idiographic analysis*. Such correlations have been computed in prior studies of self–other agreement (Pelham, 1993) as well as assumed similarity (Krueger, 2000).

There are two major advantages in using the idiographic approach. First, it allows the researcher to study moderators of person perception phenomena. If, for instance, there was an interest in showing that depressed people were less likely to assume that others were similar to themselves, one could correlate a measure of depression with an idiographic measure of assumed similarity. Second, an idiographic analysis provides a single value, instead of several different values for each variable. Because of this aggregation, idiographic analyses may provide a more powerful overall test of a phenomenon.

There are, however, several key drawbacks to the use of such methods. First, the process is computationally complex; one must compute elaborate statistics for each person. Second, one must decide which idiographic measure to use and each might yield very different results. For instance, self and other can be correlated with each other, or the sum of absolute differences can be measured. The researcher needs to carefully consider which type of idiographic measures to employ (Cronbach & Gleser, 1953). Third, there might be self–other agreement, but the source of that agreement may be mean differences between the variables rated. In such a case, a person's self-rating would correlate not only with the others' rating of him or her but also with others' ratings of a third person. This problem, called *stereotype accuracy* (Cronbach, 1955), can be eliminated by proper statistical analyses. Computational complexity, choosing the appropriate index, and stereotype accuracy are difficulties in idiographic analyses, but they can be overcome.

We next illustrate an idiographic analysis using the Study 2 data from Kenny, Horner, Kashy, and Chu (1992). In that study, there are 10 ratings of personality, two for each of the Big Five. There were 27 groups of four women who rated the three other participants at zero acquaintance as well as making self-ratings. Zero acquaintance means that the women have not interacted; they are making personality ratings based on appearance and nonverbal behaviors. We decided to use a correlational index. Note that for this study, we are computing the idiographic index for dyad, not person. For instance, we can compute Jane's assumed similarity to Sue, Helen, and Jennifer.

To remove stereotype accuracy as a potential problem, we followed the advice of Kenny and Acitelli (1994) by subtracting from each score its mean on that particular variable across all persons. We computed the variable means separately for perceptions of the self and for perceptions of the other. Had we not done these mean subtractions, we would have found spurious large levels of both assumed similarity and self–other agreement.

We computed a self–other agreement correlation by correlating a person's self-ratings with how the person was seen by a particular other. We computed the assumed similarity correlation by correlating the self-ratings with how the self saw a particular other. Thus for each person, there are three sets of assumed similarity correlations, and three sets of self–other agreement correlations, one for each interaction partner. The average assumed similarity correlation was .195 and the average self–other agreement correlation was .030.

Because we have assumed similarity and self–other agreement for each dyad, we can perform an SRM analysis on these measures. With this analysis we could ask four interesting questions:

1. Do some people assume that their partners are similar to them and other people do not (actor variance in assumed similarity)? Does Jane think that she is similar to Sue, Helen, and Jennifer?
2. Are some people seen as very similar to others, and other people are seen as not very similar to others (partner variance in assumed similarity)? Do Sue, Helen, and Jennifer think they are similar to Jane?
3. Do some people's self-ratings tend to agree with their partners' ratings of them, and other people's self-ratings tend to show low agreement (actor variance in self–other agreement)? Do Sue, Helen, and Jennifer see Jane the way she sees herself?
4. Do some perceivers tend to agree with people's self-ratings and others tend not to agree (partner variance in self–other agreement)? Does Jane see Sue, Helen, and Jennifer the way they see themselves?

The third question has been called *expressivity* (Snodgrass, Hecht, & Ploutz-Snyder, 1988) or the *good-target hypothesis* (Funder, 1995) and the fourth question has been called *perceptivity* (Snodgrass, Hecht, & Ploutz-Snyder, 1988) or the *good-judge hypothesis* (Colvin & Bundick, 2001).

We do find evidence that some people assume similarity more than others; the answer to question 1 is yes. We also find that some people have more self–other agreement than do others; the answer to question 3 is yes. This result may seem surprising in that the mean level of self–other agreement is essentially zero. If there are differences in self–other agreement, then for some selves, others can predict their self-ratings and for other selves, the correlation between self and other is negative. Our explanation of the result is as follows. Some people are more prototypical and for these people there are positive self–other correlations. However, others are counter-prototypical and so for these people the average self–other correlation is negative.

Some (e.g., Pelham, 1993) have argued that idiographic analyses yield superior information to more traditional nomothetic analyses, in which each variable is analyzed using person as the unit of analyses. Kenny and Winquist (2001) have shown that when appropriate analyses are done (e.g., effects resulting from stereo-type accuracy are removed), the results from the two sets of analyses tend to be very similar. To show this, we also conducted a nomothetic analysis on the Kenny et al. data and averaged those analyses across the 10 variables, and found the following: The average assumed similarity correlation across the 10 variables is .158, whereas the average self–other agreement correlation is only .050. Note the results are essentially the same as the findings in our idiographic analysis.

As we have stated earlier, the major advantage of the idiographic analyses is the possibility of discovering who shows more or less of the given effect. We can then examine which persons show more self–other agreement or more assumed similarity; that is, we can conduct a person moderator analysis. For example, we also found that people who assume more similarity see others more favorably.

We have in this section concentrated on idiographic analyses of assumed similarity and self–other agreement. However, other self-perception indices can be subjected to an idiographic analysis. In particular, meta-accuracy, the ability of a person to know how others view him or her, could be analyzed by idiographic methods.

SUMMARY

The relationship between self-perceptions and perceptions of others is bidirectional: To understand ourselves, we need to understand others and to understand others, we need to understand ourselves. This complex interplay of self-perceptions with other-perceptions and metaperceptions is discussed in this chapter. To understand how a person sees her or himself, we need to also understand how the person sees others, how others see the person, and how the person thinks others see him or her.

We have used the social relations model as a model for the study of these processes. Although this can be very complicated, it potentially offers us new insights into the relationship between self-perception and the perceptions of others. We hope this chapter has illustrated that utility and that researchers take advantage of the approach.

ACKNOWLEDGMENT

We thank Linda Albright and Micha Strack who provided us with helpful comments on an earlier draft of the chapter.

REFERENCES

Albright, L., Forest, C., & Reiseter, K. (2001). Acting, behaving, and the selfless basis of metaperception. *Journal of Personality and Social Psychology, 81*, 910–921.

Albright, L., & Malloy, T. E. (1999). Self-observation of social behavior and metaperception. *Journal of Personality and Social Psychology, 77*, 726–734.

Albright, L., & Malloy, T. E. (2006). *Metaperception and self-perception in acquainted and unacquainted groups*. Unpublished data.

Allport, G. W. (1937) *Personality: A psychological interpretation*. New York: Holt.

Andersen, S. M., & Chen, S. (2002). The relational self: An interpersonal social-cognitive theory. *Psychological Review, 109*, 619–645.

Anderson, C., Srivastava, S., Beer, J. S., Spataro, S. E., & Chatman, J. E. (2006). Knowing your place: Self-perceptions of status in social groups. *Journal of Personality and Social Psychology, 91*, 1094–1110.

Bales, R. F., & Cohen, S. P. (1979). *SYMLOG: A system for the multiple level observation of groups*. Glencoe, IL: The Free Press.

Brewer, M. B. (1991). The social self: On being the same and different at the same time. *Personality and Social Psychology Bulletin, 17*, 475–482.

Christensen, P. N., Stein, M. B., & Means-Christensen, A. (2003). Social anxiety and interpersonal perception: A social relations model analysis. *Behaviour Research and Therapy, 43*, 1355–1371.

Colvin, C. R., & Bundick, M. S. (2001). In search of the good judge of personality: Some methodological and theoretical concerns. In J. Hall & F. J. Bernieri (Eds.), *Interpersonal sensitivity: Theory and measurement* (pp. 47–65). Mahwah, NJ: Lawrence Erlbaum Associates, Inc.

Cronbach, L. J. (1955). Processes affecting scores on "understanding of others" and "assumed similarity." *Psychological Bulletin, 52*, 177–193.

Cronbach, L. J., & Gleser, G. C. (1953). Assessing similarity between profiles. *Psychological Bulletin, 50*, 456–473.

Donahue, E. M., Robins, R. W., Roberts, B. W., & John, O. P. (1993). The divided self: Concurrent and longitudinal effects of psychological adjustment and social roles on self-concept differentiation. *Journal of Personality and Social Psychology, 64*, 834–846.

Felson, R. B. (1981). Self- and reflected appraisal among football players: A test of the Meadian hypothesis. *Social Psychology Quarterly, 44*, 116–226.

Festinger, L. (1954). A theory of social comparison processes. *Human Relations, 7*, 117–140.

Frey, F. E., & Tropp, L. R. (2006). Being seen as individuals versus as group members: Extending research on metaperception to intergroup contexts. *Personality and Social Psychology Review, 10*, 265–280.

Funder, D. C. (1995). On the accuracy of personality judgment: A realistic approach. *Psychological Review, 102*, 652–670.

Gibbons, F. X., Benbow, C. P., and Gerrard, M. (1994). From top dog to bottom half: Social comparison strategies in response to poor performance. *Journal of Personality and Social Psychology, 67*, 638–652.

Gilovich, T., Savitsky, K., & Medvec, V. H. (1998). The illusion of transparency: Biased assessments of others' ability to read our emotional states. *Journal of Personality and Social Psychology, 75*, 332–346.

Heine, S. J., & Lehman, D. R. (1997). The cultural construction of self-enhancement: An examination of group-serving biases. *Journal of Personality and Social Psychology, 72*, 1268–1283.

James, W. (1890). *The principles of psychology* (Vol. I). New York: Holt.

Jones, E. E., & Nisbett, R. E. (1972). The actor and the observer: Divergent perceptions of the causes of behavior. In E. E. Jones, D. E. Kanouse, H. H. Kelley, R. E. Nisbett, S. Valins, & B. Weiner (Eds.), *Attribution: Perceiving the causes of behavior* (pp. 79–94). Hillsdale, NJ: Lawrence Erlbaum Associates, Inc.

Jung, T. (2006). *Perceptions of personality in South Korea*. Unpublished raw data.

Kenny, D. A. (1994). *Interpersonal perception: A social relations analysis*. New York: Guilford Press.

Kenny, D. A., & Acitelli, L. K. (1994). Measuring similarity in couples. *Journal of Family Psychology, 8*, 417–431.

Kenny, D. A., & DePaulo, B. M. (1993). Do people know how others view them? An empirical and theoretical account. *Psychological Bulletin, 114*, 145–161.

Kenny, D. A., Horner, C., Kashy, D. A., & Chu, L. (1992). Consensus at zero acquaintance:

Replication, behavioral cues, and stability. *Journal of Personality and Social Psychology*, 62, 88–97.

Kenny, D. A., & La Voie, L. (1984). Separating individual and group effects. *Journal of Personality and Social Psychology*, 71, 928–936.

Kenny, D. A., & Malloy, T. E. (1988). Partner effects in social interaction. *Journal of Nonverbal Behavior*, 12, 34–57.

Kenny, D. A., Mohr, C., & Levesque, M. (2001). A social relations variance partitioning of dyadic behavior. *Psychological Bulletin*, 127, 128–141.

Kenny, D. A., & West, T. V. (2007). *Using the social relations model to estimate self-enhancement effects via structural equation modeling*. Manuscript in preparation.

Kenny, D. A., & Winquist, L. A. (2001). The measurement of interpersonal sensitivity: Consideration of design, components, and unit of analysis. In J. A. Hall & F. J. Bernieri (Eds.), *Interpersonal sensitivity: Theory and measurement* (pp. 265–302). Englewood Cliffs, NJ: Lawrence Erlbaum Associates, Inc.

Kinch, J. W. (1963). A formalized theory of self-concept. *American Journal of Sociology*, 68, 481–486.

Krueger, J. (2000). The projective perception of the social world: A building block of social comparison processes. In J. Suls & L. Wheeler (Eds.), *Handbook of social comparison: Theory and research* (pp. 323–351). Dordrecht, The Netherlands: Kluwer Academic Publishers.

Kwan, V. S. Y., John, O. P., Kenny, D. A., Bond, M. H., & Robins, R. W. (2004). Reconceptualizing individual differences in self-enhancement bias: An interpersonal approach. *Psychological Review*, 111, 94–110.

Laing, R. D., Phillipson, H., & Lee, A. R. (1966). *Interpersonal perception: A theory and a method of research*. New York: Springer-Verlag.

Leary, M. R., & Downs, D. L. (1995). Interpersonal functions of the self-esteem motive: The self-esteem system as a sociometer. In M. H. Kernis (Ed.), *Efficacy, agency, and self-esteem* (pp. 123–144). New York: Plenum Press.

Levesque, M. J. (1997). Meta-accuracy among acquainted individuals: A social relations analysis of interpersonal perception and metaperception. *Journal of Personality and Social Psychology*, 72, 66–74.

Levesque, M. J., & Kenny, D. A. (1993). Accuracy of behavioral predictions at zero acquaintance: A social relations analysis. *Journal of Personality and Social Psychology*, 65, 1178–1187.

Malloy, T. E., Albright, L., Kenny, D. A., & Winquist,, L. (1997). Interpersonal perception and metaperception in non-overlapping social groups. *Journal of Personality and Social Psychology*, 72, 390–398.

Marcus, D. K., & Miller, R. S. (2003). Sex differences in judgments of physical attractiveness: A social relations analysis. *Personality and Social Psychology Bulletin*, 29, 325–335.

Markus, H. R., & Kitayama, S. (1991). Culture and the self: Implications for cognition, emotion and motivation. *Psychological Review*, 98, 222–253.

Oliver, P. V. (1988). *Effects of need for social approval on first interaction among members of the opposite sex*. Doctoral dissertation, University of Connecticut.

Pelham, B. W. (1993). The idiographic nature of human personality: Examples of the idiographic self-concept. *Journal of Personality and Social Psychology*, 64, 665–677.

Robins, R. R., Mendelsohn, G. A., Connell, J. B., & Kwan, V. S. Y. (2004). Do people agree about the causes of behavior? A social relations analysis of behavior ratings and causal attributions. *Journal of Personality and Social Psychology*, 86, 334–344.

Santuzzi, A. M. (in press). Perceptions and metaperceptions of negative evaluation: Group composition and interpersonal accuracy in a social relations model. *Group Processes and Intergroup Relations*.

Sedikides, C., Gaertner, L., & Toguchi, Y. (2003). Pancultural self-enhancement. *Journal of Personality and Social Psychology, 84*, 60–79.

Shechtman, Z., & Kenny, D. A. (1994). Metaperception accuracy: An Israeli study. *Basic and Applied Social Psychology, 15*, 451–465.

Snodgrass, S. E., Hecht, M. A., & Ploutz-Snyder, R. (1988). Interpersonal sensitivity: Expressivity or perceptivity? *Journal of Personality and Social Psychology, 74*, 238–249.

Snyder, C. R., & Fromkin, H. L. (1980). *Uniqueness: The human pursuit of difference*. New York: Plenum Press.

Spitzberg, B. H., & Cupach, W. R. (1984). *Interpersonal communication competence*. Beverly Hills, CA: Sage.

Strack, M. (2004). *Sozialperspektivitat: Theoretische bezuge, forschuungsmethodik und wirtschaftpsychologische praktikabilitat eins beziehungsdiagnostischen konstrukts*. Göttingen Germany: Universitätsverlag Göttingen.

Tajfel, H., & Turner, J. C. (1986). The social identity theory of intergroup behavior. In S. Worchel & W. G. Austin (Eds.), *Psychology of intergroup relations* (pp. 7–24). Chicago: Nelson-Hall.

Taylor, S. E., & Brown, J. D. (1988). Illusion and well-being: A social psychological perspective on mental health. *Psychological Bulletin, 103*, 193–210.

Turner, J. C., Hogg, M. A., Oakes, P. J., Reicher, S. D., & Wetherell, M. C. (1987). *Rediscovering the social group: A self-categorization theory*. New York: Blackwell.

Vorauer, J., & Kumhyr, S. M. (2001). Is this about you or me? Self-versus other-directed judgments and feelings in response to intergroup interaction. *Personality and Social Psychology Bulletin, 27*, 706–719.

Yingling, J. (1980). *Judgments of interpersonal competence in dyadic context*. Unpublished data.

7

Self-Regulation and Close Relationships

ROY F. BAUMEISTER and TYLER F. STILLMAN

Self-regulation refers to the ways in which the mind exerts controls over its drives, functions, and states. Self-regulation is thus essential for keeping innate, base tendencies at bay in favor of more civilized behavior (Vohs & Baumeister, 2004). Self-regulation can be thought of as the self acting on itself for some higher or desired purpose, such as inhibiting the urge to make a cutting remark for the sake of harmoniousness, getting off the couch to go for a jog in the interest of health, or refraining from eating meat for the sake of one's ethical or religious beliefs.

Close relationships are benefited greatly by self-regulation. A mother who cannot control her temper—a husband who gambles away his paycheck—will undoubtedly discover that poor self-regulation damages relationships. However, we propose that the connection between self-regulation and close relationships is reciprocal: Healthy close relationships not only follow good self-regulation, they actually strengthen self-regulation. In short, our assertion is that being in a healthy relationship aids in self-regulation, and the capacity to self-regulate benefits close relationships.

The term "self-regulation" is essentially interchangeable with the term "self-control." However, there is a subtle connotative difference between the two which merits mentioning. "Self-regulation" hints at bringing the self in line with a preferred state on a regular basis through either conscious or nonconscious processes, whereas "self-control" tends to be associated with conscious impulse control (Vohs & Baumeister, 2004). Most authors do not draw this distinction and view the terms as synonymous. This chapter focuses primarily on conscious self-regulation, and the two terms are used interchangeably.

There is a general belief among psychologists and laypersons that self-control is beneficial to performance in a variety of domains—such as academics or sports. This appears to be a safe assumption. In fact, inquiries into the degree to which self-control is beneficial have yielded some startling findings. A recent study investigating the contributions of both IQ and self-control on academic perform- ance found that self-control was a much better predictor of academic performance than was IQ (Duckworth & Seligman, 2005). Thus a domain typically viewed as highly dependent on intelligence is actually more dependent on self-regulation. The impact of self-control on close relationships may prove to be similarly surprising, both in the strength of the relationship and also the bidirectional nature of the relationship.

While we do not make a distinction between self-control, self-regulation, or self-discipline, one distinction that must be made is between *trait* self-control and *state* self-control. Trait self-control is what is most frequently understood when people refer to a person's capacity for self-control or self-regulation. It is the extent to which individuals are able to control their baser impulses over time and in different situations. Thus when someone is considered to have the trait of good self-control, the assumption is that the person overrides impulses consistently and in a variety of contexts. Indeed, there is empirical evidence that an individual's trait self-control is a stable quality over time (Gottfredson & Hirschi, 1990).

Whereas trait self-control is relatively consistent, state self-control is by definition transitory. It varies over time and across situations in a way that trait self-control does not. State self-control may fluctuate insofar as the ability to override all of one's less desirable drives is dependent on a common, limited self-regulatory resource. Thus when self-regulatory resources are low, one is "ego-depleted" and self-control failure is more likely (Baumeister, Bratslavsky, Muraven, & Tice, 1998; Baumeister & Heatherton, 1996; Muraven, Tice, & Baumeister; 1998; Schmeichel & Baumeister, 2004). Ego depletion occurs when a consistent or focused demand is made on the self-regulatory resources, temporarily using them up. During this time of reduced resources, the individual is less able to self-regulate. Time without self-control demands is required to replenish self-regulatory reserves. Experimentally, self-regulatory depletion has been demonstrated in over 40 published experiments resulting from a broad variety of self-regulatory tasks ranging from the refraining of eating tempting foods to prolonged orthographical tasks, to controlling one's mood (Baumeister, Schmeichel, & Vohs, in press). This variety of experimental manipulations which results in reduced self-regulatory control offers essential support to the proposition that exerting control over one's self saps a common self-regulatory resource. An example of ego depletion, or state self-control, is as follows. If a newly married woman spends a long evening with her in-laws during which she is constantly biting her tongue, she is consequently in a temporary state of weakened self-regulation capacity, and she is more likely to snap at her partner, kick her dog, break her diet, or indulge other relationship-harming impulses even if these are things she would not do with self-regulatory resources intact. Clearly, state self-control must be taken into account when discussing the harmonious functioning of a relationship.

State and trait self-control may be better understood in relation to broader theories of self-regulation. One such broad theory into which the present discussion of self-control fits is the Test–Operate–Test–Exit (TOTE) System (Carver & Scheier, 1981; Powers, 1973). The initial test phase consists of the self determining one's standing relative to a goal or desired state. For instance, if someone's goal is a happy marriage, a test phase might consist of comparing one's feelings toward a partner relative to the goal of a harmonious relationship. If there is no difference between a desired goal and an individual's current state, then the process does not advance to "operate." However, the "operate" phase begins if there is a discrepancy between one's goals (i.e., a happy marriage) and one's state (i.e., hostile feeling towards one's mate). The "operate" phase involves the self acting to achieve a goal. Thus, in the marriage example, an individual who detects a difference between their current feelings toward their mate and their marital goals will act so as to bring themselves in line with the goal, for instance by trying to better one's feelings about one's partner. The next "test" phase determines whether the action was efficacious in bringing about the desired goal or state. If a gap persists between the goal and the individual's current state, then the self returns to the "operate" phase. When a discrepancy no longer exists, then the individual "exits" the feedback loop. This has been described as a discrepancy-reducing loop, because the aim is to eliminate discrepancies between goal and state (Carver, 2004).

The "operate" phase is unique in the TOTE feedback loop in that it constitutes a deliberate effort or action. It is essentially the self acting on the self, or self-regulation. The capacity to "operate" is therefore dependent on self-regulatory resources (Schmeichel & Baumeister, 2004). Those with compromised state self-control may be unable to effectively "operate," while those with their complete self-control resources will have a greater capacity to act. Similarly, those with good trait self-control will more consistently act on the self in an effective manner than those with poor trait self-control, thereby achieving goals such as healthy relationships.

NATURAL SELECTION AND THE ORIGIN OF SELF-CONTROL

Everyone experiences self-control failures in the course of life. One line of inquiry is the reasons people fail to effectively control themselves (e.g., Baumeister, Heatherton, & Tice, 1994). An equally intriguing question is why people are able to exercise self-control at all as opposed to simply acting on impulse. The answer may lie in evolution. Evolutionary psychology has thus far been centered on the less noble side of human relationships, focusing on male sexual opportunism and the female pursuit of resources through mate selection. However, this is only part of the story of nature's influence on close relationships. Humans have a consistent and profound longing for close interpersonal connectedness. This desire has been called the *need to belong* (Baumeister & Leary, 1995). This longing for closeness may be a result of the fact that human survival has largely come to depend on living and associating with other people. Human ancestors who were part of a tribe or social group were more likely to survive than those who were on their own. In short, being allowed to be part of a group has become essential for survival. Given the high value of social acceptance and the deadly consequences of social rejection, a faculty that increased the likelihood of group membership is something that would have increased survival. Heatherton and Vohs (1998) have argued that self-control evolved in humans because the ability to manage one's actions and responses is crucial to accessing the life-sustaining benefits of group membership. They contend that human ancestors who were best able to restrain responses and modify behaviors were more likely to maintain social and dyadic relationships. Individuals in human evolutionary past who were unable to control themselves were not granted the benefits of group membership, such as hunting as a group, and died off. Similarly, socially excluded individuals would have had a more difficult time finding a mate and passing on their genes. Again, the argument for an evolutionary origin to self-regulation is that group membership is essential for survival and reproduction, and self-regulation is required for group membership. For instance, those in the evolutionary past who tried to initiate sex with the mate of an alpha male, or who were unable to accept an equitable sharing of food, would have found themselves exiled from the group, while those who were able to exercise restraint would have been allowed to retain the benefits of group membership. On the Heatherton and Vohs view (1998), self-control is more than just good for relationships; the origin of self-control is inextricably linked to the value of relationships with others.

Close relationships as the basis for the evolution of self-control has logical appeal, but empirical evidence of the kind describing gender-based differential reproductive strategies is presently lacking. A direct examination of parent trait self-control relative to child trait self-control would make an important contribution to the understanding of the genetic basis for self-control. However, our search yielded no such study. In the absence of clear evidence, one would expect data showing both that self-control is heritable and that self-control failures continue to be punished by social exclusion today. Indeed, there is some empirical support to this effect. In laboratory examinations of mice, genetics have been shown to affect whether the mice would impulsively take a small reward or whether they could refrain from taking it and thereby earn a larger reward, suggesting that self-control has a genetic component that can be passed on (Brunner & Hen, 1997; Otobe & Makino, 2004). This is not strong evidence of evolution, given that heritability is better suited for describing individual differences than evolved characteristics, but it does seem to indicate that there is a genetic aspect to self-control that could be passed on. Of course, a genetic contribution to self-control does not preclude social factors from influencing it. The impact of close relationships, which is one important environmental influence on self-control, will be examined shortly.

It appears that the social exile of those who have shown self-control failure is not only found in our evolutionary past. Today, people who show certain self-regulatory failures such as theft or assault are incarcerated. They are not allowed to associate with the rest of society and are not allowed to mate. Today people who are overweight find themselves socially marginalized as well (Puhl & Brownell, 2001). This might be because of the fact that obesity is perceived as a sign of self-regulatory failure, and is taken as evidence that an individual is a poor group member. Indeed, the extent to which obesity is viewed as personally controllable is predictive of negative attitudes towards overweight individuals in a variety of cultures (Crandall, D'Anello, Sakalli, Lazarus, Wieczorkowska, & Feather, 2001). The social marginalization of those considered low in self-control continues. Taken as a whole, data on the heritability of self-control and social marginalization of those who are assumed to have poor self-control are consistent with the Vohs and Heatherton argument regarding an evolutionary origin to self-control, but a great deal more data need to be gathered on this provocative proposition.

EFFECTIVE SELF-REGULATION BENEFITS CLOSE RELATIONSHIPS

Effective self-regulation should benefit close relationships in two simple ways. It should contribute directly to the harmoniousness of interactions, for instance by enabling people to remain calm and positive in circumstances that might otherwise become unpleasant. It should also contribute indirectly to the overall well-being of the relationship by avoiding problems, for instance by helping people avoid extradyadic romance (Gailliot & Baumeister, 2006; Tangney, Baumeister, & Boone, 2004).

Self-control is a valuable asset in getting along with people in general. Low self-control is related to aggression and violence in both adolescents (Feldman & Weinberger, 1994; Krueger, Caspi, Moffitt, White, & Stouthammer-Loeber, 1996) and adults (Avakame, 1998; Gottfredson & Hirschi, 1990; Latham & Perlow, 1996). In contrast, high self-control in children predicts better social functioning (Eisenberg et al., 1997; Fabes et al., 1999) and popularity (Maszk, Eisenberg, & Guthrie, 1999).

One large-scale investigation into self-regulation specified several characteristics that are associated with self-control which impact one's overall ability to get along with others (Tangney et al., 2004). These researchers found that poor self-control contributed to a number of psychopathological symptoms with the potential to disrupt interpersonal harmony, including hostile anger, paranoid ideation, somatization, depression, anxiety, and psychoticism.

In contrast, the benefits of self-regulation on close relationships were clearly demonstrated, beginning with the finding that people with good self-control reported better family cohesion, fewer family conflicts, and a more secure attachment style (although this finding is also consistent with our position that good close relationships improve self-control). In addition, good trait self-control corresponded with empathic perspective taking. Empathic perspective taking is the ability to step outside one's own point of view, which is an important trait to mutual understanding and to the success of a relationship (Davis & Oathout, 1987). Results also showed that self-control is correlated with other characteristics that improve relationship functioning, including low levels of anger, low levels of interpersonal aggression, effective anger management, emotional stability, agreeableness, conscientiousness, and taking responsibility for one's mistakes. Finally, moderation in alcohol consumption—a trait with clear implications for the well-being of close relationships—was shown to correspond with self-control. The conclusion of the Tangney et al. (2004) data seems to be that self-control supports a variety of pro-relational dimensions, consistent with our position.

A classic study on children's capacity to delay gratification offers support for the benefits of self-regulation for relationships (Mischel, Shoda, & Peake, 1988). The study began by giving children between the ages of 4 and 5 a simple choice: they could take one marshmallow immediately, or they could wait and receive two marshmallows. Two marshmallows are clearly more attractive than one marshmallow, at least for preschoolers. The temptation of the smaller reward was too much for many children, who selected immediate gratification over the better reward. The amount of time the children took before taking the smaller reward was recorded, which constituted the measure of self-control. Ten years later, these children were assessed for social competency, among other variables. Children who showed good self-control at that young age showed more social competency in their adolescence than did the children who quickly took the one marshmallow. This is evidence not only that self-regulation impacts relationships, but also that the association is enduring.

Of course, people all have moments in which their behavior falls short of ideal. Selfishness invariably leads to acts that hurt one's partner, even among the most dedicated and considerate mates. If an otherwise thoughtful wife temporarily loses her temper with her husband, the offended husband might feel a keen urge for justice and retaliation. However, it is after a hurtful act by one partner that the other partner's self-control appears of vital importance (Finkel & Campbell, 2001). How the offended partner responds to the hurtful act has profound effects on the well-being of the relationship (Rusbult, Verette, Whitney, Slovik, & Lipkus, 1991). The term *accommodation* refers to the willingness to inhibit destructive responding in favor of constructive responding, after one has been offended by one's partner (Rusbult et al., 1991).

The impulse to respond to a partner's hurtful behavior with further negativity is often strong. To respond without negativity (or, optimally, with kindness and love) is difficult, costly, and effortful (Rusbult et al., 1991; Yovetich & Rusbult, 1994). If one does not have the necessary self-regulatory resources to accommodate, there will be no accommodation and the harmful behavior will be reciprocated. Finkel and Campbell (2001) demonstrated a positive correlation between trait self-control and accommodation across four studies. Thus people who have good overall self-control respond better to their partner's missteps than do people with poorer trait self-control. These researchers also investigated state self-control. They discovered that when self-control resources were intact, participants in a relationship generally reported that they would accommodate in response to a partner's missteps. However, when participants were required to exert self-regulatory resources in order to suppress their emotions while watching an emotion-provoking video, there was a subsequent decrease in self-reported willingness for accommodation. The importance of self-control in responding to a partner's transgressions was supported by Vohs and Baumeister (2005), who showed that ego depletion caused destructive responses to a partner's hypothetical transgressions. This reciprocity of negativity among ego-depleted participants held true when they were thinking about current, past, and hypothetical relationships. This is an excellent demonstration of the importance of both trait and state self-control in the functioning of relationships.

Vohs and Baumeister (2005) also demonstrated that state self-control can affect whether people blame their partners for a shared failure or whether they take individual credit for a shared victory. This has been described as the self-serving bias, which is the tendency to view oneself as responsible for success while seeing external factors (such as one's partner) as responsible for failures (Sicoly & Ross, 1977). Couples worked together to create a structure out of blocks, and they were given either positive or negative feedback regarding how creative they had been. Ego-depleted participants viewed themselves as more responsible for the positive feedback and viewed their partners as more responsible for the negative feedback. Among participants whose self-regulatory resources were intact, this trend was absent and they were able to dole out both blame and credit in a relatively fair and even-handed way.

A recent investigation provides strong evidence for the importance of trait self-control to the survival of a relationship (Vohs, Baumeister, & Finkenauer, 2006). Given that people vary on trait self-control over a range from what can be considered low to moderate to high levels, there are several reasonably plausible combinations of partners' trait self-control that might best predict a relationship outcome. It is conceivable that partners with complementary levels of trait self-control would be ideal, such that a partner with high self-control would be best matched with a partner with low self-control. It is also plausible that similar levels of self-control would best predict relationship outcomes, such that the best mate for someone with low self-control would be someone with similarly low self-control. However, this study revealed that the summed total of two partners' self-control best predicts relationship outcome. Two partners with high trait self-control are most likely to have a successful close relationship. This also means that any relationship is better off if at least one of the partners has high trait self-control, although two partners high in self-control is the ideal. The linear trend also indicates that there is no apparent drawback to increasingly effective self-regulation.

Sexual Restraint

Failure to curb one's sexual appetites can do great harm to a romantic relationship. Extradyadic sexual activity can introduce serious, tangible problems such as disease and unwanted pregnancy. In relationships where a couple agrees on sexual exclusivity, there is also a risk of jealousy, resentment, and feelings of betrayal. Engaging in an extradyadic relationship has been described as one of the most damaging behaviors to a relationship (Whisman, Dixon, & Johnson, 1997). Even when a couple agrees to tolerate extradyadic sexual activity, it seems to present a risk factor for future breakups (Blumstein & Schwartz, 1983). To be sure, none of these findings establishes that the extradyadic activity directly causes harm to relationships, but the assumption that it does is widespread and plausible. The likely harm done by sexual infidelity to relationships may be the reason why extradyadic sexual relationships are viewed negatively in a variety of cultures (Sheppard, Nelson, & Andreoli-Mathie, 1995). Suppressing impulses to engage in sexual activity with alternative partners may contribute to helping sustain intimate relationships, as is suppressing the urge to consider alternative partners. To be sure, societal norms exert pressure to express one's sexuality in a socially appropriate way. However, the presence or absence of norms alone is insufficient to explain a great deal of sexual behavior, including behavior that is contrary to norms, such as infidelity. This section will review evidence that self-control is relevant to the control of sexual behavior, especially for relationship partners.

Behaviors that demonstrate an inability to effectively self-regulate, such as immoderate alcohol consumption, drug addiction, and overeating, are correlated with a lack of sexual restraint and sexual misbehavior (Koepp, Schildbach, Schmager, & Rohner, 1993). In fact, poor self-control is central to the definition of a sexual control disorder (Wiederman, 2004).

The role of self-control in sexual restraint has also been demonstrated in laboratory studies. Ego-depletion caused participants to gaze for a longer time at sexually appealing people in a magazine than did participants who were not ego-depleted (Vohs & Baumeister, 2005). Although one might expect that being in a relationship would decrease how much time participants spent looking at sexually attractive people in the pictures, the effect of ego-depletion was even greater for participants who were in a relationship. Thus people in a state of weakened self-control have limited ability to suppress the consideration of alternative sexual partners, as compared to people with their self-control resources intact. Although gazing at attractive potential mates might sound harmless, the consideration of alternative mates weakens commitment to a current relationship and can result in relationship dissolution (Rusbult, 1980).

Gailliot and Baumeister (2006) found that both trait and state self-control facilitated the suppression of sexuality across several studies. Low trait self-control was found to be correlated with higher self-reported sexual activity, more sexual thoughts, and greater self-reported willingness for infidelity. Ego depletion caused participants to solve word puzzles using more sexual words and led to an increase in self-reported willingness for infidelity in hypothetical circumstances. Further, ego-depletion caused sexually inexperienced dating partners to engage in more sexual acts of physical intimacy than they had done previously in a laboratory setting. In addition, retrospective accounts showed that respondents' inability to restrain their sexual impulses frequently occurred during times of self-regulatory exertion (as in a sexual indiscretion occurring during a diet). Clearly, state self-control has important implications for relationships that value sexual exclusivity.

In summary, there is some evidence supporting the benefits of self-control to close relationships. We are yet to come across data supporting the proposition (i.e., Kremen & Block, 1998) that the benefits of self-control are curvilinear, or in other words that self-control ceases to be an advantage and becomes a liability in the highest ranges (at a cost to spontaneity, for example). When it comes to the functioning of a relationship, the existing evidence shows that self-control is unambiguously beneficial.

POSITIVE CLOSE RELATIONSHIPS BENEFIT SELF-REGULATION

A Bidirectional Relationship

The authors' contention is that self-control not only benefits one's relationships, but that good relationships enhance one's self-control. The favorable effect of self-control on relationships is more established in the literature than the benefits of close relationships on self-control, but there is emerging evidence for our position. An early demonstration of the bidirectional causal relationship between self-control and self-presentation was provided across eight studies by Vohs, Baumeister, and Ciarocco (2005). Although self-presentation is admittedly not the same thing as a close interpersonal relationship, self-presentation is a key part of maintaining relationships (Leary, 2001). First, Vohs et al. (2005) demonstrated the role of self-control in self-presentation. Consistent with the idea that self-control is required for effective interpersonal interactions, results showed that tasks resulting in ego-depletion resulted in self-presentation degradation. Specifically, these researchers found that participants who had decreased self-control resources made poorer first impressions than those with self-control resources intact. They then assessed the impact of effortful self-presentation on self-control by assigning participants to present themselves in a manner counter to habitual patterns, or not counter to them. Results showed that effortful presentation resulted in a temporary decrease in self-control resources, as measured by decreased persistence on an unsolvable puzzle. This suggests that the relationship between self-control and interpersonal processes goes in both directions.

Developmental psychology provides evidence that relates more directly to the benefits of close relationships on self-regulation. Following Baumrind's (1971) classifications of parenting styles, permissive parents are reluctant to correct inappropriate behavior in favor of a more "hands-off" policy. In contrast, authoritative parents set consistent limits for their children, and do so in an environment of dialogue and warmth. Experimental evidence indicates that these differing styles of parenting appear to influence children's development of self-control (Mauro & Harris, 2000). In this laboratory study, parents asked their preschool age children to refrain from touching a brightly wrapped present. The parents then left the room, and the children were surreptitiously observed. Children raised by mothers who employ an authoritative parenting style were better able to resist touching the tempting gift than were children raised by permissive mothers. In other words, a parenting style more indicative of warmth and closeness was correlated with better self-control in children. Researchers using different methods likewise found a child's developmental context to be related to self-control (Neitzel & Stright, 2003). In this study, children and mothers interacted as the children completed a preliminary task. Mothers were observed as they interacted with their child during this first task. Those mothers who provided positive emotional support and encouragement had children who were more persistent and more successful at the second task, given months later, than were the children of less supportive mothers. Thus positive parental interactions corresponded with better self-regulation during early development.

The impact of healthy parent–child relationships on self-control is also seen in the problem behaviors that children avoid as well as the positive behaviors children engage in. Children and teens (age 9–17) who have healthy and positive relationships with their parents are less likely to have problems with both alcohol and marijuana (Coombs, Paulson, & Richardson, 1991). Similarly, the more frequently college students speak with their mothers about drinking, the less likely they are to engage in binge drinking (Turrisi, Wiersma, & Hughes, 2000). While these correlational studies are consistent with our hypotheses that close relationships benefit self-control, the directionality cannot clearly be determined.

A number of studies have shown that being raised by both a mother and a father corresponds with higher academic performance and achievement (Astone & McLanahan, 1991; Hetherington, Camara, & Featherman, 1983; Keith & Finlay, 1988; Mulkey, Crain, & Harrington, 1992). In other words, children who have the benefit of two close parents outperform children who have a single close parent. Of course, we are not suggesting that single parents are somehow not as close to their children as are couples, but children raised by couples do have one more close parental relationship. To be sure, there are factors other than self-control that may influence this finding, but it is nevertheless quite likely that self-control plays a central role in the superior academic achievement in two-parent homes. In short, this finding is consistent with our hypothesis but must be interpreted with appropriate caution.

These studies provide evidence that the family environment in which one is raised has implications for one's ability to self-regulate. Such findings are confirmed by a retrospective analysis of adult populations. Researchers have found that trait self-control is higher among people who report having been raised in a positive family environment than it is among people who are raised in dysfunctional families (Tangney et al., 2004), although it is conceivable that trait self-control could have biased recollections.

We have principally interpreted the parental influence on behavioral problems as indirect, or through the development of self-control, rather than directly, such as by teaching children specifically the merits of education. In other words, while the benefits of close parental relationships on children's behavioral problems can be described in terms of the development of one general trait, self-control, the benefits of parental influence could also be explained in terms of the development of specific faculties that directly influence the individual child's behavior. Researchers recently tested the question of whether parenting behaviors directly or indirectly (via self-control) influence adolescents' emotional and behavioral problems (Finkenauer, Engles, & Baumeister, 2005). Over 1300 adolescents responded to questionnaires regarding self-control, their parents, and the frequency and seriousness of behavioral and emotional problems.

Consistent with our thesis, one primary finding of this study is that parenting styles, assessed by the parenting style index (Lamborn, Mounts, Steinberg, & Dornbusch, 1991; Steinberg, Lamborn, Darling, Mounts, & Dornbusch, 1994), demonstrating a high level of acceptance (i.e., "I can talk to my parents about my problems") and a low level of psychological manipulation (i.e, "My parents treat me coldly when I fail at school") resulted in higher levels of self-control in children. Self-control in children was found to be strongly related to a reduction of both behavioral problems (delinquency and aggression) and emotional problems (depression, self-esteem, and stress). However, while self-regulation did contribute to positive emotional and behavioral factors in unique ways (unrelated to parenting style), parenting style also uniquely contributed to these factors. In other words, parental closeness benefits children through an indirect contribution via the development self-control, but also has a direct influence independent of self-control.

We think these findings are of great value to practice as well as theory. The two main traits that have been shown to contribute broadly to success in life are self-control and intelligence. Decades of interventions and experimentation have thus far failed to produce anything that is proven to yield lasting gains in intelligence, and it may be that the genetic contribution to intelligence sets an upper limit that socializing experiences are essentially unable to raise. (Admittedly, abuse, neglect, and deprivation can cause children to grow up less intelligent than their genes would have allowed.) In contrast, self-control seems much more amenable to learning and improvement. Hence instilling and strengthening self-control may be the most valuable way that parents, teachers, and others can enable children to succeed better.

Automatic Self-Control Resource Replenishment

Close relationships may be particularly useful in mitigating ego-depletion. Researchers have found that bringing one's family to mind boosts self-regulation among participants who have had their self-regulatory resources drained (Stillman, Tice, & Baumeister, 2006). In one study, participants in the control condition were given a monotonous orthographical task, while participants in the ego-depletion condition were given a similar orthographical task that was both monotonous and cognitively demanding. Participants were then supraliminally primed either with family-relevant words or control words. The priming occurred when participants constructed sentences out of a small list of words, which in the family-relevant condition contained family words like "daughter" and "father," or neutral words. The priming of family-relevant words was done to bring about the psychological presence of loved ones. Last, all participants were asked to create as many words as possible from a list of scrambled letters, with no time limit indicated. Because participants could quit the task any time they wanted to, the number of words they created was at least partly dependent on self-control, and in general participants in the depletion condition created fewer words. However, the number of words participants created in the ego-depletion condition was affected by whether they had received the family prime or not, as revealed by statistically significant interactions. Ego-depleted participants who were primed with the family (in other words, participants who were in the psychological presence of loved ones) created more words than did ego-depleted participants who were given the control prime, indicating that bringing the family to mind ameliorates state self-control.

A second study found similar results using subliminal primes. Rather than being presented with general family-related words such as "sister," participants in this study were presented with the terms they used to refer to loved ones, such as "Debra" or "Mommy." To do this, all participants were asked to complete a questionnaire regarding their preferences for certain letters of the alphabet prior to entering the lab where the actual experiment would take place. The questionnaire explained that to help account for biased answers, participants were asked to provide the names of close loved ones. The responses were surreptitiously entered into a computer that would later be used by the participants. Thus, in the family-relevant condition, participants who call their fathers "Daddy" would be subliminally presented with the word "Daddy" as they completed either an ego-depleting task requiring persistent thought control or a control task. In general participants subjected to the ego-depletion condition created fewer words than in the control task. Again, among depleted participants those who received the family-related prime created more words than did participants who received a neutral prime as revealed by a significant interaction. These researches also sought to determine whether the closeness and warmth of participants' relationships to their families would influence the effect of priming with family-related concepts; however nearly every participant reported a positive relationship with their family in general (although some had ill feelings toward particular family members). This remains an intriguing question.

Although an important amount of self-regulation aimed at maintaining or improving a relationship most likely occurs on a conscious level, the subliminal priming study is evidence that self-regulation of some kind occurs automatically and nonconsciously in the psychological presence of family. Fitzsimons and Bargh (2003) found similar self-regulatory benefits from both the conscious and nonconscious psychological presence of loved ones. They found that when participants were primed with important relationships, they put more effort into understanding someone's behavior, worked harder on a verbal task, and were more willing to help an experimenter than controls. This too is supportive evidence for the benefits of close relationships on state self-control, although the Fitzsimons and Bargh investigation was not designed specifically to assess state self-control and it therefore lacked an ego-depletion manipulation.

These studies suggest that bringing one's loved ones to mind helps boost state self-control. This temporary boost in self-control might be one reason it is so common to see pictures of people's family members everywhere people work— from cabs to cubicles. Work is almost inherently depleting, and thoughts of one's close relationships provide a buffer against ego-depletion. The underlying mechanism for this is not clear, although it is presently under investigation (Stillman, Tice, & Baumeister, 2006). One possible reason why the psychological presence of loved ones would mitigate the effects of ego-depletion is that thoughts of loved ones might cause a positive mood, and positive mood is associated with improved self-control (Tice, Bratslavsky, & Baumeister, 2001). On this view, the observed effect would be more a result of affect than of relational connectedness. If this is the reason for the reduction of ego-depletion, then ego-depletion would be reduced as much in people primed with family words as those primed with non-family words of equally positive valence. Another possibility is that social connectedness in general is the mechanism by which priming the family improves self-regulation. If this is the case, then priming words suggesting general connectedness should result in a self-control boost similar to that of family-related words. Although the proposition that bringing to mind close relationships is unique in its capacity to improve state self-control is intriguing, there is not yet sufficient evidence to rule out other interpretations.

While all important relationships require some form of self-regulation, it is logical that specific relationships call for different kinds of self-regulation goals. For example, sexual fidelity is a more important goal to one's romantic relationships than it is to one's friendships. Fitzsimons and Bargh (2003) demonstrated empirically that people do have different self-regulation goals associated with different relationships. Participants who had previously stated that they wanted to make their mothers proud performed better on a verbal task when primed with thoughts of their mothers, while participants who did not have this goal did not show improvement. Similarly, participants who were primed with the name of their best friend were more understanding of a stranger's behavior than were participants who were not primed with a best friend's name.

Social Exclusion

A different approach to studying the link between self-control and close relationships is to examine the effects of social rejection or exclusion. If close relationships benefit self-control, one would also expect the absence of relationships, or social exclusion, to harm self-control. This hypothesis was central to the recent investigation by Baumeister, DeWall, Ciarocco, and Twenge (2005).

The first part of that investigation was simply intended to confirm that social exclusion would impair self-regulation. This was shown with multiple different methods. A sense of social exclusion was created in some studies by giving people bogus feedback on a personality test, specifically telling them that their responses indicated that they were the sort of person who was likely to end up alone in life—over time, their friends would disappear, their romances and marriages would be short-lived, and they would end up spending more and more time alone. In other studies, rejection was manipulated by having participants talk together in a group to get acquainted and then privately rate which other people they would like to be paired with for an upcoming task—then telling some participants that nobody in the group had chosen them as someone with whom they would like to be paired. Both of these manipulations led to poorer self-regulation, as compared to various control conditions. That is, the socially excluded people showed poor self-regulation in the sense that they ate more snack food (cookies), consumed less of a healthy but bad-tasting beverage, and gave up faster on a frustrating task. They also performed worse on a dichotic listening task, which requires people to put on headphones and screen out information being recited in one ear so as to concentrate on what they hear in the other ear. (Dichotic listening tasks measure the control of one's attention, and so the poor performance by rejected people shows an inability to concentrate and focus on what is important.)

Thus social exclusion leads to poor self-regulation. But why? There were several possible theories. One was that social rejection makes people too emotionally upset to control themselves or concentrate. That is, socially excluded participants were too emotionally distressed to self-regulate. This is not wholly inconsistent with our hypothesis, but it would necessitate some revision. Past work has demonstrated that emotional distress damages self-regulation (Rosenthal & Marx, 1981; Tice et al., 2001; Wegener & Petty, 1994). However, there was no evidence for this. Excluded people responded more with emotional numbness than with intense emotional distress. Another possibility is that the rejection experienced by participants was simply a form of bad news, and their self-control failure was not a result of social exclusion but rather of getting negative feedback. However, a control condition in which participants were told bad news about their future (that they would most likely break many bones) yielded no such self-regulation failure. Thus these results cannot be explained simply in terms of giving participants unwelcome feedback. Another possible reason for the impaired self-regulation of rejected participants is that their self-esteem was damaged, thereby lowering their confidence in their ability to perform well. However, state self-esteem was specifically monitored in one study, revealing that there were no reliable changes to self-esteem, and that self-esteem was not related to the self-regulation measure.

Yet another theory was that rejection somehow directly disables the complex mental apparatus needed for self-control. There were several versions of this theory, including the very appealing idea that people who are rejected use up all their self-control energy trying to cope with the threat to their self-esteem and trying to make sure they don't have an emotional outburst. (That could explain the lack of emotional distress—perhaps people who get rejected find it upsetting, but they exert self-control to keep from breaking down and crying in the lab.) These ideas would all predict that rejected people would be fully unable to self-regulate, as opposed to being merely unwilling to exert themselves. To test that idea, Baumeister et al. (2005) repeated one of the experiments with the twist that some participants were offered a cash reward if they could perform well on the dichotic listening task. To the surprise of the investigators, the rejected people performed just as well as non-rejected ones when there was a cash reward at stake. This showed that exclusion does not really destroy or disable the capacity for self-regulation. Rejected people can self-regulate if they have a sufficient (selfish) reason to do so. Apparently, rejected people are normally just unwilling—rather than unable—to self-regulate. The implications of this unwillingness are relevant to a theory called "the implicit bargain."

The Implicit Bargain

Research findings about self-regulation and exclusion, especially those covered in the preceding section, have pointed toward what has come to be called the "implicit bargain" theory to link self-regulation and belongingness. This view is receiving increasing attention, although more research is needed. Hence let us describe it, though it is a bit more complicated than the other theories.

The implicit bargain theory starts by recognizing that self-regulation is costly to the self. It consumes effort and energy, so it is hard work. Moreover, it often requires frustrating or depriving the self. That is, most self-control is used for resisting temptation or making yourself do something you do not want to do. People use self-control to pull themselves out of bed when they would rather go back to sleep, to resist eating delicious but fattening food, to stifle their impulses to smoke or drink, to hold back their aggressive or sexual desires, and the like. In relationships, self-control may be used for holding one's tongue, for going along with a partner's wishes when one would rather do something different, for resisting the temptation to get romantically or sexually involved with a new partner, and the like. In a sense, the capacity for self-control is a capacity for frustrating yourself.

Why do people use self-control, if it is mainly hard work aimed at depriving themselves of what they want? The answer is that it helps them get other things that they want even more. In particular, people want to belong to groups and relationships, and self-control helps them do this. Baumeister (2005) has concluded that the key to understanding human nature is that people evolved to belong to groups and relationships in new, more complex and far-reaching ways than any other animals. Self-control thus enables people to conform to social norms, moral principles, laws, group expectations, and other standards to a much greater degree than other animals. The payoffs are immense, because people get most of what they need from their group. As just one example, most animals get their food from the natural environment around them, but people get their food from each other (i.e., mediated by their social group and network).

The implicit bargain is therefore to make the efforts and sacrifices of self-control in exchange for enjoying the immense and powerful rewards of belonging to the group. Individuals might enjoy the freedom to run amok and do whatever they feel like at all times, but they also want the satisfaction of having someone love them and care for them, and part of making a relationship succeed is a matter of behaving well so that your partner remains loyal and committed.

The implicit bargain can thus break down on either side. Certainly there is no disputing the fact that poor self-control leads to social rejection. People who fail to control themselves (e.g., by impulsive, immoral, illegal, or reckless acts) are excluded in many ways: lovers and spouses reject them; employers fire them; clubs expel them. Indeed, society as a whole excludes rule-breakers by putting them in prison, and there is evidence that poor self-control is the single most central aspect of the criminal personality (e.g., Gottfredson & Hirschi, 1990).

The other kind of breakdown—rejection leading to poor self-control—is less obvious, but it may be just as real and important. In a sense, that is what the studies by Baumeister et al. (2005) showed. When people are rejected, they cease to be willing to make the efforts and sacrifices required for self-control. They are still capable of controlling themselves, if they have a selfish reason for doing so, but they do not seem willing to make the effort without that. And why should they? According to the implicit bargain hypothesis, the main purpose of self-control is to facilitate belongingness—and so if you are not going to belong (as rejection shows), why bother making yourself follow external rules and be good according to what others think?

Limitations

Of the two propositions made in this chapter—that self-control benefits close relationships and that close relationships benefit self-control—the evidence that self-control improves close relationships is stronger. Yet it is conceivable that in some instances self-control might harm relationships. For instance, a teetotaler may exhibit good self-control, but is probably not the life of the party. Similarly, a student who devotes time and resources to academic excellence might find herself marginalized by friends who do not value educational achievements. Alternatively, someone who has recently made a decision to stop drinking or to improve their academic standing might find that close friends who do not share these goals actually hinder their progress to their pursuits. These scenarios may appear to be inconsistent with the proposed hypotheses; however, they are perhaps more illustrative of the importance of shared goals than to a fundamental flaw in the proposed bidirectional relationship. In other words it is not self-control that directly hinders the relationship, but the particular expression of self-control. Likewise, it is not the relationship that damages self-control so much as the contrasting goals of the couple that threaten the relationship.

CONCLUSIONS

Close relationships are among the most important aspects of human life (Baumeister & Leary, 1995). So important are relationships to happiness, and even to survival, that people are willing to exert control over their impulses in order to maintain them. Thus one important component for the harmonious functioning of a close relationship is self-control. However, this relationship is bidirectional. Healthy relationships foster self-control, while self-control suffers in poor relationships and following social exclusion.

There is room for a considerable amount of research to be done on this intriguing association. To begin with, the extent to which parental influence on self-control is socially influenced (such as through positive close relationships) as compared to genetic, is one vital question that remains unanswered, at least in our examination of the literature.

There are several other fertile directions this research can take. For instance, an investigation into the relative impact of state as opposed to trait self-control on different aspects of relationship functioning might yield important insights into the specific role each plays in maintaining close relationships. While a great deal is yet to be understood about the nature of self-control and close relationships, there is sufficient evidence to conclude that self-control is helpful in maintaining healthy and happy relationships, and that close relationships ameliorate the regulation of behavior.

REFERENCES

Astone, N. M., & McLanahan, S. S. (1991). Family structure, parental practices, and high school completion. *American Sociological Review*, 56, 309–320.

Avakame, E. F. (1998). Intergenerational transmission of violence, self-control, and conjugal violence: A comparative analysis of physical violence and psychological aggression. *Violence and Victims*, 13, 301–316.

Baumeister, R. F. (2005). *The cultural animal: Human nature, meaning, and social life*. New York: Oxford University Press.

Baumeister, R. F., Bratslavsky, F., Muraven, M., & Tice, D. M. (1998). Ego depletion: Is the active self a limited resource? *Journal of Personality and Social Psychology*, 74, 1252–1265.

Baumeister, R. F., DeWall, C. N., Ciarocco, N. J., & Twenge, J. M. (2005). Social exclusion impairs self-regulation. *Journal of Personality and Social Psychology*, 88, 589–604.

Baumeister, R. F., & Heatherton, T. F. (1996). Self-regulation failure: An overview. *Psychological Inquiry*, 7, 1–15.

Baumeister, R. F., Heatherton, T. F., & Tice, D. M. (1994). *Losing control: How and why people fail at self-regulation*. San Diego, CA: Academic Press.

Baumeister, R. F., & Leary, M. R. (1995). The need to belong: Desire for interpersonal attachments as a fundamental human motivation. *Psychological Bulletin*, 127, 497–529.

Baumeister, R. F, Schmeichel, B. J., & Vohs, K. D. (in press). Self-regulation and the executive function: The self as controlling agent. Chapter prepared for E. T. Higgins & A. W. Kruglanski, *Social psychology: Handbook of basic principles* (2nd ed.).

Baumrind, D. (1971). Current patterns of parental authority. *Developmental Psychology Monographs*, 4, 1–103.

Blumstein, P., & Schwartz, P. (1983). *American couples: Money, work, and sex*. New York: William Morrow.

Brunner, D., & Hen, R. (1997). Insights into the neurobiology of impulsive behavior from serotonin receptor knockout mice. In D. M. Stoff & J. J. Mann (Eds.), *Annals of the New York Academy of Sciences: Vol. 836. The neurobiology of suicide: From the bench to the clinic* (pp. 81–105). New York: New York Academy of Sciences.

Carver, C. S. (2004). *Self-regulation of action and affect*. In R. F. Baumeister & K. D. Vohs (Eds.), *Handbook of self-regulation: Research, theory, and applications* (pp. 13–39). New York: Guilford Press.

Carver, C. S., & Scheier, M. F. (1981). *On the self-regulation of behavior*. New York: Cambridge University Press.

Coombs, R. H., Paulson, M. J., & Richardson, M. A. (1991). Peer vs. parental influence in substance use among Hispanic and Anglo children and adolescents. *Journal of Youth and Adolescence*, 20, 73–88.

Crandall, C., D'Anello, S., Sakalli, N., Lazarus, E., Wieczorkowska, G., & Feather, N. T. (2001). An attribution-value model of prejudice: Anti-fat attitudes in six nations. *Personality and Social Psychology Bulletin*, 27, 30–37.

Davis, M. H., & Oathout, H. A. (1987). Maintenance of satisfaction in romantic relationships: Empathy and relational competence. *Journal of Personality and Social Psychology*, 53, 397–410.

Duckworth, A. L., & Seligman, M. E. P. (2005). Self-discipline outdoes IQ in predicting academic performance of adolescents. *Psychological Science*, 16, 939–944.

Eisenberg, N., Fabes, R. A., Shepard, S. A., Murphy, B. C., Guthrie, I. K., Jones, S., et al.

(1997). Contemporaneous and longitudinal prediction of children's social functioning from regulation and emotionality. *Child Development, 68,* 642–664.

Fabes, R. A., Eisenberg, N., Jones, S., Smith, M., Guthrie, I., Poulin, R., et al. (1999). Regulation, emotionality, and preschoolers' socially competent peer interactions. *Child Development, 70,* 432–442.

Feldman, S. S., & Weinberger, D. A. (1994). Self-restraint as a mediator of family influences on boys' delinquent behavior: A longitudinal study. *Child Development, 65,* 195–211.

Finkel, E. J., & Campbell, W. K. (2001). Self-control and accommodation in close relationships: An interdependence analysis. *Journal of Personality and Social Psychology, 81,* 263–277.

Finkenauer, C., Engles, R. C. M. E., & Baumeister, R. F. (2005). Parenting behaviour and adolescent behavioural and emotional problems: The role of self-control. *International Journal of Behavioral Development, 29,* 58–69.

Fitzsimons, G. M., & Bargh, J. A. (2003). Thinking of you: Nonconscious pursuit of interpersonal goals associated with relationship partners. *Journal of Personality and Social Psychology, 84,* 148–164.

Gailliot, M. T., & Baumeister, R. F. (2006). *Self-regulation and sexual restraint: Effects of self-control depletion and trait self-control on sexual responses.* Manuscript submitted for publication.

Gottfredson, M. R., & Hirschi, T. (1990). *A general theory of crime.* Stanford, CA: Stanford University Press.

Heatherton, T. F., & Vohs, K. D. (1998). Why is it so difficult to inhibit behavior? *Psychological Inquiry, 9,* 212–217.

Hetherington, E. M., Camara, K. A., & Featherman, D. E. (1983). Achievement and intellectual functioning of children in one-parent households. In J. Spence (Ed.), *Achievement and achievement motives* (pp. 205–284). San Francisco: Freeman.

Keith, V. M., & Finlay, B. (1988). The impact of parental divorce on children's educational attainment, marital timing, and likelihood of divorce. *Journal of Marriage and the Family, 50,* 797–809.

Koepp, W., Schildbach, S., Schmager, C., & Rohner, R. (1993). Borderline diagnosis and substance abuse in female patients with eating disorders. *International Journal of Eating Disorders, 14,* 107–110.

Kremen, A. M., & Block, J. (1998). The roots of ego-control in young adulthood: Links with parenting in early childhood. *Journal of Personality and Social Psychology, 75,* 1062–1075.

Krueger, R. F., Caspi, A., Moffitt, T. E., White, J., & Stouthamer-Loeber, M. (1996). Delay of gratification, psychopathology, and personality: Is low self-control specific to externalizing problems? *Journal of Personality, 64,* 107–129.

Lamborn, S. D., Mounts, N. S., Steinberg, L., & Dornbusch, S. M. (1991). Patterns of competence and adjustment among adolescents from authoritative, authoritarian, indulgent, and neglectful families. *Child Development, 62,* 1049–1065.

Latham, L. L., & Perlow, R. (1996). The relationship of client-directed aggressive and non-client-directed aggressive work behavior with self-control. *Journal of Applied Social Psychology, 26,* 1027–1041.

Leary, M. R. (2001). The self we know and the self we show: Self-esteem, self-presentation, and the maintenance of interpersonal relationship. In G. J. O Fletcher & M. S. Clark (Eds.), *Blackwell handbook of social psychology: Interpersonal processes* (pp. 457–477). Oxford: Blackwell.

Maszk, P., Eisenberg, N. G., & Guthrie, I. K. (1999). Relations of children's social status to their emotionality and regulation: A short-term longitudinal study. *Merrill-Palmer Quarterly, 45,* 468–492.

Mauro, C. F., & Harris, Y. R. (2000). The influence of maternal child-rearing attitudes and teaching behaviors on preschoolers' delay of gratification. *Journal of Genetic Psychology, 161,* 293–317.

Mischel, W., Shoda, Y., & Peake, P. K. (1988). The nature of adolescent competencies predicted by preschool delay of gratification. *Journal of Personality and Social Psychology, 54,* 687–696.

Mulkey, L. M., Crain, R. L., & Harrington, A. J. C. (1992). One-parent households and achievement: Economic and behavioral explanations of a small effect. *Sociology of Education, 65,* 48–65.

Muraven, M., Tice, D. M., & Baumeister, R. F. (1998). Self-control as limited resource: Regulatory depletion patterns. *Journal of Personality and Social Psychology, 74,* 774–789.

Neitzel, C., & Stright, A. D. (2003). Mothers' scaffolding of children's problem solving: Establishing a foundation of academic self-regulatory competence. *Journal of Family Psychology, 17,* 147–159.

Otobe, T., & Makino, J. (2004). Impulsive choice in inbred strains of mice. *Behavioural Processes, 67,* 19–26.

Powers, W. T. (1973). *Behavior: the control of perception.* Chicago: Aldine.

Puhl, R., & Brownell, K. (2001). Bias, discrimination, and obesity. *Obesity Research, 9,* 788–805.

Rosenthal, B. S., & Marx, R. D. (1981). Determinants of initial relapse episodes among dieters. *Obesity/Bariatric Medicine, 10,* 94–97.

Rusbult, C. E. (1980). Commitment and satisfaction in romantic associations: A test of the investment model. *Journal of Experimental Social Psychology, 16* 172–186.

Rusbult, C. E., Verette, J., Whitney, G. A., Slovik, L. F., & Lipkus, I. (1991). Accommodation processes in close relationships: Theory and preliminary empirical evidence. *Journal of Personality and Social Psychology, 60,* 53–78.

Schmeichel, B. J. & Baumeister, R. F. (2004) Self-regulatory strength. In R. F. Baumeister & K. D. Vohs (Eds.), *Handbook of self-regulation: Research, theory, and applications* (pp. 84–98). New York: Guilford Press.

Sheppard, V. J., Nelson, E. S., & Andreoli-Mathie, V. (1995). Dating relationships and infidelity: Attitudes and behaviors. *Journal of Sex and Marital Therapy, 21,* 202–212.

Sicoly, F., & Ross, M. (1977). Facilitation of ego-biased attributions by means of self-serving observer feedback. *Journal of Personality and Social Psychology, 35,* 734–741.

Steinberg, L., Lamborn, S. D., Darling, N., Mounts, N. S., & Dornbusch, S. M. (1994). Over-time changes in adjustment and competence among adolescents from authoritative, authoritarian, indulgent, and neglectful families. *Child Development, 65,* 754–770.

Stillman, T. F., Tice, D. M., & Baumeister, R. F., (2006). *The psychological presence of family improves self-control.* Manuscript in preparation, Florida State University.

Tangney, J. P., Baumeister, R. F., & Boone, A. L. (2004). High self-control predicts good adjustment, less pathology, better grades, and interpersonal success. *Journal of Personality, 72,* 271–322.

Tice, D. M., Bratslavsky, E., & Baumeister, T. F (2001). Emotional distress regulation takes precedence over impulse control: If you feel bad, do it! *Journal of Personality and Social Psychology, 30,* 53–67.

Turrisi, R., Wiersma, K., & Hughes, K. (2000). Binge drinking-related consequences in college students: The role of drinking beliefs and parent–teen communications. *Psychology of Addictive Behaviors, 14*, 342–355.

Vohs, K. D., & Baumeister, R. F. (2004). Understanding self-regulation. In R. F. Baumeister & K. D. Vohs (Eds.), *Handbook of self-regulation: Research, theory, and applications* (pp. 1–9). New York: Guilford Press.

Vohs, K. D., & Baumeister, R. F. (2005). *Romantic relationship health is determined by partners' self-control.* Manuscript in preparation, University of British Columbia.

Vohs, K. D., Baumeister, R. F., & Ciarocco, N. J. (2005). Self-regulation and self-presentation: Regulatory resource depletion impairs impression management and effortful self-presentation. *Journal of Personality and Social Psychology, 88*, 632–657.

Vohs, K. D., Baumeister, R. F., & Finkenauer, C. (2006). *Enough for the both of us: Dyadic level of self-control predicts relationship success.* Manuscript in preparation, University of British Columbia.

Wegener, D. T., & Petty, R. E. (1994). Mood management across affective states: The hedonic contingency hypothesis. *Journal of Personality and Social Psychology, 66*, 1034–1048.

Whisman, M. A., Dixon, A. E., & Johnson, B. (1997). Therapists' perspectives of couple problems and treatment issues in couple therapy. *Journal of Family Psychology, 11*, 361–366.

Wiederman, M. W. (2004). Self-control and sexual behavior. In R. F. Baumeister & K. D. Vohs (Eds.), *Handbook of self-regulation: Research, theory, and applications*. New York: Guilford Press.

Yovetich, N. A., & Rusbult, C. E. (1994). Accommodative behavior in close relationships: Exploring transformation of motivation. *Journal of Experimental Social Psychology, 30*, 138–164.

Part III

Evolutionary Perspectives

8

Immediate-Return Societies: What Can They Tell Us About the Self and Social Relationships in Our Society?

LEONARD L. MARTIN and STEVEN SHIRK

When researchers study their phenomena within a narrow range of participants (e.g., similar age, same culture), they cannot be sure if their results generalize to anyone outside of that range. This means they cannot be sure if their findings reflect context-free principles of behavior, or descriptive regularities bound to given local and historical contexts. To address this ambiguity, some social psychologists have begun to explore their findings using a wider range of samples. For example, they have compared Eastern and Western cultures (Triandis & Gelfand, 1998) or subgroups within a given culture, such as Americans of African, Asian, and European descent (Sinclair, Hardin, & Lowery, 2006).

Although important insights can be gained from such research, we believe that this research is, of all things, culturally limited. It compares groups that, although different along some dimensions, are very similar along other dimensions. For example, despite their well-documented differences, individuals in Japan and the United States live in highly technological countries, are relatively sedentary (in the sense of being non-nomadic), and are subject to the pressures of living in relatively dense populations. These are important commonalities that could lead to similarities in a number of psychological phenomena including the self and interpersonal relationships. To the extent that common cultural influences contribute to behavioral similarities, comparisons among cultures that are dominant in the world today may fail to reveal important cultural influences even though these influences are present.

To be especially informative, comparisons would have to be among cultures that share as few features as possible. In this chapter, we consider the conclusions drawn in social psychology research on the self and interpersonal relationships— but we consider them in the context of an extreme cultural comparison.

Specifically, we ask how well these conclusions hold up in certain hunter-gatherer societies.

The societies we focus on have been referred to in the anthropological literature as foraging societies, band-level societies, simple societies, egalitarian societies, or immediate-return societies. In this chapter, we use the term immediate-return societies (Woodburn, 1979, 1988) because we feel that this term captures key features of these societies, such as heightened immediacy and responsivity. For example, in immediate-return societies, individuals tend to receive feedback regarding their efforts more quickly than they do in most other societies, which are termed delayed-return societies (Barnard & Woodburn, 1988; Meillassoux, 1973).

Immediate-return societies represent an extreme minority in the world today. Although they are scattered across the world (e.g., Africa, India, South America, Asia), their combined population can be counted only in the tens of thousands (Stanford, 2001). Despite their small numbers, these societies are important to us in at least two ways. First, they are the best approximation of what life was like for our evolutionary ancestors (Marlowe, 2002). Although we cannot be sure what life was like in the distant past, we do know that it was very different from life in the modern world. There were no cities, no agriculture, and no high technology. As Marlowe (2002) put it "Even if foragers are not living fossils, surely they are the best living models of what life was like prior to agriculture" (p. 249). So, by comparing practices in our current societies with those in immediate-return societies, we can get information about ways in which our current societies may be exerting pressures on us that are dramatically different from those with which our selves and interpersonal relationships initially evolved to cope.

A second reason to consider social psychology's findings in the context of immediate-return societies is that these societies allow for the most dramatic comparisons. Immediate-return societies differ in more ways from all other existing societies than any of the other existing societies differ from one another (Burch, 1994; Testart, 1982; Woodburn, 1988). So, comparing the conclusions of social psychology research with the behaviors observed in immediate-return societies may reveal important differences in human behavior that might otherwise go unnoticed.

We begin by describing the features of immediate-return societies and comparing them to the features of delayed-return societies. Then, we describe some central findings in research on the self and relationships. After that, we discuss ways in which life in immediate-return societies suggests qualifications on those findings. Finally, we speculate on some ways in which consideration of immediate-return societies can help us function better in modern societies.

IMMEDIATE-RETURN SOCIETIES: LIVING PLACE-TO-PLACE, MOMENT-TO-MOMENT, AND PERSON-TO-PERSON

Although all immediate-return societies subsist by hunting and gathering, not all hunting and gathering societies have immediate-return cultures. By formal definition, hunter-gatherers are those who obtain less than 5% of their subsistence from farming and/or herding (Murdock, 1981). Immediate-return hunter-gatherers are those who engage in the lowest amounts of farming and/or herding (e.g., 0%) and who engage in no significant storage.

What is life like in an immediate-return society? The answer was captured succinctly by Turnbull (1962) in his depiction of the Mbuti, an immediate-return group in Africa. He observed that the Mbuti

> were more than curiosities to be filmed, and their music was more than a quaint sound to be put on records. They were a people who had found in the forest something that made their life more than just worth living, something that made it, with all its hardships and problems and tragedies, a wonderful thing full of joy and happiness and free of care. (pp. 25–26)

Similar depictions have been offered by others (Bird-David, 1992; Ingold, 1980; Sahlins, 1972).

Of course, it is easy to idealize and romanticize the immediate-return lifestyle (for a critique, see Bird-David, 1992). Even when the depictions are accurate, however, they can still be difficult to believe (e.g., Greenberg, 1999; Kenrick, 1999). As Burch (1994) noted, "immediate-return or generalized hunter-gather societies are so unlike all others that . . . it is difficult even for anthropologists who have not personally experienced one to conceive how they can exist; it is almost impossible for nonanthropologists to do so" (p. 453). It is important to keep in mind, therefore, that the characteristics of immediate-return societies we describe in this chapter are not a matter of politically biased theorizing or wishful romantic thinking. They are based on the ethnographic experiences of many researchers.

FEATURES OF IMMEDIATE-RETURN SOCIETIES

Small, Nomadic, Ever-Changing Camps

Immediate-return hunter-gatherers live in small, temporary, autonomous camps spread out among the landscape as part of a larger population. There is frequent movement of individuals in and out while a camp remains at one site, and the camps themselves may move every few weeks (Woodburn, 1979). When it comes time for a camp to move, the members may either move together or they may move separately, and they may either establish a new site or they may move to a camp already established by others. There are no special criteria for acceptance in an existing camp. When members from one camp arrive at an established camp, they are allowed to share equally in the camp's resources while they live there. In immediate-return societies, it is very easy for individuals to leave and join different camps. This so-called fission and fusion is simply a part of their life.

Because the composition of camps changes so frequently, each camp is defined primarily in terms of its present membership. There may be some stability in the composition of a camp (e.g., a family may move with the wife's mother), but nothing formally holds the members together except each individual's involvement in the current round of activity. There are no formal long-term, binding commitments (Woodburn, 1979). In immediate-return societies, individuals generally choose which relationships to pursue or abandon. They do so through visits, meal sharing, cooperative work, and even through the positioning of the openings of their huts.

Intentional Avoidance of Formal Long-Term Binding Commitments

Some behaviors that individuals in immediate-return societies perform can make them seem irresponsible from the perspective of most other cultures. For example, these individuals sometimes enter into trade arrangements with nearby villagers. They may agree to accept pots and pans from the villagers and promise to return in a few weeks with meat or honey from the forest. Their promises, however, are more likely to be broken than kept (Woodburn, 1988).

Obviously, the failure to respect formal, binding social contracts is evaluated negatively in most societies. In immediate-return societies, however, this is not the case. By avoiding such commitments, individuals in immediate-return societies also avoid the claims, debts, and future orientation that they find extremely undesirable. With a binding contract, the first party holds power over the second party until the latter delivers on his or her end of the deal. In immediate-return societies, individuals are not allowed to assert dominion over one another. So, by avoiding formal long-term, binding commitments, they reduce the possibility of social domination.

Fortunately, failure to respect formal long-term binding commitments does not cause problems in immediate-return societies. This is because individuals in these societies have few possessions and can generally get what they want through free and direct access to the natural resources. Couple this self-sufficiency with the changing composition of the camps and we see that it makes little sense for individuals in immediate-return societies to enter into formal long-term binding relationships with specific others.

It is important to keep in mind that the commitments that are avoided by individuals in immediate-return societies are those that are formal, long-term, and binding. These individuals do not avoid all commitments. A man and a woman, for example, may very well stay together for years in a monogamous relationship. It is highly unlikely, though, that the couple would formalize their relationship with a ceremony or with a "'til death do us part" vow. Rather, they will simply start living together, and that is sufficient for them and the group to recognize that they are a pair. A divorce is recognized when the two no longer live together. There is also some pressure for married couples to follow the mother of the wife when individuals move from camp to camp, but this is not a formal, binding requirement. The more general point is that in immediate-return societies, individuals are not allowed to have dominion over one another and the avoidance of formal, long-term, binding commitments is one way to facilitate autonomous, egalitarian social relationships.

Relational Autonomy

Given the ad hoc nature of their social relationships, it is not surprising to find that individuals in immediate-return societies develop a unique view of the relation between self and other. It is a view that differs from that in both individualist and collectivist societies (Triandis & Gelfand, 1998). Like those in individualist societies, members of immediate-return societies put a premium on autonomy. Their autonomy, however, does not contrast the individual with the society as it does in individualist cultures. Rather, immediate-return autonomy grows out of repeated, mutually trusting social interactions. Each individual acts with the other person in mind, and can assume that the other person will do the same (Bird-David, 1992; Ingold, 1980). As a result, the autonomy expressed in immediate-return societies incorporates significant degrees of relatedness.

On the other hand, individuals in immediate-return societies, like those in collectivist societies, develop aspects of their selves in relation to their group. In immediate-return societies, however, the social group is ad hoc in nature and does not promote formal long-term binding social commitments. As a result, there is little chance for individuals in immediate-return societies to lose themselves in their duty to the group. In other words, the relatedness individuals obtain in immediate-return societies does not come at the expense of autonomy.

Sharing

In each camp, the number of individuals is likely to be quite small (e.g., 25), the individuals are likely to be related to one another, and they are likely to have face-to-face interactions with one another on a daily basis. These features make it possible for direct person-to-person sharing to be the main source of economic distribution. Although individuals are allowed to possess some personal items (e.g., clothing, tools, weapons, small quantities of food), there is great pressure for individuals to part with any objects for which they have no immediate need (e.g., large animals obtained from a hunt).

This high degree of sharing, however, does not mean that individuals in immediate-return societies are inherently more compassionate than other individuals. Their sharing is a by-product of their social arrangements. In fact, the best explanation of the sharing appears to be "tolerated scrounging" (Marlowe, 2004b). Because individuals in immediate-return societies are not allowed to attain dominion over one another, their society has no clear mechanisms in place to sanction slackers or refuse scroungers. Doing so would place one person above another. Moreover, because the membership of the camps changes so frequently, it would be extremely difficult for individuals to keep an accurate record of who contributed and who did not. The end result is a high degree of non-contingent sharing.

Highly and Intentionally Egalitarian

Because of the high degree of non-contingent sharing, differences in resources rarely occur in immediate-return societies. When they do occur, active steps are taken to eliminate them. For example, some individuals are routinely better hunters than others. This means that a large proportion of the meat in any given camp is brought in by a small proportion of the men (Lee, 1979). These successful hunters, however, are not allowed to translate their superior hunting skills into domination over others. The group accomplishes this through a variety of leveling mechanisms.

For example, individuals in immediate-return societies meet boasting and other forms of self-aggrandizement with scorn or ridicule—and the ridicule often comes from the children. A successful hunter may leave the kill on the trail, and on entering the camp, speak of the kill only in passing and in a deprecating manner (Lee, 1968). Alternatively, the hunter can walk into camp and let the bloody arrow speak for itself. Then, other members of the camp will go into the forest, retrieve the kill, and bring it back to camp. One sure way for individuals to lose esteem in an immediate-return society is to attempt to claim that esteem for themselves.

Reverse Dominance Hierarchy

The emphasis on autonomy and egalitarianism is so strong in immediate-return societies that it produces a society with no formal leaders. Individuals with certain skills (e.g., hunting, food collecting, communication) may have more influence on a group's decisions than other individuals, but these individuals have no coercive power. Moreover, the group seeks advice from different individuals in different situations. As a result, what passes for leadership in immediate-return societies is very transient and constrained.

Because members of immediate-return societies tend to believe that one individual should not dominate another, attempts on the part of one individual to become dominant are perceived by the group as a common problem. This leads the group to exert pressure on the would-be dominator to bring him or her back in line. Boehm (1993) has referred to this pressure as a reverse dominance hierarchy.

The group equalizes would-be dominators through criticism, ridicule, and simple disobedience. In more extreme cases, the group may desert or even assassinate the would-be leader. Woodburn (1979) tells of two Hadza who attempted to impress a visiting anthropologist by getting other members of the camp to clear a path to the river. The others in the camp merely laughed and walked away. It is difficult to be a leader if there is no one to lead.

Distributed Decision Making

If immediate-return societies do not have sanctioned leaders with coercive power, then how do they make decisions that affect the group as a whole? They appear to do so through a series of individual decisions. Woodburn (1979) described how he was

> particularly mystified by the fact that when I asked [members of a Hadza camp] about their plans, I was hardly ever given an answer that turned out to be correct. Little by little it became clear that the reason was that there was no procedure for reaching joint decisions about camp moves and statements made were no more than guesses. The Hadza are not in the habit of committing themselves to plans. Camps are very unstable units with constant movement of people in and out. Movement of a whole camp depends on a series of ad hoc individual decisions not on the decision of a leader or on consensus reached in discussion. (p. 253; see also Turnbull, 1962)

Cultural Instability

In a society that values equality as highly as immediate-return societies do, there can be no single, correct version of events or values. After all, if the values of one person are considered correct, then a different set of values held by another person must be incorrect. This dichotomy implies inequality, which is actively avoided in immediate-return societies.

The concrete result is that individuals in immediate-return societies have few verbalized rules of behavior, their rituals are highly variable (and may even be dispensed with altogether), and the individuals have no single, clear idea of a moral order (Brunton, 1989). Knowledge in immediate-return societies is idiosyncratic and gained by personal experience. It is not handed down by others. As one individual put it, "None of us are quite sure of anything except of who and where we are at that particular moment" (quoted in Brunton, 1989).

Benign View of Nature

Individuals in immediate-return societies view the relationship between humans and nature in much the same way that they view relationships between humans (Ingold, 1980; Turnbull, 1962). Both involve the sharing of resources and affection. Immediate-return hunter-gatherers think of the forest as a parent and think of themselves as children of the forest. Moreover, they believe that the forest, like any good parent, is morally bound to share food and other material resources. They also believe that the forest shares equally to everyone regardless of prior reciprocal obligations. Bird-David (1992) has described these beliefs as "the cosmic economy of sharing" (p. 122).

The benign view of nature held by individuals in immediate-return societies was expressed clearly in an observation by Turnbull (1962). He observed a Mbuti hunter singing to his young son. The words of the song, Turnbull noted, "like the words of most molimo songs, were few. They simply said, 'The forest is good' " (p. 83).

Present-Oriented

In immediate-return societies, individuals usually obtain a relatively immediate yield for their labor and use this yield with minimal delay (Barnard & Woodburn, 1988). They know within a few hours, for example, if their hunt has been successful. If it has been, then they can return to the camp to eat, and if it has not, then they have time to search for an alternative food source.

This relatively immediate feedback allows members of immediate-return societies to maintain an extreme focus on the present. In the words of Forde and Douglas (1956), individuals in immediate-return societies "are bound to the momentary present, scarcely ever striking out new lines for themselves, never forecasting the distant future, and seldom making provisions for the near future. Capable of anticipating its future needs only for a very brief span. Accumulation is difficult, long-term planning is impossible" (p. 332). In immediate-return societies, individuals seem to live by the motto "If it is not here and now what does it matter where (or when) it is?" (Turnbull, 1983, p. 122).

HOW MOST OF US LIVE NOW: THE DELAYED-RETURN LIFESTYLE

A fairly accurate description of the general features of most societies in the world today can be produced simply by listing features that are the opposite of those we described for immediate-return societies. This is because most societies today are delayed-return societies (Birdsell, 1973; Burch, 1994; Testart, 1982; Woodburn, 1988). Recall that in immediate-return societies, individuals receive relatively immediate feedback regarding their efforts. In delayed-return societies, on the other hand, there is often a delay between the effort individuals exert and the feedback they receive regarding its outcome. As a result, individuals may experience long stretches of uncertainty between their efforts and their payoff, and they may find at the end of this time that their efforts did not pay off. By that time, it may be too late for them to switch to an alternate strategy. This leads individuals in delayed-return societies to focus more on the future and past than individuals in immediate-return societies (Meillassoux, 1973; Turnbull, 1962; Woodburn, 1988).

How do individuals in delayed-return societies cope with the uncertainties and delays presented to them by their culture? They have developed mechanisms designed to give them confidence that their efforts will pay off. These include such things as formal long-term binding commitments, and adherence to ideologies that justify their efforts (e.g., work ethic, just world beliefs). The former is a social mechanism that demands the cooperation of specific others. Unless both individuals in a social commitment hold up their end of the deal, there is likely to be no payoff to the efforts of one or both parties. Moreover, the motivation to uphold one's end of a deal is strengthened in delayed-return societies by the societal sanctioning of a power hierarchy. Individuals in delayed-return societies have explicit laws and give certain members of the society (e.g., police) the power to enforce those laws.

One result of this more rigid social structure is that individuals in delayed-return societies experience less fluidity in their social relationships. Being party to a formal long-term binding commitment reduces an individual's autonomy, gives one person power over another, and makes it difficult for the individuals involved to fission and fusion. The individuals are bound to one another until their commitments have been fulfilled. Significant movement between groups is also difficult in delayed-return societies because the populations are larger and more sedentary. The members of these societies also tend to be bound to given locations and resources (e.g., farms, factories, universities).

The social rules developed in delayed-return societies make it possible for individuals in these societies to lay claim to personal property even if they have much more than others. In fact, some delayed-return ideologies (e.g., just world, work ethic, capitalism) allow individuals to see the unequal distribution of resources as appropriate and perhaps even desirable. After all, it can be taken as evidence that the rules work. Individuals who do the right thing get more rewards then individuals who do the wrong thing.

Because some individuals in delayed-return societies have more power and resources than others, status and prestige become resources in themselves. They facilitate access to other resources. Competition is also valued. Gender equality, on the other hand, is decreased relative to immediate-return societies. This is because in delayed-return economies, there is increased competition and an increased need to protect resources. This places a premium on the larger sex (i.e., males). Interpersonal equality is also weakened by an increase in preferential allocation of resources to those loyal to the leader. The maintenance of the power hierarchy is seen as crucial to the maintenance of the society as a whole. Without a sanctioned power hierarchy and formal long-term binding commitments, delayed-return societies would not function. The more general effect of living in a delayed-return society is that individuals may come to see the world as generally hostile and competitive.

The hierarchical social arrangement and larger group size associated with delayed-return societies makes direct face-to-face social control difficult, if not impossible. In addition, the members of these societies do not live primarily among those to whom they are related. Together, these features make it difficult for the members of delayed-return societies to arrive at a consensus for decision making. When factions develop within the larger society, they cannot fission into more harmonious subgroups. The factions are compelled to cope with one another and often develop more polarized ingroup–outgroup attitudes. Because the larger society is composed of subgroups with different attitudes and values, the society as a whole may find it difficult to keep would-be dominators in line (i.e., reverse dominance hierarchy). The different members of a delayed-return society may not even agree on who needs to be brought back into line.

Delayed-return societies also differ from immediate-return societies in the nature of their child-rearing practices. Barry, Child, and Bacon (1959; Zern, 1983) compared hunting and fishing societies (i.e., immediate-return) with herding and farming societies (i.e., delayed-return). They noted that in hunting and fishing societies, each day's food comes from that day's catch. In addition, because of the relatively short delay between an individual's efforts and the feedback regarding the outcome of those efforts, individuals in hunting and fishing societies can meet with initial failure and still switch to an alternate plan to acquire resources. This means that deviations from the established routine are not necessarily feared. If the deviation is not successful, then the individuals can return to the original plan. As a result, the child-rearing in these societies places an emphasis on personal initiative and skill.

In herding and farming societies, on the other hand, established social rules prescribe the best known way to bring in the resources. Carelessness in the performance of one's established duties can be detrimental to the entire society, and given the delay in feedback, the society may have no time to develop an alternate strategy to obtain resources if they find that the initial plan did not work. For example, in a farming society, individuals must plow the fields, plant the seeds, water the fields, and monitor them for weeds and pests. They must also harvest the grain and store it safely. Each of these activities must be done in the right way at the right time. It will be months, though, before the farmers know if their efforts were successful. If they were not, then the consequences (e.g., hunger or starvation) are likely to be severe, widespread, and long-term. As a result, the child-rearing in these societies emphasizes obedience and rule following.

EMPIRICAL IMPLICATIONS OF THE CULTURAL DIFFERENCES

We know of no studies that directly compared individuals from immediate-return societies with those from delayed-return societies on any classic social psychology phenomena (e.g., dissonance, self-esteem, persuasion). Such direct cross-cultural comparisons would be very difficult to do given the small size and inaccessibility of immediate-return societies. On the other hand, such direct comparisons may not be necessary. Researchers can gain information by comparing individuals who differ in terms of the features that distinguish the two cultures from one another (e.g., time orientation, benign worldview). This strategy is similar to that adopted by a number of cross-cultural researchers. They can study people who differ along an individualism/collectivism dimension, for example, even if these people do not come from different cultures (Triandis & Gelfand, 1998).

What features distinguish a more immediate-return person from a more delayed-return one (Martin, 1999)? We will consider three: temporal orientation, egalitarianism, and the pursuit of long-term goals. The question is whether individuals who differ in terms of these features also differ in the extent to which they display some traditional social psychology effects. There is evidence that they do.

Self-Serving Bias

Social psychology research has suggested that individuals are highly motivated to think of themselves in positive terms (Campbell & Sedikides, 1999). For example, they often take credit for success and place the blame for failure outside of themselves (Anderson & Slusher, 1986). There is reason to believe, though, that self-serving processing is a culturally dependent phenomenon.

Recall that individuals in immediate-return societies are more likely than those in delayed return societies to maintain a present-focused temporal orientation. Boyd-Wilson, Walkey, and McClure (2002) found that individuals differing in their present focus also differed in their tendency to display a self-serving bias. Specifically, Boyd-Wilson et al. had participants complete the time competence scale (Shostrom, 1964), which includes items such as: it is important to me how I live in the here and now and I spend more time actually living. Then they asked participants to rate themselves and other people in terms of a series of trait adjectives (e.g., friendly, insecure). There is a tendency for individuals to rate themselves more favorably than others in terms of their possession of positive traits (Alicke, 1985). This is a self-serving bias. Boyd-Wilson et al. found this bias, but only among participants who were moderate in their present focus. Those who were either very high or very low in their present focus rated themselves equal to other people in terms of their possession of positive traits.

According to Boyd-Wilson, McClure and Walkey (2004), being present-focused is related to positive well-being and a lack of defensiveness. This is why the present-focused participants were less self-serving. The accuracy of participants very low in present focus, on the other hand, was assumed to be the result of depressive realism (Alloy & Abramson, 1988). Only participants with a moderate focus on the present were inaccurate and unrealistic. In other words, only participants with a moderate focus on the present showed a self-serving bias. The main point of these findings, for present purposes, is that the extent to which participants displayed a self-serving bias, a well-established social psychology phenomenon, was shown to be a function of at least one of the features that distinguish immediate-return societies from delayed-return societies.

Blaming the Victim

Social psychology research has revealed that individuals often display a number of biases when they assign causes to the behavior of other people. For example, individuals may assign more responsibility to other people for the unfortunate events they experience than for the fortunate events they experience—even if they are in no way responsible for the events (Lerner & Simmons, 1966). There is reason to believe, though, that blaming the victim is a culturally bound phenomenon.

Recall that individuals in immediate-return societies are more likely than those in delayed-return societies to endorse an egalitarian social structure. They are also more likely to pursue short-range goals in non-binding relationships. Individual differences along these two dimensions have been shown to moderate the tendency to blame innocent victims. Lambert and Raichle (2000), for example, had participants complete a measure of social dominance orientation and then read a scenario depicting a date rape. Participants were asked how much blame they assigned to the female victim and how much to the male perpetrator. Lambert and Raichle found that the higher a participant's social dominance orientation, the more he or she blamed the female and exonerated the male. In other words, blaming an innocent victim was higher among participants who displayed features common to delayed-return societies (i.e., desire to maintain social hierarchies) than among participants who displayed features common to immediate-return societies (e.g., desire for egalitarian social relations).

According to Hafer (2000), the belief that the world is just is especially important to individuals who are committed to the pursuit of long-term goals. After all, if the world is not just, these people would have no confidence that their long-term efforts would pay off. Because of the centrality of this belief to their continued goal pursuit, these committed individuals are highly motivated to maintain their belief in a just world. The suffering of innocent people, however, challenges that belief, so individuals committed to the pursuit of long-term goals may be especially likely to blame innocent victims for their unpleasant fates. Assigning blame to innocent victims allows these individuals to restore their belief in a just world (i.e., the person deserved his or her fate) and have greater confidence that their long-range efforts will pay off.

To test this hypothesis, Hafer asked participants to describe their long-term plans or to describe the university courses they were currently taking, then she had the participants watch a videotape in which a female student described how she had contracted a sexually transmitted disease. Some participants heard that the student had contracted the disease by accident (broken condom), whereas others heard that the student contracted the disease through her own negligence (chose not to use a condom). Consistent with the hypothesis that the existence of innocent victims is threatening to individuals committed to long-term goals, Hafer found that participants who had been asked to write about their long-terms goals were more likely than those asked to write about their classes to blame, derogate, and dissociate themselves from the innocent victim. There were no differences between groups in the rating of the non-innocent victim. In other words, participants displaying features common to delayed-return societies (commitment to long-term goals) were more likely to blame an innocent victim.

In sum, we have seen that several features that distinguish immediate-return societies from delayed-return societies can moderate the occurrence of several well-established social psychology phenomena. This moderation may be revealed, however, only by studying cultures that are extremely different from one another, or at least by studying individuals who differ in the ways that these cultures differ from one another.

THEORETICAL IMPLICATIONS OF THE CULTURAL DIFFERENCES

In this section, we consider some ways in which the differences between immediate-return societies and delayed-return societies might have implications for additional topics. These are topics central to interpersonal behavior for which research relevant to the immediate/delayed distinction has not yet been investigated. Namely, we speculate on some ways in which the differences associated with immediate-return and delayed-return societies might moderate effects related to attachment, interdependence, social exclusion and self-esteem, and self-evaluation maintenance.

Attachment

A number of theorists (e.g., Hazan & Shaver, 1994) have suggested that the social interactions individuals have throughout their life are shaped in large part by the emotional attachment they form with their primary caregiver during infancy. If the primary caregiver provides consistent nurturance and security to the infant, then the infant develops a strong, secure emotional attachment with the caretaker. This attachment is especially important as the infant begins to explore his or her environment. In the course of this exploration, the infant may encounter objects that arouse feelings such as fear and uncertainty. These feelings, in turn, may curtail the infant's exploration and motivate him or her to seek out the caregiver. If the infant experiences nurturance and security on returning to the caregiver, then the infant can gain the strength it needs to return to reduce the fear and uncertainty and resume the exploration. A secure attachment in infancy may also make it easier for individuals to establish satisfying relationships later in their life (Hazan & Shaver, 1994).

If the primary caregiver does not provide nurturance and security, or provides them inconsistently, then infants will fail to develop a secure attachment. When this happens, infants may be reluctant to explore their environment and later in life they may have difficulty establishing satisfying relationships. Individuals with insecure attachments may also experience depression, moodiness, tension, and emotional instability.

What can life in immediate-return societies tell us about this view of social development? Although it does not argue against this view, it does suggest that the attachment process might unfold slightly differently in immediate-return societies. Consider first of all that, compared to infants in delayed-return societies, those in immediate-return societies spend proportionately less time with their mother (Marlowe, 2005). They spend relatively more time with grandmothers, aunts, uncles, siblings, and even non-related individuals. Thus the early attachments formed in immediate-return societies may be less focused on one particular person. This raises the possibility that individuals in immediate-return societies may feel more comfortable than those in delayed-return societies in relying on the social group during times of stress.

Consider also that, compared to children in delayed-return societies, those in immediate-return societies spend more time interacting with their peers and do so at an earlier age (Marlowe, 2005). After age 3 or 4, the children are left in a safe place near the camp to be watched over by one adult while the other adults go out hunting and gathering. As a result, the children learn at a very early stage that they can derive nurturance and security from others their own age. This learning is likely to ease the transfer of attachment from the primary caregiver to the peers. This transfer might also happen sooner in immediate-return societies than in delayed-return societies.

Finally, recall that the attachment with the caregiver is important primarily when the infant confronts a stressful situation. While there are certainly dangers individuals in immediate-return societies must face, individuals in these societies also have a more benign view of nature. They learn from infancy that they can trust one another and that "the forest is good" (Turnbull, 1962). They are also socialized for autonomy. This means that infants in immediate-return societies may experience less frequent need to resort to the safety of their primary attachment figure.

Together, these differences suggest that it is possible for infants to develop secure attachments to multiple caregivers, live in an environment in which fear-based reliance on the caregiver is relatively rare, and still develop satisfactory social relationships throughout their life. Thus current social psychology theorizing may be placing too much emphasis on attachment to a single primary caregiver, and may be overestimating the difficulty involved in the transfer of attachment from the primary caregiver to others.

Social Exclusion and Self-Esteem

The early bond individuals establish with their caregivers is not the only affective bond in which social relationships can play an important role. Several theorists have suggested that humans have a need for belongingness (Baumeister & Leary, 1995; Ryan & Deci, 2000). This need is satisfied when individual have social interactions that are pleasant, frequent, and stable, and that demonstrate concern for one another's welfare. Not surprisingly, satisfaction of this need is related to psychological well-being, including self-esteem and a meaningful existence (Williams, 2001).

The relation between social interactions and self-esteem was detailed by Leary, Tambor, and Terdal (1995). They proposed that individuals possess a built-in ability and motivation to monitor the extent to which other individuals appear to value and accept them. If individuals detect signs that they are being excluded by others who are important to them, then they experience negative feelings and they may alter their behavior in ways that put them back in the good graces of the others.

Leary also proposed that the negative feelings that accompany social exclusion are what we refer to as self-esteem. Specifically, the negative feelings that are elicited when individuals detect signs of exclusion constitute a large part of what we call low self-esteem, whereas the positive feelings that are elicited when individuals do not detect signs of exclusion (or do detect signs of inclusion) constitute a large part of what we call high self-esteem.

What can life in immediate-return societies tell us about this view of social relationships, affect, and self-esteem? Consider first of all that individuals in immediate-return societies experience a high degree of autonomy. They are socialized for self-initiative, can survive in the forest on their own, and are not bound by formal long-term binding commitments. They can also fission to other groups if they are receiving signs of exclusion from their current group, and immediate-return societies practice automatic social acceptance. Thus there is little chance that individuals in immediate-return societies would ever face complete social exclusion or suffer severe consequences if they were to be excluded.

There is also a great deal of cultural instability in immediate-return societies (Brunton, 1989). Thus there are few formal, verbalizable rules that individuals in immediate-return societies could violate that would lead them to be excluded. The end result is that social exclusion in the strong sense of that term is unlikely in immediate-return societies. It is unlikely, therefore, that the evolutionary mechanism that gave rise to the relationship between social exclusion and self-esteem was differential survival in the literal sense (Leary et al., 1995).

It seems more likely that individuals who reacted empathically to the plight of others were likely to be favored by other members of the group. These favored individuals, in turn, would attain a reproductive advantage over group members who were not moved by the plight of the other members of the group (e.g., sexual selection). A second possibility is that social groups composed primarily of individuals who responded with personal feelings to the plight of others out-reproduced groups composed of less empathic individuals (Sloan-Wilson & Sober, 1994). In other words, the evolutionary mechanism that gave rise to the social exclusion/self-esteem link may have been more social than individual.

Self-Esteem Maintenance

Another role that social interactions can play in the development of an individual's self-esteem was articulated by Tesser (1988). He proposed that in evaluating their self-worth, individuals take into consideration at least three pieces of information. They consider their own performance relative to others, the relevance of the other person as a standard of comparison (referred to as closeness), and the relevance of the performance domain for the individual's self-esteem. For example, individuals evaluate themselves favorably if they outperform a close other on a task that is relevant to their own self-esteem. They evaluate themselves unfavorably if they perform worse than a close other on a task that is relevant to their own self-esteem. Individuals can also develop a favorable self-evaluation if they are outperformed by a close other on a task that is not relevant to their own self-esteem. In this case, the favorable evaluation comes vicariously, from what Cialdini (1976) referred to as basking in reflected glory (e.g., my son, the doctor).

Because each of the components of the self-evaluation judgment has a subjective component, individuals have some ability to change the experience of these components. For example, they can increase the psychological distance between themselves and close others if these others have outperformed them on a task that is relevant to assessing their self-esteem (Pleban & Tesser, 1981) and they can decrease the psychological relevance of a task on which they have been out-performed by a close other (Tesser & Campbell, 1980). Individuals may even attempt to lower (i.e., sabotage) the performance of a close other if the other person outperforms them on a self-relevant task (Tesser & Smith, 1980).

What can life in immediate-return societies tell us about this view of self-esteem and interpersonal relationships? The first thing to consider is that immediate-return societies are highly egalitarian. Their sharing is relatively non-contingent and individuals are not allowed to profit personally from any superior skills they might possess. Thus self-esteem per se is not a commodity and there are no social status hierarchies. Consider also that most members of the camp are relatively competent in the sense of being able to satisfy most of their needs through unrestricted access to the natural resources. Although some hunters are generally better than others, hunting has a low probability of success even for the better hunters, so it is difficult to base one's self-esteem on such an unstable performance domain. It is also difficult for individuals in immediate-return societies to associate their self-worth with their behavior because of the leveling mechanisms. The bottom line, therefore, is that in immediate-return societies one's performance relative to others may not be associated strongly with one's self-evaluation.

What about the evidence that individuals psychologically alter the factors that influence their self-evaluation (i.e., closeness, relevance, performance)? Observation of life in immediate-return societies raises the possibility that individuals may not be doing this in order to maintain a favorable self-evaluation. For example, when individuals distance themselves from a close other who has outperformed them on a self-relevant task, they may be engaging in a form of fission. Individuals in immediate-return societies do not tolerate domination or self-aggrandizement. A close other who outperforms a person may be primed for both, so being around such a person may prompt thoughts of fission; that is, thoughts of increasing the distance between one's self and a potential self-aggrandizer. This distancing is less likely to happen if the superior performance of the other benefits the group, as with a successful hunt or reflected glory.

In sum, observation of life in immediate-return societies raises the possibility that behaviors that have been interpreted as being in the service of self-esteem may actually be in the service of maintaining equality and harmony within the group. From this perspective, any positive self-evaluation that accompanies the behaviors is a by-product, not the goal. When individuals engage in behavior that helps the group, they feel good. This interpretation fits with the assumption that groups whose members maintained equality and harmony out-reproduced groups whose members were more selfishly oriented (Sloan-Wilson & Sober, 1994).

Interdependence

What factors other than early attachment and the need for belongingness bind individuals to social relationships? Why do individuals stay in some relationships but not others? Questions such as these have been addressed in the context of

Interdependence Theory (e.g., Thibaut & Kelley, 1959). This theory focuses on the rewards and costs individuals accrue in their interpersonal relationships. Rewards and punishments in the context of the theory are defined very broadly and range from concrete (e.g., money) to abstract (e.g., social status).

If the ratio of rewards to costs an individual is receiving in his or her current relationship is higher than the level individuals are used to getting in relationships, then the individual will generally be satisfied in the relationship. Being satisfied, however, does not necessarily mean that the individuals will stay. If individuals experience a level of satisfaction in their current relationship that is higher than the level they believe they could obtain in other relationships, then they will stay. Although the current relationship may not be very good, it affords a higher level of satisfaction than they believe they could obtain in other relationships. Alternatively, if individuals experience a level of satisfaction in their current relationship that is below what they believe they could obtain in other relationships, then they will leave, even if their current level of satisfaction is high.

A second variable that determines commitment to a relationship is the level of an individual's investment (Rusbult & Buunk, 1993). Investments are resources individuals have provided to a relationship that they cannot retrieve if they were to leave the relationship. These include such things as time, self-disclosure, mutual friends, or shared material possessions. The higher the investment, the more likely it is that individuals will stay in a relationship even if they find it unsatisfactory.

What can life in immediate-return societies tell us about this view of relationship interdependence? Obviously, individuals in immediate-return societies exchange rewards and costs and make decisions about staying or leaving relationships. In fact, they do so much more frequently than individuals in delayed-return societies. They engage in considerable face-to-face sharing and interaction on a daily basis. They also make almost daily decisions about whether to leave or stay in a certain camp. Thus they are likely to be quite practiced in considering rewards, costs, satisfaction, and alternatives.

In fact, in immediate-return societies, individuals can come and go with ease and without paying any economic penalty. Their relationships in immediate-return societies are generally voluntary and freely terminable. Thus relationships in immediate-return societies may be influenced more by satisfaction than by investments. Individuals in delayed-return societies, on the other hand, enter into long-term, formal, binding commitments (e.g., legal marriage) and often receive delayed feedback regarding the outcomes of their efforts. As a result, they may experience more pressure to stay in relationships in which they are not satisfied.

Communal and Exchange Relationships

Clark and Mills (1979) distinguished between communal relationships and exchange relationships. In the former, individuals provide benefits to address the needs of their relationship partner. They also provide these benefits in a relatively non-contingent manner and they show little concern about the evenness or balance of each transaction. In exchange relationships, on the other hand, individuals provide benefits as a way to ensure future benefits or as a way to return past benefits received. The individuals in these relationships keep careful track of their costs and benefits and are aware that the receipt of a benefit incurs an obligation to return a comparable benefit.

It should be obvious by now that immediate-return hunter-gatherers shun exchange relationships. Such relationships imply dominance, inequality, and formal, binding commitments. Moreover, the sharing in immediate-return societies is largely non-contingent and the individuals do seem concerned about the needs of their fellow group members. As we noted earlier, though, the abundant, non-contingent sharing in immediate-return societies is a by-product of their culture; thus it tells us little about the motivation of the specific individuals. In fact, individuals in immediate-return societies often grumble about the amount of sharing required of them, and they often attempt to by-pass the mandatory sharing (e.g., sneak food into camp at night). As Marlowe (2004a) noted with regard to the Hadza, individuals in immediate-return societies have "donor-fatigue," and when they have a chance to escape from forced sharing, they do. So, while the societal norms in immediate-return societies clearly dictate that relationships should be communal, the individuals in those societies display some ambivalence over this norm.

These observations suggest that researchers exploring costs and benefits in relationships need to consider not only the overt behavior but also the subjective experience of the participants. An individual could engage in non-contingent sharing, yet not be really oriented communally toward the relationship. Similarly, two people could be led by the situation to participate in an exchange relationship, yet one may enjoy the arrangement, whereas another may feel alienated by it.

More generally, it appears that interpersonal relationships in any society reflect the dynamic interplay between self-interest and societal norms. In immediate-return societies, the dynamics have settled in a range closer to communal relationships, whereas in delayed-return societies the dynamics have settled closer to exchange relationships. In fact, delayed-return societies are defined, in part, by their emphasis on formal, binding commitments (i.e., exchange relationships). Moreover, in delayed-return societies, individuals have developed ideologies (e.g., social dominance orientation, Protestant work ethic, just world beliefs) that not only permit selfishness and inequality, but that also turn them into desirable traits. So, if our species really did evolve in the context of social relationships approximating those in current immediate-return societies, then our current delayed-return societies may be requiring us to behave in ways that are discordant with our natural tendencies—or that at least overemphasize our individualistic side of the self–other dynamic.

SUMMARY AND IMPLICATIONS

We have suggested that social psychology research might reveal new insights into basic social psychology processes if it were to move beyond its current focus on one or a few cultures. Even most cross-cultural research, we have argued, is limited to the extent that it compares cultures that have a great deal in common (i.e., all delayed-return cultures). The most dramatic comparison, hence the most information, may be gained by comparing findings obtained in the prominent societies in the world today with findings obtained in immediate-return societies.

The main hurdle to adopting this suggestion is that it is very difficult to conduct research on immediate-return societies. These societies are rare, small, and generally difficult to access. An alternative strategy, therefore, is to identify the central dimensions on which immediate-return societies and delayed-return societies differ and see if individuals within a given culture also differ on those dimensions. This is similar to the strategy taken in research on individualism and collectivism. Researchers have developed scales to measure the extent to which individuals express individualistic as opposed to collectivistic values (Triandis & Gelfand, 1998), then they use these individual differences to predict differences in other psychological variables (e.g., cooperation, sensitivity to context).

A similar strategy could be used to see if the differences associated with immediate-return societies and delayed-return societies are psychologically meaningful. For example, researchers could develop measures of the extent to which individuals support equality as opposed to status hierarchies, are focused on the present as opposed to the future, or engage in formal long-term binding commitments. If individuals differ along these dimensions, then they may also differ in their display of the various social psychology phenomena we have addressed in this chapter (self-esteem, relationship investment, attachment). Research using this strategy may help us understand the extent to which social psychology research is revealing aspects of basic human nature as opposed to by-products of our current delayed-return culture.

REFERENCES

Alicke, M. D. (1985). Global self-evaluation as determined by the desirability and controllability of trait adjectives. *Journal of Personality and Social Psychology, 49*, 1621–1630.

Alloy, L. B., & Abramson, L. Y. (1988). Depressive realism: Four theoretical perspectives. In L. B. Alloy (Ed.), *Cognitive processes in depression* (pp. 223–265). New York: Guilford Press.

Anderson, C. A., & Slusher, M. P. (1986). Relocating motivational effects: A synthesis of cognitive and motivational effects on attributions for success and failure. *Social Cognition, 4*, 270–292.

Barnard, A., & Woodburn, J. (1988). Property, power and ideology in hunter-gatherer societies: An introduction. In T. Ingold, D. Riches, & J. Woodburn (Eds.), *Hunters and gatherers 2: Property, power, and ideology* (pp. 4–31). Oxford: Berg Publishers.

Barry, H., III, Child, I. L., & Bacon, M. K. (1959). Relation of child training to subsistence economy. *American Anthropologist, 61*, 51–63.

Baumeister, R. F., & Leary, M. R. (1995). The need to belong: Desire for interpersonal attachments as a fundamental human motivation. *Psychological Bulletin, 117*, 497–529.

Bird-David, N. (1992). Beyond "The original affluent society": A culturalist reformulation. *Current Anthropology, 33*, 115–137.

Birdsell, J. B. (1973). A basic demographic unit. *Current Anthropology, 14,* 337–356.

Boehm, C. (1993). Egalitarian behavior and reverse dominance hierarchy. *Current Anthropology, 34,* 227–254.

Boyd-Wilson, B. M., McClure, J., & Walkey, F. H. (2004). Are well-being and illusory perceptions linked? The answer may be yes, but . . . *Australian Journal of Psychology, 56,* 1–9.

Boyd-Wilson, B. M., Walkey, F. H., & McClure, J. (2002). Present and correct: We kid ourselves less when we live in the moment. *Personality and Individual Differences, 33,* 691–702.

Brunton, R. (1989). The cultural instability of egalitarian societies. *Man, 24,* 673–681.

Burch, E. S., Jr. (1994). The future of hunter-gatherer research. In E. S. Burch, Jr. & L. J. Ellanna (Eds.), *Key issues in hunter-gatherer research* (pp. 441–503). Oxford: Berg Publishers.

Campbell, W. K., & Sedikides, C. (1999). Self-threat magnifies the self-serving bias: A meta-analytic integration. *Review of General Psychology, 3,* 23–43.

Cialdini, R. B. (1976). Basking in reflected glory: Three (football) field studies. *Journal of Personality and Social Psychology, 34,* 366–375.

Clark, M., & Mills, J. S. (1979). Interpersonal attraction in exchange and communal relationships. *Journal of Personality and Social Psychology, 37,* 12–24.

Forde, D., & Douglas, M. (1956). Primitive economics. In H. L. Shapiro (Ed.), *Man, culture, and society* (pp. 330–344). New York: Oxford University Press.

Greenberg, J. (1999). On imagined cultures and real ones, and the evolution and operation of human goal striving. *Psychological Inquiry, 10,* 220–224.

Hafer, C. L. (2000). Investment in long-term goals and commitment to just means drive the need to believe in a just world. *Personality and Social Psychology Bulletin, 26,* 1059–1073.

Hazan, C., & Shaver, P. R. (1994). Attachment as an organizational framework for research on close relationships. *Psychological Inquiry, 5,* 1–22.

Ingold, T. (1980). *The appropriation of nature: Essays on human ecology and social relations.* Iowa City: University of Iowa Press.

Kenrick, D. (1999). Of hunter-gatherers, fundamental social motives, and person–situation interactions. *Psychological Inquiry, 10,* 226–229

Lambert, A. J., & Raichle, K. (2000). The role of political ideology in mediating judgments of blame in rape victims and their assailants: A test of the just world, personal responsibility, and legitimization hypotheses. *Personality and Social Psychology Bulletin, 26,* 853–863.

Leary, M. R., Tambor, E. S., & Terdal, S. K. (1995). Self-esteem as an interpersonal monitor: The sociometer hypothesis. *Journal of Personality and Social Psychology, 68,* 518–530.

Lee, R. B. (1968). What hunters do for a living, or, how to make out on scarce resources. In R. B. Lee & I. DeVore (Eds.), *Man the hunter* (pp. 30–48). Chicago: Aldine Publishing Company.

Lee, R. B. (1979). *The !Kung San: Men, women, and work in a foraging society.* Cambridge: Cambridge University Press.

Lerner, M., & Simmons, C. H. (1966). Observer's reaction to the "innocent victim": Compassion or rejection? *Journal of Personality and Social Psychology, 4,* 203–210.

Marlowe, F. (2002). Why the Hadza are still hunter-gatherers. In S. Kent (Ed.), *Ethnicity, hunter-gatherers, and the "other": Association or assimilation in Africa* (pp. 247–275). Washington, DC: Smithsonian Institution Press.

Marlowe, F. W. (2004a). Dictators and ultimatums in an egalitarian society of hunter-gatherers: The Hadza of Tanzania. In J. Henrich, R. Boyd, S. Bowles, H. Gintis, C. Camerer, & E. Fehr (Eds.), *Foundations of human sociality: Economic experiments and ethnographic evidence from fifteen small-scale societies* (pp. 168–193). Oxford: Oxford University Press.

Marlowe, F. W. (2004b). What explains Hadza food sharing? *Research in Economic Anthropology, 23,* 69–88.

Marlowe, F. W. (2005). Who tends Hadza children? In B. Hewlett and M. Lamb (Eds.), *Hunter-gatherer childhoods: Evolutionary, developmental and cultural perspectives* (pp. 177–190). New Brunswick: Transaction.

Martin, L. L. (1999). I-D compensation theory: Some implications of trying to satisfy immediate-return needs in a delayed-return culture. *Psychological Inquiry, 10,* 195–208.

Meillassoux, C. (1973). On the mode of production of the hunting band. In P. Alexandre (Ed.), *French perspectives in African studies* (pp. 187–203). Oxford: Oxford University Press for the International African Institute.

Murdock, G. P. (1981). *Atlas of world cultures.* Pittsburgh, PA: University of Pittsburgh Press.

Pleban, R., & Tesser, A. (1981). The effects of relevance and quality of another's performance on interpersonal closeness. *Social Psychology Quarterly, 44,* 278–285.

Rusbult, C. E., & Buunk, B. P. (1993). Commitment processes in close relationships: An interdependence analysis. *Journal of Social and Personal Relationships, 10,* 175–204.

Ryan, R. M., & Deci, E. L. (2000). Self-determination theory and the facilitation of intrinsic motivation, social development, and well-being. *American Psychologist, 55,* 68–78.

Sahlins, M. (1972). *Stone Age economics.* Chicago: Aldine-Atherton, Inc.

Shostrom, E. L. (1964). An inventory for the measurement of self-actualization. *Educational and Psychological Measurement, 2,* 207–218.

Sinclair, S., Hardin, C. D., & Lowery, B. S. (2006). Self-stereotyping in the context of multiple social identities. *Journal of Personality and Social Psychology, 90,* 529–542.

Sloan-Wilson, D., & Sober, E. (1994). Reintroducing group selection to the human behavioral sciences. *Behavioral and Brain Sciences, 17,* 585–654.

Stanford, C. B. (2001). *The hunting apes: Meat eating and the origins of human behavior.* Princeton, NJ: Princeton University Press.

Tesser, A. (1988). Toward a self-evaluation maintenance model of social behavior. In L. Berkowitz (Ed.), *Advances in experimental social psychology* (Vol. 21, pp. 181–227), New York: Academic Press.

Tesser, A., & Campbell, J. (1980). Self-definition: The impact of the relative performance and similarity of others. *Social Psychology Quarterly, 43,* 341–346.

Tesser, A., & Smith, J. (1980). Some effects of task relevance and friendship on helping: You don't always help the one you like. *Journal of Experimental Social Psychology, 16,* 582–590.

Testart, A. (1982). The significance of food storage among hunter-gatherers: Residence patterns, population densities, and social inequalities. *Current Anthropology, 23,* 523–537.

Thibaut, J. W., & Kelley, H. H. (1959). *The social psychology of groups.* Oxford: Wiley.

Triandis, H. C., & Gelfand, M. J. (1998). Converging measurement of horizontal and vertical individualism and collectivism. *Journal of Personality and Social Psychology, 74,* 118–128.

Turnbull, C. M. (1962). *The forest people.* New York: Simon & Schuster.

Turnbull, C. M. (1983). *The Mbuti pygmies: Change and adaptation*. New York: Holt, Rinehart, & Winston.

Williams, K. (2001). *Ostracism: The power of silence*. New York: Guilford Press.

Woodburn, J. C. (1979). Minimal politics: The political organization of the Hadza of North Tanzania. In W. A. Shack & P. S. Cohen (Eds.), *Politics in leadership: A comparative perspective* (pp. 244–266). Oxford: Clarendon Press.

Woodburn, J. (1988). African hunter-gatherer social organization: Is it best understood as a product of encapsulation? In T. Ingold, D. Riches, & J. Woodburn (Eds.), *Hunters and gatherers 1: History, evolution and social change*. Oxford: Berg Publishers.

Zern, D. S. (1983). The relationship of certain group-oriented and individualistically oriented child-rearing dimensions to cultural complexity in a cross-cultural sample. *Genetic Psychology Monographs, 108*, 3–20.

9

Evolutionary Accounts of Individual Differences in Adult Attachment Orientations

JEFFRY A. SIMPSON, LANE BECKES, and
YANNA J. WEISBERG

Attachment theory (Bowlby, 1969, 1973, 1980) is one of the most comprehensive theories of personality and social development in the history of psychology. Bowlby's keen observations and deep insights into the psychological and emotional ties that bind individuals together, combined with his expansive theoretical vision to merge core principles from different disciplines—ranging from ethology, to evolutionary biology, to psychiatry, to control systems theory, to cognitive psychology—was a remarkable intellectual feat.

Many social scientists are familiar with the basic principles of attachment theory and some of the many generative findings the theory has produced with respect to infants, children, adolescents, and adults. What many people do not fully appreciate, however, is that attachment theory is an evolutionary theory of personality and social development "from the cradle to the grave" (Belsky, 1999; Simpson, 1999). One of the primary goals of this chapter is to illustrate how and why attachment theory is so "evolutionary" at its core. To do so, we review how and why different models that seek to explain the development of distinct attachment "patterns" (in children) and "styles" or "orientations" (in adults) are grounded on principles borrowed from one of the broadest and most important evolutionary theories—life history theory (see Kaplan & Gangestad, 2005).

The chapter is divided into eight sections. In the first section, we review the basic tenets of attachment theory and describe the two attachment dimensions in adults: anxiety and avoidance. We also discuss what each dimension measures and the kinds of interpersonal functioning and relationship outcomes that each predicts. Following this, we discuss how disparate empirical findings can be understood from Mikulincer and Shaver's (2003) process model of attachment, which suggests that the primary proximate function of adult attachment orientations is to regulate, control, and mitigate negative affect in stressful situations.

In the second section, we describe life history theory and indicate how attachment theory fits with other major middle-level evolutionary theories. Most of our attention is devoted to showing how principles of attachment theory intersect with basic principles of life history, which has inspired several new theoretical models linking attachment patterns (in children) or orientations (in adults) to major developmental, social, and interpersonal outcomes across the lifespan. In the third section, we review some of these models, highlighting their core principles, assumptions, and claims in relation to one another. Most of our attention focuses on models advanced by Main (1981) and Cassidy and Berlin (1994), Belsky, Steinberg, and Draper (1991; and also Belsky, 1999), Chisholm (1993, 1996), Kirkpatrick (1998), and Hazan and Zeifman (1999).

In the fourth and fifth sections, we speculate about whether and how certain neurobiological systems may have been co-opted during evolutionary history to serve some of the evolutionary functions proposed by different attachment/life history models. In the sixth section, we discuss connections between stress, the attachment system in children and adults, and different developmental pathways and life-course trajectories. We propose that a deeper appreciation of certain biologically based systems could inform and advance our understanding of particular evolved functions that individual differences in adult attachment orientations may serve. In the seventh section, we speculate about how sociometer theory intersects with attachment and the neurobiological models described in earlier sections. We conclude by highlighting why attachment theory is such a broad, rich, and generative theory of personality and human development across the entire lifespan.

ATTACHMENT THEORY

Bowlby (1969, 1973, 1980) believed that early interactions with significant others instill attitudes and beliefs that then shape expectations of what relationships and relationship partners should be like in the future. These attitudes and beliefs, which are a core component of working models, ostensibly involve "if/then" propositions that specify the behaviors and responses expected from attachment figures in attachment-relevant situations (e.g., *if* I am upset, *then* I can rely on my partner for comfort and support). A vast body of research has highlighted the multiple ways in which working models influence information processing and interpersonal functioning within close relationships. Working models, for instance, affect whether and how individuals selectively attend to and perceive their partners, how they make important inferences and judgments about their partners' actions, how they think, feel, and behave in certain interpersonal contexts, and what they preferentially remember—or fail to remember—about their partners' past actions (see Rholes & Simpson, 2004).

Two orthogonal dimensions define individual differences in adult attachment (Brennan, Clark, & Shaver, 1998; Griffin & Bartholomew, 1994). The first dimension, labeled *avoidance*, reflects the degree to which people feel comfortable with closeness and emotional intimacy in relationships. Individuals who score higher on avoidance are less invested in their relationships and yearn to remain psychologically and emotionally independent of their partners (Hazan & Shaver, 1994). The second dimension, termed *anxiety*, taps the degree to which people worry and ruminate about being rejected or abandoned by their partners. Prototypically secure people score lower on both dimensions.

During the past 20 years, a considerable amount of research has identified fundamental correlates of each adult attachment dimension. For example, more securely attached adults (who score lower on both the anxiety and avoidance dimensions) hold more positive views of both themselves and close others, which permits them to maintain more optimistic and benevolent views of their relationships and partners (Hazan & Shaver, 1994). Indeed, one of the primary goals of securely attached individuals is to actively build greater closeness and intimacy with their romantic partners (Mikulincer, 1998). As a consequence, more securely attached adults tend to have happier, better functioning, and more stable romantic relationships than more insecure people do (see Feeney, 1999, for a review).

More anxiously attached adults (who score higher on the anxiety dimension and lower on avoidance) have negative self-views and guarded but hopeful views of close others. These mixed perceptions presumably lead highly anxious persons to doubt their worth as relationship partners, feel resentful of past attachment figures, worry about future relationship loss or abandonment, and remain vigilant to cues that current partners might be pulling away either psychologically or emotionally (Cassidy & Berlin, 1994). One of the main goals of highly anxious individuals is to achieve greater felt security with their romantic partners (Mikulincer, 1998), which often leads them to smother and sometimes scare away their partners. Not surprisingly, the romantic relationships of highly anxious people tend to be unsatisfying, not very well adjusted, and often tumultuous (Feeney, 1999).

Highly avoidant adults (who score higher on the avoidance dimension) have either positive self-views (in the case of dismissing avoidants) or negative self-views (in the case of fearful avoidants), along with more negative views of attachment figures (Bartholomew, 1990). One of the overarching goals of highly avoidant individuals is to maintain independence, control, and autonomy in their relationships (Mikulincer, 1998), which may partially explain why highly avoidant persons have less close and satisfying relationships that often terminate prematurely (Feeney, 1999).

Mikulincer and Shaver (2003) have developed a process model that describes the psychological pathways through which individuals who have different attachment orientations navigate. According to their model, different attachment orientations reflect different styles of managing and coping with stressful experiences. Grounded in attachment theory (Bowlby, 1969), the model claims that signs of possible threat activate the attachment system, which motivates most people to seek greater physical or psychological proximity to their attachment figures. Because more securely attached people are confident that their attachment figures will be available, attentive, and responsive to their needs, secure persons readily turn to their romantic partners to help alleviate and dissipate their distress. This problem-focused coping strategy often quells the attachment system, allowing more secure persons to resume other important life tasks.

The pathways are different for highly anxious and highly avoidant individuals. Highly anxious persons tend to be uncertain about whether they can count on their attachment figures to be available, attentive, and responsive in times of stress, a realization that amplifies their distress and insecurity. At the same time, however, they remain hopeful that their attachment figures might—at some point—be sufficiently responsive to their needs. This, in turn, motivates highly anxious people to adopt hypervigilant coping strategies, which generate continued distress and cognitive rumination, both of which keep their attachment systems chronically activated (Simpson & Rholes, 1994).

Highly avoidant individuals believe that seeking proximity to their attachment figures is neither a viable nor a desirable option. This belief impels highly avoidant people to recruit deactivation or "avoidant" coping strategies, which facilitate the suppression of negative emotions and cognitions and promote continued independence and autonomy. Even though their attachment systems may seem "deactivated," highly avoidant people may experience elevated physiological arousal and distress despite the fact that they appear calm.

Mikulincer and Shaver's (2003) model, therefore, proposes that one key function of adult attachment orientations is to regulate negative emotions, especially when they occur in interpersonal contexts. A similar position has been advocated by other scholars in the attachment field (e.g., Kobak & Sceery, 1988; Mikulincer & Florian, 1998; Simpson, 1990). The issue of whether emotion regulation might serve evolutionary functions (e.g., enhancing survival, generating differential reproduction) is not addressed in most attachment models, including the Mikulincer and Shaver model. Other evolutionary-based models, however, have attempted to link different attachment patterns (in children) or orientations (in adults) with differential survival or reproduction across the lifespan.

LIFE HISTORY THEORY

Life history theory (LHT) is a very broad evolutionary theory. It addresses how and why individuals allocate their time, energy, and resources to different traits, behaviors, and important life tasks when they make trade-off decisions that could have a bearing on their reproductive fitness (i.e., the replication of their genes in future generations). More specifically, LHT considers the selection pressures in our ancestral past that should have influenced when and the conditions under which organisms channel time, energy, and resources to physical development, growth, reproduction, body repair, and aging. In a sense, LHT specifies when, how, and why other middle-level evolutionary theories, such as host–parasite coevolution theory (Tooby, 1982), reciprocal altruism theory (Trivers, 1971), sexual selection and parental investment theory (Trivers, 1972), parent–offspring conflict theory (Trivers, 1974), and attachment theory (Bowlby, 1969), interrelate and unfold across the life-course of individuals. Given its focus on how the allotment of time, effort, and resources should be tied to differential reproductive fitness over the lifespan, LHT provides a novel framework for understanding personality and social development, one not offered by non-evolutionary developmental theories.

According to LHT, individuals can increase their reproductive fitness via two routes (Parker & Maynard Smith, 1991). On the one hand, they can consciously or unconsciously "invest" in traits or attributes that affect the timing of their mortality (i.e., the age at which they deteriorate and die). Alternately, they can "invest" in traits or attributes that influence the timing of their fertility (i.e., the age and rate at which they reproduce). Most important traits and attributes have diametrically opposite effects on mortality and fertility (Kaplan & Gangestad, 2005). That is, traits or attributes that improve fertility through more frequent or intense mating often shorten survival because many of the traits that make individuals (particularly men) more attractive to the opposite sex compromise their immune systems (Grafen, 1990). Moreover, the allocation of greater energy and resources to growth during development usually retards fertility when individuals are young, but enhances it once individuals are sexually mature (Stearns, 1992). And the allocation of time, energy, and resources to ensure that one's children grow to be strong and healthy typically limits one's own future fertility and long-term survival.

According to LHT, individuals must negotiate three basic trade-offs during their lives: (1) whether to invest in present (immediate) reproduction versus future (delayed) reproduction; (2) whether to invest in higher quantity versus higher quality of offspring; and (3) whether to invest in more mating versus parenting effort. How each trade-off is resolved should hinge on a host of factors, including the nature and demands of the local environment (e.g., how harsh it is, the prevalence of pathogens and disease, the need for biparental rearing), the skills, abilities, and resources available to an individual at a given point in time, the skills, abilities, and resources possessed by others (e.g., kin, potential mates, competitors), and so on.

Several scholars (e.g., Belsky et al., 1991; Cassidy & Berlin, 1994; Chisholm, 1993, 1996; Main, 1981) have conjectured that, during evolutionary history, the quality of care parents provided to their children may have conveyed valuable information about the nature, demands, and resources in the local environment in which children were being raised. This premise has motivated attachment theorists to develop lifespan models explaining how early social experiences with caregivers could shape the formation of internal working models in children, eventually guiding individuals down different developmental trajectories (pathways) that implicate central LHT traits and attributes, such as differential rates or patterns of physical growth, reproductive development, mating strategies, and ultimately parenting practices directed toward their own children. In the next section, we review and evaluate six lifespan attachment models, each of which centers one or more of the three basic life history trade-offs discussed above.

LIFE HISTORY ATTACHMENT MODELS

The Main/Cassidy and Berlin Model

Both Main (1981) and Cassidy and Berlin (1994) suggest that the three patterns of attachment observed in young children—secure, anxious-avoidant (avoidant), and anxious-resistant (preoccupied)—might be evolved conditional strategies that emerge in response to the quality of care that children receive from their primary caregivers. These models focus on coherent behavioral strategies and tactics that should have promoted survival through the perils of childhood.

According to Main (1981), the primary behavioral strategy enacted by most children is to seek proximity, care, and protection from attachment figures (typically caregivers) when children are afraid, distressed, fatigued, or ill. This is the modal strategy enacted by children who are securely attached to their caregivers. If, however, caregivers are unable or unwilling to provide sensitive and contingent care, avoidance may have evolved as a "secondary" adaptive behavioral strategy because it could have ensured some degree of proximity and contact with less committed, frustrated, or overburdened caregivers without driving them away. In parallel fashion, Cassidy and Berlin (1994) claim that the intense and exaggerated expressions of attachment needs displayed by anxious (preoccupied) children may reflect another secondary evolved strategy, one designed to gain greater attention and care from caregivers who might be motivated to provide high-quality care, but do so intermittently or unpredictably. Both models, however, address only the immediate needs and survival of children rather than complete life-course trajectories (see Belsky, 1999).

The Belsky Model

Belsky and his colleagues (Belsky, 1999; Belsky et al., 1991) specify how early social experiences may generate different developmental pathways that culminate in distinct reproductive (mating) strategies in adulthood. According to this model, different attachment patterns or styles may be adaptive, in that they promote future decisions about reproduction and childrearing that should be well suited to the particular environmental demands experienced within an individual's lifetime. More specifically, experiences in nuclear families are believed to be a good barometer of conditions in the surrounding environment, which subsequently affect the physical and psychological development of the individual.

The Belsky et al. (1991) model contains distinct stages that result in the specific reproductive/mating strategies that individuals eventually adopt in adulthood. Belsky et al. claim that: (1) certain contextual factors experienced in the nuclear family life (e.g., the amount of stress, the level of resources) affect (2) the quality of parenting within the family (e.g., how sensitive or attentive parents are to their children's needs). These early social experiences in turn impact (3) the psychological and behavioral development of the child (e.g., his or her attachment pattern and internal working models), which then impact (4) somatic development (i.e., when sexual maturity occurs), and finally (5) the adoption of short-term or long-term reproductive/mating strategies in adulthood.

According to this model, secure attachment patterns and styles develop in response to caregivers who—given local rearing environments—provide contingent, sensitive care. This leads the child to infer that: (1) the world is not excessively dangerous, (2) other people can be trusted and counted on, and (3) relationships tend to be enduring, rewarding, and satisfying (Belsky, 1999). Over time, secure individuals preferentially value close, committed relationships. Given the quality of care that they received as children, secure individuals are also inclined to give better care to and investment in their own offspring. Indeed, more securely attached persons do have more satisfying romantic relationships (Simpson, 1990), and they generally are more sensitive and responsive to their child's needs (Rholes, Simpson, & Blakely, 1995).

Avoidant attachment styles are believed to develop from consistently rejecting parenting practices that may partially stem from unpredictable, resource-poor, or harsh environments. Such environmental conditions should shunt avoidant persons down a short-term (i.e., quantity-focused) reproductive pathway, culminating in greater mating effort (e.g., more interest and effort devoted to short-term mating relationships), and less emphasis on providing high-quality care and parenting. Highly avoidant adults are, in fact, more unrestricted in their sociosexual orientation (Simpson & Gangestad, 1991), and they are less committed to and trusting of their romantic partners (Simpson, 1990).

Anxious (preoccupied) attachment is characterized by exaggerated demands for care and attention in the hope of garnering more time, attention, and resources from caregivers. According to Belsky (1999), this tendency could reflect a conflict of interest between parents and their preoccupied child over the "proper" allocation of resources (see Trivers, 1974). Belsky, however, believes that anxious attachment may have evolved to induce dependency in selected children, permitting parents to have a "helper-at-the-nest" to facilitate their own reproductive success when additional help is required to raise offspring. To gain favor and greater attention from their parents, anxiously attached children might have found it rewarding to help their parents raise and care for their siblings. Hence, anxious (preoccupied) attachment styles are not linked to any particular mating or reproductive strategy in adulthood.

Belsky et al.'s model does not imply that individuals develop and then retain the same attachment orientation from the cradle to the grave, regardless of changing partners or environmental experiences. According to attachment theory (Bowlby, 1973), individuals can and often do experience changes in working models and attachment orientations, especially when they encounter new or model-incongruent relationship experiences later in development (Fraley & Brumbaugh, 2004; Simpson, Rholes, Campbell, & Wilson, 2003). Thus, although social experiences often sustain existing attachment models and orientations during social development, predictable changes can and do occur.

The Chisholm Model

Chisholm (1993, 1996) conjectures that attachment patterns and styles could be a psychobiological mechanism for optimizing future life history trade-off decisions. Unlike the Belsky et al. model, which emphasizes trade-offs between quantity versus quality of offspring, Chisholm concentrates on trade-offs between present (immediate) versus future (delayed) reproduction. According to Chisholm, mortality rates in the local rearing environment ought to influence parenting and caregiving practices. When local mortality rates are high, individuals (both parents and eventually their children) should adopt short-term reproductive strategies in which current fertility is emphasized. When mortality rates are lower, in contrast, they should adopt long-term mating strategies and slower reproduction, resulting in fewer children who are given better care and more individual attention.

The types of caregiving that result from local mortality rates, therefore, should serve as a cue of the degree of risk or uncertainty in the local environment. On average, low mortality rates should be associated with more benign and plentiful environments, allowing for better and more attentive parental care. Offspring who receive such care should, in turn, develop secure working models and action tendencies that are well suited to such environments. More secure children should then follow a developmental trajectory in which growth, delayed maturation, high-quality pair-bonds, and strong parental investment all occur. More insecure working models and attachment patterns/styles, on the other hand, should flow from local environments that encourage insensitive or unresponsive parenting. Avoidant attachment, for instance, should be witnessed when parents are *unwilling* to invest in their offspring, regardless of their actual ability to do so. Such parents should dismiss or ignore their children's emotional needs and should directly or indirectly communicate their unwillingness to invest in them. Their children should then be launched down a developmental pathway in which survival takes precedence over growth, and adult romantic relationships are viewed with cynicism and skepticism. During adulthood, highly avoidant individuals should—and often do—enter short-term, uncommitted sexual relationships, are less willing to invest in their offspring, channel their energies and resources more toward mating effort than parenting effort, and place less importance on investing in offspring (see Chisholm, 1996).

Chisholm argues that anxious (preoccupied) attachment might be an adaptation to parental *inability* to invest, which may be a consequence of deficient or limited resources. The parents of these children should provide inconsistent or unpredictable care, but they should *not* be chronically rejecting or emotionally callous. Highly anxious children should try to extract as many resources as possible from their parents, and they should reach sexual maturity at an earlier age. As adults, highly anxious persons should engage in more short-term mating, be willing but perhaps not fully able to invest in their offspring, channel their energies and resources more toward parenting effort than mating effort, and behave less consistently toward their own children (see Chisholm, 1996).

Although the Belsky and Chisholm models both predict that cues from rearing environments should influence the development of attachment orientations and mating strategies over time, the models have some key differences. As mentioned earlier, although both are grounded in life history theory, they deal with different life history decisions. Belsky's model focuses on trade-offs between quantity versus quality of offspring, whereas Chisholm's model addresses trade-offs between current versus future reproduction. The models also differ with respect to views of anxious attachment. Belsky's model concentrates on how unpredictable caregiving fosters dependence in children, leading them to doubt their capacity to be autonomous. Chisholm's model, on the other hand, emphasizes parents' inability to invest in offspring and how that then expedites sexual development en route to the enactment of short-term mating strategies.

The Hazan and Zeifman Model

Hazan and Zeifman (1999; Zeifman & Hazan, 1997) argue that adult pair-bond relationships are an instantiation of attachment relationships earlier in life. They point out many similarities between childhood attachment to caregivers and adult attachment to close peers and romantic partners. Infants and adults, for example, both display similar reactions to separation from or loss of attachment figures. Moreover, people look for qualities in mates that are similar to those they valued in their caregivers, such as kindness and similarity. Emotionally bonded children and adults both tend to behave similarly when seeking close contact, physical intimacy, and affection from others. And both parent–child and adult–adult attachment relationships pass through similar stages of development.

Hazan and Zeifman contend that the primary purpose of attachment in adult relationships is to forge stable and enduring pair-bonds so partners can provide better mutual support and raise children successfully. Pair-bonding is presumed to enhance the survival and reproductive fitness of mates and their offspring. Indeed, adult mating strategies are meaningfully associated with the pair-bond status of one's parents, with father absence and marital discord predicting earlier sexual maturation, the enactment of short-term mating strategies in adulthood, and less stable marriages (see Belsky, 1999). Children who have more pair-bonded parents, by comparison, should adopt long-term mating strategies and emphasize quality rather than quantity when they have their own children (see Hazan & Zeifman, 1999). More pair-bonded partners also contribute to their reproductive success by providing each other with more support, which is linked with better long-term physical and mental health and more regular ovulation patterns in women. Considering this evidence, Hazan and Zeifman believe that the primary function of attachment in adulthood is to facilitate enduring emotional bonds between partners that, on average, enhance their reproductive success.

The Kirkpatrick Model

Kirkpatrick (1998) also believes that adult attachment orientations have evolved to enhance reproductive fitness in response to early childhood experiences, but he questions whether security and protection are the primary functions of adult attachment. Instead, Kirkpatrick claims that components of the caregiving system (e.g., love) might have been co-opted during evolutionary history to sustain long-term romantic pair-bonds in adulthood, and that adult attachment styles may reflect alternate reproductive/mating strategies.

According to life history theory, one of the largest trade-offs is between allocating time and energy to mating effort versus parenting effort. Kirkpatrick proposes that it was not always adaptive or advantageous for women and men to pursue long-term, monogamous mating strategies. Consequently, adult attachment styles may have served as a mechanism for choosing the best mating strategy given a particular rearing environment, based on both the nature of early childhood experiences and the quality of early parenting. People who have received consistently sensitive and responsive parenting should develop more secure working models and, therefore, should enact long-term, committed mating strategies. Such individuals should also develop greater trust and intimacy in their relationships, and they ought to fall in love fairly easily. More avoidant individuals, in contrast, should have less committed romantic relationships, should pursue short-term mating strategies, and should have more unrestricted sociosexual orientations. Highly anxious persons should generally desire and pursue long-term mating strategies. Their insatiable desire to be with their partners, however, may drive partners away (see Kirkpatrick, 1998).

In sum, Kirkpatrick (1998) believes that features of the caregiving system—especially love acting as a "commitment device"—could have been co-opted to cement and stabilize long-term pair-bonds. Thus, whereas Hazan and Zeifman (1999) believe that attachment bonds that evolved to keep children in close proximity to their caregivers may have been co-opted to cement adult romantic pair-bonds, Kirkpatrick claims that love is the primary reason behind pair-bond maintenance, and he views adult attachment orientations as alternate evolved mating strategies.

Summary of Models

Each of the models outlined above posits that different attachment styles might be evolved mechanisms through which individuals adjust their reproductive trajectories in response to early environmental cues. The Belsky (1999) and Chisholm (1996) models emphasize how cues reflecting the quality of the local rearing environment generate different attachment orientations in adulthood that are better suited to those environments. The Hazan and Zeifman (1999) and Kirkpatrick (1998) models stress the evolutionary importance of maintaining adult pair-bonds and the primary emotions that accompany different reproductive strategies. All of these models hypothesize that early stress and insecure attachment patterns result in mating activities indicative of an r-selected strategy, whereas early experiences that entail less stress and secure attachment styles lead to reproductive activities indicative of a K-selected strategy. In general, r-selected strategies are associated with lower investment in mates and offspring, more opportunistic mating, and an emphasis on early and frequent mating. Although each theory addresses slightly different life history components such as high versus low parental investment, immediate versus future mating, short-term versus

long-term mating strategies, committed versus opportunist mating, and developmental trends toward growth versus survival and early reproduction, each one
deals with the general theme of r- versus K-selected reproductive strategies.

   In the next section, we integrate features of these models within a broader
model that specifies the proximate mechanisms through which some of these life
history differences might unfold. We also attempt to integrate life history theories
of attachment with neurobiological, social, and developmental evidence regarding
the effects and functions of attachment patterns and styles.

NEUROBIOLOGY OF ATTACHMENT

Attachment patterns and styles are believed to be evolved mechanisms that helped
individuals match their behavior to the social and physical environments they were
likely to encounter during their lives. Given the connection between the difficulty
of the physical environment and the tenor of the social environment, attachment orientations should have helped individuals to better navigate the social
environments in which they lived, and to enact more adaptive behaviors.

   One of the most exciting new areas of inquiry is the neurobiology of
attachment mechanisms and processes. One important contribution to the neurobiology of attachment has been the discovery that infant bio-regulation is
contingent on what transpires between infants and their mothers (Hofer, 1995).
Hofer has demonstrated that, by removing or selectively adding specific components of normal mother–infant interaction in rats (e.g., milk, warmth, tactile
stimulation), certain biological and behavioral systems increase or decrease
independently (such as heart rate and activity level, respectively). Hofer believes
that these aspects of mother–infant interaction could be "hidden regulators" of the
biological and behavioral systems of infants. If so, mother–infant attachment could
be a regulatory phenomenon, whereby certain hidden regulators condition infants
to prefer stimuli that are repeatedly associated with these regulators and provide
physiological homeostasis.

   From a life history perspective, this sort of dynamic regulation should be
influenced by the characteristics of the local environments in which infants are
raised. Poor regulation may be associated with being reared in harsh or resource-
deficient environments, whereas better regulation might emanate from safe or
resource-rich environments. If, during evolutionary history, certain cues in local
environments were valid indicators of the type of environments that individuals
would probably inhabit during most of their lives, psychological adaptations that
set different activation thresholds, baseline levels, and reactivity levels in these
systems could have evolved. To the extent that individual differences in attachment orientations are manifestations of evolved psychological mechanisms, these
cues may have produced developmental differences in the reactivity and activation
thresholds of certain systems that operate in mother–infant interactions and relationships (see Simpson & Rholes, 1994). This hypothesis would be supported if,
for example, bio-behavioral systems that should have led to selection benefits
ancestrally are the primary ones tied to early attachment experiences, while

other important systems (e.g., thermal regulation) are not associated with early attachment experiences.

Brain Systems Supporting Attachment and Social Bonds

Panksepp and colleagues (e.g., Nelson & Panksepp, 1998; Panksepp, 1999) suggest that social bonds might be mediated by an integrated "social emotion system" that has two affective components (subsystems). The first subsystem mediates the separation distress response, and the second one mediates social reward or contact comfort. The separation distress subsystem has been studied extensively in non-human mammals, primarily via the application of electrical stimulation to certain parts of the brain to discern effects on distress vocalizations (e.g., Jurgens & Ploog, 1988; Kyuhou & Gemba, 1998; Panksepp, 1999; Robinson, 1967). The brain areas involved in the separation distress subsystem include the dorsomedial thalamus, the ventral septal area, the preoptic area, the bed nucleus of the stria terminalis, the anterior cingulate cortex, and some sites in the amygdala and hypothalamus. Panksepp (1999) believes that this organization may be an exaptation (i.e., an adaptation built on earlier adaptations) of pain circuits. This interpretation has received support from recent fMRI studies in humans showing that activation of a "physical pain" area of the anterior cingulate cortex occurs when people experience *social* exclusion (Eisenberger, Lieberman, & Williams, 2003).

Among the neurochemicals that increase activity in the separation distress subsystem are corticotrophin releasing factor (CRF) and glutamate (Panksepp, 1999; Panksepp, Siviy, & Normansell, 1985), with glutamate probably being the core neurochemical. CRF, however, is an important neurotransmitter involved in the activation of stress circuitry, which has been of interest to those who study the interaction between the stress system and separation distress. Most studies have found a positive relation between CRF and distress vocalizations in most species. Some failures to find this link (e.g., Insel & Harbaugh, 1989) led Harvey and Hennesy (1995) to look more closely at the association between CRF and distress vocalizations.

In an important study of rat pups, Harvey and Hennesy (1995) found that CRF and distress vocalizations have a curvilinear relation, with both lower and higher levels of CRF being associated with *declines* in distress vocalizations. This finding could offer a crucial insight into a possible misconception held by some attachment theorists about the connection between threatening stimuli (particularly predators) and attachment system activation. Kirkpatrick (1998) has suggested that one fundamental difference between adult and infant attachment is that the attachment system overrides other behavioral systems when infants are confronted with predators or other major threats. Adults, however, do not always seek immediate protection from their "caregivers" in similar circumstances. This assumption—that the *attachment system* evolved principally to protect vulnerable infants and children from acute predation per se—could be at odds with what is currently being learned about the functioning of different neurobiological systems. According to Panksepp (1999), the fear system that governs the "fight or flight" response should *not* trigger separation distress, because such displays might lead predators to the location of the distressed child. Furthermore, research on links between the separation distress subsystem and the fear system in non-human animals suggests that the separation distress subsystem tends to activate fear circuits, but activation of the fear system does not necessarily elicit separation distress (e.g., Pettijohn, Wong, Ebert, & Scott, 1977; Davis, Gurski, & Scott, 1977).[1]

Another group of neurochemicals down-regulate activation of the separation distress subsystem. Interestingly, some of these neurochemicals also appear to affect other attachment-relevant systems, particularly the social reward/contact comfort subsystem (Nelson & Panksepp, 1998, Panksepp, 1999; Panksepp et al., 1985). These neurochemicals include endogenous opioids, oxytocin, vasopressin, and prolactin. Endogenous opioids tend to be released in the presence of social stimuli, including milk transfer and somatosensory body contact between mothers and their newborn rat pups (Blass & Fitzgerald, 1988). Opioid antagonists typically block these behavioral effects. This suggests that opioid release may generate differences between rat pups that receive milk or body contact and those that do not. Endogenous opioids have a strong rewarding effect that often produces euphoric feelings, and they are powerful conditioning agents. They can condition preferences for stimuli that are presented not only before or during opioid release (Carr, Fibiger, & Phillips, 1988), but also future opioid release when organisms are re-exposed to the same stimuli (Siegel, 1979). A final piece of evidence suggesting the importance of opioids in regulating attachment and social bonding is that lower levels of opioids often increase social motivation in many species (e.g., Martel, Nevison, Simpson, & Keverne, 1995; Panksepp, Najam, & Soares, 1980).

Endogenous opioids, along with other neurochemicals released by the social reward/contact comfort subsystem, might also have an impact on the development of internal working models. The powerful conditioning effects of this subsystem may generate selective preferences for stimuli repeatedly associated with the activation of its circuits. For example, through classically conditioned interactions that produce preferences for stimuli repeatedly associated with the release of opioids, people may develop strong preferences and motivations to approach certain stimuli. More importantly, opioids and other social reward neurochemicals might generate strong conditioned behavioral tendencies toward caregivers, both in children and adults. Among anxiously attached individuals, for instance, hyperactivation of support-seeking behavior may occur because it induces the reward inherent in the social reward/contact comfort subsystem. Among avoidantly attached persons, behavior toward caregivers may revolve around maintaining a comfortable emotional distance that children and adults have learned to regulate to maximize social reward subsystem activity without driving their caregivers away. More specifically, if parents persistently reject or are hostile to efforts by their children to gain support, their children should not learn to avoid them completely; they should learn what distance and level of contact is possible and provides the most reinforcement (see Main, 1981).

In addition to endogenous opioids, oxytocin and vasopressin also down-regulate distress vocalizations (Nelson & Panksepp, 1998; Panksepp, 1999). These neuroregulators are related peptides, and both have effects similar to endogenous opioids. Oxytocin, however, may inhibit tolerance to opioids (Krivan, Szabo, Sarnyai, Kovacs, & Telegdy, 1995). Similar to the effects of drug addiction, tolerance to opioids occurs when more and more of a neurochemical is necessary to induce the original positive effects. Although oxytocin has many of the same properties as opioids with respect to the social reward subsystem, it has an opposite effect on social interaction. Increases in oxytocin stimulate more affiliation, especially the onset of maternal behaviors (Pedersen, Ascher, Monroe, & Prange, 1982; Pedersen, Caldwell, Walker, Ayers, & Mason, 1994).

It is important to note that all of the neural systems and chemicals involved in mother–infant attachment also seem to be implicated in other types of attachment relationships and processes (Panksepp, 1999). Furthermore, both the social reward/contact comfort subsystem and the separation distress subsystem operate throughout the lifespan. This fact is important for those seeking to understand ties between the attachment system, the caregiving system, and the sexual/mating system. Indeed, sex, maternal behavior, and attachment behavior all stimulate the release of oxytocin (Nelson & Panksepp, 1998, Panksepp, 1999), and endogenous opioids tend to be released during sexual activity and certain mother–infant interactions. And all of these associations are likely to involve the social reward/contact comfort subsystem.

Some of the evidence reviewed above supports Kirkpatrick's (1998) ideas about the function of "love" in close relationships. The integrated social emotion system (i.e., the separation distress subsystem and the social reward/contact comfort subsystem) might regulate and stabilize relationships across the lifespan. Other evidence, however, supports Hazan and Zeifman (1999), who argue that the infant attachment system "reorganizes" during social development to promote adult pair-bonding. Indeed, Shapiro and Insel (1989) found that, in female rats, oxytocin receptor density shifts from being highest in separation distress areas of the brain in infant rats to being highest in sociosexual areas in adult rats. This suggests that there may, in fact, be a single "social emotion system" that integrates the social reward/contact comfort and separation distress subsystems. This system might undergo receptor reorganization during puberty and parenthood so that behaviors critical for later life tasks can be successfully carried out.

NEUROBIOLOGY AND THE STRUCTURE OF ATTACHMENT

It is tempting to contemplate how our neurobiological account of attachment might map on to Mikulincer and Shaver's (2003) two-dimensional model of attachment. According to their model, individuals who score high on the anxiety dimension use hyperactivation strategies, whereas those who score high on avoidance utilize deactivating strategies, especially when the attachment system is activated. In a parallel fashion, the separation distress subsystem tends to elicit support seeking, and chronic activation of this subsystem ought to generate hyperactivation tendencies. The social reward/contact comfort subsystem, in contrast, regulates avoidance behaviors. Higher activation thresholds in this subsystem could result in less support seeking, perhaps in response to learning histories in which support seeking has not been rewarded.

These two subsystems, however, probably do not map directly on to the attachment anxiety and avoidance dimensions. Mikulincer and Shaver's (2003) model posits that people who score low on both anxiety and avoidance should be most securely attached. According to our model, however, the greatest disregulation should exist when the separation distress subsystem has low activation thresholds, and the social reward/contact comfort subsystem has high thresholds. This suggests that the dimensions underlying the Mikulincer and Shaver model of attachment and the social emotion system are not identical and could lie at 45 degree angles. For instance, high attachment anxiety may be characterized by having a lower (i.e., easier-to-trigger) threshold on the separate distress subsystem and a higher (i.e., more-difficult-to-trigger) threshold on the social reward/contact comfort subsystem. High attachment avoidance, on the other hand, could be characterized by having a higher threshold on both the separation distress and the social reward/contact comfort subsystems. Preliminary evidence supporting this possibility is discussed below. We believe that integrating these neurobiological models could appreciably enhance our understanding of the nature and structure of the attachment system.

This neurobiological account of attachment structure focuses on only one component of working models—affect. Working models, however, also contain important cognitive and behavioral components. We suspect that the integrated social emotion system may be more relevant to the affective component of working models. This system should mediate learning processes that could shape the cognitive and behavioral components of working models through conditioning processes, particularly in early childhood. As individuals grow, however, they may develop multiple memory structures for the same object or stimulus (Wilson, Lindsey, & Schooler, 2000), some of which are implicit and others of which are explicit.

This could have important implications for understanding continuity and change of working models across the lifespan. The affective component may be largely toned by early social experiences tied to evolved mechanisms that forecast an individual's future environment. This could establish different activation thresholds for the two subsystems orchestrated by the social emotion system in different people. Early in life, these processes might also affect the learning of implicit cognitive and behavioral representations of attachment figures and relationships. Later in life, individuals are likely to develop explicit representations of attachment partners and relationships. These explicit representations may be more malleable and based on more recent experiences, and they might change more easily over the lifespan as individuals enter and leave different relationships. Implicit cognitive and behavioral representations, however, should continue to be shaped by basic learning and conditioning principles, but they may be less malleable.

In the next section, we sketch a theoretical account of how the social emotion system might generate continuity in attachment working models across time. We also discuss how working models could guide behavior in romantic and caregiving relationships. One goal of this section is to draw connections between ultimate, phylogenetic, ontogenetic, and proximate causes of attachment behavior, providing a fuller conceptualization of attachment processes across the lifespan.

STRESS, ATTACHMENT, AND DEVELOPMENT

The stress system plays a vital role in the regulation of the integrated social emotion system. For example, it regulates the separation distress subsystem and is regulated by contact comfort (Blass, 1996; Panksepp, 1999). The stress system could, therefore, be an important mechanism through which early attachment experiences translate into different mating and parenting strategies in adulthood. Indeed, the fact that the stress system develops slowly suggests that postnatal experiences may have important effects on calibrating the development of individual differences in stress reactivity and regulation (Gunnar & Davis, 2003).

Relatively little is known about whether the quality of caregiving infants receive translates into differential stress reactivity. In rats, greater maternal licking and grooming result in adult progeny that have lower CRF responses (i.e., less fearful reactions to novel stimuli; Caldji, Tannenbaum, Sharma, Francis, Plotsky, & Meaney, 1998; Levine, 1994). Some primates also display lower stress responses to threatening stimuli when they have access to their mothers (Levine & Weiner, 1988). Mineka, Gunnar, and Champoux (1986) found that monkeys that experienced contingent, responsive stimulation in the form of levers and pulleys they could use to obtain rewards exhibited less fear to novelty and were more willing to explore new environments than monkeys that were given the same rewards.

Several studies have also found that secure attachment relationships in humans are associated with lower cortisol levels (a neurochemical that indexes stress reactions) in the Strange Situation (Gunnar, 2000; Spangler & Scheiche, 1998). Gunnar and Davis (2003) have also confirmed that early adverse rearing conditions predict elevated cortisol levels in children, even after they are removed from negative conditions. In adult romantic relationships, attachment styles affect behavior more strongly in different kinds of stressful situations, ranging from fear-induction (Simpson, Rholes, & Nelligan, 1992) to interpersonal conflicts (Simpson, Rholes, & Phillips, 1996). Stress, therefore, is an important factor in the expression of working models and attachment styles later in life. Most of the current evidence suggests that (1) greater stress early in life and less sensitive parenting exacerbate disregulation of the stress system that may last into adulthood, and (2) this disregulation could explain several extant findings in the adult attachment literature.[2]

In safe, predictable environments in which parents are able and willing to invest in their children, moderate activation thresholds should develop in the separation distress and social reward/contact comfort subsystems. This, in turn, should generate a well-regulated stress system, one that is appropriately "responsive" to local environmental conditions. However, in highly stressful or demanding environments in which investment and support are deficient, individuals should develop higher activation thresholds for separation distress. This would prevent these individuals from clamoring for attention and resources that caregivers are unable or unwilling to grant. In these harsh environments, it might also be beneficial for individuals to have higher activation thresholds for the social reward/ contact comfort subsystem. In highly stressful and unsupportive environments, it may be necessary to form relationships cautiously and to take advantage of relationships opportunistically when possible. In these environments, individuals could easily invest in and trust the wrong people, especially if emotional bonds are developed too quickly. This account explains many of the preferences and behaviors of highly avoidant people. Moreover, according to this line of thinking, highly avoidant individuals should be able to divert or suppress socially mediated stress reactions in certain situations (which they can; see Fraley, Garner, & Shaver, 2000), but they should have greater difficulty down-regulating stress reactions once they are triggered.

In environments where caregivers are willing but unable to provide consistently good care and support, it might be beneficial for individuals to have lower separation distress subsystem activation thresholds. This would facilitate stronger bids for attention and nurturance, increasing the likelihood that some support will eventually be received. It might also be beneficial for such individuals to develop higher social reward/contact comfort subsystem activation thresholds. In these environments, finding comfort too quickly or easily could produce complacency in relationships, meaning that one could lose some of the benefits of having a lower separation distress threshold. Instead, individuals in these environments ought to remain vigilant so they can obtain support whenever it becomes available. This account explains many of the preferences and behaviors of highly anxious people. It also leads one to predict that more anxious individuals should be highly aroused by socially mediated stress reactions, and should be slower to return to baseline arousal levels after stressors have subsided. Recent evidence supports some of these speculations (see Powers, Pietromonaco, Gunlicks, & Sayer, 2006).[3]

Alternate accounts somewhere between these two systems are also possible. For example, in extremely dangerous environments in which care and support are mandatory for infant survival, parenting may take a more preoccupied, vigilant, and intrusive form. This may lead children to develop very low activation thresholds in both subsystems, which in turn should generate unusually high rates of support seeking and ease-of-comforting and, therefore, rapid emotional bonding. Children reared in such extreme environments may be afraid of novelty and become enmeshed with their parents, resulting in the "helper-at-the-nest" pattern described by Belsky (1999). Although this pattern may appear similar to the "regular" anxious attachment pattern, its outcomes may be unique. Individuals who display the "helper-at-the-nest" pattern, for instance, should show atypically high reactivity to novelty and social stressors, but may recover more quickly.

Self-Regulation, Stress, and the Social Emotion Systems

Although the account presented above explains the existence of individual differences in attachment patterns and orientations, it does not explain how these patterns/orientations lead to differential reproductive outcomes and parenting behaviors in adulthood. One mediating mechanism through which differential thresholds in the integrated social emotion system could have effects on reproductive strategies and parenting is self-regulation.

Baumeister and his colleagues (e.g., Baumeister & Vohs, 2003; Muraven & Baumeister, 2000) believe that self-regulation (i.e., the act of exerting self-control) requires the use of finite energy. Indeed, when individuals use self-regulatory resources to control their behavior in one context, they find it difficult to do so in other contexts. Interestingly, self-regulatory processes are hampered by stress and emotion regulation. Because of this, insecurely attached individuals—who may have social emotion system thresholds that exacerbate stress—should be particularly vulnerable to self-regulatory failures, especially in stressful social contexts. They may, for example, be more inclined to behave automatically in line with their working models, which might lead them to engage in impulsive or destructive interpersonal behaviors (Baumeister & Vohs, 2003).

Highly avoidant individuals have working models that create and sustain emotional distance and may encourage certain opportunistic interpersonal behaviors. To the extent that they have difficulties or concerns about managing social stress reactions, highly avoidant persons should be prone to self-regulatory failures that culminate in impulsive interpersonal behaviors, such as having sex purely for self-gratification or responding with hostility to their children, regardless of what their children have done. Highly anxious persons, in contrast, have working models that involve emotional neediness and foster hyper-vigilance. When they encounter difficulties with managing social stress, they may also be susceptible to self-regulatory failures that trigger impulsive interpersonal behaviors, such as having sex to elevate flagging self-esteem, or displaying parenting behaviors that fluctuate between intrusiveness and outbursts of anger.

TIES TO SOCIOMETER THEORY

According to sociometer theory (Leary, Tambor, Terdal, & Downs, 1995), changes in self-esteem alert people to how socially included and accepted they are at a given point in time. When people are less connected to or included by others, they should experience declines in state self-esteem because of the prospect of social exclusion or isolation. The integrated social emotion system we have outlined might be a neural manifestation of this sociometer. Our theoretical account does not discount the possibility that the two subsystems underlying the social emotion system could be involved in signaling social isolation or rejection via temporary feelings of lower self-worth. As we have discussed, early attachment experiences may "tune" these subsystems to environmental cues, which could then affect levels of state and perhaps even trait self-esteem. More specifically, negative early attachment experiences might increase vulnerability to experiencing low self-esteem via the calibration of the social emotion system. Perceptions of current environmental events might then determine whether state self-esteem remains stable, decreases, or increases as individuals stimulate separation distress scenarios in their minds and experience "social pain" (see MacDonald & Leary, 2005).

CONCLUSIONS

In this chapter, we have reviewed different life history-based theories of attachment and have tried to link them with specific neurobiological mechanisms and psychological processes. Mounting evidence suggests that early environmental stress and unpredictability affect caregiving practices, which then begin to mold attachment experiences and internal working models. During development, these experiences may generate differences in the calibration and/or regulation of the social emotion system, the modulation of sexual development, and perhaps the development of conditioned responses to attachment figures. Regulation of the integrated social emotion system, in turn, might mediate stress reactivity to social stressors, which could combine with conditioned behavioral and emotional responses to attachment figures to further shape working models. Patterns of stress reactivity might also be linked to self-regulation depletion processes, which could influence the enactment of certain impulsive behaviors, especially those associated with mating and parenting strategies.

Attachment theory is unique among interpersonal theories in that it explicitly addresses multiple levels of analysis. Tinbergen (1963) proposed that complete theories must address questions at four levels of analysis to explain a given trait, behavior, or phenomenon fully. Specifically, complete theories explain how and why a given trait or behavior evolved (ultimate causation), whether, how, and why its evolution is tied to the development of the trait or behavior in other species (phylogeny), how and why it develops in a particular manner during the life-course of individuals (ontogeny), and what kinds of stimuli elicit, sustain, or terminate its expression (proximate causation). Most interpersonal theories in social and personality psychology focus almost entirely on proximate causation. This is unfortunate because people bring vestiges of their past—memories of how they were raised and treated by significant others, working models that affect mating and parenting in adulthood, and perhaps neurological systems that have been shaped by selection pressures and then calibrated by ontogenetic experiences— with them into adulthood. Bowlby (1969, 1973, 1980) developed a theory that attempts to addresses *all* of Tinbergen's levels of analysis (see Simpson, 1999). This is why attachment theory has become one of the most important, generative, and influential theories of personality and social behavior "from the cradle to the grave" in the history of psychology.

NOTES

1. The fear circuit could also have an inverted U-shaped relation with the separation distress system, just CRF does. If so, less fear-invoking events could activate separation distress vocalizations.

2.　Even if these factors contribute to stress disregulation in adulthood, disregulation may also be mediated by other systems. For example, both the separation distress subsystem and the social reward/contact comfort subsystem might interact in important ways with the stress system. Activation of the separation distress subsystem ought to increase stress levels, whereas activation of the social reward/contact comfort subsystem should usually lower stress. Given the interactive nature of these systems, it may be difficult to determine whether disregulation of the stress system in adults is attributable to specific developmental experiences that may have impacted the stress system earlier in life. Indeed, early stress and early attachment experiences could calibrate the separation distress subsystem *and* the social reward/contact comfort subsystem, with secure and insecure working models producing different activation thresholds in these two subsystems.

3.　Because the social emotion system should have developed different reactivity thresholds, these effects should *not* be witnessed in most non-social contexts. If, however, early attachment experiences exert direct effects on the stress system, stress reactions to non-social situations could also become disregulated.

REFERENCES

Bartholomew, K. (1990). Avoidance of intimacy: An attachment perspective. *Journal of Social and Personal Relationships*, *1*, 147–178.

Baumeister, R. F., & Vohs, K. D. (2003). Self-regulation and the executive function of the self. In M. R. Leary & J. P. Tangney (Eds.), *Handbook of self and identity* (pp. 197–217). New York: Guilford Press.

Blass, E. M. (1996). Mothers and their infants: Peptide-mediated physiological, behavioral and affective changes during suckling. *Regulatory Peptides*, *66*, 109–112.

Blass, E. M., & Fitzgerald, E. (1988). Milk-induced analgesia and comforting in 10-day-old rats: Opioid mediation. *Pharmacology, Biochemistry, and Behavior*, *29*, 9–13.

Bowlby, J. (1969). *Attachment and loss. Vol. 1. Attachment*. New York: Basic Books.

Bowlby, J. (1973). *Attachment and loss. Vol. 2. Separation*. New York: Basic Books.

Bowlby, J. (1980). *Attachment and loss. Vol. 3. Loss*. New York: Basic Books.

Belsky, J. (1999). Modern evolutionary theory and patterns of attachment. In J. Cassidy & P. R. Shaver (Eds.), *Handbook of attachment: Theory, research, and clinical applications* (pp. 141–161). New York: Guilford Press.

Belsky, J., Steinberg, L., & Draper, P. (1991). Childhood experience, interpersonal development, and reproductive strategy: An evolutionary theory of socialization. *Child Development*, *62*, 647–670.

Brennan, K. A., Clark, C. L., & Shaver, P. R. (1998). Self-report measurement of adult attachment: An integrative overview. In J. A. Simpson & W. S. Rholes (Eds.), *Attachment theory and close relationships* (pp. 46–76). New York: Guilford Press.

Caldji, C., Tannenbaum, B., Sharma, S., Francis, D., Plotsky, P. M., & Meaney, M. J. (1998). Maternal care during infancy regulates the development of neural systems mediating the expression of fearfulness in the rat. *Proceedings of the National Academy of Science*, *95*, 5335–5340.

Carr, G. D., Fibiger, H. C., & Phillips, A. G. (1988). Conditioned place preference as a measure of drug reward. In J. M. Liebman & S. M. Cooper (Eds.), *The neuropharmacological basis of reward* (pp. 264–319). Oxford: Clarendon Press.

Cassidy, J., & Berlin, L. (1994). The insecure/ambivalent pattern of attachment: Theory and research. *Child Development*, *65*, 971–991.

Chisholm, J. (1993). Death, hope, and sex: Life history theory and the development of reproductive strategies. *Current Anthropology, 34*, 1–24.

Chisholm, J. (1996). The evolutionary ecology of attachment organization. *Human Nature, 7*, 1–38.

Davis, K. L., Gurski, J. C., & Scott, J. P. (1977). Interaction of separation distress response with fear in infant dogs. *Developmental Psychobiology, 10*, 203–212.

Eisenberger, N. I., Lieberman, M. D., & Williams, K. D. (2003). Does rejection hurt? An fMRI study of social exclusion. *Science, 302*, 290–292.

Feeney, J. A. (1999). Adult romantic attachment and couple relationships. In J. Cassidy & P. R. Shaver (Eds.), *Handbook of attachment: Theory, research, and clinical applications* (pp. 355–377). New York: Guilford Press.

Fraley, R. C., & Brumbaugh, C. C. (2004). A dynamical systems approach to conceptualizing and studying stability and change in attachment security. In W. S. Rholes & J. A. Simpson (Eds.), *Adult attachment: Theory, research, and clinical implications* (pp. 86–132). New York: Guilford Press.

Fraley, R. C., Garner, J. P., & Shaver, P. R. (2000). Adult attachment and the defensive regulation of attention and memory: Examining the role of preemptive and postemptive defensive processes. *Journal of Personality and Social Psychology, 79*, 816–826.

Grafen, A. (1990). Biological signals as handicaps. *Journal of Theoretical Biology, 144*, 517–546.

Griffin, D., & Bartholomew, K. (1994). Models of the self and other: Fundamental dimensions underlying measures of adult attachment. *Journal of Personality and Social Psychology, 67*, 430–445.

Gunnar, M. R. (2000). Early adversity and the development of stress reactivity and regulation. In C. A. Nelson (Ed.), *The Minnesota symposia on child psychology: The effects of early adversity on neurobehavioral development* (Vol. 31, pp. 163–200). Mahwah, NJ: Lawrence Erlbaum Associates, Inc.

Gunnar, M. R., & Davis, E. P. (2003). Stress and emotion in early childhood. In R. M. Lerner, M. A. Easterbrooks, & J. Mistry (Eds.), *Handbook of psychology: Developmental psychology* (Vol. 6, pp. 113–134). Hoboken, NJ: Wiley.

Harvey, A., & Hennesy, M. (1995). Corticotropin-releasing factor modulation of the ultrasonic vocalization rate of isolated rat pups. *Developmental Brain Research, 87*, 125–134.

Hazan, C., & Shaver, P. R. (1994). Attachment as an organizational framework for research on close relationships. *Psychological Inquiry, 5*, 1–22.

Hazan, C., & Zeifman, D. (1999). Pair bonds as attachments: Evaluating the evidence. In J. Cassidy & P. R. Shaver (Eds.), *Handbook of attachment: Theory, research, and clinical applications* (pp. 336–354). New York: Guilford Press.

Hofer, M. A. (1995). Hidden regulators: Implications for a new understanding of attachment, separation, and loss. In S. Goldberg, R. Muir, & J. Kerr (Eds.), *Attachment theory: Social, developmental, and clinical perspectives*. Hillsdale, NJ: Analytic Press.

Insel, T. R., & Harbaugh, C. R. (1989). Central administration of corticotrophin releasing factor alters rat pup isolation calls. *Pharmacology, Biochemistry, and Behavior, 32*, 197–201.

Jurgens, U., & Ploog, D. (1988). On the motor coordination of monkey calls. In J. D. Newman (Ed.), *The physiological control of mammalian vocalization* (pp. 21–41). New York: Plenum Press.

Kaplan, H. S., & Gangestad, S. W. (2005). Life history theory and evolutionary psychology.

In D. M. Buss (Ed.), *The handbook of evolutionary psychology* (pp. 68–95). Hoboken, NJ: Wiley.

Kirkpatrick, L. (1998). Evolution, pair-bonding, and reproductive strategies: A reconceptualization of adult attachment. In J. A. Simpson & W. S. Rholes (Eds.), *Attachment theory and close relationships* (pp. 353–393). New York: Guilford Press.

Kobak, R. R., & Sceery, A. (1988). Attachment in late adolescence: Working models, affect regulation, and representations of self and others. *Child Development*, 59, 135–146.

Krivan, M., Szabo, G., Sarnyai, Z., Kovacs, G. L., & Telegdy, G. (1995). Oxytocin blocks the development of heroin-fentanyl cross-tolerance in mice. *Pharmacology, Biochemistry, and Behavior*, 52, 591–594.

Kyuhou, S., & Gemba, H. (1998). Two vocalization-related subregions in the midbrain periaqueductal gray of the guinea pig. *Neuroreport: An International Journal for the Rapid Communication of Research in Neuroscience*, 9, 1607–1610.

Leary, M. R., Tambor, E. S., Terdal, S. K., & Downs, D. L. (1995). Self-esteem as an interpersonal monitor: The sociometer hypothesis. *Journal of Personality and Social Psychology*, 68, 518–530.

Levine, S. (1994). The ontogeny of the hypothalamic–pituitary–adrenal axis: The influence of maternal factors. *Annals of the New York Academy of Sciences*, 746, 275–288.

Levine, S., & Weiner, S. G. (1988). Psychendocrine aspects of mother–infant relationships in non-human primates. *Psychoneuroendocrinology*, 13, 143–154.

MacDonald, G., & Leary, M. R. (2005). Why does social exclusion hurt? The relationship between social and physical pain. *Psychological Bulletin*, 131, 202–223.

Main, M. (1981). Avoidance in the service of attachment: A working paper. In K. Immelmann, G. Barlow, L. Petrinovich, & M. Main (Eds.), *Behavioral development: The Bielefeld interdisciplinary project* (pp. 651–693). New York: Cambridge University Press.

Martel, F. L., Nevison, C. M., Simpson, M. J. A., & Keverne, E. B. (1995). Effects of opioid receptor blockade on the social behavior of rhesus monkeys living in large family groups. *Developmental Psychobiology*, 28, 71–84.

Mikulincer, M. (1998). Attachment working models and the sense of trust: An exploration of interaction goals and affect regulation. *Journal of Personality and Social Psychology*, 74, 1209–1224.

Mikulincer, M., & Florian, V. (1998). The relationship between adult attachment styles and emotional and cognitive reactions to stressful events. In J. A. Simpson & W. S. Rholes (Eds.), *Attachment theory and close relationships* (pp. 143–165). New York: Guilford Press.

Mikulincer, M., & Shaver, P. R. (2003). The attachment behavioral system in adulthood: Activation, psychodynamics, and interpersonal processes. In M. P. Zanna (Ed.), *Advances in experimental social psychology* (pp. 53–152). San Diego, CA: Academic Press.

Mineka, S., Gunnar, M. R., & Champoux, M. (1986). Control and early socio-emotional development: Infant rhesus monkeys reared in controllable versus uncontrollable environments. *Child Development*, 57, 1241–1256.

Muraven, M., & Baumeister, R. F. (2000). Self-regulation and depletion of limited resources: Does self-control resemble a muscle? *Psychological Bulletin*, 126, 247–259.

Nelson, E. E., & Panksepp, J. (1998). Brain substrates of infant–mother attachment: Contributions of opioids, oxytocin, and norepinephrine. *Neuroscience and Biobehavioral Reviews*, 22, 437–452.

Panksepp, J. (1999). *Affective neuroscience: The foundations of human and animal emotions*. New York: Oxford University Press.

Panksepp, J., Najam, N., & Soares, F. (1980). Morphine reduces social cohesion in rats. *Pharmacology, Biochemistry, and Behavior, 11*, 131–134.

Panksepp, J., Siviy, S. M., & Normansell, L. A. (1985). Brain opioids and social emotion. In M. Reite & T. Fields (Eds.), *The psychobiology of attachment and separation* (pp. 3–49). New York: Academic Press.

Parker, G., & Maynard Smith, J. (1991). Optimality theory in evolutionary biology. *Nature, 348*, 27–33.

Pedersen, C. A., Ascher, J. A., Monroe, Y. L., & Prange, A. J. (1982). Oxytocin induces maternal behavior in virgin female rats. *Science, 216*, 648–649.

Pedersen, C. A., Caldwell, J. D., Walker, C., Ayers, G., & Mason, G. A. (1994). Oxytocin activates the postpartum onset of rat maternal behavior in the ventral tegmental and medial preoptic areas. *Behavioral Neuroscience, 108*, 1163–1171.

Pettijohn, T. F., Wong, T. W., Ebert, P. D., & Scott, J. P. (1977). Alleviation of separation distress in three breeds of young dogs. *Developmental Psychobiology, 10*, 373–381.

Powers, S., Pietromonaco, P., Gunlicks, M., & Sayer, A. (2006). Dating couples' attachment styles and patterns of cortisol reactivity and recovery in response to a relationship conflict. *Journal of Personality and Social Psychology, 90*, 613–628.

Rholes, W. S., & Simpson, J. A. (Eds.) (2004). *Adult attachment: Theory, research, and clinical implications*. New York: Guilford Press.

Rholes, W. S., Simpson, J. A., & Blakely, B. S. (1995). Adult attachment styles and mothers' relationships with their young children. *Personal Relationships, 2*, 35–54.

Robinson, B. W. (1967). Vocalizations evoked from the forebrain in Macaca Mulata. *Physiology and Behavior, 2*, 345–354.

Shapiro, L. E., & Insel, T. R. (1989). Ontogeny of oxytocin receptors in rat forebrain: A quantitative study. *Synapse, 4*, 259–266.

Siegel, S. (1979). The role of conditioning in drug tolerance and addiction. In J. D. Keehan (Ed.), *Psychopathology in animals*. New York: Academic Press.

Simpson, J. A. (1990). Influence of attachment styles on romantic relationships. *Journal of Personality and Social Psychology, 59*, 971–980.

Simpson, J. A. (1999). Attachment theory in modern evolutionary perspective. In J. Cassidy & P. R. Shaver (Eds.), *Handbook of attachment: Theory, research, and clinical applications* (pp. 123–150). New York: Guilford Press.

Simpson, J. A., & Gangestad, S. W. (1991). Individual differences in sociosexuality: Evidence for convergent and discriminant validity. *Journal of Personality and Social Psychology, 60*, 870–883.

Simpson, J. A., & Rholes, W. S. (1994). Stress and secure base relationships in adulthood. In D. Perlman & K. Bartholomew (Eds.), *Attachment processes in adulthood* (pp. 181–204). London: Jessica Kingsley.

Simpson, J. A., Rholes, W. S., Campbell, L., & Wilson, C. L. (2003). Changes in attachment orientations across the transition to parenthood. *Journal of Experimental Social Psychology, 39*, 317–331.

Simpson, J. A., Rholes, W. S., & Nelligan, J. S. (1992). Support seeking and support giving within couples in an anxiety-provoking situation: The role of attachment styles. *Journal of Personality and Social Psychology, 62*, 434–446.

Simpson, J. A., Rholes, W. S., & Phillips, D. (1996). Conflict in close relationships: An attachment perspective. *Journal of Personality and Social Psychology, 71*, 899–914.

Spangler, G., & Schieche, M. (1998). Emotional and adrenocortical responses of infants to the Strange Situation: The differential functions of emotion expression. *International Journal of Behavioral Development, 22,* 681–706.

Stearns, S. C. (1992). *The evolution of life histories.* Oxford: Oxford University Press.

Tinbergen, N. (1963). On the aims and methods of ethology. *Zeitschrift für Tierpsychologie, 20,* 410–433.

Tooby, J. (1982). Pathogens, polymorphism, and the evolution of sex. *Journal of Theoretical Biology, 97,* 557–576.

Trivers, R. L. (1971). The evolution of reciprocal altruism. *Quarterly Review of Biology, 46,* 35–57.

Trivers, R. L. (1972). Parental investment and sexual selection. In B. Campbell (Ed.), *Sexual selection and the descent of man* (pp. 136–179). New York: Aldine de Gruyter.

Trivers, R. L. (1974). Parent–offspring conflict. *American Zoologist, 24,* 249–264.

Wilson, T. D., Lindsey, S., & Schooler, T. (2000). A model of dual attitudes. *Psychological Review, 107,* 101–126.

Zeifman, D., & Hazan, C. (1997) Attachment: The bond in pair-bonds. In J. A. Simpson & D. T. Kenrick (Eds.), *Evolutionary social psychology* (pp. 237–263). Hillsdale, NJ: Lawrence Erlbaum Associates, Inc.

Part IV

Reciprocal Influences of Self and Other, II: Close Relationships and Changing the Self

10

How Close Others Construct and Reconstruct Who We Are and How We Feel About Ourselves

ARTHUR ARON, SARAH KETAY, SUZANNE RIELA, and ELAINE N. ARON

*T*he self-expansion model of motivation and cognition in close relationships (Aron & Aron, 1986; Aron, Aron, & Norman, 2001) has two fundamental principles:

1. *Motivational principle:* People seek to expand their potential efficacy—that is, a major human motive is what has previously been described as effectance, competence, or exploration. (See especially, Aron, Norman, & Aron, 1998.)
2. *Inclusion-of-other-in-the-self principle:* One way people seek to expand the self is through close relationships, because in a close relationship the other's resources, perspectives, identities, and self-soothing and self-exciting capacities are experienced, to some extent, as one's own (as "included in the self"). (See especially, Aron, Mashek, & Aron, 2004.)

In this chapter we first review each of these aspects of the model and then suggest some possible implications of this model for (1) the content and structure the self-concept and (2) how one feels about that self-concept (one's self-esteem). A final section explores implications for some major theoretical perspectives relevant to the self.

SELF-EXPANSION MOTIVATION

The posited desire to expand the self is a general motive to enhance one's potential efficacy, encompassing well-known models of competence motivation, self-efficacy, self-improvement, exploration, curiosity, and intrinsic motivation (e.g., Bandura, 1977; Gecas, 1989; Ryan & Deci, 2000; Taylor, Neter, & Wayment, 1995;

White, 1959). Seeking self-expansion is not generally a conscious motive; feeling expanded may often be a conscious state (though not called by that name of course). Also, self-expansion operates both directly, as a general drive to enhance potential efficacy, and also through more specific evolved motivational modules, such as need to belong and sexual desire. Finally, rapid self-expansion, as often occurs when forming a new romantic relationship, is posited to result in high levels of excited positive affect.

These abstract ideas can be made more concrete by considering the Self-Expansion Questionnaire (SEQ; Lewandowski & Aron, 2002), a measure of the extent to which a person experiences a relationship partner as facilitating increased knowledge, skill, abilities, mate value, positive life changes, and novel experiences. Example items include "How much does your partner help to expand your sense of the kind of person you are?", "How much does your partner provide a source of exciting experiences?", "How much has knowing your partner made you a better person?", and "How much do you see your partner as a way to expand your own capabilities?" The SEQ is internally consistent and unifactorial, suggesting that these various experiences represent a coherent construct, and has demonstrated discriminant and convergent validity in relation to other relationship variables.

Below we briefly review four relevant research programs, each in the context of romantic love.

Self-Expansion Motivation Research Program 1: Developing a New Relationship Expands the Self

Aron, Paris, and Aron (1995) tested 325 students five times, once every 2½ weeks over 10 weeks. At each testing, participants answered a series of questions, including whether they had fallen in love since the last testing, plus a 3-minute timed task in which they listed as many self-descriptive words or phrases as came to mind in response to, "Who are you today?" Responses were coded for 19 content domains, such as family roles, occupations, and various emotions. As predicted, there was a significantly greater increase in number of self-content domains in the self-descriptions from before to after falling in love, as compared to changes before to after other testing sessions for those who fell in love, or as compared to typical between-test changes for participants who did not fall in love. In a sense, there was a literal expansion of self. A follow-up with a new sample of 529, included standard self-efficacy and self-esteem scales. As predicted, there were significantly greater increases in these variables from before to after falling in love. In both studies, effects were maintained when measures of mood change were controlled statistically.

Self-Expansion Motivation Research Program 2: Losing a Self-Expanding Relationship Contracts the Self

Lewandowski, Aron, Bassis, and Kunak (2006) first tested this idea in two questionnaire studies. Individuals who had recently experienced a break-up rated pre-dissolution self-expansion on the SEQ. Post-dissolution diminished self-concept was assessed in Study 1 by the direct question, "To what extent did you feel as though you lost part of who you are, as a result of the break-up?"; in Study 2, by content analysis for number of negative thoughts minus number of positive thoughts in response to the open-ended question, "How were you affected by the break-up of your relationship?" In both studies, pre-dissolution self-expansion predicted more diminished self-concept. Study 3 was a priming experiment. Participants first completed a task that increased the salience of either highly self-expanding or non-self-expanding aspects of their current relationship; they were then led through a guided imagery task in which they imagined breaking up with their partner. At the start and end of the experiment, all participants completed the open-ended "Who are you today?" listing used by Aron et al. (1995). As predicted, there was a significantly greater decline in the number of self-concept domains before to after imagining the break-up for those in the high, versus those in the low self-expansion prime condition. This result is exactly parallel, in the opposite direction, to what was found by Aron et al. (1995) for those who fell in love versus those who did not. Further, the impact of pre-dissolution self-expansion seems to be quite specific to this aspect of relationship quality since results in all three studies remained robust after controlling for pre-dissolution closeness. Finally, we should note that while loss of a self-expanding relationship seems to de-expand the self, some elements included in the self from the relationship (e.g., information gained) should survive relationship loss.

Self-Expansion Motivation Research Program 3: The Process of Rapid Expansion is Affectively Positive

Rapid expansion is posited to be highly pleasurable. Thus, in addition to a desire to *be* expanded (to possess high levels of potential efficacy), a key motivator is the desire to experience the *process* of expanding, to feel one's self increasing rapidly in potential self-efficacy. This is similar to Carver and Scheier's (1990) conception of self-regulatory process, in which people are portrayed as monitoring the rate at which they are making progress toward goals, and as experiencing positive affect when the perceived rate exceeds an expected rate. Indeed, they propose that accelerations in the rate cause feelings of exhilaration. Our notion of being motivated to experience the expanding process is also similar to Pyszczynski, Greenberg, and Solomon's (1997) "growth-expansion system." According to these authors, people seek the sense of exhilaration that accompanies expanding their skills and understanding, and it is the *process* of expanding skills and understanding that produces the exhilaration rather than the *product* or end state of having attained a new skill or understanding.

The major relevant work is a series of studies testing a predicted increase in relationship quality in long-term relationships from joint participation in self-expanding activities. This work emerged from a consideration of the well-documented typical decline in satisfaction and love after the "honeymoon period" (e.g., Tucker & Aron, 1993). When people begin a relationship, there may be an exhilarating period in which they spend hours talking, engaging in intense risk-taking and self-disclosure. From our perspective, this initial exhilarating period is one in which the partners are expanding their selves at a rapid rate by virtue of the intense exchange. Once they know each other fairly well, opportunities for further rapid expansion of this sort inevitably decrease. When rapid expansion occurs in the context of the relationships there is a high degree of satisfaction and love; when expansion is slow or nonexistent, there is little emotion, perhaps even boredom. Further, if slow expansion follows a period of rapid expansion, the loss of enjoyable emotion may be disappointing and attributed to deficiencies in the relationship.

In one series of experiments (e.g., Aron, Norman, Aron, McKenna, & Heyman, 2000, Studies 3–5) dating and married couples from the community came to our lab for what they believed was an assessment session involving questionnaires and being videotaped while interacting. Indeed, they completed questionnaires, participated together in a task that was videotaped, and then completed more questionnaires. However, unknown to participants, the questionnaires before were a pretest; those after, a posttest; and the task itself, an experimentally manipulated procedure in which some couples engaged in an expanding activity that was novel and challenging and those in the control condition engaged in a more mundane activity. (In the expanding activity the couple were tied together on one side at the wrists and ankles and then took part in a task in which they crawled together on mats for 12 meters, climbing over a barrier at one point, while pushing a foam cylinder with their heads. The task was timed and the couple received a prize if they beat a time limit; but the situation was rigged so that they all just barely succeeded on the next to last trial.) In all three experiments, as predicted, there was a significantly greater increase in relationship satisfaction and love in the expanding condition. The first study demonstrated the basic effect. The second included a no-activity control condition, and found that the effect was specifically due to increased satisfaction in the self-expansion condition (and not to decreased satisfaction in the mundane condition). The third experiment included short videotaped discussions of standardized topics before and after the interaction task and replicated the earlier findings using measures based on blind coding of the videotaped interactions.

The implications have been further clarified in two additional experiments. In one (Aron & Norman, 2007), a member of each couple carried out the crawling task as described above alone, while the partner was or was not made salient. (Instructions for which way to push the foam cylinder with one's head were given in a lit arrow that was directly beneath a TV monitor. In the partner-salient condition, the monitor itself was "accidentally" left on and showed the partner filling out a questionnaire; in the control condition, the monitor was off.) The result was a greater increase in satisfaction and love in the partner-salient condition, suggesting that the effect of self-expanding activities on relationships requires that the partner be salient; otherwise, the effect does not generalize to the relationship. The other additional experiment (Lewandowski & Aron, 2006) had couples do tasks systematically constructed to be either high or low in novelty/challenge or, independently, high or low in arousal (in a 2 × 2 design). The results were significant effects for high versus low novelty/challenge, but no significant effect for high versus low arousal. (Interestingly, a parallel study using the same tasks, but on romantic attraction between strangers at initial meeting, showed significant effects for arousal, but not for novelty/challenge; Lewandowski & Aron, 2004.)

Self-Expansion Motivation Research Program 4: The Nature of Passionate Love

Aron and Aron (1991) hypothesized that passionate love is best conceptualized as a strong goal-oriented motivation to merge with the partner. That is, passionate love is the experience associated with an intense desire to expand the self by including a particular other person in the self. Thus passionate love is not a distinct emotion in its own right (like happiness, sadness, or anger). Rather, it can evoke a variety of emotions according to whether and how the desire is fulfilled or frustrated. This view contrasts with views of passionate love as a specific emotion in its own right (e.g., Gonzaga, Keltner, Londahl, & Smith, 2001; Shaver, Morgan, & Wu, 1996; Shaver, Schwartz, Kirson, & O'Connor, 1987).

The status of love as a specific emotion has been controversial. It is clearly highly emotional. It functions in many ways like other emotions and Shaver et al. (1987) found "love" to be the most common response when asked to list a proto-typic emotion. Love has even been included as a "primary emotion" in many affect schemes. However, love, and especially passionate love, differs from most specific emotions in that it tends to be hard to control, is not associated with any specific facial expression, and is focused on a very specific reward. Thus some affect theorists (e.g., Ekman, 1992) have pointedly not included it among the basic emotions.

To examine how love differs from emotions, Acevedo and Aron (2004) conducted a series of studies in which participants were asked to think about an experience of love or an emotion such as anger or happiness, and then check which emotions they felt from a long list of emotions (from Shaver et al., 1987). In each of seven studies, using a variety of procedures and samples from three different cultures, people significantly checked many more negative valence emotions for love than they did for happiness or other strong positive emotions, or positive valence items for negative emotions.

Another series of studies (Acevedo, Gross, & Aron, 2005) focuses on up- and down-regulation of emotion. Preliminary results from interviews and question-naires suggest that people can down-regulate feelings of passionate love about as easily as emotions such as anger, fear, and happiness. However, it is much more difficult than anger and so forth to up-regulate (increase) feelings of passionate love. Respondents had no more trouble than for other conditions thinking of times they had wanted to up-regulate passionate love (to make themselves experience passionate love for someone for whom they did not feel it). But unlike anger and so forth, there were very, very few cases where they reported having been successful.

In yet another approach, we examined the neural correlates of passionate love (Aron, Fisher, Mashek, Strong, Li, & Brown, 2005). Here the hypothesis is that passionate love should consistently engage brain regions associated with intense reward (such as the caudate nucleus and associated dopamine system), but should be much less consistent across subjects in engaging brain regions associated with specific emotions (such as the orbital frontal cortex, anterior cingulate cortex, and amygdala). Thus we conducted an fMRI study with 17 participants who were all very intensely, and very recently, "in love" (verified by interviews and question-naire responses). While in the scanner, participants viewed images of their beloved and of a familiar neutral individual of the same sex and age as their partner. Consistent with predictions, there was significantly greater consistent activation across subjects in reward areas (but not in emotion areas) when viewing the image of their beloved than when viewing the control image. Further, the degree of greater activation when viewing the image of the beloved was strongly correlated with a self-report measure of intensity of passionate love, in spite of the considerably restricted range of scores.

Taken together, we think the tendency of passionate love to generate more opposite valence emotions compared to emotions, to be more difficult to up-regulate than emotions, and to engage common reward areas across subjects but not common emotion areas, lends considerable support to the self-expansion model hypothesis that it should be considered a goal-oriented state rather than a specific emotion. This hypothesis derives from the central idea in the self-expansion model that people seek close relationships to expand the self by including others in the self, and that passionate love represents the experience of a perceived opportunity for very rapid expansion of the self.

Self-Expansion Motivation Research Conclusions

In sum, the motivational aspect of the self-expansion model proposes that a major human motive, which occurs in diverse contexts including close relationships, is the desire to expand one's ability to accomplish goals, both directly and through enhancing the efficacy of the partner or the relationship as a unit. We have described four lines of research examining implications of this idea in the context of romantic love, which appear to support predictions from the model, as well as demonstrate its heuristic value for generating novel hypotheses relevant to important theoretical and practical issues.

Before concluding this section on the self-expansion motive, we wish to make clear that we see it as an aspect of every living system, and perhaps of the universe itself, if we may be so metaphysical. After all, the Big Bang does seem to be about self-expansion, as does the development from single to multi-cell organisms, reptiles' development of the sense of territory as an extension of the self into the environment, mammals' sense of their offspring and social group as an extension of the self, and finally humans' ability to sense anything or anyone, or everything and everyone, as part of the self. Was any of this conscious? Probably not. Was it governed by a "motive"? We would say yes, in the sense that every organism seeks to expand its potential efficacy, and that humans (and other mammals) seek to expand this efficacy, especially through relationships with others.

INCLUDING OTHERS IN THE SELF

According to the self-expansion model, this general motivation to expand the self often leads to a desire to enter and maintain a particular close relationship, in part because close relationships are an especially satisfying, useful, and human means to self-expansion. (Although we continue to use the term "*self*-expansion" in the relationship context, the inclusion and resulting expansion is typically mutual.) Specifically, in a close relationship, each includes to some extent in his or her self the other's resources, perspectives, and identities. Below we briefly elaborate on each of these aspects. (People also self-expand in ways besides including others in the self, a point to which we will return at the end of the chapter. But for most humans, the inclusion of other persons is a particularly important opportunity for self-expansion because of the complexity and richness of another human being, and because social linkages are so important in our species.)

Including Others' Resources in the Self

"Resources" refers to the material, knowledge-related (conceptual/informational/ procedural), and social assets that facilitate the achievement of goals. Perceiving one's self as including a relationship partner's resources refers to perceiving one's self as having access to those resources, as if, to some extent, the close other's resources were one's own (e.g., "I can do this because my partner will show me how"). This perceived inclusion of another's resources is particularly central from a motivational point of view because it means that the outcomes (rewards and costs) the other incurs are to some extent experienced as one's own. Thus, for example, helping the close other is helping the self; interfering with the other is interfering with the self (e.g., "I'll be quiet while my partner reads the instructions"). This analysis also implies that the other's acquisition and loss of resources are experienced to some extent as if they were happening to one's own resources.

As noted, one implication is that we treat to some extent a close other's outcomes as if they were our own. In the first direct test of this principle (Aron, Aron, Tudor, & Nelson, 1991, Experiment 1 and Follow-ups 1 and 2), participants took part in an allocation game in which they made a series of decisions allocating money to self, best friend, or another person. Allocations to best friend were consistently similar to those for self, but allocations to non-close others consistently favored self. Importantly, these results held up whether or not the other would know who was responsible for the allocations. Several other studies using a variety of paradigms and theoretical orientations support the prediction from the model that people react to a close other's outcomes as if the outcomes were their own (e.g., Beach, Tesser, Fincham, Jones, Johnson, & Whitaker, 1998; De La Ronde & Swann, 1998; Gardner, Gabriel, & Hochschild, 2002; McFarland, Buehler, & MacKay, 2001; Medvene, Teal, & Slavich, 2000). Many of these predictions would also follow from interdependence models of "transformation of motivation" (e.g., Kelley & Thibaut, 1979). Indeed, the idea of including other in the self has been linked directly with such models in work on "cognitive interdependence" (Agnew, Van Lange, Rusbult, & Langston, 1998). Our view is that transformation of motivation occurs both through coming to see the other *as* the self through shared/overlapping constructions of self and other, as well as through the kinds of subjective exchange-like processes that are emphasized in much of the traditional interdependence theorizing.

Including Others' Perspectives in the Self

This aspect of inclusion refers to experiencing (consciously or unconsciously) the world to some extent from the partner's point of view. For example, when a long-term married individual attends a ballet, the ballet may be experienced not only through the individual's own eyes but also, as it were, through the spouse's eyes. Thus when another person is included in the self, various self-related attributional and cognitive biases should also apply with regard to that person.

Several studies have indeed found that the usual actor–observer difference in the tendency to make situational versus dispositional attributions (Jones & Nisbett, 1971) is smaller when the other is someone close to self, such as a best friend or romantic partner. These studies were all based on Sande, Goethals, and Radloff's (1988) paradigm in which participants rate each of a series of 11 trait pairs (e.g., "serious–carefree") for whether the first, the second, neither, or both are true of a target person. Consistent with the usual bias, people make more situational ("both") choices when rating themselves than when rating other people in general. However, consistent with the model of inclusion of close others in the self, Sande et al. found that this difference between self and other was greatly reduced when the other was a liked, familiar person. Focusing specifically on *close* others, Aron et al. (1991, Introduction to Experiment 1) found that participants rated "both" for 4.5 traits for self, 3.46 for best friend, and 2.71 for non-close other (friend vs. non-close other, $p < .01$). Further, Aron and Fraley (1999) found that the extent to which participants used "both" when rating a romantic partner was significantly positively correlated with subjectively rated "closeness" to the partner ($r = .21$) and that it significantly predicted whether the couple were still together 3 months later ($r = .30$).

Another relevant series of studies adapted a paradigm developed by Lord (1980), focusing on the conceptual perspective of seeing oneself as background to experience while seeing other people as figural. Participants are presented a series of 60 nouns, for each of which they are to form a vivid, elaborated image of a particular person (self or someone else) interacting with the object the noun represents. Later, participants are given a surprise free recall test for the nouns. As predicted from his model of self as background to experience, Lord found consistently *fewer* nouns recalled that were imaged with self, versus nouns imaged with media personalities. In our studies (Aron et al., 1991; Experiment 2 and Follow-up), participants also imaged nouns with a close other, their mother. Our results replicated Lord's for self and non-close other (media personality or mother's best friend). But *also*, as predicted from our model, nouns imaged with the *close* other were recalled about the same as those imaged with self. Further, one of these studies included a measure of closeness to mother. The degree of the effect (mother minus mother's friend difference) correlated strongly ($r = .56$) with closeness (but not with rated similarity with mother). Thus, just as one's own perspective is a background to experience, one's perspective gained through close others may also serve as a background to experience; and the closer the others are, the more this is the case.

Including Others' Identities in the Self

"Identity" refers to features that distinguish a person from other people and objects—primarily the characteristics, memories, and other features that locate the person in social and physical space. In relation to the cognitive aspects in general (that is, perspectives and identities), we have described our model as implying shared cognitive elements of self and close others (Aron & Fraley, 1999). Some general support for the notion that we include close others' identities in the self can be gleaned from research on "the self-reference effect." In their meta-analysis, Symons and Johnson (1997) reported a consistent overall better memory for words studied in relation to self than for words studied in relation to other persons. However, importantly, across the 65 studies with relevant data, they also found that there were significantly smaller differences between self-reference memory facilitation and other-reference memory facilitation when the other was someone close to self. Thus being in a close relationship does seem to subvert (though not eliminate entirely) the seemingly fundamental cognitive distinction between self and other.

However, our model also posits that this apparent subversion by close relationships of the self–other distinction is due, specifically, to the other becoming "part of the self"—to the very structure of the self changing, such that the self includes the other in its very make-up. For example, the model implies that one's own and a close other's traits may actually be confused or interfere with each other. To test this idea, we evaluated the patterns of response latencies in making me/not me decisions ("does the trait describe me?") about traits previously rated for their descriptiveness of self and of spouse (Aron et al., 1991, Experiment 3 and Follow-up). On traits on which the self matched the partner (the trait was true of both or false of both), me/not-me responses were faster than when a trait was mismatched for self and partner (true for one, false for the other). Further, Aron and Fraley (1999) found that the degree of this match–mismatch response-time effect (serving as a measure of overlap of self and other) correlated significantly with self-report measures of relationship quality, and significantly predicted increases in subjective closeness over a 3-month period. Using this same response-time paradigm, Smith, Coats, and Walling (1999) replicated both the overall difference between close and non-close others and the correlation with the magnitude of self-reported closeness to the close other. Smith and colleagues eloquently articulated why such patterns may result: "If mental representations of two persons . . . overlap so that they are effectively a single representation, reports on attributes of one will be facilitated or inhibited by matches and mismatches with the second" (p. 873). Researchers using this paradigm have also shown that people include the qualities of their ingroup in the self (Smith et al., 1999; Tropp & Wright, 2001) and that it is possible to induce some degree of inclusion of a stranger in the self by instructions to take the role of the other (Galinsky & Moskowitz, 2000; see also Davis, Conklin, Smith, & Luce, 1996, for a related result).

Another series of studies (Mashek, Aron, & Boncimino, 2003) focused on the prediction that people especially confuse information associated with self with information associated with close others. Participants rated one set of traits for self, a different set of traits for a close other, and still other traits for one or more familiar non-close others. Participants were then given a surprise recognition task in which they were presented with each trait and asked for which person they had rated it. The focus of the analysis was on confusions—traits participants remembered having rated for one person when they had actually rated them for a different person. In all three studies, results were as predicted. When participants did not correctly recognize a trait as having been originally rated for self, they were significantly more likely to remember it as having been rated for the partner than as having been rated for a media personality; similarly, when participants did not correctly recognize a trait as originally rated for partner, they were significantly more likely to remember it as having been rated for self than for the media personality. These results all held up controlling for various potential confounds, such as greater tendency to recall any trait as having been rated for self, valence and extremity of ratings, and similarity to the close other.

Yet another line of relevant research is work using the Inclusion of Other in the Self (IOS) Scale (Aron, Aron, & Smollan, 1992). The scale consists of seven pairs of circles overlapping to different degrees, from which respondent select the pair (degree of overlap) that best describes a particular relationship. It has high reliability and discriminant, convergent, and predictive validity—with levels that match or exceed those of other measures of closeness that are typically more complex and lengthy. The scale has been widely used in relationship research (for a review, see Agnew, Loving, Le, & Goodfriend, 2004), and correlates with such non-obvious measures as the effect size in the match–mismatch response-time paradigm (e.g., Aron & Fraley, 1999) and the number of plural pronouns such as "we" and "us" used spontaneously in relationship descriptions (Agnew et al., 1998). A meta-analysis of predictors of dating relationship dissolution (Le, Smoak, & Agnew, 2006) found a mean effect size for the IOS scale of $d = -.78$, with minimal variance among studies. Perhaps the IOS Scale has been so successful because the metaphor of overlapping circles representing self and other corresponds to how people actually process information about self and other in relationships.

Finally, preliminary fMRI data suggest an overlap of the neural systems related to self and close others (Aron, Whitfield, & Lichty, 2007). While in the scanner, participants heard their own name, the name of a familiar other, and common names that did not refer to people well known to the participant. Rated closeness to the familiar other (outside the scanner) predicted significantly greater similarity in the overall pattern of brain activation when hearing one's own name and when hearing the familiar other's name, as compared to the similarity in the overall pattern of brain activation when hearing one's own name and when hearing a common name of a stranger.

Is it Familiarity?

Close others are typically also highly familiar, but several findings suggest that the various inclusion effects are specifically due to closeness. In the Symons and Johnson (1997) meta-analysis, there was little difference in average effect size between studies using familiar versus non-familiar others as non-self targets; rated familiarity did not correlate with the Lord paradigm effects in Aron et al. (1991), while rated closeness did; direct measures of familiarity (amount of time and diversity of activities shared with partner) did not predict the attribution effects or the match–mismatch effects in the Aron and Fraley (1999) study, while rated closeness and IOS scores did; and Mashek et al. (2003) found that the source memory confusion effect was stronger for a college student's best friend (a very close but moderately familiar other) than for his or her father (a moderately close but very familiar other).

Including Others in Self Conclusion

In sum, the idea that close relationship partners treat each other's resources, perspectives, and identities to some extent as their own has been supported in studies using diverse methods including self-reports, allocation tasks, memory and response time procedures, and neuroimaging, and does not appear to be the result of a mere familiarity effect.

IMPLICATIONS FOR UNDERSTANDING THE SELF

Development, Content, and Structure of the Self-Concept

Extending James (1890/1948), we take the following general view. People add to what they identify as themselves (as "me") to the extent that the addition (e.g., a person or event) affects outcomes for a person's current conception of self. Originally, the self is probably composed of one's bodily sensations and the liveliest aspects of the stream of consciousness. But very quickly, the infant's self incorporates a sense of his or her entire body, caregiver, name, and perhaps even blankets, crib, clothing, and so forth. Over time, more and more aspects of the environment become part of the self. The degree to which an object is likely to be included and deeply embedded is a function of one's largely unconscious perception of how much one is affected by outcomes associated with it (a favorite blanket lost, the caregiver being attentive) and how long these outcomes are sensed as likely to affect one. Also, an important source of the sense of being affected, at least for the infant, is the degree to which negative affects are soothed or ended and positive affects stimulated, including curiosity and self-expansion through the excitement of learning and interacting.

Given this general view of the development of the self-concept, we believe the self-expansion model more specifically adds the following.

1. *People are especially likely to include what or who will increase their*

ability to accomplish goals over time. Thus resources such as knowledge, abilities, wealth, and social status, are more important than specific physical possessions or brief experiences, unless they add to wealth, status, and so forth.

2. *Other people are especially ideal to be included in the self as this seems to be the very premise of the adaptation of social animals.* When forming a long-term relationship with a desirable other person, one has access to the other's physical resources, social status, perspectives, knowledge, and help with emotional regulation. And given the expectation of a long-term relationship, one will have these benefits for a long time; this begins with the infant's bond with the caregiver.

3. *Other people with whom one has a close relationship are especially likely to be included in the self to the extent one is interdependent with them.* That is, following Kelley and Thibaut's (1979) model, the very meaning of a close relationship is that my outcomes are dependent on (are affected by) your outcomes and our joint outcomes.

4. *If close others become significant parts of the content of the self, then the contents of the self are subject to significant fluctuations as relationships change.* Such changes are particularly likely to impact the self to the extent the other or the relationship is perceived (1) to offer self-expanding resources, (2) to make his or her resources available to self, and (3) to be interdependent with self.

Self-Esteem

We think of self-esteem as the value one places on oneself, the good or bad feelings that accompany salience of the self. There are at least two general ways in which we think the self-expansion model may offer unique insights into understanding self-esteem.

First, to the extent someone is included in the self, one's self-esteem is partly a function of the value placed on the person (or the person's perceived resources, perspectives, identities, and self-soothing or self-exciting/expanding affects). If a close other is felt to be a wonderful person (as when my child is highly successful), then to the extent this close other is included in myself, I feel myself to be wonderful. Similarly, if I feel the other is terrible (for example, if my child became a criminal), I feel myself to be terrible. The same could be said for objects such as a lovely or shabby home, or a strong or weak ability to read. But because a great deal of oneself consists of close others included in the self (as per the previous section on construction of the self-concept), the value of these others plays a huge role in self-esteem. This also applies to issues of acceptance and rejection following ideas like those of Leary and McDonald (2003). That is, my self-esteem is strongly affected by the degree of social acceptance or rejection I sense my close others to enjoy or suffer.

This effect on self-esteem can feed back on the relationship. Thus, rather than lower my self-esteem, I may distance myself from the close other. Also, once I have developed a particular level of self-esteem for myself overall, whatever the cause, that will naturally extend to close others. Similarly, if I feel myself overall to be very negative, this is likely to taint my perception of anyone who is close to me. Of course other processes are also likely to be at work here; for example, if I see myself negatively, I am likely to assume my partner sees me that way, as noted by Murray, Rose, and Holmes (2005). However, we would add that if seeing myself negatively leads to seeing my partner as more positive by comparison, this might lead back to my seeing myself more positively. Thus including other in the self could lead to a kind of equilibrium in how I see myself and my partner.

Second, as described earlier, we posit that love for a particular other occurs fundamentally because we sense that including that other in the self offers substantial potential for self-expansion. Thus *self-love* (certainly an aspect of self-esteem) should vary especially strongly with how much one senses oneself to be able to accomplish whatever one desires, and to have the ability to include whatever or whoever adds to that potential efficacy.

Further, our model equates *passionate* love with experienced or hoped for *rapid* self-expansion. Thus one should feel a surge of self-love (a "passionate self-love") when one is experiencing some major, rapid inclusion of new perspectives, resources, and identities in the self. Indeed, when falling in love with another, if it is unambiguously reciprocated, one is likely to show such a rapid increase in self-esteem (Aron et al., 1995, Study 2).

But the parallels may go much further. In a romantic relationship, as one becomes accustomed to having the resources and so forth that the partner provides, the exhilaration from the rapid movement towards the goal inevitably slows down. The same thing may occur with self-esteem. As one becomes accustomed to some substantial new development in one's life (e.g., marriage, graduation), the sense of expansion decreases, and so does self-esteem. Finally, it may well be that the way people can recover a sense of high self-esteem is the same way they can recover feelings of passionate love: participate in novel and challenging activities with self being salient (e.g., learn something new, travel somewhere exotic).

RELATION TO OTHER MODELS

Here we give some examples of possible implications of the self-expansion model for issues raised by various other self-relevant theoretical models.

Approaches of Cooley, Mead, Role Theory, Symbolic Interactionism, and Narrative Psychology

According to these approaches, we know who we are by how others see us and by what is expected of us. The self is constructed in the context of a shared meaning system. That is, the self is a location in the shared social nexus with a set of socially defined expectations. Here is what we would add: When others are included in the self, there can be a confusion of one's location in the social nexus with that of the close other. Thus one aspect of a close other that I take on to myself is the other's social roles and expectations. (For example, if my partner is a star athlete I may spontaneously expect myself—perhaps quite incorrectly—to have high athletic ability.) Indeed, these concepts that are seen to shape individual experience and behavior in these kinds of models are also applicable to our reactions and urgings to those to whom we are close. (It is, for example, very easy to be embarrassed by the social mistakes of close others.)

Transference

Andersen and Chen (2002), following ideas developed in the context of psychodynamic thinking, have emphasized that our understanding of and reactions to a new person are often shaped by the new person's similarity to people who have been important in our lives. Thus our response to the new person may be inappropriately similar to that for the old one. The self-expansion model adds that what we transfer onto a new person is someone who is already part of the self. This means, as transference models emphasize, that we see the previous other in the new person. But we would add that, because the previous other was in the self, we include (to some extent) the new person in the self. Then, the self is expanded to include aspects of the new person that were not already included in the self based on the old person. One implication is that I may feel that I have access to the resources, perspectives, and identities of the new person (perhaps incorrectly if no relationship is formed with the new person). This may be a major way that people develop new aspects of the self, some of which turn out to be misleading when tested. (Of course, the self may also associate failures or obstacles to self-expansion with a close other, then transfer those onto a similar person or a person with whom one is in a similar situation, and expect to fail with or be obstructed by the new person.)

Attachment Theory

We see the attachment system (Bowlby, 1969) as a product of the long evolution of social animals that has become even more crucial, and flexible, in primates and then in humans. One way to think about this direction of evolution is that a long childhood provides time for the child to include the family's resources, knowledge, perspectives, and so forth into the self. That is, childhood is a long expansion of the self by including others into it. One does not think of the first weeks of life, while attachment is already developing, as a time when cognition is strong. But expansion of the self is not limited to conscious intention manifested through thought and action. Stern (1985), at least, would argue (and studies of newborns verify; e.g., Simpson, 1999) that much is happening psychologically even in the first days of life—newborns recognize and prefer their mother's voice and scent, human voices, and looking at human faces, especially eyes. These preferences involve affects and motivations as well as perception. That is, newborns do seem to prefer to "include" knowledge of others. By 3 months they have developed a "core sense of self" (Stern, 1985, p. 26) and others, especially the primary care giver. They seem to be busily including others into the self in the sense of learning from them what is rewarded with smiles and what is dangerous or leads to refusal to share resources through facial and bodily expressions and tones of voice.

If including the resources of the other is not already occurring in a cognitive sense, the groundwork is certainly being laid. But of course the infant actually is including the other in the self—first the other's physical regulation of the newborn through the other's resources, then by 3 months the other's emotional and social regulation through mutual gaze, and so on with increasing development. From the beginning the infant has ways of self-expanding by communicating "yes" as well as "no"—that is, "I want more of that," or "I wish to include more of that." Caregivers respond by providing (or not) what the infant wants.

Disruptions of this natural inclusion of each other into their selves, leading to insecure attachments, create expectations about the others' responses to this desire to include the other. These in turn lead to individual differences in self-expansion motivation and strategies (Aron & Aron, 2006). That is, we hypothesize that attachment style differences would lead to different self-expansion strategies beside including others, as well as reduced self-expansion motivation through early frustration of it or punishment of it being directed towards certain domains.

Affectively Based Self- and Other-Organizations and Splitting

People sometimes organize knowledge about the self into niches or aspects that are either all positive or all negative (e.g., Graham & Clark, 2006; Showers & Kevlyn, 1999; Showers & Kling, 1996). This research has also shown that we make a similar organization of our knowledge of a close other. What the self-expansion model adds is that to the extent the close other is part of the self, these two aspects of the self-organizations are inter-related into a system. For example, if one has a valenced self-organization, activating a negative about oneself or the other can activate a set of negatives about both self and other. If my close other forgets to wash the dishes, I may disproportionately recall how much both my partner *and myself* are irresponsible. Some specific hypotheses are (1) degree of valenced categorization of self and other should be similar to the extent other is included in the self; (2) to the extent one has valenced categorization of self and to the extent other is included in the self, when a particular valence is made salient for either, it should activate the same valence thoughts about both; and (3) when a particular valence is made salient about self and one has valenced organization, if thoughts of the other do not match this valence, it should decrease the extent to which one feels the other is included in the self.

Empathy

Empathy models emphasize spontaneous response to another's suffering. Studies have already shown that we are empathic for those we include in self (Cialdini, Brown, Lewis, Luce, & Neuberg, 1997) and taking the perspective of the other increases including other in the self (Davis et al., 1996, Galinsky & Moskowitz, 2000). An additional implication is that empathy can feed back to construct and change the self and how one feels about oneself. For example, we hypothesize that

(1) to the extent a person is included in the self, if that person is threatened, the self is threatened; but (2) to the extent a close other is felt to be threatened, we may exclude the other from the self (to avoid reducing one's own opportunities for self-expansion).

Self-Esteem Maintenance Theory (SEM)

Tesser (1988) predicted that individuals will reflect (take onto themselves) another's successes when these do not represent a negative social comparison for self, but they will contrast with the other when the other's success creates a negative social comparison. Reflection processes are exactly what one would expect if other is included in the self. Lockwood, Dolderman, Sadler, and Gerchak (2004) found that for close others, we may minimize comparison by subjectively strengthening salience of the social bond. The reason may be that when the other is part of self, the other's success is my success. Thus, similar to the empathy suggestions, we hypothesize (1) to the extent a person is included in the self (and holding constant similarity), and to the extent that person succeeds, one feels that the self has succeeded; and (2) to the extent a person succeeds (and holding constant similarity), we are motivated to include them in the self to the extent their success signals resources for future success (i.e., if their success appears to be pure chance and does not provide any new resources, one would not have the same reaction). These hypotheses differ from the standard SEM models in that those models typically treat similarity and closeness as identical (as a unit relation). We argue however that similarity and closeness can be separated and have opposite effects. Similarity to one who has succeeded can create contrast or comparison because one feels one could or should have had the same outcome. But for closeness (when defined as including other in the self), the effects should be entirely to encourage reflection.

Self-Concept Clarity, Other-Concept Clarity, and Relational Schemas

These approaches (e.g., Baldwin, 2005; Campbell, Trapnell, Heine, Katz, Lavallee, & Lehman, 1996; Gurung, Sarason, & Sarason, 2001) focus on the extent to which one has well-defined and stable concepts of self and others, and the extent to which one has clear and accessible if–then, self–other linkages. Several possible predictions follow from the self-expansion model related to these constructs: (1) to the extent someone is included in the self and the person is different from self, there should be less self-concept clarity; thus closeness can sometimes undermine the clarity of just who one is, which could well lower one's self esteem; (2) to the extent someone is included in self and I have a clear self-concept, this interferes with having a clear concept of the other; and (3) finally, because a relational schema is a cognitive construction involving a self- and other-construct, to the extent self and other are confused, the relational schema should be less well defined (though only after controlling for familiarity and experience with the other).

SUMMARY AND CONCLUSION

The self-expansion model is based on a motivational principle that people seek to expand their potential efficacy, and an inclusion-of-other-in-the-self principle that one way in which people seek to expand the self is through close relationships in which they come to experience the other's resources, perspectives, and identities as their own. We first reviewed research that lends support to this model in the context of close relationships and then explored some new ideas about ways the model may bear on our understanding of the self: We briefly elaborated a suggestion that the self-concept consists, to a considerable extent, of what we have included in the self from close others (also noting that the contents of the self-concept are thus likely to be highly affected by changes in relationships). For similar reasons we suggested that self-esteem should be heavily influenced by the esteem we hold for close others, and went on to add some specific ways that ideas from the model regarding love may apply to self-esteem considered as self-love. Finally, we considered some ways that the self-expansion model may generate new hypotheses relevant to various influential self-related theories.

Overall, our goal has been to stimulate new thinking about the self, using our model, which has quite explicit views about the self, although developed for understanding close relationships. We expect that some of our speculations may not survive empirical tests. But we hope to have provided some conceptual resources, perspectives, and identities that readers can include in their scientific self; and that including these in their self will expand their potential efficacy in developing a systematic knowledge of how we construct and reconstruct who we are and how we feel about ourselves.

REFERENCES

Acevedo, B., & Aron, A. (2004). *Love: More than just a feeling?* Paper presented at the Annual Meeting of the Society for Personality and Social Psychology, Austin, TX, January 2004.

Acevedo, B., Gross, J., & Aron, A. (2005). *Up- and down-regulation of love versus other emotions.* Research in progress.

Agnew, C. R., Loving, T. J., Le, B., & Goodfriend, W. (2004). Thinking close: Measuring relational closeness as perceived self-other inclusion. In D. Mashek & A. Aron (Eds), *Handbook of closeness and intimacy* (pp. 103–115). Mahwah, NJ: Lawrence Erlbaum Associates, Inc.

Agnew, C. R., Van Lange, P. A. M., Rusbult, C. E., & Langston, C. A. (1998). Cognitive interdependence: Commitment and the mental representation of close relationships. *Journal of Personality and Social Psychology, 74,* 939–954.

Andersen, S. M., & Chen, S. (2002). The relational self: An interpersonal social-cognitive theory. *Psychological Review, 109,* 619–645.

Aron, A., & Aron, E. N. (1986). *Love as the expansion of self: Understanding attraction and satisfaction.* New York: Hemisphere.

Aron, A., & Aron, E. N. (1991). Love and sexuality. In K. McKinney & S. Sprecher (Eds.),

Sexuality in close relationships (pp. 25–48). Hillsdale, NJ: Lawrence Erlbaum Associates, Inc.

Aron, A., & Aron. E. N. (2006). Romantic relationships from the perspectives of the self-expansion model and attachment theory: Partially overlapping circles. In M. Mikulincer & F. S. Goodman (Eds.), *The dynamics of romantic love: Attachment, caregiving, and sex* (pp. 359–382). New York: Guilford Press.

Aron, A., Aron, E. N., & Norman, C. (2001). The self expansion model of motivation and cognition in close relationships and beyond. In M. Clark & G. Fletcher (Eds.), *Blackwell handbook of social psychology, Vol. 2: Interpersonal processes* (pp. 478–501). Oxford: Blackwell.

Aron, A., Aron, E. N., & Smollan, D. (1992). Inclusion of Other in the Self Scale and the structure of interpersonal closeness. *Journal of Personality and Social Psychology*, 63, 596–612.

Aron, A., Aron, E. N., Tudor, M., & Nelson, G. (1991). Close relationships as including other in the self. *Journal of Personality and Social Psychology*, 60, 241–253.

Aron, A., Fisher, H., Mashek, D., Strong, G., Li, H., & Brown, L. (2005). Reward, motivation and emotion systems associated with early-stage intense romantic love. *Journal of Neurophysiology*, 94, 327–337.

Aron, A., & Fraley, B. (1999). Relationship closeness as including other in the self: Cognitive underpinnings and measures. *Social Cognition*, 17, 140–160.

Aron, A., Mashek, D., & Aron, E. N. (2004). Closeness, intimacy, and including other in the self. In D. Mashek & A. Aron (Eds.), *Handbook of closeness and intimacy* (pp. 27–41). Mahwah, NJ: Lawrence Erlbaum Associates, Inc.

Aron, A., & Norman, C. (2007). *Couple participation in self-expanding activities and relationship quality: Is shared participation necessary?* Manuscript in preparation.

Aron, A., Norman, C. C., & Aron, E. N. (1998). The self-expansion model and motivation. *Representative Research in Social Psychology*, 22, 1–13.

Aron, A., Norman, C. C., Aron, E. N., McKenna, C., & Heyman, R. (2000). Couples' shared participation in novel and arousing activities and experienced relationship quality. *Journal of Personality and Social Psychology*, 78, 273–283.

Aron, A., Paris, M., & Aron, E. N. (1995). Falling in love: Prospective studies of self-concept change. *Journal of Personality and Social Psychology*, 69, 1102–1112.

Aron, A., Whitfield, S., & Lichty, W. (2007). Whole brain correlations: Examining similarity across conditions of overall patterns of neural activation in fMRI. In S. Sawilowsky (Ed.), *Real data analysis* (pp. 365–369). Charlotte, NC: American Educational Research Association/Information Age Publishing.

Baldwin, M. W. (2005). Understanding and modifying the relational schemas underlying insecurity. In M. W. Baldwin & S. D. Dandeneau (Eds.), *Interpersonal cognition* (pp. 33–61). New York: Guilford Press.

Bandura, A. (1977). Self-efficacy: Toward a unifying theory of behavioral change. *Psychological Review*, 84, 191–215.

Beach, S. R., Tesser, A., Fincham, F. D., Jones, D. J., Johnson, D., & Whitaker, D. J. (1998). Pleasure and pain in doing well, together: An investigation of performance-related affect in close relationships. *Journal of Personality and Social Psychology*, 74, 923–938.

Bowlby, J. (1969). *Attachment and loss: Vol. 1. Attachment*. New York: Basic Books.

Campbell, J. D., Trapnell, P. D., Heine, S. J., Katz, I. M., Lavallee, L. F., & Lehman, D. R. (1996). Self-concept clarity: Measurement, personality correlates, and cultural boundaries. *Journal of Personality and Social Psychology*, 70, 141–156.

Carver, C., & Scheier, M. (1990). Principles of self-regulation, action, and emotion. In

E. T. Higgins & R. M. Sorrentino (Eds.), *Handbook of motivation and cognition: Foundations of social behavior* (Vol. 2). New York: Guilford Press.

Cialdini, R. B., Brown, S. L., Lewis, B. P., Luce, C., & Neuberg, S. L. (1997). Reinterpreting the empathy–altruism relationships: When one into one equals oneness. *Journal of Personality and Social Psychology*, 73, 481–494.

Davis, M. H., Conklin, L., Smith, A., & Luce, C. (1996). Effect of perspective taking on the cognitive representation of persons: A merging of self and other. *Journal of Personality and Social Psychology*, 70, 713–726.

De La Ronde, C., & Swann, W. B., Jr. (1998). Partner verification: Restoring shattered images of our intimates. *Journal of Personality and Social Psychology*, 75, 374–382.

Ekman, P. (1992). An argument for basic emotions. *Cognition and Emotion*, 6, 169–200.

Galinsky, A. D., & Moskowitz, G. B. (2000). Perspective-taking: Decreasing stereotype expression, stereotype accessibility, and in-group favoritism. *Journal of Personality and Social Psychology*, 78, 708–724.

Gardner, W. L., Gabriel, S., & Hochschild, L. (2002). When you and I are "we", you are not threatening: The role of self-expansion in social comparison. *Journal of Personality and Social Psychology*, 82, 239–251.

Gecas, V. (1989). Social psychology of self-efficacy. *American Sociological Review*, 15, 291–316.

Gonzaga, G. C., Keltner, D., Londahl, E. A., & Smith, M. D. (2001). Love and the commitment problem in romantic relations and friendship. *Journal of Personality and Social Psychology*, 81, 247–262.

Graham, S. M., & Clark, M. S. (2006). Self-esteem and organization of valenced information about others: The "Jekyll and Hyde"-ing of relationship partners. *Journal of Personality and Social Psychology*, 90, 652–665.

Gurung, R. A. R., Sarason, B. R., & Sarason, I. G. (2001). Predicting relationship quality and emotional reactions to stress from significant-other-concept clarity. *Personality and Social Psychology Bulletin*, 27, 1267–1276.

James, W. (1948). *Psychology*. Cleveland, OH. Fine Editions Press. (Original work published 1890.)

Jones, E. E., & Nisbett, R. (1971). The actor and the observer: Divergent perceptions of the causes of behavior. In E. E. Jones, D. E. Kanouse, H. H. Kelley, R. E. Nisbett, S. Valins, & B. Weiner (Eds.), *Attribution: Perceiving the causes of behavior* (pp. 79–94). Morristown, NJ: General Learning Press.

Kelley, H. H., & Thibaut, J. W. (1979). *Interpersonal relations: A theory of interdependence*. New York: Wiley-Interscience.

Le, B., Smoak, D., & Agnew, C. R. (2006). *A meta-analytic examination of predictors of dissolution in dating relationships*. Paper presented at the International Assocation for Relationship Research meeting, Rethymnon, Crete, July.

Leary, M. R., & McDonald, G. (2003). Individual differences in self-esteem: A review and theoretical integration. In M. Leary & J. P. Tangney (Eds.), *Handbook of self and identity* (pp. 401–418). New York: Guilford Press.

Lewandowski, G. W., & Aron, A. (2002). *The Self-Expansion Scale*. Paper presented at the Third Annual Meeting of the Society for Personality and Social Psychology, Savannah, GA.

Lewandowski, G. W., & Aron, A. (2004). Distinguishing arousal from novelty and challenge in initial romantic attraction. *Social Behavior and Personality*, 32, 361–372.

Lewandowski, G. W., Jr. & Aron, A. (2006). *The effects of novel/challenging versus arousing activities on couples' experienced relationship quality*. Manuscript under review.

Lewandowski, G. W., Aron, A. P., Bassis, S., & Kunak, J. (2006). *Losing a self-expanding relationship: Implications for the self-concept. Personal Relationships, 13,* 317–331.

Lockwood, P., Dolderman, D., Sadler, P., Gerchak, E. (2004). Feeling better about doing worse: Social comparisons within romantic relationships. *Journal of Personality and Social Psychology, 87,* 80–95.

Lord, C. G. (1980). Schemas and images as memory aids: Two modes of processing social information. *Journal of Personality and Social Psychology, 38,* 257–269.

Mashek, D. J., Aron, A., & Boncimino, M. (2003). Confusions of self and close others. *Personality and Social Psychology Bulletin, 29,* 382–392.

McFarland, C., Buehler, R., & MacKay, L. (2001). Affective responses to social comparisons with extremely close others. *Social Cognition, 19,* 547–586.

Medvene, L. J., Teal, C. R., & Slavich, S. (2000). Including the other in self: Implications for judgments of equity and satisfaction in close relationships. *Journal of Social and Clinical Psychology, 19,* 396–419.

Murray, S. L., Rose, P., & Holmes, J. G. (2005). Putting the partner within reach: A dyadic perspective on felt security in close relationships. *Journal of Personality and Social Psychology, 88,* 327–347.

Pyszczynski, T. A., Greenberg, J., & Solomon, S. (1997). Why do we need what we need? A terror management perspective on the roots of human social motivation. *Psychological Inquiry, 8,* 1–20.

Ryan, R. M., & Deci, E. L. (2000). Self-determination theory and the facilitation of intrinsic motivation, social development, and well-being. *American Psychologist, 55,* 68–78.

Sande, G. N., Goethals, G. R., & Radloff, C. E. (1988). Perceiving one's own traits and others': The multifaceted self. *Journal of Personality and Social Psychology, 54,* 13–20.

Shaver, P. R., Morgan, H. J., & Wu, S. (1996). Is love a "basic" emotion? *Personal Relationships, 3,* 81–96.

Shaver, P. R., Schwartz, J., Kirson, D., & O'Connor, C. (1987). Emotion knowledge: Further exploration of a prototype approach. *Journal of Personality and Social Psychology, 52,* 1061–1086.

Showers, C. J., & Kevlyn, S. B. (1999). Organization of knowledge about a relationship partner: Implications for liking and loving. *Journal of Personality and Social Psychology, 76,* 958–971.

Showers, C. J., & Kling, K. (1996). Organization of self-knowledge: Implications for recovery from sad mood. *Journal of Personality and Social Psychology, 70,* 578–590.

Simpson, J. A. (1999). Attachment theory in modern evolutionary perspective. In J. Cassidy & P. R. Shaver (Eds.), *Handbook of attachment* (pp. 115–140). New York: Guilford Press.

Smith, E., Coats, S., & Walling, D. (1999). Overlapping mental representations of self, in-group, and partner: Further response time evidence and a connectionist model. *Personality and Social Psychology Bulletin, 25,* 873–882.

Stern, D. N. (1985). *The interpersonal world of the infant.* New York: Basic Books.

Symons, C. S., & Johnson, B. T. (1997). The self-reference effect in memory: A meta-analysis. *Psychological Bulletin, 121,* 371–394.

Taylor, S. E., Neter, E., & Wayment, H. A. (1995). Self-evaluative processes. *Personality and Social Psychology Bulletin, 21,* 1278–1287.

Tesser, A. (1988). Toward a self-evaluation maintenance model of social behavior. In L. Berkowitz (Ed.), *Advances in experimental social psychology* (Vol. 11, pp. 288–338). San Diego, CA: Academic Press.

Tropp, L. R., & Wright, S. C. (2001). Ingroup identification as the inclusion of ingroup in the self. *Personality and Social Psychology Bulletin, 27*, 585–600.

Tucker, P., & Aron, A. (1993). Passionate love and marital satisfaction at key transition points in the family life cycle. *Journal of Social and Clinical Psychology, 12*, 135–147.

White, R. W. (1959). Motivation reconsidered: The concept of competence. *Psychological Review, 66*, 297–333.

11

The Relational Self in Transference: Intrapersonal and Interpersonal Consequences in Everyday Social Life

SERENA CHEN and SUSAN M. ANDERSEN

At one time or another, most of us have been cognizant of ourselves behaving differently around someone close to us, whether a romantic partner, friend, or parent. When Joe is with his domineering parents, he shifts away from his usually assertive demeanor toward a more submissive one. With her best friend, Sarah "lets her hair down," revealing thoughts, feelings, and behaviors reserved just for this friend. Indeed, spouses often bring out the best (or worst) in each other. All of these instances suggest the special nature of people's actions in relation to close others.

In this chapter, we describe our theory and research on the cognitive, emotional, motivational, and behavioral tendencies people exhibit in relation to their significant others. Together, these self-aspects constitute what we call *relational selves*. Our theoretical perspective is distinct in part because it is grounded in transference, the phenomenon whereby aspects of past relationships, including the associated relational selves, re-surface in encounters with new others. As such, our work speaks to not only the relational nature of the self in interactions with significant others, but also its re-emergence in day-to-day encounters with new people.

Below, we first describe the social-cognitive model of transference on which our theory of the relational self is based, followed by this theory's key postulates. We then turn to evidence that relational selves are activated in the context of transference, thereby eliciting a host of intrapersonal and interpersonal consequences. From there, we compare and contrast our work with a number of other perspectives on the self and relationships, including several represented in this volume. Finally, we consider relational selves in the context of the broader self system.

LOCATING THE RELATIONAL SELF IN TRANSFERENCE

Clinicians view transference (Freud, 1912/1958; Sullivan, 1953) as a tool by which the therapist allows himself or herself to be the object of the client's transference as a means of helping the client resolve maladaptive relational patterns. By contrast, we take a social-cognitive approach, which specifies the mental structures and processes that account for the occurrence of transference within therapeutic settings and in daily life.

The Social-Cognitive Model of Transference

Our model of transference assumes that mental representations of significant others are stored in memory, constituting warehouses of knowledge about these important individuals, including beliefs about their physical and personality attributes, as well as their internal states, such as their thoughts and feelings (Andersen & Cole, 1990; Andersen & Glassman, 1996; Andersen, Glassman, & Gold, 1999; Chen, 2003). Because of the emotional and motivational import of significant others, these representations are infused with affect and motivation. Significant-other representations are considered to be exemplars (e.g., Smith & Zárate, 1992), each designating a specific individual rather than a social category or type, such as "Blacks" or "politicians" (e.g., Andersen & Klatzky, 1987; Cantor & Mischel, 1979). Although they may contain generic knowledge—that is, generalizations about the significant other—it is this person that accounts for the associations among such knowledge, rather than a generic category label. Exemplar- and category-based processing are distinguishable in various ways (e.g., Smith & Zárate, 1992), but the activation and use of exemplars follow general principles of knowledge accessibility (e.g., Higgins, 1996a).

We define transference as occurring when a perceiver's representation of a significant other is activated in an encounter with a new person—for example, because of the person's physical resemblance to the significant other, or to the overlap of his or her personality attributes with the significant other's. Upon such activation, the perceiver interprets the person in ways derived from the significant-other representation, and responds to the person in ways that reflect the self–other relationship. Although nomothetic, social-cognitive processes—namely, the activation and use of mental representations—account for the occurrence of transference, we maintain that the content and meaning of significant-other representations are idiographic, unique to each perceiver.

Research has shown that significant-other representations are chronically accessible, implying they are in a constant state of high activation readiness (e.g., Higgins & King, 1981), but has also shown that transient cues further increase their accessibility (Andersen, Glassman, Chen, & Cole, 1995). Transient activation can occur based on priming, which involves incidental cues in the environment, or based on applicability, which involves attended-to cues in a stimulus person. In each case, the "match" between stored knowledge and the cues heightens the likelihood of knowledge activation and use (Higgins, 1996a; see also Andersen, Moskowitz, Blair, & Nosek, 2007). The vast majority of research on transference has used applicability to transiently activate significant-other representations. Specifically, we have used attributes of a significant other to characterize a stimulus person to increase the accessibility of the corresponding significant-other representation. In other words, the attribute-based resemblance of the person to the significant other triggers transference. We view such applicability-based cues as an analog for those perceivers encounter in ordinary, face-to-face interactions (Chen & Andersen, 1999; Chen, Andersen, & Hinkley, 1999).

To study transference, we use a two-session paradigm that involves both idiographic and nomothetic elements. In a pretest session participants name a significant other (e.g., parent, friend), and then generate descriptors to characterize this person. Several weeks later, they are led to anticipate an interaction with another participant in an ostensibly unrelated session. Participants then go through a learning phase in which they are presented with descriptors allegedly about their upcoming partner. For participants in the "Own" condition, some of these descriptors are derived from ones they previously generated about their significant other. In other words, their partner resembles their own significant other, thus triggering transference. By contrast, "Yoked" participants are shown descriptors about someone else's significant other and thus transference is not elicited. Own and Yoked participants are paired on a one-to-one basis so that the descriptive stimuli used across conditions are identical, but differ in their meaning and significance to Own versus Yoked participants.

After the learning phase, transference is assessed using one or both of two standard measures. One is a recognition-memory test that measures representation-derived inferences about the partner. Such inferences are indexed by participants' confidence that they learned descriptors about the partner that are true of their significant other, but were not actually presented. In short, this measure taps participants' inference that the partner is more like their significant other than is the case. The other measure, which asks participants to evaluate their partner, assumes that the affect associated with significant-other representations is elicited upon activation of these representations (Fiske & Pavelchak, 1987). Evidence for transference takes the form of Own participants evaluating the partner more positively when the partner resembled their own positively (vs. negatively) regarded significant other, with no such pattern among Yoked participants. In short, this measure taps whether participants evaluate their partner as they evaluate their significant other.

Over 15 years of research has documented transference using these measures. Included in this body of work is evidence that transference may occur nonconsciously (Glassman & Andersen, 1999; see also Andersen, Reznik, & Glassman, 2005; Chen, Fitzsimons, & Andersen, 2006). In other words, people need not consciously draw analogies between significant and new others for transference to occur. Inferences and evaluations of new others derived from significant-other representations are core to the phenomenon, but transference also elicits a myriad of consequences involving the selves people are with their significant others.

A Transference-Based Approach to the Relational Self

Our theory of the relational self (Andersen & Chen, 2002) assumes that every individual possesses a repertoire of relational selves, each reflecting aspects of the self with a particular significant other. Extending the social-cognitive model of transference, we posit that significant-other representations and relational selves are linked by knowledge reflecting the typical patterns of relating to the significant other. As a result of such linkages, when a significant-other representation is activated, this activation spreads to the relevant relational self, leading the perceiver to experience the self as he or she does when with the significant other. In working self-concept terms, transference elicits a shift in the content of the working self-concept toward relational-self knowledge. In this respect, our theory coheres with numerous theoretical approaches that discuss contextual variability in the self (e.g., Baldwin, 1992; Cantor, Markus, Niedenthal, & Nurius, 1986; Crocker & Wolfe, 2001).

Our theory is especially closely tied to Mischel and Shoda's (1995) model of personality, which posits that each individual's personality is composed of a unique pattern of IF–THEN relations. IFs are objective situations, and THENs are the outward responses people exhibit in them. IF–THEN relations are mediated by the "psychological situations" that are elicited by objective situations. These psychological situations derive from cognitive-affective units, such as encodings, expectations, and goal strategies. The model posits cross-situational malleability in the self, but captures stability at the level of a person's overall pattern of IF–THEN relations. Applied to our theory, IFs are situations in which transference occurs, and THENs are responses reflecting the relevant relational self. These IF–THENs are mediated by cognitive-affective units contained within the activated significant-other representation and relational self. Malleability in the self lies in the activation of different significant-other representations and relational selves across contexts, but stability is found in the consistent activation of particular representations and relational selves in the same contexts.

Finally, we assume that relational selves consist of attribute- and role-based aspects of the self with significant others. They also include positive and negative self-evaluations, the affect experienced when with a significant other, the goals pursued in the relationship, the self-regulatory strategies used, and the behaviors enacted. Like significant-other representations, the content of relational selves is largely idiographic, but also includes socially shared facets, like the role occupied with significant others and the standards others hold for the self.

ACTIVATING RELATIONAL SELVES IN TRANSFERENCE

We now turn to evidence for the activation of relational selves in transference. Reflecting the wide-ranging content of relational selves, when such activation occurs, people exhibit a host of intrapersonal and interpersonal responses in their interactions with new others.

Self-Definition and Self-Evaluation

When a significant-other representation is activated, the working self-concept should be infused in part with associated relational-self knowledge. Thus the perceiver's subjective self-definitions and self-evaluations should come to reflect this relational self. Several studies support this. In one study, participants did five feature-listing tasks at pretest (Hinkley & Andersen, 1996). They first described themselves as a baseline self-concept measure. They then described both a positively and a negatively regarded significant other, after which they described themselves as they are when with each person, as a baseline measure of each relational self. In the second session, participants were presented with descriptors about a new person who either did (Own condition) or did not (Yoked condition) resemble their positive or negative significant other. Afterward, they listed descriptors to characterize themselves at that moment (assessing their working self-concept), and classified each listed descriptor as positive or negative (assessing self-evaluation).

To assess shifts in the working self-concept toward the relational self, we first calculated the overlap between the descriptors of participants' baseline working self-concept and each relational self. Controlling for this pretest overlap, participants in the Own condition, for whom transference was elicited as a result of the new person's resemblance to one of their significant others, showed a greater shift in their working self-concept toward the relevant relational self, relative to Yoked participants. This finding held for both positive and negative significant others. Also in evidence were shifts in self-evaluation reflecting the overall evaluation of the significant other. Specifically, we summed the positive and negative classifications that participants ascribed to those self-descriptors in the second session that overlapped with their pretest relational self. Own participants evaluated these overlapping descriptors more positively when the new person resembled their positive, rather than negative, significant other. This effect was not seen among Yoked participants. Hence, when transference occurs, both self-definition and self-evaluation shift to reflect the relevant relational self.

Similar evidence exists for significant others who are positively evaluated, but around whom one experiences a dreaded self (Reznik & Andersen, 2005). Activating the representation of such a significant other should elicit this dreaded self, thus producing negative shifts in self-definition and self-evaluation. To test this, it was assumed that all people can think of a significant other who they love but around whom they behave badly (i.e., have a dreaded self), as well as a significant other with whom they are at their best (i.e., have a desired self). Using the transference paradigm, participants learned about a new person who resembled a positive significant other (Own condition) associated with either a dreaded or a desired self, or learned about a person who resembled someone else's significant other (Yoked condition).

Once again, Own participants' working self-concept shifted toward the relevant relational self—namely, the dreaded self when the new person resembled the significant other around whom participants are at their worst, and the desired self when the person resembled the significant other with whom participants are at their best. Moreover, the self-descriptors involved in the shift were evaluated more negatively in the dreaded-self condition, and more positively in the desired-self one, in the Own relative to the Yoked condition. Hence, when the dreaded or desired self is activated in transference, self-evaluation reflecting the valence of the relational self arises, even though the valence of the significant-other representation was held constant.

Finally, research has examined the impact of accepting significant others on stigmatized individuals' self-evaluations (Tapias & Chen, 2006). The hypothesis was that significant others who pair their acceptance with an acknowledgement of the negativity of a stigmatizing attribute that individuals believe they have will foster positively evaluated relational selves. Activating the representation of such a significant other should therefore elicit positive self-evaluations. In this research, just prior to encountering a new person, self-perceived overweight women visualized an accepting significant other who acknowledged their overweight stigma. The applicability of the significant other's views to inferring those of the new person was varied—for example, by leading participants to believe that the views of close others are similar and thus applicable to inferring the views of strangers, or different from and thus inappropriate for inferring the views of strangers. The results showed that priming a stigma-acknowledging, accepting significant other led participants to evaluate themselves more positively in anticipation of meeting the new person when the significant other's views were applicable to the new person's, relative to conditions involving non-acknowledging or inapplicable significant others.

Expectations of Acceptance or Rejection

Numerous theoretical perspectives highlight the important role played by people's expectations of significant others' acceptance and rejection (e.g., Downey & Feldman, 1996). We assume that such expectations are stored in the linkages between significant-other representations and relational-self knowledge, such that they play out in transference encounters. Indeed, several transference studies have shown that participants in the Own condition expect more acceptance from an upcoming partner when the partner resembled a positively versus negatively regarded significant other, a pattern not observed among Yoked participants (Andersen, Reznik, & Manzella, 1996; Reznik & Andersen, 2005).

The research on significant others and stigma also assessed stigmatized women's acceptance and rejection expectations about an upcoming partner (Tapias & Chen, 2006). Several studies showed that priming participants with a stigma-acknowledging, accepting significant other led to more expected acceptance from the partner, compared to priming a non-acknowledging significant other, when the significant others' views were applicable to inferring the partners' views. Moreover, expectations carried through to the end of the interaction, in that participants primed with an acknowledging and applicable significant other were most likely to report that their partner accepted them after the interaction.

On the other hand, recent work on physically or psychologically abusive family members in transference (Berenson & Andersen, 2006) arranged that female participants with and without an abusive parent expected to interact with a partner who resembled this parent (Own condition) or did not (Yoked condition). The results showed that Own but not Yoked participants with an abusive parent expected more rejection from the new person than did their counterparts without an abusive parent. They were also more likely to report disliking, mistrusting, and being indifferent toward the person.

Goals and Motives

Significant others enable people to satisfy the fundamental need for connection (Andersen, Reznik, & Chen, 1997; Baumeister & Leary, 1995). This desire to be emotionally close, to connect, should be stored in the linkages binding significant-other representations and relational selves, and thus activated in transference. Indeed, several studies have shown that Own but not Yoked participants were more motivated to be emotionally open with, and not distant from, a new person who resembled a positively rather than a negatively evaluated significant other (Andersen et al., 1996; Berk & Andersen, 2000; Reznik & Andersen, 2007).

Research has also explored the self-evaluative motives pursued when relational selves are activated. Given that people seek self-verifying appraisals from significant others (e.g., Swann, De La Ronde, & Hixon, 1994), it was hypothesized that self-verification motives are activated along with the relational self in transference (Kraus & Chen, 2007). Consistent with this, participants reported wanting the new person who resembled their significant other (vs. not) to evaluate them more in a manner that verified their core relational self-views.

Evidence for the activation of goal-related elements of relational selves can also be found outside the transference context. For example, research has shown that subliminal exposure to the name of a significant other leads people to behave in line with goals associated with this other (Fitzsimons & Bargh, 2003). Moreover, activation of a significant-other representation increases the accessibility of the goals associated with the other, as well as goal commitment and persistence, particularly when participants are close to this other and believe he or she values the goal (Shah, 2003a). Significant others' expectations about one's goal attainment also color one's own appraisals of the difficulty of attaining the relevant goal (Shah, 2003b).

Other work has assessed how chronically unsatisfied goals with significant others play out in transference (Berk & Andersen, 2007). Specifically, self-reported hostility increases when a representation of a positive significant other with whom one chronically experiences unsatisfied (vs. satisfied) goals for affection is activated in an encounter with a new person. Moreover, when the new person resembles a family member—a significant other who was not chosen and is thus "irrevocable"—these increases in hostility were linked to behaviors in an experimental task that were designed to solicit acceptance from the person.

Elicitation and Disruption of Affect

The affect-laden nature of significant-other representations suggests that the emotional meaning of significant-other relationships should be elicited in transference

(Andersen & Baum, 1994). To test this, the immediate facial movements of participants while reading each descriptor about a new person in the learning phase of the transference paradigm were covertly videotaped (Andersen et al., 1996). Naive judges then rated the pleasantness of participants' facial expressions of emotion. The results showed that Own but not Yoked participants expressed more pleasant facial affect when their positive rather than negative significant-other representation was activated. Thus transference elicits the affect associated with the significant other.

Further evidence comes from the research on abusive significant others (Berenson & Andersen, 2006). In this work, beyond learning about an upcoming partner who did or did not resemble a parent who was or was not abusive, participants were told that the partner was becoming tense and irritable "at this moment" (or was not). Own participants with an abusive parent actually reported less dysphoric mood in response to this irritability cue, showing relatively "flat affect," while this cue spiked the dysphoric mood of abused participants in the Yoked condition. No such differences emerged among non-abused participants. Thus, despite reports of rejection expectations, dislike, mistrust, and indifference by abused women, noted earlier, these women may show a kind of "emotional numbing" response in transference, reflecting the emotional shutdown they used to cope with their abusive relationship.

Affect reflecting the overall affective tone of a relationship tends to be chronically experienced in the relationship. However, circumstances external and internal to the person may disrupt this affect, which should be detectable in transference. Indeed, one study showed that negative affect ensues when the representation of a positively regarded significant other is activated with a new person whose role (e.g., "novice") vis-à-vis the self is incongruent with the significant other's role (e.g., "authority figure") (Baum & Andersen, 1999). Such role violations disrupt the positive affect typically enjoyed in positive significant-other relationships, presumably because such role incongruence signals that the goals one typically pursues in the significant-other relationship are unlikely to be met.

Disrupted positive affect may also occur when the representation of a positive significant other associated with a dreaded self is activated. In the research on dreaded selves (Reznik & Andersen, 2005), Own participants expecting to meet a new person who resembled such a significant other showed less positive and more negative mood relative to participants in the Yoked condition. By contrast, activating the representation of a positive significant other associated with a desired self elicited positive affect compared to the Yoked condition

Finally, research has also examined the emotional states evoked by activating a representation of a parent with whom one has a secure, preoccupied, dismissive, or fearful attachment (Andersen, Bartz, Berenson, & Keczkemethy, 2006). Evoking transference involving a parent to whom one is securely attached produced increases in positive affect (relative to the corresponding Yoked condition, an effect not seen in the preoccupied, dismissive, or fearful conditions). Greater positive affect was also seen among secure relative to insecurely attached participants in the Own versus Yoked conditions. At a more specific level, transference involving a parent with whom participants had a preoccupied attachment led to increases in anxiety relative to the Yoked condition, an effect not seen in the other groups. Finally, transference in the dismissive attachment condition produced large decreases in hostility compared to the Yoked condition, in which hostility was greatly elevated relative to that shown by other participants. This suggests the kind of suppressed emotion—namely, suppressed hostility—characteristic of avoidant relationships in the context of transference.

Self-Regulation

Two primary forms of self-regulation have been studied in the context of transference. The first pertains to efforts to meet significant-other-related standards, and the second to strategic responses aimed at defending the self and one's relationship in the face of threat.

In the first case, research has drawn on self-discrepancy theory (Higgins, 1987), which maintains that people are aware of the standpoints of significant others on their actual, ideal, and ought selves (in addition to their own standpoints). As such, significant-other standpoints are likely to be stored as part of relational selves, and the activation of a relational self should activate the ideal and ought self-guides held by the relevant significant other. To the degree that actual–ideal discrepancies exist, dejection-related affect should ensue, whereas actual–ought discrepancies should elicit agitation-related affect.

To test these predictions, participants who had an ideal or ought self-discrepancy from the standpoint of a parent learned descriptors about a new person who did or did not resemble this parent (Reznik & Andersen, 2007). Activating the parent representation should activate the associated relational self, including the ideal or ought self-discrepancy from the parent's standpoint. Indeed, ideal-discrepant participants reported more dejection-related affect, whereas ought-discrepant participants reported more agitation-related affect, as reflected by hostility.

Regulating the self with respect to ideal standards reflects a promotion regulatory focus, (a focus on attaining positive outcomes), whereas self-regulation in the service of ought standards reflects a prevention focus (a focus on preventing negative outcomes) (e.g., Higgins, 1996b). If activating a parent representation activates the self-discrepancy from this parent's standpoint, the self-regulatory focus with respect to this other should also emerge in transference. Ideal-discrepant participants in the above research should therefore show greater approach tendencies toward their partner, whereas ought-discrepant participants should show more avoidance. Supporting this, ideal-discrepant Own participants reported less motivation to avoid their partner in anticipation of meeting him or her, relative to after learning the meeting would not occur (at which point promotion was no longer relevant). By contrast, ought-discrepant Own participants reported more avoidance motivation before relative to after learning the meeting would not occur (at which point prevention was no longer relevant). This asymmetrical approach/avoidance pattern was not seen among Yoked participants.

Research on the second form of self-regulation has examined both self- and relationship-protective responses. For example, in the research on shifts in self-definition and self-evaluation toward the relational self, recall that participants learned about a new person who did or did not resemble a positive or negative significant other (Hinkley & Andersen, 1996). Afterward, Own participants described themselves with self-descriptors that overlapped with ones they listed earlier to describe the relational self with this significant other, and evaluated these relational-self attributes in line with their evaluation of the significant other. However, Own participants in the negative significant-other condition evaluated the *non*-relational-self attributes of their working self-concept more favorably than participants in all other conditions, presumably as a defensive response to the threat incurred by the shift toward the negative relational self.

Such findings were replicated in the research on dreaded selves (Reznik & Andersen, 2005). Recall that when the representation of a positive significant other associated with a dreaded self was activated, Own but not Yoked participants' self-descriptors shifted in content and evaluation toward the relevant relational self. In addition, Own participants in the dreaded-self condition recruited the most positive self-attributes in their overall working self-concept. Thus, although self-evaluation shifted to reflect the negative valence of the relevant relational self (i.e., a dreaded self), a countervailing, self-protective response was also seen.

Regarding relationship-protective self-regulation, recall the facial affect research showing that Own but not Yoked participants' facial expressions when reading descriptors about their upcoming partner were more pleasant when the partner resembled a positive rather than a negative significant other (Andersen et al., 1996). In this research, regardless of whether the partner resembled a positive or negative significant other, participants were presented with both positively and negatively valenced descriptors about him or her. Being confronted with negative descriptors about a new person that also characterize a positive significant other poses a threat to participants' positive views of this other, thus prompting a self-regulatory response aimed at curbing the threat. Indeed, Own participants responded to negative descriptors about their partner that reflected disliked qualities of their positive significant other with more pleasant facial affect relative to participants in any other condition and, moreover, relative to positive descriptors about this same significant other. Hence, the overall evaluation of the significant other drove facial affect, such that Own participants' prior evaluation of the negative descriptors was reversed in their facial affect, presumably as a relationship-protective response (for related findings, see Murray & Holmes, 1993).

The research on abusive significant others offers converging evidence (Berenson & Andersen, 2006). Even when previously abused, Own relative to Yoked participants expressed more positive facial affect when presented with descriptors about an upcoming partner who resembled a positively regarded parent. Thus, although they reported higher rejection expectations, dislike, mistrust, and indifference, as noted, their facial affect was just as positive as that of non-abused participants. Moreover, both abused and non-abused Own participants showed more positive facial affect in response to learning that the new person was becoming tense and irritable (compared with Yoked participants). In essence, both groups appeared to transform the negative, irritability cue into positive affect. Thus, even when maladaptive and potentially dangerous relationships are involved (among those who were abused), activating the associated significant-other representation and relational self evokes self-regulatory responses that protect these relationships.

Interpersonal Behavior

Finally, when the relational self is activated, this includes expectations regarding the significant other's acceptance or rejection, which should have implications for behavior in transference encounters. Indeed, wide-ranging research shows that perceivers' expectations about a target person are often fulfilled by virtue of perceivers' tendency to act in line with these expectations and the target's tendency to respond in kind. Such a self-fulfilling cycle has in fact been demonstrated in transference.

In this work, participants (perceivers) were exposed to descriptors about another participant (target) with whom they then had an audiotaped conversation (Berk & Andersen, 2000). The target resembled the perceiver's own (or a yoked participant's) positive or negative significant other. The pleasantness of the affect expressed in participants' conversational behavior was coded. It was hypothesized that the relational self associated with the positive or negative significant other should be activated in transference in such a way that people behave in line with their positive or negative assumptions, respectively, thus eliciting confirmatory behavior in the target. Indeed, the target expressed more pleasant affect when he or she resembled the perceiver's positive rather than negative significant other; no such effect was seen in the Yoked conditions. Thus, assumptions derived from perceivers' relational selves are activated in transference, and thereby elicit confirmatory behavior in targets.

Conceptually similar results were found in the research on stigma (Tapias & Chen, 2006). Participants primed with an acknowledging and accepting significant other prior to interacting with a new person to whom the significant other's views were seen as applicable reported higher expectations of acceptance, as noted. In addition, however, they displayed less negative affect and self-disclosed more, relative to participants primed with non-acknowledging or inapplicable significant others. Moreover, these participants were evaluated more favorably by independent judges viewing a videotape of their interaction with the new person. These positive effects on stigmatized people's interpersonal behavior, and in turn others' evaluations of them, suggest a means by which self-fulfilling cycles of rejection initiated by stigma-based expectations of rejection may be circumvented.

COMPARING AND CONTRASTING PERSPECTIVES

Our theory of the relational self inspired much of the research described above, but our data cohere with and complement findings emerging from several other bodies of work. In this section, we highlight points of convergence and divergence between our theoretical approach and three prominent lines of work that similarly address the self and relationships. In doing so, we suggest ways in which our perspective and the others may mutually inform one another (for further discussion, see Chen, Boucher, & Tapias, 2006).

Relational Schemas

According to Baldwin (1992), a relational schema consists of schemas of the self and the significant other in the self–other relationship, which are linked by an interpersonal script. This script consists of if–then contingencies of interaction (e.g., "If I assert myself, then my mother will treat me with respect") that embody expectations about how significant others will respond to the self, built from past interpersonal experiences. People derive rules of self-inference from repeated exposure to such if–then contingencies. For example, the contingency "If I make a mistake, then others will criticize and reject me" may give rise to the self-inference rule "If I make a mistake, then I am unworthy" (Baldwin, 1997, p. 329).

Numerous parallels exist between our theory and the relational schema perspective. First, the self-schema component of relational schemas is akin to our relational-self construct, as both refer to the self in the relevant relationship, and both are viewed as distinct from knowledge about significant others. In addition, the interpersonal script component of relational schemas fits our assumption regarding linkages between relational-self and significant-other knowledge. Positing such linkages is important because it distinguishes relational schema and transference perspectives from models that conceptualize the impact of relationships on the self in terms of the *internalization* of significant-other elements into the self, rather than in terms of self-aspects formed *in relation to* significant others.

The two perspectives also converge in assumptions about chronic and transient sources of activating relational-self knowledge. In relational schema terms, when contextual cues activate a significant-other schema, this triggers associated if–then rules that shift views of the self toward self-conceptions in the relevant relationship (Baldwin, 1997). Research has also shown that relational schemas may be chronically accessible (e.g., Baldwin, Keelan, Fehr, Enns, & Koh-Rangarajoo, 1996), implying that at times little contextual cuing is needed to activate them.

Theoretical parallels notwithstanding, research on relational schemas and transference has tended to differ in emphasis and methodology, differences that suggest ways in which the two bodies of work might extend one another. For example, although both perspectives assume that relational-self knowledge is formed on the basis of repeated activation of particular self-aspects in interactions with significant others, relational schema research offers particular precision regarding the mechanisms underlying this formation. Namely, self-inferences are derived through the repeated use of if–then rules, which are procedural knowledge structures that dictate the self-inferences that follow given particular responses from significant others (Baldwin, 1997). Such if–then rules are readily incorporated into our transference-based view of the relational self. When a significant-other representation is activated, if–then self-inference rules (derived from repeated interactions with the relevant significant other) may be activated, thus leading to the shift toward relational-self aspects that occurs in transference.

As another example, as transference refers to the re-surfacing of prior relationships in interactions with *new* others, our research has relied on attribute-based cues in a *new* person that match the attributes of a perceiver's significant other to activate a significant-other representation and its associated relational self. In other words, the activation cues we use emanate directly from new people themselves. Because the new person's resemblance to the significant other is fairly minimal, the activation of transference is relatively implicit. By contrast, although subliminal priming of significant-other faces has been used to activate relational schemas (Baldwin, Carrell, & Lopez, 1990), most relational schema research has had participants consciously visualize that they are interacting with an actual significant other (e.g., Baldwin & Sinclair, 1996). Hence, relational schemas have often been activated by procedures that refer directly to significant others, rather than by cues in a new person with whom past relational dynamics are subsequently played out. One implication here is that it may be worthwhile to examine whether and how the consequences of activated relational schemas play out in interactions with new people.

Of interest, research on relational schemas has also shown that novel cues (e.g., auditory tones) that are repeatedly paired with elements of relational schemas can activate these schemas (e.g., Baldwin & Main, 2001). If–then contingencies can also serve as activation cues, in that harboring expectations about an interaction partner's responses (Pierce & Lydon, 1998), or being exposed to an interaction pattern that resembles if–then dynamics with a significant other (Baldwin, Fehr, Keedian, Seidel, & Thompson, 1993), can activate relational schemas. Applied to transference, such studies suggest that in daily social encounters, transference may be elicited not only by people who resemble a significant other, but also by cues incidentally associated with a significant other, or cues reflecting the dynamics of the relationship.

Attachment Theory

Attachment theory maintains that internal working models of the self and others are formed in the course of early interactions with attachment figures (Bowlby, 1969/1982). Caring and responsive attachment figures foster the formation of a model of the self as competent and worthy of love, and of others as caring and available. By contrast, attachment figures who are inconsistently responsive or are neglectful give rise to insecure models—for example, a model of the self as unworthy of love and of others as uncaring.

Various points of convergence and divergence can be found between the attachment-theoretical view of the self and our conception of the relational self. First, although early infant and adult attachment research focused on attachment figures, defined as individuals who serve a specific set of functions (e.g., secure base), more recent work on adults has shown the utility of applying attachment theory to a broader circle of significant others (e.g., Baldwin et al., 1996), whether or not they meet all of the criteria for attachment figures. Thus, working models of the self can involve attachment figures or significant others more generally, which fits our interest in the impact of significant others, attachment figures or otherwise, on the self.

On the other hand, most adult attachment research has treated attachment as an individual difference variable (e.g., Hazan & Shaver, 1987), resulting in working models of the self often being treated as if they reflect the self-concept as a whole, while their relational origins fade into the background. For example, some research has used global self-esteem as a measure of these self models (e.g., Griffin & Bartholomew, 1994). Although some attachment experiences may become so internalized that treating them as general trait characteristics makes sense, self models that derive from interactions with significant others and designate the self in relation to these specific others are what we call relational selves. Consistent with our focus on relational selves linked to specific significant others, mounting research shows that people possess both general and relationship-specific attachment models (e.g., Klohnen, Weller, Luo, & Choe, 2005; Overall, Fletcher, & Friesen, 2003; Pierce & Lydon, 2001). Overlap may exist across levels, but general and relationship-specific working models have differential predictive power.

On a different note, attachment theory maintains that working models of the self and others are complementary and intertwined (e.g., Bowlby, 1973; Collins & Read, 1994), implying they exert their effects in tandem. This fits well with our view that linkages exist between relational-self and significant-other knowledge, although most attachment research does not explicitly refer to such linkages. Exceptions are studies conceptualizing individual differences in attachment in terms of differences in the nature of the if–then contingencies stored in relational schemas (Baldwin et al., 1993).

Consistent with transference and relational schema findings, working models can be activated by transient or chronic sources of accessibility (e.g., Mikulincer & Arad, 1999). However, attachment theory is unique in positing that physical or psychological threats in the environment activate the attachment system, and thus working models (Bowlby, 1969/1982). A key function of attachment figures is to provide a safe haven; thus, people should seek proximity to these figures in the face of threat. Indeed, research has shown that threat-related, semantic stimuli (e.g., separation) increase the accessibility of representations of attachment figures among those securely attached (Mikulincer, Gillath, & Shaver, 2002). More pertinent to the activation of working models of the self, threat (i.e., failure feedback) has been shown to polarize the chronic self-evaluations of insecurely attached individuals (e.g., anxious-ambivalent individuals' negative self-evaluations are exacerbated) (Mikulincer, 1998).

How might attachment and transference research inform one another? As noted, attachment working models have often been treated as an individual difference, implying that people have working models that hold across relationships. By contrast, our work has focused on specific significant others and associated relational selves. Yet the notion that people have more generalized conceptions of significant others and relational selves paves the way for widening the scope of the transference phenomenon. Namely, a new person may activate a more generalized significant-other representation (e.g., family members), thus shifting the working self-concept toward self-aspects experienced with multiple family members.

Our work on transference also informs adult attachment work. In fact, recent findings suggest that transference may constitute a mechanism by which attachment working models arise in current encounters and manage to persist over time (Andersen et al., 2006; Brumbaugh & Fraley, 2006). That is, attachment working models may persist not only because they are activated in interactions with attachment figures themselves, but also because they are activated in encounters with new people who resemble these figures.

Including Other in the Self

The inclusion-of-other-in-self (IOS) approach (Aron, Aron, Tudor, & Nelson, 1991) posits that close relationships involve the incorporation of close others (e.g., their perspectives and attributes) into the self-concept. Is our conception of the relational self akin to this? Generally no. Although the IOS approach distinguishes self-knowledge from significant-other knowledge, its core assumption is that closeness leads to self–other overlap. By contrast, we view relational-self and significant-other knowledge as linked but separate, as the relational self reflects how the self relates to, rather than internalizes, significant others. Research adopting a relational schema approach provides a useful illustration of this distinction by showing that people's self-construals assimilate to their relationship partners on the affiliation dimension, but complement their partners on the control dimension (Tiedens & Jimenez, 2003). Thus, self-conceptions may be similar to or different from conceptions of significant others, but what matters is self–other linkages— that is, how the self relates in interactions with significant others. By contrast, the IOS approach highlights overlapping aspects of the self and significant others to the exclusion of complementary ones, which may be equally relevant to the relational self.

Other points of divergence become apparent when one considers the IOS measure, which consists of seven pairs of circles, with one circle in each pair designating the self and the other circle designating a significant other (Aron, Aron, & Smollan, 1992). The degree of overlap between the circles varies, with more overlap indicating greater inclusion of the other in the self. Although this measure is usually administered with respect to a specific significant other, there is some ambiguity as to which "self" is being assessed. To illustrate, research shows that entering a new relationship yields self-concept expansion, due partly to the inclusion of the relationship partner (Aron, Paris, & Aron, 1995). In this work, participants were asked to describe themselves without reference to the relationship. Thus it is unclear whether the "self" here refers to self-conceptions in the relationship or to the global self-concept. In fact, IOS theorizing is silent on whether contextual variations, relationship or otherwise, have implications for how much others are included, whereas variations in the relational context are central to our transference-based view of the relational self.

Overall, from an IOS perspective, significant others influence the self by being incorporated into the general self-concept, whereas we argue that significant others prompt the formation of self-aspects reflecting the self when relating to others. Thus, IOS may or may not afford predictions about how an individual will respond to significant or new others, whereas relational selves provide a direct basis for such predictions. Nonetheless, it is intriguing to consider how the two approaches might be integrated. For example, it is certainly possible for a person to interact with significant or new others in ways derived from significant others themselves; that is, relational selves may include some aspects of significant others, even though they are not defined solely by them. Or, perhaps relational-self and significant-other knowledge are especially tightly intertwined in relationships involving a high degree of inclusion.

THE RELATIONAL SELF IN THE BROADER SELF SYSTEM

Relational aspects of the self designate only one of multiple levels of self-representation. In this final section, we locate the relational self in the broader self system by comparing and contrasting the relational self with individual and collective self-aspects.

Relational Self versus Individual and Collective Selves

The individual self refers to aspects of the self that make a person unique and separate from others (e.g., Brewer & Gardner, 1996; Turner & Onorato, 1999). Relational-self aspects may also be unique, but they are the result of connections to others rather than separation from them. Although collective-self aspects, which reflect the self as a group member (Luhtanen & Crocker, 1992; Tajfel & Turner, 1986), also result from connections to others, relational selves involve connections to known significant others, whereas collective selves designate connections with individuals whose identities may or may not be known (Hogg & Turner, 1985; Prentice, Miller, & Lightdale, 1994). Also, whereas activating a collective self leads one to become an interchangeable member of the group (Turner, Oakes, Haslam, & McGarty, 1994), activating a relational self leads people to become the self they are when with a significant other, not to become interchangeable with him or her.

In working self-concept terms, different contextual cues are likely to activate each level of self-representation. Whereas relational selves tend to be activated by cues denoting the significant other or the relationship dynamics with the other, any number of cues may activate individual self-aspects. For example, cues in an office setting may activate an array of individual self-aspects for a given person, but may not activate any specific relational self. Further, self-categorization theory argues that collective selves are activated when differences among members of one's ingroup are perceived to be smaller than differences between the ingroup and outgroup (Turner et al., 1994). Such perceptions of intra- and intergroup differentiation have no direct bearing on the activation of relational selves.

On an empirical level, research has shown that when an outperforming friend is seen as separate from the self (i.e., when the individual self is activated), his or her performance is threatening, thus leading people to judge the friend more harshly than an outperforming stranger (Gardner, Gabriel, & Hochschild, 2002). However, when the friend is linked to the self (i.e., when a relational self is activated), his or her performance is not threatening, resulting in more favorable evaluations of the friend than the stranger. Supporting the relational–collective distinction, research has shown that people possess attachment working models of the self as a group member that are distinct from working models associated with significant others (Smith, Murphy, & Coats, 1999). Thus, people possess distinct beliefs about and evaluations of themselves in relation to significant others versus a group.

Relations and Interplay among Selves

Are different levels of self-definition as distinct outside of the laboratory as theory and research would have it? It is certainly plausible that there is some overlap across a person's individual, relational, and collective selves. Put differently, people may possess a set of core attributes that are ever-present in the working self-concept (e.g., Markus & Kunda, 1986). However, overlapping content may manifest itself in unique ways at each self level. For example, even if a person's individual and collective selves overlapped to a degree, resource allocations may serve the individual self when this self is activated, but go against it in favor of the collective self when the latter is salient (e.g., Turner, Brown, & Tajfel, 1979). Also, different standards of comparison are used at different self levels (e.g., Brewer & Weber, 1994), implying that the same content may be judged differently when ascribed to different self levels.

On another note, it is intriguing to consider possible forms of interplay across self levels. For example, relationships may be of critical relevance in social identity, by facilitating perceptions of common bonds that generalize to the group level (Andersen, Downey, & Tyler, 2005). Hence, relationships may be a vehicle for forming or shifting social identities (Davis-Lipman, Tyler, & Andersen, 2007). Indeed, research has shown that activation of a significant-other representation activates the significant other's ethnicity, which is then applied to a new person in transference (i.e., the new person is assumed to have this same ethnicity), at least when the significant other shares the perceiver's ethnic background (Saribay & Andersen, in press). The perceiver's own ethnic identity is also activated, leading to increased intergroup bias. Hence, there are clearly links between self levels, although more research is needed to precisely outline their interplay.

SUMMARY AND FUTURE DIRECTIONS

To summarize, we presented a theory of the relational self grounded in the social-cognitive phenomenon of transference. Relational selves refer to self-knowledge reflecting the person one is in relation to specific significant others. Because such self-knowledge is linked to knowledge about the corresponding significant others, when transference occurs upon activation of a significant-other representation in an encounter with a new person, the associated relational self is activated in tandem. As a result, the working self-concept shifts to reflect the self in relation to the particular significant other—as revealed in self-definitions and self-evaluations, as well as a constellation of affective, cognitive, motivational, self-regulatory, and behavioral responses—only now in relation to a new person.

When considering our findings on relational selves, along with those coming from related theoretical approaches, what emerges is a portrait of a self that is shaped by significant others far more than is typically recognized in the Western literature on the self—until recently. As this volume shows, the past few decades have witnessed an explosion of interest in the impact of significant others on the self. Although the exact nature of relational selves, and their number and importance relative to other facets of the self, may vary across people as a function of culture, gender, and countless individual differences, the emerging consensus is that every individual possesses a repertoire of relational selves, derived from interactions with his or her significant others. In short, relational selves are as core to understanding self and identity as any other self-component.

Looking ahead, it will be important to uncover the full range of processes associated with activated relational selves within and beyond the transference context. A key aim should be to characterize the manner in which processes in the service of relational selves converge or depart from processes at other self levels. From another vantage point, viewing relational selves as core self-elements raises intriguing questions about their role in imparting coherence and clarity in the self. On a related note, future research should grapple with the degree to which people view relational selves as reflecting their "true self," thereby conferring feelings of authenticity and self-determination. Judging from the theory and data amassed thus far, future work is likely only to strengthen the growing view that significant others exert far-ranging influences on the self in the context of significant-other relationships and day-to-day encounters with new others.

REFERENCES

Andersen, S. M., Bartz, J., Berenson, K., & Keczkemethy, C. (2006). *Triggering the attachment system in transference: Evoking specific emotions through transiently activating a parental representation.* Unpublished manuscript, New York University.

Andersen, S. M., & Baum, A. B. (1994). Transference in interpersonal relations: Inferences and affect based on significant-other representations. *Journal of Personality, 62,* 4, 460–497.

Andersen, S. M., & Chen, S. (2002). The relational self: An interpersonal social-cognitive theory. *Psychological Review, 109,* 619–645.

Andersen, S. M., & Cole, S. W. (1990). "Do I know you?": The role of significant others in general social perception. *Journal of Personality and Social Psychology, 59,* 384–399.

Andersen, S. M., Downey, G., & Tyler, T. R. (2005). Becoming engaged in community: Personal relationships foster social identity. In G. Downey, C. Dweck, J. Eccles, &

C. M. Chatman (Eds.), *Navigating the future: Social identity, coping, and life tasks* (pp. 210–251). New York: Russell Sage Foundation.

Andersen, S. M., & Glassman, N. S. (1996). Responding to significant others when they are not there: Effects on interpersonal inference, motivation, and affect. In R. M. Sorrentino & E. T. Higgins (Eds.), *Handbook of motivation and cognition* (Vol. 3, pp. 262–321). New York: Guilford Press.

Andersen, S. M., Glassman, N. S., Chen, S., & Cole, S. W. (1995). Transference in social perception: The role of chronic accessibility in significant-other representations. *Journal of Personality and Social Psychology, 69,* 41–57.

Andersen, S. M., Glassman, N. S., & Gold, D. (1998). Mental representations of the self, significant others, and nonsignificant others: Structure and processing of private and public aspects. *Journal of Personality and Social Psychology, 75,* 845–861.

Andersen, S. M., & Klatzky, R. L. (1987). Traits and social stereotypes: Levels of categorization in person perception. *Journal of Personality and Social Psychology, 53,* 235–246.

Andersen, S. M., Moskowitz, D. B., Blair, I. V., & Nosek, B. A. (2007). Automatic thought. In E. T. Higgins & A. W. Kruglanski (Eds.), *Social psychology: Handbook of basic principles* (2nd ed.). New York: Guilford Press.

Andersen, S. M., Reznik, I., & Chen, S. (1997). The self in relation to others: Cognitive and motivational underpinnings. In J. G. Snodgrass & R. L. Thompson (Eds.), *The self across psychology: Self-recognition, self-awareness, and the self-concept* (pp. 233–275). New York: New York Academy of Science.

Andersen, S. M., Reznik, I., & Glassman, N. S. (2005). The unconscious relational self. In R. Hassin, J. S. Uleman, & J. A. Bargh (Eds.), *The new unconscious.* New York: Oxford University Press.

Andersen, S. M., Reznik, I., & Manzella, L. M. (1996). Eliciting transient affect, motivation, and expectancies in transference: Significant-other representations and the self in social relations. *Journal of Personality and Social Psychology, 71,* 1108–1129.

Aron, A., Aron, E. N., & Smollan, D. (1992). Inclusion of other in the self scale and structure of interpersonal closeness. *Journal of Personality and Social Psychology, 63,* 596–612.

Aron, A., Aron, E. N., Tudor, M., & Nelson, G. (1991). Close relationships as including other in the self. *Journal of Personality and Social Psychology, 60,* 241–253.

Aron, A., Paris, M., & Aron, E. N. (1995). Falling in love: Prospective studies of self-concept change. *Journal of Personality and Social Psychology, 69,* 1102–1112.

Baldwin, M. W. (1992). Relational schemas and the processing of information. *Psychological Bulletin, 112,* 461–484.

Baldwin, M. W. (1997). Relational schemas as a source of if–then self-inference procedures. *Review of General Psychology, 1,* 326–335.

Baldwin, M. W., Carrell, S. E., & Lopez, D. F. (1990). Priming relationship schemas: My advisor and the Pope are watching me from the back of my mind. *Journal of Experimental Social Psychology, 26,* 435–454.

Baldwin, M. W., Fehr, B., Keedian, E., Seidel, M., & Thompson, D. W. (1993). An exploration of the relational schemata underlying attachment styles: Self-report and lexical decision approaches. *Personality and Social Psychology Bulletin, 19,* 746–754.

Baldwin, M. W., Keelan, J. P. R., Fehr, B., Enns, V., & Koh-Rangarajoo, E. (1996). Social-cognitive conceptualization of attachment working models: Availability and accessibility effects. *Journal of Personality and Social Psychology, 71,* 94–109.

Baldwin, M. W., & Main, K. J. (2001). Social anxiety and the cued activation of relational knowledge. *Personality and Social Psychology Bulletin, 27*, 1637–1647.

Baldwin, M. W., & Sinclair, L. (1996). Self-esteem and "if . . . then" contingencies of interpersonal acceptance. *Journal of Personality and Social Psychology, 71*, 1130–1141.

Baum, A., & Andersen, S. M. (1999). Interpersonal roles in transference: Transient mood effects under the condition of significant-other resemblance. *Social Cognition, 17*, 161–185.

Baumeister, R. F., & Leary, M. R. (1995). The need to belong: Desire for interpersonal attachments as a fundamental human motivation. *Psychological Bulletin, 117*, 497–529.

Berenson, K. R., & Andersen, S. M. (2006). Childhood physical and emotional abuse by a parent: Transference effects in adult interpersonal relationships. *Personality and Social Psychology Bulletin, 32*, 1509–1522.

Berk, M. S., & Andersen, S. M. (2000). The impact of past relationships on interpersonal behavior: Behavioral confirmation in the social-cognitive process of transference. *Journal of Personality and Social Psychology, 79*, 546–562.

Berk, M. S., & Andersen, S. M. (2007). *The sting of lack of affection: Chronic goal dissatisfaction in transference*. Manuscript submitted for publication.

Bowlby, J. (1973). *Attachment and loss: Vol. II. Separation: Anxiety and anger*. New York: Basic Books.

Bowlby, J. (1982). *Attachment and loss: Vol. I. Attachment* (2nd ed.). New York: Basic Books. (Original work published in 1969.)

Brewer, M. B., & Gardner, W. (1996). Who is this "we"? Levels of collective identity and self representations. *Journal of Personality and Social Psychology, 71*, 83–93.

Brewer, M. B., & Weber, J. G. (1994). Self-evaluation effects of interpersonal versus intergroup social comparison. *Journal of Personality and Social Psychology, 66*, 268–275.

Brumbaugh, C. C., & Fraley, R. C. (2006). Transference and attachment: How do attachment patterns get carried forward from one relationship to the next? *Personality and Social Psychology Bulletin, 32*, 552–560.

Cantor, N., Markus, H., Niedenthal, P., & Nurius, P. (1986). On motivation and self-concept. In R. M. Sorrentino and E. T. Higgins (Eds.), *Handbook of motivation and cognition: Foundations of social behavior* (pp. 96–121). New York: Guilford Press.

Cantor, N., & Mischel, W. (1979). Prototypicality and personality. Effects on free recall and personality impressions. *Journal of Research in Personality, 13*, 187–205.

Chen, S. (2003). Psychological-state theories about significant others: Implications for the content and structure of significant-other representations. *Personality and Social Psychology Bulletin, 29*, 1285–1302.

Chen, S., & Andersen, S. M. (1999). Relationships from the past in the present: Significant-other representations and transference in interpersonal life. In M. P. Zanna (Ed.), *Advances in experimental social psychology* (Vol. 31, pp. 123–190). San Diego, CA: Academic Press.

Chen, S., Andersen, S. M., & Hinkley, K. (1999). Triggering transference: Examining the role of applicability in the activation and use of significant-other representations in social perception. *Social Cognition, 17*, 332–365.

Chen, S., & Boucher, H. C., & Tapias, M. P. (2006). The relational self revealed: Integrative conceptualization and implications for interpersonal life. *Psychological Bulletin, 132*, 151–179.

Chen, S., Fitzsimons, G. M., & Andersen, S. M. (2006). Automaticity and close relationships. In J. A. Bargh (Ed.), *Social psychology and the unconscious: The automaticity of higher mental processes* (pp. 133–172). New York: Psychology Press.

Collins, N. L., & Read, S. J. (1994). Cognitive representations of attachment: The structure and function of working models. In K. Bartholomew & D. Perlman (Eds.), *Advances in personal relationships* (Vol. 5, pp. 53–90). Philadelphia: Jessica Kingsley Publishers.

Crocker, J., & Wolfe, C. T. (2001). Contingencies of self-worth. *Psychological Review, 108*, 593–623.

Davis-Lipman, A., Tyler, T. R., & Andersen, S. M. (2007). Building community one relationship at a time: Consequences for seeking and acceptance of help. *Social Justice Research*.

Downey, G., & Feldman, S. (1996). Implications of rejection sensitivity for intimate relationships. *Journal of Personality and Social Psychology, 70*, 1327–1343.

Fiske, S. T., & Pavelchak, M. (1986). Category-based versus piecemeal-based affective responses: Developments in schema-triggered affect. In R. M. Sorrentino & E. T. Higgins (Eds.), *Handbook of motivation and cognition* (pp. 167–203). New York: Guilford Press.

Fitzsimons, G. M., & Bargh, J. A. (2003). Thinking of you: Nonconscious pursuit of interpersonal goals associated with relationship partners. *Journal of Personality and Social Psychology, 84*, 148–164.

Freud, S. (1958). *The dynamics of transference. Standard edition* (Vol. 12, pp. 99–108). London: Hogarth. (Original work published 1912.)

Gardner, W. L., Gabriel, S., & Hochschild, L. (2002). When you and I are "we," you are no longer threatening: The role of self-expansion in social comparison processes. *Journal of Personality and Social Psychology, 82*, 239–251.

Glassman, N. S., & Andersen, S. M. (1999). Activating transference without consciousness: Using significant-other representations to go beyond what is subliminally given. *Journal of Personality and Social Psychology, 77*, 1146–1162.

Griffin, D., & Bartholomew, K. (1994). Models of self and other: Fundamental dimensions underlying measures of adult attachment. *Journal of Personality and Social Psychology, 67*, 430–445.

Hazan, C., & Shaver, P. (1987). Romantic love conceptualized as an attachment process. *Journal of Personality and Social Psychology, 52*, 511–524.

Higgins, E. T. (1987). Self-discrepancy: A theory relating self and affect. *Psychological Review, 94*, 391–340.

Higgins, E. T. (1996a). Knowledge activation: Accessibility, applicability, and salience. In E. T. Higgins & A. W. Kruglanski (Eds.), *Social psychology: Handbook of basic principles* (pp. 133–168). New York: Guilford Press.

Higgins, E. T. (1996b). Ideals, oughts, and regulatory focus: Affect and motivation from distinct pains and pleasures. In P. M. Gollwitzer & J. A. Bargh (Eds.), *The psychology of action: Linking cognition and motivation to behavior* (pp. 91–114). New York: Guilford Press.

Higgins, E. T., & King, G. A. (1981). Accessibility of social constructs: Information processing consequences of individual and contextual variability. In N. Cantor & J. F. Kihlstrom (Eds.), *Personality, cognition and social interaction* (pp. 69–121). Hillsdale, NJ: Lawrence Erlbaum Associates, Inc.

Hinkley, K., & Andersen, S. M. (1996). The working self-concept in transference: Significant-other activation and self-change. *Journal of Personality and Social Psychology, 71*, 1279–1295.

Hogg, M. A., & Turner, J. C. (1985). Interpersonal attraction, social identification and psychological group formation. *European Journal of Social Psychology, 15,* 51–66.

Kraus, M. W., & Chen, S. (2007). *Automatic activation of self-evaluative goals in relationship contexts: Striving to be known by significant others.* University of California, Berkeley. Manuscript under review.

Klohnen, E. C., Weller, J. A., Luo, S., & Choe, M. (2005). Organization and predictive power of general and relationship-specific attachment models: One for all, all for one? *Personality and Social Psychology Bulletin, 31,* 1665–1682.

Luhtanen, R., & Crocker, J. (1992). A collective self-esteem scale: Self-evaluation of one's social identity. *Personality and Social Psychology Bulletin, 18,* 302–318.

Markus, H., & Kunda, Z. (1986). Stability and malleability of the self-concept. *Journal of Personality and Social Psychology, 51,* 858–866.

Mikulincer, M. (1998). Adult attachment style and affect regulation: Strategic variations in self-appraisals. *Journal of Personality and Social Psychology, 75,* 420–435.

Mikulincer, M., & Arad, D. (1999). Attachment working models and cognitive openness in close relationships: A test of chronic and temporary accessibility effects. *Journal of Personality and Social Psychology, 77,* 710–725.

Mikulincer, M., Gillath, O., & Shaver, P. R. (2002). Activation of the attachment system in adulthood: Threat-related primes increase the accessibility of mental representations of attachment figures. *Journal of Personality and Social Psychology, 83,* 881–895.

Mischel, W., & Shoda, Y. (1995). A cognitive-affective system theory of personality: Reconceptualizing situations, dispositions, dynamics, and invariance in personality structure. *Psychological Review, 102,* 246–268.

Murray, S. L., & Holmes, J. G. (1993). Seeing virtues in faults: Negativity and the transformation of interpersonal narratives in close relationships. *Journal of Personality and Social Psychology, 65,* 707–722.

Overall, N. C., Fletcher, G. J. O., & Friesen, M. D. (2003). Mapping the intimate relationship mind: Comparisons between three models of attachment representations. *Personality and Social Psychology Bulletin, 29,* 1479–1493.

Pierce, T., & Lydon, J. E. (1998). Priming relational schemas: Effects of contextually activated and chronically accessible interpersonal expectations on responses to a stressful event. *Journal of Personality and Social Psychology, 75,* 1441–1448.

Pierce, T., & Lydon, J. E. (2001). Global and specific relational models in the experience of social interactions. *Journal of Personality and Social Psychology, 80,* 613–631.

Prentice, D. A., Miller, D. T., & Lightdale, J. R. (1994). Asymmetries in attachment to groups and to their members: Distinguishing between common-identity and common-bond groups. *Personality and Social Psychology Bulletin, 20,* 484–493.

Reznik, I., & Andersen, S. M. (2005). *Becoming the dreaded self: Diminished self-worth with positive significant others in transference.* Unpublished manuscript, New York University.

Reznik, I., & Andersen, S. M. (2007). Agitation and despair in relation to parents: Activating emotional suffering in transference. *European Journal of Personality, 21,* 281–301.

Saribay, S. A., & Andersen, S. M. (in press). Relational to collective: Significant-other representations, ethnic categories, and intergroup perceptions. *Personality and Social Psychology Bulletin.*

Shah, J. (2003a). Automatic for the people: How representations of significant others implicitly affect goal pursuit. *Journal of Personality and Social Psychology, 84,* 661–681.

Shah, J. (2003b). The motivational looking glass: How significant others implicitly affect goal appraisals. *Journal of Personality and Social Psychology, 85*, 424–439.

Smith, E. R., Murphy, J., & Coats, S. (1999). Attachment to groups: Theory and measurement. *Journal of Personality and Social Psychology, 77*, 94–110.

Smith, E. R., & Zárate, M. A. (1992). Exemplar-based social judgment. *Psychological Review, 99*, 3–21.

Sullivan, H. S. (1953). *The interpersonal theory of psychiatry.* New York: Norton.

Swann, W. B., Jr., De La Ronde, C., & Hixon, J. G. (1994). Authenticity and positivity strivings in marriage and courtship. *Journal of Personality and Social Psychology, 66*, 857–869.

Tajfel, H., & Turner, J. C. (1986). The social identity theory of intergroup behavior. In S. Worchel & W. G. Austin (Eds.), *Psychology of intergroup relations* (pp. 7–24). Chicago: Nelson-Hall.

Tapias, M. P. & Chen, S. (2006). *Significant-other acceptance and stigma.* Manuscript in preparation.

Tiedens, L. Z., & Jimenez, M. C. (2003). Assimilation for affiliation and contrast for control: Complementary self-construals. *Journal of Personality and Social Psychology, 85*, 1049–1061.

Turner, J. C., Brown, R. J., & Tajfel, H. (1979). Social comparison and group interest in ingroup favouritism. *European Journal of Social Psychology, 9*, 187–204.

Turner, J. C., Oakes, P. J., Haslam, S. A., & McGarty, C. (1994). Self and collective: Cognition and social context. *Personality and Social Psychology Bulletin, 20*, 454–463.

Turner, J. C., & Onorato, R. S. (1999). Social identity, personality, and the self-concept: A self-categorization perspective. In T. R. Tyler, R. M. Kramer, & O. P. John (Eds.), *The psychology of the social self* (pp. 11–46). Mahwah, NJ: Lawrence Erlbaum Associates, Inc.

12

Changes in Working Models of the Self in Relationships: A Clinical Perspective

JOANNE DAVILA and MELISSA RAMSAY MILLER

*T*his chapter focuses on how working models of the self change in the context of relationships from both clinical and social/personality perspectives. Extensive literatures in both traditions describe how the self develops and is regulated in the context of relationships, but the literatures on change in models of self are smaller and less explicit. Yet, the notion of change is important in both traditions, with both recognizing the necessity of change. We begin this chapter by describing prominent models of the self in relationships from clinical and social/personality perspectives, and we discuss how we might define models of self that take into account these different perspectives. The next section describes theories of development and change in the self in relationships from social/personality and clinical perspectives. The final section discusses common themes across these two traditions.

MODELS OF THE SELF IN RELATIONSHIPS

Social/Personality Models

A long tradition among social/personality psychologists views the self in the context of relationships, particularly with regard to the development of self-views and self-esteem. Cooley's (1902/1983) and Mead's (1956) early theories, which formed the basis for numerous contemporary models of the self, suggested that people look to others to understand the self. These early and more contemporary theories hold, at their base, that how we see ourselves, our beliefs and feelings about the self, are dependent on how others see us.

Leary's sociometer model of the self (e.g., Leary, Tambor, Terdal, & Downs, 1995; see Leary, Chapter 5 in this volume) argues that self-esteem is a manifestation of what people assess to be their relational value. That is, people regularly assess how valued they are by others, and these assessments determine how they feel about the self. As such, state self-esteem varies in direct response to perceptions of relational value.

Murray and her colleagues' work reflects similar ideas, but they have focused specifically on romantic relationships—in particular, on how individuals use their relationships to affirm their ideas about themselves (Murray, Holmes, & Griffin, 2000; Murray, Chapter 1 in this volume). Beliefs about a partner's regard determine people's own self views, such that individuals feel worse or better about themselves depending on the level of negative or positive perceived regard from a partner (Murray, Griffin, Rose, & Bellavia, 2003).

Andersen also provides a model of how sense of self is dependent on experiences with significant others (e.g., Andersen & Chen, 2002; Chen & Andersen, Chapter 11 in this volume). Building on the psychodynamic notion of transference, Andersen argues that people hold a set of "relational selves" that are each linked with a specific significant other in their life. How the self is experienced and expressed depends on which significant other is being referenced in a particular situation. For example, models of the self in relation to the father that were originally constructed in that relational context are likely to be activated when one is with someone who is similar to one's father, and will guide one's behavior toward that person.

Aron's work also speaks to how significant others can affect the sense of self, albeit in a somewhat different manner and for somewhat different motives (e.g., Aron & Aron, 1986; Aron, Ketay, Riela, & Aron, Chapter 10 in this volume). Aron's model proposes that, in close relationships, people begin to include aspects of their partner into their own self-concept. This "self-expansion," or the inclusion of another's qualities into one's own has important implications for relationship functioning, as well as for the self, in that the partners we are with affect how we view ourselves. For example, a person who becomes romantically involved with a philanthropic partner is likely to begin to see themselves as caring and giving.

The theories described above provide a representative set of examples of the ways in which social/personality psychologists understand how relationships affect models of the self. Each posits that the self is understood within the context of relationships, though they diverge on the specific process by which this may occur (e.g., general assessment of relational value, perceptions of partner's regard, changing activation of relational schemas, or taking on of partner's qualities). Another important theory, attachment theory (Bowlby, 1969, 1973, 1980), crosses both social/personality and clinical (as well as developmental) perspectives.

Bowlby proposed that, out of early relational experiences, people develop internal working models of the self, others, and relationships that guide thoughts, feelings, and behaviors. The notion is that the child learns about the self, particularly about the worth of the self, in the context of the treatment provided by caregivers. When caregivers respond to children during times of need in an available, consistent, caring manner, children develop the sense that they are worthy. When caregivers are unresponsive or uncaring, children develop the sense that they are not valued by others. Social/personality psychologists and others have applied this notion to adult relationships, and have documented that adult romantic relationships serve attachment functions (e.g., Feeney, 2004; Hazan & Shaver, 1987; Trinke & Bartholomew, 1997; Waters, 1997). Thus the same processes of determining self-worth in response to caregiver availability can occur with adult romantic partners.

Despite differences in specific processes by which the relational context may affect the self, as noted earlier, all of the social/personality models reviewed together suggest that beginning with our earliest experiences in childhood, we come to develop our sense of self from the relationships in our lives, and we continue to use those relationships (consciously and/or unconsciously) as a way to assess who we are and what we are worth.

Clinical Models

Clinical approaches to understanding the self in relationships have come to similar conclusions. Stern (1985), in theorizing about how the self develops in infancy, suggests it is in large part through interactions with caregivers. As adults begin to view the infant in particular ways and behave correspondingly, the infant begins to experience the self in new ways based on those interactions. Moreover, the subjective sense of self may develop and be validated by adults' affective attunement to the infant. To the extent that adults are sensitive to the infant's emotional experiences and can reflect them back in a manner that conveys a shared affect state, the infant will develop a more clear and coherent sense of self. These ideas are similar to those of Bowlby, but Stern's model focuses more specifically on emotional attunement and validation than on the broader constructs of parental availability and secure base functioning that are key to attachment theory.

Self-psychological models (Kohut, 1977; see also St. Clair, 1986) make hypotheses similar to those of Bowlby and Stern in suggesting that the sense of self develops from the relationship between parents and child. Although no self is present at birth, parents treat the child as if there is a self. Doing so leads to the development of an organized and complex self-system. Furthermore, a coherent and positive sense of self develops only when parents have an empathic relationship with the child, one in which they can validate the child's qualities and feelings, and provide positive role models for self construction. Self-psychological models differ from the other clinical models in that they are particularly focused on the development of healthy and maladaptive forms of narcissism, rather than on more broad aspects of self-development and regulation, but a discussion of this is beyond the scope of this chapter.

The object-relations perspective also locates the origins of the self in early parent–child relationships, and suggests that early experiences result in images of self, other, and a connecting affective link (e.g., Kernberg, 1976; see also St. Clair, 1986). While Stern and self-psychology emphasize the role of actual relationships in creating an ongoing context for self development, object-relations theory places self development within the individual as a challenge that must be negotiated for healthy development. A healthy sense of self is believed to be reflected in the ability to integrate good and bad aspects of the self, and to recognize the boundaries between self and others. Therefore, object-relations theories are more intrapsychic than interpersonal in their models of how children negotiate the developmental task of ego (i.e., self) integration, but, like the other clinical theories, they espouse the notion that self-image is closely related to images of others. That is, the experience of the self is directly linked to how others are experienced.

It was from object-relations theories that attachment theory grew. Although in agreement with object-relations scholars about the importance of early relationships for the development of intrapsychic representations of self and others, Bowlby diverged by placing greater emphasis on how actual interpersonal experiences (rather than intrapsychic ones) shape representations early on and, importantly, on an ongoing basis over time. Compared to attachment theory, the psychoanalytic models described above, although consistent in their ideas about how the self develops in a relational context, have much less to say about the relational context in which the self is maintained or continues to develop over time. In these models, after development in childhood, the self is viewed as an intrapsychic structure. Although many scholars attest to the intersubjectivity of the self—that the sense of self exists in the context of images of others—this is still thought to occur in the mind. It is the case, though, that psychoanalytic models, particularly contemporary relational ones, espouse the role of early relational experiences in current functioning; for example, that the sense of self in relationships can underlie the repetition of interpersonal patterns and be manifested in transferential relationships.

Besides the psychoanalytic and attachment models, there are few explicit clinical models of the self in relationships. Rogers (1951), coming from a humanistic perspective, discussed the central role of consistent, non-contingent positive regard from others in order to develop and maintain a healthy sense of self. In attempting to understand the self in the context of depression, Blatt and others (e.g., Beck, 1983; Blatt & Zuroff, 1992) have postulated that one risk factor for depression involves a sense of self that is excessively dependent on others. Cognitive models have given self-schemas a primary role in understanding psychopathology, suggesting that both the content of self-models (e.g., self-evaluations) and self-schematic processing (e.g., selective attention to certain aspects of the self) can drive emotional and behavioral dysfunction (e.g., Beck, Rush, Shaw, & Emery, 1979). However, although these models can accommodate the role of relationships in the sense of self, the models are by no means specific about *where* and *how* the sense of self develops, giving no special attention to interpersonal factors (although see Gotlib & Hammen, 1992, for an exception, with regard to depression).

In sum, the clinical perspectives, other than relational psychoanalytic and attachment theories, have somewhat less to say about ongoing self-in-relationship processes than do the social/personality perspectives, which focus explicitly on how such processes may operate in the course of relationships in everyday, normative functioning. However, both social/personality and clinical perspectives share the view that key features of the sense of self are developed in the context of relationships, beginning with the earliest relationships in childhood.

"Models" of Models of the Self

Having reviewed theories of how self-models develop in the context of relationships, we move to the question of how the different models construe the structural and process-oriented features of self-models. That is, what are the different "models" of self-models? The length of this chapter prohibits a detailed treatment of this topic, but we briefly review relevant features to facilitate a common language that can be used throughout our discussion.

In social/personality psychology, one of the most prominent models for defining the self is the self-schema (Markus, 1977). Borrowing from cognitive psychology, the self is thought of as cognitively represented by a set of information that is organized and linked in the mind. The self-schema contains general attributes and specific traits and beliefs about the self, including evaluative components, such as those beliefs typically thought to represent self-esteem (e.g., Rosenberg, 1979), as well as goals. The self-schema is thought to function much like any other schema, for example by directing attention to schema-relevant and schema-consistent information. The self-schema also may operate in conscious awareness or automatically, outside of conscious processing. Consistent with this, it has become clear that self-esteem is represented both explicitly, in consciously held beliefs, attitudes, and feelings, and implicitly, in non-conscious ones (e.g., Greenwald & Farnham, 2000). So, from a social/personality perspective, self-models largely can be defined in cognitive terms as the conscious and non-conscious cognitions and feelings that individuals hold about the self.

A similar definition can be applied to self-models from the perspective of attachment theory. Although attachment scholars still question precisely how to define Bowlby's construct of internal working models and how they function, attempts at doing so by social/personality psychologists have drawn heavily on the self-schema concept. For example, internal working models of the self are seen as cognitive-affective structures that are habitual, generalized, and operate largely unconsciously on thoughts, behavior, and emotion. More specifically, Collins and Read (1994) suggest that internal working models contain memories of attachment-relevant experiences, beliefs, attitudes, and expectations about the self (and others), attachment-relevant goals and needs, and plans and strategies to achieve goals. Attachment scholars recognize that this information is represented and operates at both conscious and non-conscious levels to guide functioning over time.

Clinical models of self-models, other than cognitive ones, which have drawn heavily on schema-based conceptualizations, have been less explicit about what the self is, although they all agree, in some ways, that self-models can be held both consciously and non-consciously. Psychoanalytic models focus heavily on non-conscious information and processes. Cognitive models, although focused largely on conscious material, clearly recognize the power of non-conscious aspects of the self in their attention to "automatic thoughts" and underlying schemas. Cognitive models also tend to focus on the content of self-models, whereas psychoanalytic models tend to focus more on processes, such as self-protection (i.e., defense), ego integration, and self-reflection. Interestingly, some of these processes are consistent with those described by social/personality psychologists. For example, social/personality research on self-serving biases, self-enhancement, self-verification, and various defenses shows that people are motivated to protect the self (for a review see Moskowitz & Tesser, 2005). Both social/personality and psychoanalytic scholars agree that people benefit from a coherent sense of self. For example, Campbell, Assanand, and Di Paula (2003) have demonstrated that possessing a clear, stable, and differentiated self-concept is associated with better psychological adjustment. Similarly, psychoanalytic scholars have recognized the importance of reflective functioning, or mentalizing, which involves the capacity to conceive of and think about the mental states of the self and others and to link these representations to behavior (Fonagy, Steele, Steele, Moran, & Higgitt, 1991). For instance, individuals with reflective self-awareness would have a meta-awareness of who they are and why they behave the way they do, thus allowing them to predict and explain their own behavior and maintain a sense of self-coherence. This capacity aids in functioning in a manner similar to self-clarity in that both are thought to be essential to individuals in forming and maintaining integrated identities (Fonagy & Target, 1997). In line with this, such mentalizing is associated with positive outcomes, including prevention of depression relapse (Teasdale, Moore, Hayhurst, Pope, Williams, & Segal, 2002), change in psychotherapy (Karlsson & Kermott, 2006), and attachment security (Slade, Grienenberger, Bernbach, Levy, & Locker, 2005).

So, although there are important differences in how scholars from different traditions view self-models, there also are important similarities that can allow us to have some common language to function in the service of translation and integration. It is safe to say that both social/personality and psychoanalytic perspectives agree that information about the self is, at least in part, represented mentally, in the form of beliefs, attitudes, and feelings about the self; that mental representations can be consciously held and accessible, as well as non-consciously held and operate outside of awareness; and that processes involved in keeping the self consistent, coherent, and safe are regularly operating both in and out of awareness. With this common foundation in mind, we turn to a discussion of change processes.

CHANGE IN MODELS OF SELF IN RELATIONSHIPS

The primary goal of this chapter is to discuss how models of self in relationships change. To do so, we review how the different perspectives conceptualize change, and then provide a more integrated discussion of how change may come about.

Social/Personality Models of Change

Social/personality psychologists have focused largely on naturally occurring change processes in the content of self-models. That is, changes that are not planned or pursued with the explicit assistance of another, such as a therapist, or with self-change as a specific goal. Instead, these changes, although perhaps motivated at some level, occur largely in response to naturally occurring circumstances in the interpersonal environment.

Importantly, before going into detail about what promotes naturally occurring change, it is necessary to point out that, at least from the schema-based conceptualization of self-models, change is not the natural state. Rather, self-schemas follow the rules of schema-consistent processing. As such people are more likely to confirm their self-schemas than to change them. In addition, most theory and research relevant to change in self-models focuses on changes in states rather than traits, and on consciously accessible self-models rather than non-conscious ones, although there are notable exceptions (e.g., Andersen & Chen, 2002; Davila & Cobb, 2003).

Much of the literature that we include was not developed in the context of understanding change, but it is relevant. For example, social-comparison theories (Festinger, 1954; Tesser, 1988) provide a way of understanding naturalistic change in that people's self-views can change in response to whether they compare themselves favorably or unfavorably to others (e.g., Krones, Stices, Batres, & Orjada, 2005; Tesser & Paulhus, 1983). Also, as alluded to earlier, Leary's sociometer model (Leary et al., 1995) provides hypotheses about how change in state self-esteem occurs in the context of relationships, although it is not a model of change per se. Specifically, state self-esteem will fluctuate in response to people's assessments of their relational value. Therefore, according to both models, on a day-to-day or even moment-to-moment basis, state self-esteem may be changing depending on assessments of the interpersonal environment. Whether and how this leads to changes in trait self-esteem is not known, but to the extent that there are significant changes in the environment that would allow for lasting changes in the way one's relational value is assessed or how one compares oneself to others, then changes in trait self-esteem might follow. We return to this when we discuss change from the perspective of attachment theory.

Andersen's model of relational selves (Andersen & Chen, 2002), as well as Baldwin's (1992) model of relational schemas are similar to sociometer and social comparison theories in that they predict that models of self can change in a moment-to-moment way depending on the interpersonal environment. However, the relational selves and schema models describe ways this occurs outside of awareness. That is, people are not necessarily actively comparing themselves to others or assessing their interpersonal environments. Rather, people's self-models are changing in an automatic or unconscious manner in response to interpersonal circumstances. In addition, the relational selves and schema models suggest that people hold multiple models of self in relation to different people, and the sense of self will depend on whichever one happens to be activated. Thus these models speak most directly to state change, but suggest that trait change might be promoted if a particular self-model could be more chronically activated.

Self-presentation models also have implications for understanding changes in self in the context of relationships. Schlenker and Pontari (2000) argue that self-presentation is a necessary strategy used to create a desired impact on others, which may come to affect self-assessments, and, ultimately, self-presentations may become "real." Importantly, Schlenker and Pontari suggest that this process depends on social validation of the presented self. When it is approved or accepted it may be more likely to be internalized. Therefore, this model espouses a model of change in the self that has the potential to lead to trait change, in which the self may be shaped by interactions with and feedback from others. People may "try out" a sense of self, and may ultimately take it on with positive feedback from others.

Attachment scholars have provided explicit predictions about circumstances that can lead to change in models of self in the context of relationships. Specifically, changes in internal working models of self will occur when attachment models are disconfirmed and elaborated with new information (Bowlby, 1988; Collins & Read, 1994). Moreover, the situations likely to result in such disconfirmation are those that represent changes in caregiving environment and other emotionally significant and long-lasting interpersonal circumstances (Collins & Read, 1994). Indeed, research supports these hypotheses, both at the state and the trait levels. For example, negative changes in state self-models occur in response to assessments of interpersonal loss (Davila & Sargent, 2003) and relationship break-ups (Kirkpatrick & Hazan, 1994). Negative changes in trait self-models are associated with experiencing stressful interpersonal circumstances during childhood or in adulthood (e.g., Davila & Cobb, 2003; Weinfeld, Sroufe, & Egeland, 2000). Therefore, tests of predictions from attachment theory have provided some of the clearest evidence of how models of the self change, both at state and trait levels, in response to naturally occurring changes in the interpersonal environment.

The predictions about change from attachment theory have been informed by developmental and clinical theory and are not the "property" of social/personality psychology per se, although social/personality researchers have conducted a good deal of the work in this area. However, there are a number of explicit models of change in self-models in the context of relationships that are uniquely social/personality psychological. For example, Aron's theory of self-expansion in romantic relationships (Aron & Aron, 1986) states that the self changes to include aspects of the other, and that such change is lasting, at least in the context of the particular relationship. Whether such self-change persists following the dissolution of a relationship and the engagement in a new relationship is unknown.

Rusbult, Kumashiro, Stocker, and Wolf (2005) also suggest that romantic relationships can change an individual's sense of self. In the "Michelangelo effect," Rusbult and colleagues suggest that people's selves are sculpted by partners. Specifically, partners can help people become more of their ideal selves through selective perceptual and behavioral affirmation of aspects of the self that reflect the ideal. In a sense, partners can bring out the best in people and then help people maintain it. Of course, less than ideal selves can also be sculpted. But in either case, the model suggests that romantic partners can foster and help sustain changes in self-models. Again, whether these changes are lasting across relationships over time is unknown.

One final example of a model that is relevant to change in self-models in the context of relationships comes from the notion of transportation into narrative. The use of narrative for understanding, developing, and changing one's sense of self is not uniquely social/personality psychological, but it has gained increasing interest among social and personality psychologists. Generally speaking, narrative scholars believe, like self-presentation theorists, that the narratives, or stories, that people tell about the self are developed and can change in the context of our interpersonal worlds (e.g., Bruner, 2002). Scholars also have suggested that people can use the narratives of others (e.g., through literature) as a way to construct and change the self. As Green (2005) notes, looking to fictional or non-fictional others provides opportunities for social comparison and suggestions for alternate selves. Furthermore, becoming immersed in the life of a character may allow for a safe way to try out new ways of being. As such, in construing change in self-models in the context of relationships, both actual and imaginal relationships may be important.

Clinical Models of Change

Not surprisingly, in contrast to social/personality models, which focus on naturally occurring change, clinical models focus on change that is planned and pursued with the explicit assistance of another, typically a therapist. Also, unlike social/personality models, trait level change is explicitly the goal, although this may come about through processes of state change. Like social/personality models, however, clinical models also emphasize both conscious and non-conscious processes, and also recognize that change is not a natural state, often making intervention a challenging process.

There are few specific models of clinical change that explicitly involve the self in the context of relationships. As noted earlier, a number of theoretical perspectives are consistent with the notion that the self develops in the context of relationships and that the self is a relational phenomenon, but some of the perspectives that focus explicitly on change in models of the self define the active ingredient of change in non-relationship based ways, and some of the perspectives that define the active ingredient of change in relationship based ways do not focus explicitly on change in models of self.

For example, cognitive therapies are specifically designed to change self-schemas, but the approach is non-relational. Although cognitive models recognize that maladaptive self-schemas and distorted self-beliefs often have interpersonal content (e.g., "I am not valued by others"), the technique to bring about change is cognitive restructuring, in which evidence for maladaptive beliefs is questioned and examined, and new, more realistic beliefs are developed. This process may be indirectly relational in that people may engage in "experiments" in which they look for evidence for their distorted beliefs in their relationships and then test out new beliefs. But it is the cognitive restructuring that is thought to be the key mechanism of change.

A variety of other approaches also recognize that the self is important, although it is not the main focus of treatment. Experiential therapy provides some focus on resolving conflict in the self in the context of relationships (e.g., expression of emotions, identification of unmet needs, and increasing assertiveness) through simulated dialogue techniques in which the client enacts split-off emotions or aspects of the self in relation to a significant other (Elliott, Watson,

Goldman, & Greenberg, 2004). In mindfulness therapy there is a focus on self-reflection and engagement with the self's experience in the here and now as a means of changing problematic patterns of thinking or behaving and of becoming more accepting of the self (Kabat-Zinn, 1990). In dialectical behavior therapy (Linehan, 1993), typically used for clients with borderline personality disorder, there is an emphasis on skills training designed, in part, to help people become more accepting of the self and develop better self-regulation through techniques such as mindfulness, distress tolerance, and emotion regulation.

In contemporary psychoanalytic therapy, though there is variability between theorists, the processing of the transference, both in the therapy relationship and with other significant relationships, is believed to be the means by which change in the self occurs. As people understand and interpret patterns of relating to themselves and others that are based on internalized prior relationship experiences, they may newly internalize aspects of the therapy relationship (and themselves in it) to produce change in self views and in the self in relation to others (Buckley, 1994). For example, in transference-focused psychotherapy, changes in the self have been demonstrated through achievement of a secure attachment style and development of greater differentiation and relatedness in thoughts about self and others (Levy, Kelly, Meehan, Reynoso, Clarkin, & Kernberg, 2006).

Interestingly, psychoanalytic approaches are similar in some ways to what Bowlby (1988) described as a therapeutic approach for changing models of self in the context of relationships: (1) provide patients with a secure base from which they can explore painful aspects of their life by being supportive and caring; (2) help patients explore past and present relationships, including expectations, feelings, and behaviors; (3) help patients examine the relationship with the therapist and how it may relate to relationships or experiences outside of therapy; (4) encourage awareness of how current relationship experiences may be related to past ones; and (5) help patients feel, think, and act in new ways that are unlike past relationships. Essentially, Bowlby proposed a method of intervention that would allow for the development of the very thing he suggested would lead to change—a new, emotionally significant interpersonal environment (the therapeutic relationship), that would disconfirm existing models and replace them with new ones.

The therapeutic relationship clearly plays an important role in Bowlby's ideas. Indeed, it can be seen as a new, hopefully secure attachment relationship. Although the importance of the therapy relationship, or therapeutic alliance, was once disputed or written off as a "non-specific" component of treatment separate from the active ingredients for change (see Goldfried & Davila, 2006), the importance of the alliance for fostering change is now more accepted. Indeed, it may be in the alliance that we see the most direct and explicit way of conceptualizing change in self-models in relationships from a clinical perspective.

According to Bordin (1979), the therapeutic alliance is composed of three factors: The presence of a bond between therapist and client, where the client views the therapist as caring, understanding, and knowledgeable, an agreement between client and therapist regarding the goals of treatment, and an agreement on the means by which goals may be achieved. In this conceptualization, the alliance serves as the context in which interventions of any sort can take place. Bordin's first component, the presence of a bond, is the component most typically thought of as relevant to the alliance, and speaks most to the nature of the relationship between therapist and client. Perhaps its implications for change in the self were best described by Rogers (1951) who said,

> the client moves from the experiencing of himself as an unworthy, unacceptable, and unlovable person to the realization that he is accepted, respected, and loved, in this limited relationship with the therapist . . . as the client experiences the attitude of the acceptance which the therapist holds toward him, he is able to take and experience this same attitude toward himself. (pp. 159–160)

This sentiment has been echoed in different ways by clinicians from a variety of orientations. Beck et al. (1979), in describing cognitive therapy for depression, note that a prerequisite for successfully conducting therapy is to be warm, empathic, and accepting. From a psychoanalytic perspective, Luborsky (1984) notes that insight and understanding cannot be useful unless they occur in a supportive relationship. Strupp and Binder (1984) consider the defining characteristic of therapy to be the human relationship, and suggest that the essence of change is in the human experience in which the client feels understood and from this develops a new understanding of the self and behavior.

In sum, then, from a clinical perspective, perhaps the most significant vehicle for changing models of self in relationships is the therapeutic relationship itself.

INTEGRATED PERSPECTIVES ON CHANGE

As the reader has likely recognized, there are important consistencies across social/personality and clinical models of change. However, there also are a number of ways in which each perspective can inform the other. In this section, we describe a set of themes that emerge in the work from the two perspectives as a means of integration, and as a catalyst for further elaboration by each tradition.

Change in Self-Models Happens in the Context of an Actual Relationship

Both the social/personality and clinical perspectives strongly agree that change in models of self happens in the context of an actual relationship. From the clinical perspective, the therapy relationship provides both a direct and an indirect vehicle for change in self-models. The relationship between therapist and client can provide a new, emotionally significant experience of acceptance that allows the client to experience the self in a new manner. As such, models of self in relationships can change with a new relationship experience. But what are the mechanisms of this?

Social/personality perspectives provide a range of possibilities, all of which may play a role. For example, consistent with the models of Leary et al. (1995) and Murray and colleagues (e.g., Murray et al., 2000, 2003), when a therapist behaves in an accepting, empathic manner over time, clients may begin to assess their relational value more positively and may perceive more positive regard from their "partner," the therapist. Both would facilitate at least temporary increases in state self-esteem that, over time, might begin to affect trait self-esteem. This may be how Rogerian interventions have their effect. Similarly, consistent with Rusbult et al.'s (2005) Michelangelo effect, having a "partner" (the therapist), who selectively affirms healthy aspects of the self can bring about change. As such, the therapist becomes the sculptor, much in the way a romantic partner may be. Functional analytic psychotherapy (FAP; Kohlenberg & Tsai, 1994) is based, in part, on this idea. In FAP, the therapy relationship is seen as the primary mechanism of change, and the therapist responds with natural contingencies that increase improvements and decrease problem behaviors. Importantly, the notion of natural reinforcers (i.e., naturally occurring, typical responses to behavior), as compared to contrived ones (i.e., planned, non-typical responses) is key, in that FAP and other radical behavioral approaches argue that change is most likely to emerge and be maintained with natural reinforcers. This suggests that people hoping to sculpt the selves of their romantic partners are best doing so through the use of natural contingencies. Indeed, a recent study indicates the efficacy of couple's therapy that is based in large part on this principle (Christensen, Atkins, Berns, Wheeler, Baucom, & Simpson, 2004).

It also is worth considering whether self-expansion theory (Aron & Aron, 1986) might illuminate how the therapy relationship provides the context for change. Might the client come to incorporate aspects of the therapist in the self? Certainly one goal of therapy is for clients to internalize the new experience of the self in the context of the therapy relationship, as well as to learn and utilize new skills that have been developed. In that way, the client has incorporated aspects of the therapy in the self. Hence, although clients may not directly incorporate aspects of the therapist into the self, they may incorporate aspects of the relationship.

Social/personality models of change, thus, may provide specific, testable hypotheses about how the therapy relationship manifests in change in self-models. Clinical models also may direct social/personality models to aspects of the change process that have not been of focus. For example, there is likely to be an emotional component involved in how self-models change in relationships and, compared to the social-cognitive aspects of the self, this component has been overlooked by social/personality psychologists. Perhaps this accounts for, or is a function of, the tendency to focus on state level changes. A general principle of therapeutic change that pertains to the emotional component of self-models is the facilitation of a corrective experience (Goldfried & Davila, 2006). Although contemporary perspectives on this principle emphasize that it may occur at a variety of levels, using a range of techniques, it is generally agreed that it involves a new emotional experience (Alexander & French, 1946). Another general principle of therapeutic change is ongoing reality testing, in which patients are encouraged to continue to engage in new behaviors and new ways of viewing the self, as well as actively processing these new experiences over time (Goldfried & Davila, 2006). Therefore, consistent with what Bowlby (1969) proposed, trait level changes in models of self may be most likely to come about in the face of ongoing, emotionally significant, interpersonal experiences. To further understand when and how models of self will be self-confirming, fluctuating at the state level, or changing at the trait level, a consideration of the emotional impact of relationship experiences and their duration may be warranted.

This discussion raises an additional issue. Social/personality models of change have developed out of an attempt to specify normative aspects of social cognitive functioning. Although valenced aspects of the self (e.g., self-esteem) have been a major focus, pathological variations in the self have garnered less attention. As such, there has been little need for social/personality models of significant, lasting character change. Clinical models, on the other hand, are explicitly about lasting character change, as that is the business of clinical psychology. Still, it is clear that each would benefit from a consideration of the other.

Change in Self-Models is Not Always Dependent on the Presence of an Actual Relationship

Having made a case for the importance of an actual relationship in facilitating change, we now acknowledge that such a relationship may not always be necessary. As noted earlier, it has been suggested that fictional or non-fictional others can be used to stimulate change in self-models (Green, 2005). A number of clinical techniques are consistent with this. For example, computer- or internet-based treatment programs that do not include an actual therapist may be effective for certain problems (e.g., Carlbring et al., 2005; Newman, Kenardy, Herman, & Taylor, 1997). In addition, the use of imaginal exposure, in which clients imagine themselves in challenging situations behaving in new ways, is a commonly used, effective technique. That such interventions work suggests that an imagined relationship experience that allows for new ways of being may be effective in bringing about change in self-models. This has the potential to provide a rich opportunity for research on change in models of self in relationships for scholars in both the social/personality and the clinical traditions.

Change in Self-Models Happens through the Creation of a New Story for the Self

From the social/personality perspective, both the narrative and self-presentation traditions are consistent with this. This notion is more implicit in the clinical perspective, although there is an emphasis on case formulation. Following an initial assessment of a client, a case formulation is developed. Although there are differences across orientations in what the formulation includes, it is generally conceived of as a working hypothesis or "story" about the client's presenting problems and how they have developed and been maintained. This formulation then drives the intervention process in that it aids in the identification of goals, and strategies to reach those goals, and this information is often shared with the client either initially or over time. Inherent in this process, then, is the idea that the client will (eventually) come to share in the formulation, and, consequently, understand the self in a manner consistent with it. Therefore, in this way, part of the process of therapy is clients' recognizing and adopting a new understanding of the self, who they currently are, and who they can be in the future.

Because there are differences across orientations in what a formulation might include, both in content and structure (see Eells, 1997), this raises the question of whether there is one "right" formulation or story for each person. If case formulations can differ across orientations for the same person, and if new narratives of the self can emerge from the potentially random event of choosing to read a particular book, and if people can present themselves in a variety of ways depending on the needs in different settings, then is the creation of a new story for the self unlimited? What constrains the potential self-stories that will fit for each individual? Certainly environmental factors do, particularly the relationships in which the individuals are engaged, as we have suggested throughout this chapter. But other than that, we know relatively little about factors that determine which particular new story for the self will be adopted.

However, we do know something about the kinds of factors that may make the adoption of a new self-story more or less likely. For example, consistent with schema-activation models, as a new story is developing or being considered for adoption, the more that story is activated and processed the more likely it is it will be adopted (e.g., Wyer & Srull, 1981). This idea is consistent with certain treatments designed to help people cope with traumatic experiences. Traumatic material is often avoided, as it overwhelms people's coping capacity and does not fit into their sense of self. Therefore, treatments have focused on helping people tell their story of the trauma, both for the purpose of exposure to extinguish anxiety, and for the purpose of processing the traumatic material so it becomes a non-threatening part of the person's sense of self (e.g., Horowitz, 2003; Riggs, Cahill, & Foa, 2006).

Generally speaking, from a clinical perspective, exposure to new experiences and enactment of new behaviors are likely to work towards the development and acceptance of a new self-story, particularly in the context of a supportive therapeutic relationship (Goldfried & Davila, 2006). As research on self-presentation has suggested (see Schlenker & Pontari, 2000), presenting oneself in a particular way may become real over time, particularly when there is social validation for doing so. However, as Schlenker and Pontari (2000) note, new roles may not be accepted if they are too discrepant from the existing sense of self. This suggests a "small steps" approach to clinical intervention for both the therapist and the client, who need to be mindful that while they may both want significant change, it may only come about gradually. This idea provides a good transition to our next theme.

Change in Self-Models is Hard and May Take Time

Social/personality and clinical psychologists both recognize that change in self-models, particularly at the trait level, can be a very difficult endeavor, that may take a great deal of time. As noted earlier, this notion is inherent in our understanding of how self-schemas operate, in that they tend to be self-confirming. It also is inherent in Bowlby's (1973) notion of internal working models, in that they tend to assimilate rather than accommodate information. And, we believe, most clinicians would readily agree that people often hold hard and fast to old models of self even when they desire change. People often know of no other way to be and, perhaps, may even be motivated to maintain their existing self-view (see Swann, 1996), as it may contribute to a sense of safety or security. It may be that things that are known, even if they are undesirable, are more comfortable than the unknown.

However, social/personality research has shown that people do show great fluctuation in state level thoughts and feelings about the self. From an anecdotal viewpoint, this is true in clinical situations as well, as improvement in therapy is by no means a linear process. As such, an important goal for future research would be to examine if, when, and how changes in state models of the self are related to and/ or effect changes in trait models of the self. As suggested earlier, one answer may lie in the emotional significance of potentially change-promoting experiences. Another answer may lie in the extent of the experience, with chronic or repeated experiences being more powerful. Another answer, not mutually exclusive of the prior two, may lie in the newness of the experience. According to contemporary relational psychodynamic perspectives (e.g., Messer & Warren, 1995), which identify the core of psychopathology as being reflected in repetitive maladaptive interpersonal patterns in which people engage, one of the most important aspects of therapy is to not repeat or replay those patterns in the therapy relationship. Rather, it is to provide the client with a new interpersonal experience. Perhaps each instance in therapy that fails to repeat prior experiences or fails to confirm current self-models promotes temporary state change, which, over time, develops into trait change. Consistent with the idea that people can hold multiple relational- and self-schemas (e.g., Baldwin, Keelan, Fehr, Enns, & Koh-Rangarajoo, 1996), these state changes in self-models may develop slowly and at first only be activated in the moment, but later come to be more chronically activated or dominant.

Change in Self-Models Develops from a Balance between Self-Enhancement and Self-Verification

Although we have not introduced the notions of self-enhancement and self-verification prior to this point because they are not specifically relational, they are relevant to change in self-models because they make opposing predictions about change. The self-verification model (Swann & Read, 1981) suggests that people are motivated to verify, or confirm, their beliefs about the self, regardless of their content or valence. As such, self-verification promotes stability rather than change. The self-enhancement model (e.g., Shrauger, 1975) suggests that people are motivated to feel good about the self, implying that people will attempt to confirm existing positive beliefs, but change negative ones. As such, self-enhancement would promote stability in one case and change in another.

That people might hold negative beliefs that they are motivated to both confirm and enhance (i.e., change) may seem impossible on the one hand, but this is a situation with which clinicians are likely to be familiar. People typically present to therapy wanting to feel better, but find giving up existing models difficult. When working with clients with maladaptive beliefs about self and others, who engage in repetitive maladaptive interpersonal patterns, the pull exists for the therapist to fall into the pattern and engage in the maladaptive cycle that confirms negative self-views and discourages change. As noted earlier, this replaying of the maladaptive pattern would be counter-therapeutic. However, that does not mean that self-verification needs should be ignored, nor does it mean that therapy should focus exclusively on self-enhancement. Swann (1997) has argued that self-verification in the context of therapy may allow clients to feel as if they know themselves, which may foster a sense of mastery and control. In addition, it may reduce feelings of alienation through feeling understood by the therapist. As Swann (1997) notes, the perception of the patient that "you know all my shortcomings but still like me" (p. 179) may be beneficial. McWilliams (1999), a psychoanalyst, takes this sentiment even further:

> Supporting people's self-esteem by giving them only positive reactions is not protecting or creating reasonable self-esteem; it is fostering illusion . . . One of the reasons that people's self-esteem improves during psychoanalysis is that, in contrast to the notion that authorities should reframe everything as good, the patient has exposed much that is bad and shameful, and the analyst has not shrunk from understanding those loathed parts of the self. The patient has been accepted by someone who knows all his or her faults, not someone who needs to minimize or distort. If superficial emotional support did anything substantial for a person's self-esteem, then anyone with friends would not need psychotherapy. (p. 161)

McWilliams' statement clearly speaks to her belief in the need for self-verification. Her ideas, like those of Swann, also are consistent with the recent emphasis on clinical interventions that promote both acceptance and change. The notion is that change is most likely to occur when people can be accepting of their experiences and of the self (see Hayes, Jacobson, Follette, & Dougher, 1994). In these models, acceptance does not imply submission or giving up. Rather, it implies a non-evaluative stance. Once people are no longer harshly judging the self, they may be better able to engage in new activities that promote change. Based on these ideas, and on the importance of an accepting therapeutic stance, and in line with Rogers' (1951) beliefs that clients will internalize the therapist's acceptance, it seems that change in self-models in the context of the therapy relationship will be best promoted through attention to both self-enhancement and self-verification needs. Whether this is the case in relationships outside of therapy (i.e., in naturally occurring change settings) is unknown, although the efficacy of couples' treatments that promote acceptance would suggest so (Christensen et al., 2004).

CONCLUDING COMMENTS

In this chapter, we have focused primarily on changes in models of self in the context of relationships, with an emphasis on the relational processes that may promote change. As we hope our discussion demonstrates, there is ample evidence from both the social/personality and clinical perspectives that models of self are closely linked with relational experiences, and that relationships, both naturally occurring as well as therapeutic, provide a very important context for change. However, there are multiple pathways to promoting change in self-models. Change may occur through cognitive, behavioral, and emotional channels, in the context of real and imagined relationships. Change may be affected by conscious and non-conscious processes and may happen separately at state and trait levels. Change must be actively pursued, yet balanced by acceptance. The existence of these multiple pathways provides fertile ground for continued research. In addition, although not covered in detail but inherent in aspects of our discussion, self-models span a broad continuum from healthy (e.g., positive and coherent), to mildly dysfunctional (e.g., low self-esteem or clarity), to severely pathological (e.g., narcissistic and borderline personality disorders). Certainly changing the self-models of individuals with severe pathology may be most difficult, but it is worth considering whether change processes would operate in a similar manner across the continuum. It is also worth further examination of exactly what must be learned in the context of relationships to lead to change. One key message, as this chapter has pointed out, regards the validation of one's sense of self-worth in relation to others. However, as suggested by the self-presentation, narrative, and self-expansion models, there may also be broader issues of identity. Finally, again, although not explicitly covered, it is inherent in any discussion of models of self in relationships that models of self and models of other go hand in hand. Part of the way self-models change is through corresponding change in models of others. If our sense of self develops and changes in the context of our relationships, then our sense of others will do the same.

AUTHOR NOTE

Joanne Davila and Melissa Ramsay Miller, Department of Psychology, SUNY Stony Brook. Preparation of this chapter was supported by NIMH R01 MH063904-1A2. Correspondence can be addressed to Joanne Davila, Department of Psychology, SUNY Stony Brook, Stony Brook, NY, 11794-2500. E-mail: joanne.davila@stonybrook.edu

REFERENCES

Alexander, F., & French, T. M. (1946). *Psychoanalytic therapy: Principles and applications.* New York: Ronald Press.

Andersen, S. M., & Chen, S. (2002). The relational self: An interpersonal social-cognitive theory. *Psychological Review, 109,* 619–645.

Aron, A., & Aron, E. N. (1986). *Love as the expansion of self: Understanding attraction and satisfaction.* New York: Hemisphere.

Baldwin, M. W. (1992). Relational schemas and the processing of social information. *Psychological Bulletin, 112,* 461–484.

Baldwin, M. W., Keelan, J. P. R., Fehr, B., Enns, V., & Koh-Rangarajoo, E. (1996). Social-cognitive conceptualization of attachment working models: Availability and accessibility effect. *Journal of Personality and Social Psychology, 71*, 94–109.

Beck, A. T. (1983). Cognitive therapy for depression: New perspectives. In P. J. Clayton & J. E. Barrett (Eds.), *Treatment of depression: Old controversies and new approaches* (pp. 265–290). New York: Raven Press.

Beck, A. T., Rush, A. J., Shaw, B. F., & Emery, G. (1979). *Cognitive therapy for depression.* New York: Guilford Press.

Blatt, S. J., & Zuroff, D. C. (1992). Interpersonal relatedness and self-definition: Two prototypes for depression. *Clinical Psychology Review, 12*, 527–562.

Bordin, E. S. (1979). The generalizability of the psychoanalytic concept of the working alliance. *Psychotherapy: Theory, Research, and Practice, 16*, 252–260.

Bowlby, J. (1969). *Attachment and loss: Vol. 1. Attachment.* New York: Basic Books.

Bowlby, J. (1973). *Attachment and loss: Vol. 2. Separation: Anxiety and anger.* New York: Basic Books.

Bowlby, J. (1980). *Attachment and loss: Vol. 3. Loss.* New York: Basic Books.

Bowlby, J. (1988). *A secure base.* New York: Basic Books.

Bruner, J. (2002). *Making stories: Law, literature, life.* New York: Farrar, Straus, & Giroux.

Buckley, P. (1994). Self psychology, object relations theory and supportive psychotherapy. *American Journal of Psychotherapy, 48*, 519–529.

Campbell, J. D., Assanand, S., & Di Paula, A. (2003). The structure of the self-concept and its relation to psychological adjustment. *Journal of Personality, 71*, 115–140.

Carlbring, P., Nilsson-Ihrfelt, E., Waara, J., Kollenstam, C., Buhrman, M., Kaldo, V., et al. (2005). Treatment of panic disorder: Live therapy vs. self-help via the Internet. *Behaviour Research and Therapy, 43*, 1321–1333.

Christensen, A., Atkins, D. C., Berns, S., Wheeler, J., Baucom, D. H., & Simpson, L. E. (2004). Traditional versus integrative behavioral couple therapy for significantly and chronically distressed married couples. *Journal of Consulting and Clinical Psychology, 72*, 176–191.

Collins, N. L., & Read, S. J. (1994). Cognitive representations of attachment: The structure and function of working models. *Advances in Personal Relationships, 5*, 53–90.

Cooley, C. H. (1902/1983). *Human nature and the social order.* New Brunswick, NJ: Transaction Books.

Davila, J., & Cobb, R. (2003). Predicting change in self-reported and interviewer-assessed adult attachment: Tests of the individual difference and life stress models of attachment change. *Personality and Social Psychology Bulletin, 29*, 859–870.

Davila, J., & Sargent, E. (2003). The meaning of life (events) predicts change in attachment security. *Personality and Social Psychology Bulletin, 29*, 1383–1395.

Eells, T. D. (1997). *Handbook of psychotherapy case formulation.* New York: Guilford Press.

Elliott, R., Watson, J. C., Goldman, R. N., & Greenberg, L. S. (2004). *Learning emotion-focused therapy: The process-experiential approach to change.* Washington, DC: American Psychological Association.

Feeney, B. C. (2004). A secure base: Responsive support of goal strivings and exploration in adult intimate relationships. *Journal of Personality and Social Psychology, 87*, 631–648.

Festinger, L. (1954). A theory of social comparison processes. *Human Relations, 7*, 117–140.

Fonagy, P., Steele, M., Steele, H., Moran, G. S., & Higgitt. A. C. (1991). The capacity for understanding mental states: The reflective self in parent and child and its significance for security of attachment. *Infant Mental Health Journal, 12,* 201–218.

Fonagy, P., & Target, M. (1997). Attachment and reflective function: Their role in self-organization. *Development and Psychopathology, 9,* 679–700.

Gotlib, I. H., & Hammen, C. L. (1992). *Psychological aspects of depression: Toward a cognitive-interpersonal integration.* Oxford: John Wiley & Sons.

Goldfried, M. R., & Davila, J. (2006). The role of relationship and technique in therapeutic change. *Psychotherapy: Theory, Research, Practice, Training, 42,* 421–430.

Green, M. C. (2005). Transportation into narrative worlds: Implications for the self. In A. Tesser, J. V. Wood, & D. A. Stapel (Eds.), *On building, defending, and regulating the self: A psychological perspective* (pp. 53–74). New York: Psychology Press.

Greenwald, A. G., & Farnham, S. D. (2000). Using the Implicit Association Test to measure self-esteem and self-concept. *Journal of Personality and Social Psychology, 79,* 1022–1038.

Hayes, S. C., Jacobson, N. S., Follette, V. M., & Dougher, M. J. (1994). *Acceptance and change: Content and context in psychotherapy.* Reno, NV: Context Press.

Hazan, C., & Shaver, P. R. (1987). Romantic love conceptualized as an attachment process. *Journal of Personality and Social Psychology, 52,* 511–534.

Horowitz, M. J. (2003). *Treatment of stress response syndromes.* Washington, DC: American Psychiatric Publishing, Inc.

Kabat-Zinn, J. (1990). *Full catastrophe living: Using the wisdom of your mind to face stress, pain and illness.* New York: Dell.

Karlsson, R., & Kermott, A. (2006). Reflective-functioning during the process in brief psychotherapies. *Psychotherapy: Theory, Research, Practice, Training, 43,* 65–84.

Kernberg, O. (1976). *Object relations theory and clinical psychoanalysis.* New York: Jason Aronson.

Kirkpatrick, L. A., & Hazan, C. (1994). Attachment styles and close relationships: A four-year prospective study. *Personal Relationships, 1,* 123–142.

Kohlenberg, R. J., & Tsai, M. (1994). Functional analytic psychotherapy: A radical behavioral approach to treatment and integration. *Journal of Psychotherapy Integration, 4,* 175–201.

Kohut, H. (1977). *The restoration of the self.* New York: International Universities Press.

Krones, P. G., Stice, E., Batres, C., & Orjada, K. (2005). In vivo social comparison to a thin-ideal peer promotes body dissatisfaction: A randomized experiment. *International Journal of Eating Disorders, 38,* 134–142.

Leary, M. R., Tambor, E. S., Terdal, S. K., & Downs, D. L. (1995). Self-esteem as an interpersonal monitor: The sociometer hypothesis. *Journal of Personality and Social Psychology, 68,* 518–530.

Levy, K. N., Kelly, K. M., Meehan, K. B., Reynoso, J. S., Clarkin, J. F., & Kernberg, O. F. (2006). Change in attachment patterns and reflective function in a randomized control trial of transference-focused psychotherapy for borderline personality disorder. *Journal of Consulting and Clinical Psychology, 74,* 1027–1040.

Linehan, M. M. (1993). *Cognitive-behavioral treatment of borderline personality disorder.* New York: Guilford Press.

Luborsky, L. (1984). *Principles of psychoanalytic psychotherapy: A manual for supportive-expressive treatment.* New York: Basic Books.

Markus, H. R. (1977). Self-schemata and processing information about the self. *Journal of Personality and Social Psychology, 35,* 63–78.

McWilliams, N. (1999). *Psychoanalytic case formulation.* New York: Guilford Press.

Mead, G. H. (1956). *The social psychology of George Herbert Mead* (A. Strauss, Ed.) Chicago: University of Chicago Press.

Messer, S. B., & Warren, C. S. (1995). *Models of brief psychodynamic therapy: A comparative approach.* New York: Guilford Press.

Moskowitz, G. B., & Tesser, A. (2005). *Social cognition: Understanding self and others.* New York: Guilford Press.

Murray, S. L., Griffin, D. W., Rose, P., & Bellavia, G. M. (2003). Calibrating the sociometer: The relational contingencies of self-esteem. *Journal of Personality and Social Psychology, 85,* 63–84.

Murray, S. L., Holmes, J. G., & Griffin, D. W. (2000). Self-esteem and the quest for felt security: How perceived regard regulates attachment processes. *Journal of Personality and Social Psychology, 78,* 478–498.

Newman, M. G., Kenardy, J., Herman, S., & Taylor, C. B. (1997). Comparison of palmtop-computer-assisted brief cognitive-behavioral treatment to cognitive-behavioral treatment for panic disorder. *Journal of Consulting and Clinical Psychology, 65,* 178–183.

Riggs, D. S., Cahill, S. P., & Foa, E. B. (2006). Prolonged exposure treatment of posttraumatic stress disorder. In V. M. Follette & J. I. Ruzek (Eds.), *Cognitive-behavioral therapies for trauma* (pp. 65–95). New York: Guilford Press.

Rogers, C. R. (1951). *Client-centered therapy.* Boston: Houghton Mifflin.

Rosenberg, M. (1979). *Conceiving the self.* New York: Basic Books.

Rusbult, C. E., Kumashiro, M., Stocker, S. L., & Wolf, S. T. (2005). The Michelangelo phenomenon in close relationships. In A. Tesser, J. V. Wood, & D. A. Stapel (Eds.), *On building, defending, and regulating the self: A psychological perspective* (pp. 1–30). New York: Psychology Press.

Schlenker, B. R., & Pontari, B. A. (2000). The strategic control of information: Impression management and self-presentation in daily life. In A. Tesser, R. B. Felson, & J. M. Suls (Eds.), *Psychological perspectives on self and identity* (pp. 199–232). Washington, DC: American Psychology Association.

Schrauger, J. S. (1975). Responses to evaluation as a function of initial self-perceptions. *Psychological Bulletin, 82,* 581–596.

Slade, A., Grienenberger, J., Bernbach, E., Levy, D., & Locker, A. (2005). Maternal reflective functioning, attachment, and the transmission gap: A preliminary study. *Attachment and Human Development, 7,* 283–298.

St. Clair, M. (1986). *Object relations and self psychology: An introduction.* Monterey, CA: Brooks/Cole.

Stern, D. N. (1985). *The interpersonal world of the infant: A view from psychoanalysis and developmental psychology.* New York: Basic Books.

Strupp, H. H., & Binder, J. L. (1984). *Psychotherapy in a new key: A guide to time-limited dynamic psychotherapy.* New York: Basic Books.

Swann, W. B., Jr. (1996). *Self-traps: The elusive quest for higher self-esteem.* New York: Freeman.

Swann, W. B., Jr. (1997). The trouble with change: Self-verification and allegiance to the self. *Psychological Science, 8,* 177–180.

Swann, W. B., Jr., & Read, S. J. (1981). Self-verification processes: How we sustain our self-conceptions. *Journal of Experimental Social Psychology, 17,* 351–372.

Teasdale, J. D., Moore, R. G., Hayhurst, H., Pope, M., Williams, S., & Segal, Z. V. (2002). Metacognitive awareness and prevention of relapse in depression: Empirical evidence. *Journal of Consulting and Clinical Psychology, 70,* 275–287.

Tesser, A. (1988). Toward a self-evaluation maintenance model of social behavior. In

L. Berkowitz (Ed.), *Advances in experimental social psychology* (Vol. 21, pp. 181–227). New York: Academic Press.

Tesser, A., & Paulhus, D. (1983). The definition of self: Private and public self-evaluation management strategies. *Journal of Personality and Social Psychology, 44*, 672–682.

Trinke, S. J., & Bartholomew, K. (1997). Hierarchies of attachment relationships in young adulthood. *Journal of Social and Personal Relationships, 14*, 603–625.

Waters, E. (1997). *The secure base concept in Bowlby's theory and current research*. Paper presented at the Society for Research in Child Development, Washington, DC, April 1997.

Weinfeld, N. S., Sroufe, L. A., & Egeland, B. (2000). Attachment from infancy to early adulthood in a high-risk sample: Continuity, discontinuity, and their correlates. *Child Development, 71*, 695–702.

Wyer, R. S., & Srull, T. K. (1981). Category accessibility: Some theoretical and empirical issues concerning the processing of social stimulus information. In E. T. Higgins, C. P. Herman, & M. P. Zanna, (Eds.), *Social cognition: The Ontario Symposium* (Vol. 1, pp. 395–420). Hillsdale, NJ: Lawrence Erlbaum Associates, Inc.

13

Time for Some New Tools: Toward the Application of Learning Approaches to the Study of Interpersonal Cognition

MARK W. BALDWIN, JODENE R. BACCUS, STÉPHANE D. DANDENEAU, and MAYA SAKELLAROPOULO

*T*he last two decades have witnessed the steady growth of research into interpersonal cognition, largely driven by one experimental modus operandi. Indeed it was just two decades ago that Gordon Bower (1986) wrote a chapter for clinical researchers suggesting that they might benefit from trying out a useful little technique developed by cognitive psychologists, called "priming." He predicted that just like a child given a toy hammer, they would soon find that everything they observed would start to look like a nail that needed pounding. Those of us studying relationship cognition have been using this particular hammer for quite some time now, to activate relationship representations (e.g., Baldwin & Holmes, 1987), significant other concepts (Andersen & Cole, 1990), relationship motives (Fitzsimons & Bargh, 2003) and secure-base feelings (Mikulincer & Shaver, 2003). Indeed, just about any aspect of interpersonal cognition one might name has been open to a good hammering, and we have been able to observe reverberations throughout the information-processing system.

Perhaps, though, it is time for a few new tools. In our lab we have been exploring the usefulness of what might broadly be termed learning paradigms. Bargh and Ferguson (2000), in their provocative article showing the links between behaviorism and the current social cognitive literature, examined such notions as activation, automatic and implicit processing, and the situational control of behavior, to conclude that many of the assumptions of social cognition are consistent with those typically associated with learning theory. We share this view, and we have begun to press beyond this and ask whether conditioning paradigms and the like might therefore be handy tools for examining cognition about relationships. After all, if activation patterns of social knowledge play a key role in interpersonal life, might it be possible and beneficial to find ways of modifying those activation patterns in a relatively enduring way?

We start by defining and reviewing the context of our work, which is the rich interpersonal cognition literature developed largely through the use of priming paradigms. Then we outline our recent findings using learning approaches, and discuss the applicability of this new tool to other lines of interpersonal research.

THE PROCESSING OF INTERPERSONAL INFORMATION

The field's interest in examining relationship cognition followed from a growing awareness that humans likely do not reflect on independent social objects, such as self and other, in isolation from each other as much as they think about such entities *in interaction with* each other. The sense of self is unarguably affected by its social surroundings: Social life is made up of sometimes confusing and ambiguous, sometimes harsh and hurtful, sometimes clear and comprehensible social cues, through which we all need to navigate in order to properly communicate and interact with our environment. The self-concept, and personality more generally, are largely a function of one's style of thinking about and interacting with this social environment.

Social cognitive formulations of personality have provided a framework for work on interpersonal cognition, and also lend themselves to our discussion of learning theories that follows. The Cognitive-Affective Processing System (CAPS) model of Mischel and Shoda (1995; broadly based on Mischel, 1973) has influenced much work in this area, and we draw on this model as well. Particularly appealing is the ability of this approach to account for both stability and a significant amount of variablity in people's interpersonal behavior across relationships. Specifically, behavior is seen as taking the form of *if . . . then . . .* patterns, whereby particular situations tend to lead to particular types of behaviors. In terms of relationships, the *ifs* are specific interpersonal contexts, and the *thens* are the experiences, behaviors, and self-perceptions that are cued (Andersen & Saribay, 2005; Holmes & Cameron, 2005).

The core elements in the model are the "cognitive-affective units" that underlie people's response to situations. Essentially Mischel and Shoda (1995) have done a remarkable job of organizing the social cognitive literature into some component elements, and it will be useful to review these before examining detailed examples in the domain of self–other cognition and learning. The first component element is *encoding*: How is a situation, a stimulus, or a person (including the self) construed? Even this first stage of social perception involves several processes, including selective attention to specific kinds of stimuli, and the application of schemas and associative networks that are activated to characterize the social situation. A second element involves *behavior-outcome expectancies*, for example of the sort "If I do X, the other person will do Y." *Motivation* and *affect* enter as the third and fourth types of cognitive-affective units: People's goals and values determine the types of outcomes they seek (or try to avoid) and, when these outcomes are anticipated or actually experienced, affective states of anxiety, joy, security, and so on are likely to ensue. Finally, people have specific *competencies, skills, and self-regulatory strategies* that they use to try to achieve their goals.

In an important extension of the Mischellian approach, Cantor and Kihlstrom (1985) elaborated a theory of social intelligence, carefully analyzing the nuts and bolts of social cognition by drawing on some additional concepts from the cognitive literature. Particularly helpful is the distinction between declarative and procedural knowledge (Anderson, 1983). *Declarative* knowledge represents facts and events. It includes semantic, abstract knowledge (e.g., categories, schemas) as well as memories from one's past, and it is generally thought to be represented in associative networks. *Procedural* knowledge, by contrast, includes skills and habits, such as how to ride a bicycle, how to tie one's shoe, or how to avoid an argument with one's spouse. Procedural knowledge can also include cognitive skills and habits, such as attribution-making or trait inference. Procedural knowledge is assumed to function implicitly, or outside of awareness, whereas declarative knowledge can influence both explicit and implicit processes.

In applying such ideas within the relationships literature, various domain-specific models of interpersonal cognition have been developed by different research teams. For example, much work has been done on attachment theory: Bowlby (1973), writing at the same time as Mischel was generating his pioneering social cognitive analysis of personality, described attachment working models as including expectancies about the significant other's availability and responsiveness. In several recent articles, Mikulincer and Shaver (2003, 2005) have expanded on Bowlby's model, and integrated a massive amount of attachment research into an elegant theory of internal working models. Their analysis identifies a set of three information-processing modules that guide attachment-relevant behavior. The first is a component that monitors the environment for threats; the second is a component that monitors the availability of attachment figures to provide support; and the third is a component that assesses various strategies for coping with distress. These modules function according to the kinds of cognitive-affective units described in the CAPS model, such as encoding, expectancies, and so on. While declarative knowledge underlies expectancies and views of self and other, procedural knowledge guides attention as well as the selection of attachment behavioral strategies.

As we shall review in a moment, similar analyses have been carried out in the rejection sensitivity (e.g., Pietrzak, Downey, & Ayduk, 2005), self-evaluation (e.g., Leary, 2005; Murray & Holmes, 2000), and transference and relational self (e.g., Andersen & Chen, 2002) domains, among others. Our own work (e.g., Baldwin, 1992; Baldwin, Keelan, Fehr, Enns, & Koh-Rangarajoo, 1996; Dandeneau & Baldwin, 2004) generally falls in the self-evaluation and attachment domains. Most recently, Murray, Holmes & Collins (2006) have offered a provocative model of the declarative and procedural knowledge that determines feelings of felt security in close relationships; we will return to this model later in the chapter.

Although there are important differences among these domain-specific analyses, various writers (e.g., Pietrzak et al., 2005) have pointed out that the overlap among different constructs and lines of research is considerable. For example, most researchers have postulated some form of associative-network model by which the mind represents self, others, and relationships. Most of us have used the kinds of priming techniques mentioned by Bower (1986)—including activation paradigms and also reaction-time tests of knowledge accessibility—to test these ideas. Working to a large extent in parallel, different research groups have converged on similar sorts of principles. What have we established so far? Consider the following selective review of some of the principles for which evidence has emerged across different domains; a list we have compiled with an eye toward phenomena that have been demonstrated via priming methods, and which might also be amenable to learning interventions:

- People have declarative knowledge structures representing self-with-other, which are likely to be in the form of associative networks linking self-representations, other-representations, and interpersonal scripts for typical interaction patterns (Baldwin, 1992). Interpersonal scripts can be characterized as exhibiting an *if . . . then . . .* pattern: For example, Fehr (2005) collected people's expectations of the kinds of interaction patterns that tend to be found in intimate friendships, and identified prototypical scripts such as "If I need to talk, my friend will listen" and "If I am in trouble, my friend will help me." Bretherton (1990) similarly argued that attachment scripts consist of safe haven expectations such as "If I get hurt, Mommy will take care of me." Research has documented that various clinical problems such as pathological mourning (Baccus & Horowitz, 2005), perfectionism (Hermans, 2005), and vulnerability to depression (e.g., Scarvalone, Fox, & Safran, 2005) can reflect distortions in interpersonal scripts. For example, highly dependent individuals (according to their scores on the Depressive Experiences Questionnaire) tend to expect that if they were to act submissively toward their father, he would respond warmly (Mongrain, 1998).

- People typically have multiple models for different kinds of self-with-other experiences, and these can be activated using a range of priming techniques such as visualizations of specific significant others, or even exposure to a significant other's name or photo. Activated relationships influence affect: For example, people in warm relationships automatically evaluate their partner positively on an Implicit Association Test (Zayas & Shoda, 2005), and show increased positive affect if the relationship is primed (e.g., Andersen, Reznik, & Manzella, 1996; Mikulincer, Hirschberger, Nachmias, & Gillath, 2001). Activated relationships also influence the experience of others and the self: People primed with a relationship in which they feel secure (versus avoidant or anxious), for example, tend to be drawn to secure individuals as potential dating partners (Baldwin et al., 1996), are more willing to turn to others for social support when under stress (Pierce & Lydon, 1998), and are more open to threatening or unexpected information (Mikulincer & Arad, 1999). Conversely, people primed with a critical significant other tend to become more self-critical (e.g., Baldwin, Carrell, & Lopez, 1990; Baldwin & Holmes, 1987).

Andersen and colleagues' research on the relational self (e.g., Andersen & Chen, 2002), to which we return later in the chapter, elegantly documents the extent to which people hold multiple models of self-with-other that can be activated by characteristics of a new acquaintance.

- Interpersonal cognitive structures create baseline expectancies about the likely course of novel experiences, as revealed by the way people encode the environment on reaction-time measures of hypervigilance or biased attention. For example, individuals with social anxiety (Mogg & Bradley, 2002), high rejection sensitivity (Pietrzak et al., 2005), or low self-esteem (Dandeneau & Baldwin, 2004), show attentional biases toward rejection-related targets on Stroop, lexicial decision, and visual probe tests.

- Expectancies function at least in part via spreading activation. When the *if* of a behavior-outcome expectancy is activated, activation automatically spreads to the associated *then*. For example, when *trust* is activated for avoidantly attached individuals, this facilitates lexical-decision reaction times for the expected outcome of being *hurt* (Baldwin, Fehr, Keedian, Seidel, & Thompson, 1993).

- Interpersonal cognitive structures can define elements of a goal hierarchy. If a significant-other representation is activated, activation spreads to related goals. For example, activating *Dad* can lead to facilitated responses to words relating to achievement (Shah, 2003); activating *Mom* can lead some students to actually perform better on a verbal achievement task, but only if the student has a goal of pleasing their mother by academic success (see Fitzsimons, Shah, Chartrand, & Bargh, 2005). Situation-behavior implementation intentions can also function according to spreading activation: In men who sexually harass, priming power activates thoughts of sex (Bargh, Raymond, Pryor, & Strack, 1995), and among avoidantly attached individuals, priming intimacy activates the goal of control (Mikulincer, 1998).

- Relationship cognition shows a high level of motivated processing. Work by Murray and colleagues, for example, has documented the remarkable degree to which relationship partners typically hold illusions about the uniquely marvelous characteristics of their partner (Murray & Derrick, 2005; Murray & Holmes, 2000). Commitment research has documented several types of defensive responses that are activated when a relationship commitment is threatened: If the threat is an attractive alternative, for example, committed relationship partners are quick to devalue the potential interloper (e.g., Lydon, Burton, & Menzies-Toman, 2005; Rusbult, Lange, Wildschut, Yovetich, & Verette, 2000).

- Interpersonal expectancies are not easily disconfirmed or extinguished. Often people avoid situations where they anticipate negative outcomes, and so never open themselves to disconfirming evidence (e.g., Alden, Teschuk, & Tee, 1992). If they do find themselves in a situation with the potential for new learning, either they act in such a way to produce expectancy-confirming reactions from others via self-fulfilling prophecy dynamics (e.g., Berk & Andersen, 2000; Downey, Freitas, Michaelis, & Khouri, 1998), or their activated expectancy leads them to interpret their partner's response in such a biased manner that no new learning is possible. These factors mean that interpersonal cognition often settles into a self-sustaining feedback loop or vicious cycle that is hard to break.

For a field that is only a couple of decades old we have come a long way, and we have learned a lot. We have designed reaction-time measures to assess people's automatic and unconscious reactions to interpersonal stimuli. We have developed a powerful set of priming techniques to activate the knowledge structures that define social experience. And we have begun to develop a common language to describe the elements and dynamics of interpersonal cognition, as they appear in different domains of social interaction. This body of work represents a real achievement. Still, perhaps it is time for some new tools to allow us to examine not just the functioning of existing cognitive structures, but also their development and change.

TIME FOR SOME NEW TOOLS

Is it reasonable to consider new paradigms based on trying to change patterns of interpersonal cognition? Reading through even our brief and highly selective review leaves one with the feeling that because people's knowledge structures about interpersonal life impose such a powerful bias in how novel information is processed, they must be deeply entrenched, rigid, and impervious to change. Of course we know that cognitive conservatism does tend to be the rule, but the CAPS approach (Mischel & Shoda, 1995), reminds us that personality shows a complex interplay of stability and variability. Recall that in the early days of Adult Attachment Theory, the implicit assumption in much of the literature was that people developed a single attachment "style" early in life, which fairly rigidly defined their relationships from there on in. Social cognitive analyses, however, suggested that there should be the possibility of substantial variability as a result of the activation of different working models (e.g., Baldwin & Fehr, 1995; Baldwin et al., 1996), and subsequent research has illuminated the cognitive-affective processing units that contribute to both variability and stability in attachment behavior (e.g., Mikulincer & Shaver, 2003). And, while there is more to be done in this area, several studies have supported Bowlby's notion that working models are subject to revision, documenting the kinds of relationship experiences (e.g., interpersonal loss, marriage) that can contribute to lasting changes in people's chronic attachment orientations (Davila, Burge, & Hammen, 1997).

Given that there is the opportunity for learning and change within relationships, we have wondered what possibilities may exist for the experimental manipulation of this learning. What possibilities might there be for people to intentionally apply the principles of learning theory to modify their interpersonal cognition patterns? Could people alter their attachment working models? Their tendency to experience transference reactions with certain kinds of people? Their expectancy of rejection and the self-critical reactions that come with it? We believe the answer is Yes. We suspect that virtually any element of interpersonal cognition that has been identified in priming research, including expectations, activation patterns, attentional biases, and goal structures, is open to deliberate modification through the application of learning principles. In the remainder of this chapter, we review our research using learning paradigms, and outline how the application of these paradigms to other areas of interpersonal research may shed new light on the development, expression, and modification of interpersonal patterns of relating.

In our recent research we have mostly explored two broad approaches, which map loosely onto the distinction between declarative and procedural knowledge (Anderson, 1983; Cantor & Kihlstrom, 1985). First we examine the possibility of modifying the organization and activation of people's associative networks, the core declarative knowledge structures that define categories of people, relationship situations, and so forth. Then we examine the possibility that people's information-processing procedures, including the initial stages of stimulus encoding, can be modified through repetitive practice.

Associative Learning

Associations provide the structure of interpersonal cognition. The importance of associations is well recognized by the CAPS model (Mischel & Shoda, 1995) we have been discussing. On the face of it, the focus of some CAPS research on *if . . . then . . .* situation-behavior patterns makes it look like a fairly mechanical stimulus–response (S-R) behaviorist formulation, without much room for the nuances of human cognition. But as we know, not even behaviorists are S-R, reflex-arc behaviorists anymore. Rather, observable S-R patterns of behavior are assumed to reflect cognitive units including S-S* (stimulus–stimulus) associations between different aspects of a situation, and R-S* (response–stimulus) expectancies of how specific behaviors tend to lead to specific outcomes (e.g., Bolles, 1972; Pearce & Bouton, 2001). Even though a dinner bell might lead an organism—whether canine or Homo sapiens—to start salivating, this is not generally thought to be a cognitively unmediated response but rather is because the bell activates a representation of a juicy steak (see, e.g., Bargh & Ferguson, 2000; Dickinson, 1989; Shoda & Smith, 2004). As Donald O. Hebb once argued, cells that fire together tend to wire together, so eventually the activation of one cognitive/neural element automatically spreads to the other element.

Associative structures, which link specific memories, expectancies, feelings, and abstract beliefs about self and other in an integrated network, have been studied extensively. A very securely attached individual, for example, may have her self represented as a lovable, devoted fiancée, which is associated with a view of other as a sensitive, caring fiancé. Also, as mentioned earlier, the *if . . . then . . .* expectancies in interpersonal scripts can be thought of as associations. We have been particularly interested in the sometimes profound impact of expectancies involving acceptance and rejection. Among low self-esteem individuals, for example, priming *failure* facilitates reaction times to *rejection* targets (Baldwin & Sinclair, 1996), revealing contingent expectations about social acceptance even when the target words are presented after only a 250 ms delay (Baldwin, Baccus, & Fitzsimons, 2004). One could say the low self-esteem person "believes" that failure tends to produce social rejection, but it would be more accurate to see this phenomenon as reflecting the automatic activation of rejection expectancies, produced by strong associative links. This spreading activation leads to the bad feelings: Low self-esteem feelings are presumed in interpersonal models of self-esteem to be produced by the activation of such rejection expectancies (e.g., Leary & Baumeister, 2000).

Cued Activation   Our first foray into learning paradigms involved asking a basic question: Can we modify activation patterns for rejection and acceptance information? It turns out this is actually rather straightforward. In what we have come to call *cued activation* studies, a simple association is first created between a conditioned stimulus, such as a novel computer tone, and an unconditioned inter-personal stimulus, such as an image of an accepting other. Lexical decision manipulation checks confirm that sounding the tone facilitates reaction times to related target words, and inhibits reaction times to inconsistent target words (e.g., in this case, acceptance versus rejection words; Baldwin & Main, 2001). Later, while the participant is in the midst of a supposedly unrelated task, the conditioned computer tone can be played in the background. As a result of this cue a variety of cognitive processes, behaviors, and emotions are triggered, inducing positive or confident feelings about the self.

One study that explored the possibility of reconfiguring interpersonal knowledge in this way (Baldwin & Main, 2001) focused on the sometimes debilitating phenomenon of social anxiety, which is thought to involve expectancies of rejecting or embarrassing social outcomes. To establish a realistic context we borrowed a technique from the social anxiety literature, setting up a getting-acquainted scenario and making it as anxiety-provoking as possible. First, though, all the undergraduate women participating in the study were conditioned to form associations between one computer tone and social approval, and between a different tone and social disapproval. The conditioning manipulation involved the participants answering a questionnaire and getting bogus feedback about whether their answers were socially desirable (indicated by pictures of smiling, accepting faces; signaled by a specific tone) or undesirable (indicated by pictures of frowning, rejecting faces; signaled by a different tone). This feedback was entirely bogus and had nothing to do with their answers, but it did establish novel associations between specific tones and specific social outcomes (acceptance and rejection). Later, we had the participant engage in a brief interaction with an aloof male confederate who was blind to experimental condition. His instructions were to be only minimally responsive: giving one-word answers to questions, allowing long silences, and generally making the situation as anxiety-provoking as possible for the female participant. During this agonizing conversation, one of the tones sounded repeatedly in the background (this was explained by the experimenter as being part of an unrelated computer task occurring in the back of the room). In line with the principle of cued activation, women who heard the conditioned acceptance tone were found not only to experience more positive, relaxed feelings during the interaction than the women exposed to the conditioned rejection tone, but also to behave in a more poised manner (as rated by their confederate inter- action partner) than their rejection tone counterparts. Interestingly, these findings were particularly evident among the chronically highly self-conscious women, who rated themselves as far less socially anxious if they had been cued with the acceptance tone, as opposed to the rejection tone, during the interaction.

In short, an elementary classical conditioning paradigm was effective in modifying people's associative structure regarding acceptance and rejection. This shows how closely people are attuned to this type of feedback, and how readily they learn acceptance and rejection contingencies even in relation to a priori noninterpersonal cues. We have done half a dozen studies using this and other similar cued activation approaches to activate acceptance versus rejection. The results are often straightforward, but sometimes not, and the complex findings are often the most intriguing. For example, the effects of the conditioned tones are sometimes moderated by individual difference variables in interesting ways. In two studies of self-evaluations in performance situations, whereas women's self- evaluations were bolstered by the cued activation of acceptance versus rejection, men actually showed higher self-evaluations on the cued activation of rejection— possibly reflecting a defensive reaction (Baldwin, Granzberg, Pippus, & Pritchard, 2003). In another study, only people with a relatively secure chronic attachment orientation showed a conditioning pattern where a cue for acceptance led them to anticipate warmth from others even if they failed (Baldwin & Kay, 2003; Baldwin & Meunier, 1999; Ratelle, Baldwin, & Vallerand, 2005, for other cued activation studies). Although there are some complexities to the data, the important point is that these cued activation studies clearly demonstrate the possibility of modifying longstanding associative structures and activation patterns through surprisingly basic, repetitive learning tasks.

Mind you, life would be rather strange if people were to go about their daily lives periodically cued by strategically timed computer tones. Might classical con- ditioning be used to modify more ecologically valid associations? We wonder about applying this basic principle to other lines of interpersonal research. Consider for example the important work by Andersen and colleagues on transference and the relational self (e.g., Andersen & Saribay, 2005). This work shows that when a new person shares a few characteristics with your past significant other, you tend to go beyond the information given and infer other common traits and characteristics between the two people (Andersen & Chen, 2002). You will even start to antici- pate patterns of relating, and to experience aspects of yourself, in a way consistent with experiences in the activated significant relationship. Theoretically, represen- tations of the significant other, and of self-with-other, are stored as links in mem- ory, and specific characteristics of a novel person can serve as cues to activate the entire associative structure. As an example, if you have come to associate your father's booming baritone voice with mocking criticism, a novel person with a similar tone will evoke the expectation of a caustic remark. Might it be possible to influence such transference reactions with classical conditioning paradigms? Simplest might be to create a novel association, for example that red hair and a fondness for Radiohead music tends to be associated with curiosity, acceptingness, and generosity (see, e.g., Lewicki, 1985). More challenging would be to try to modify an existing structure, by repeatedly pairing a booming voice with warm, supportive feedback. In any case, applying learning paradigms to the study of transference might afford new opportunities for an even more fine-grained analysis of how the cognitive links between the self and specific significant others are formed, and how they might be modified.

Conditioning Implicit Self-Esteem   Our most recent conditioning studies have focused on self-esteem. Historically, research has explored self-esteem as an explicit construct. Explicit self-esteem refers to self-evaluations that are consciously and deliberately made, which can be assessed using self-report measures (e.g., the Rosenberg Self-Esteem Scale). Recently, an unconscious component, implicit self-esteem, has been defined as a self-evaluation that occurs automatically and outside of awareness (Farnham, Greenwald, & Banaji, 1999). Indirect methods used to measure implicit self-esteem include the Implicit Association Test (IAT) and the Name Letter Task. In both cases, participants' automatic self-attitude is assessed; in the IAT reaction times to self- and evaluation-related words in a "self-good" block are compared to a "self-bad" block (Greenwald & Farnham, 2000), and in the traditional Name Letter Task, the liking of one's own name letter initials (versus other letters) is assessed (e.g., Bosson, Swann, & Pennebaker, 2000).

Past research into explicit self-esteem (e.g., Leary, 2005) has supported the idea that self-esteem is strongly influenced by interpersonal feedback and expectations, and recent research in our laboratory has explored the theory that implicit self-esteem is also interpersonally based. That is, we hypothesize that implicit self-esteem arises automatically from cognitive associations between "self" and "acceptance" versus "self" and "rejection."

To explore the interpersonal basis of implicit self-esteem, we turn to a form of classical conditioning that involves the associative transfer of valence, called *evaluative conditioning*. Evaluative conditioning occurs when the liking of a stimulus changes as a result of pairing that stimulus with other positive or negative stimuli (De Houwer, Thomas, & Baeyens, 2001). A common evaluative conditioning paradigm involves pairing pictures initially rated as "neutral" by participants with other pictures that the participant had previously rated as "liked" or "disliked." Following this pairing, participants tend to rate the neutral picture according to the affective valence of the picture with which it was paired.

As applied to implicit self-esteem, we theorized that repeated pairing of the self with social rejection or acceptance—whether in our lab session or across a lifetime—might transfer the affect associated with "being accepted" or "being rejected" to the self. We therefore designed a procedure to create this kind of pairing, via a repetitive computer game. To activate the self we used the presentation of self-relevant information, such as a person's first name or birthday. For social acceptance, we used photographs of smiling faces. We predicted that repeated pairing of self and acceptance would eventually create a self–*accepted* link. As a result, when the person thought about "self," this would automatically activate feelings of acceptance that would be experienced as self-esteem.

First, participants were asked to enter into a computer six self-relevant pieces of information: first name, birthday, hometown, ethnicity, phone number, and street name. Following this, participants were instructed that they would see a word appear in one of four quadrants on the computer screen, and were told to use the computer mouse to click on this word as quickly as possible. After clicking on a word, an image would briefly appear on the screen (400 ms) in the quadrant where the word had appeared. After the image disappeared, another word would appear in one of the four quadrants, and participants were again to click on that word.

The words that appeared in the boxes were either self-relevant (i.e., entered in by the participant at the beginning of the task) or non-self-relevant. In the experimental version of the task, participants' self-relevant information was always followed by an image of a smiling face so that "self" would become associated with acceptance. A frowning or a neutral face followed non-self-relevant items. In the control condition, both self-relevant and non-self-relevant information were followed by a random selection of smiling, frowning, and neutral faces. In total, participants were presented with 240 trials, 80 of which were self-relevant. The important methodological detail here is that participants in both conditions saw the three facial expressions presented an equal number of times, and saw the same amount of self-relevant versus non-self-relevant information—the only difference was in the pairing. Any condition effects could not be attributed to mere priming mechanisms therefore, since participants in the experimental and control conditions saw the same number of smiling and frowning faces.

Across several studies using this task, we have found that participants in the experimental condition show significantly higher implicit self-esteem scores after completing the task, compared to participants in the control condition. This finding has been found using both the Name Letter Task and the IAT as dependent measures. Beyond self-esteem effects, we have found that the conditioning also influences behavioral intentions. Drawing from past research on aggression, we designed a vignette measure that asks subjects how likely they would be to administer a noxious blast of noise to someone who had rejected or insulted them. We have found the self-esteem conditioning manipulations makes undergraduates (Baccus, Baldwin, & Packer, 2004) and also children between the ages of 9 and 15 (Baccus, Baldwin, & Milyavskaya, 2006) less eager to lash out at others.

In our most recent research, we have extended this paradigm to the topic of social anxiety. In one study (Baccus, Baldwin, & Primiano, 2006), participants completed either the experimental or the control version of the conditioning task. After this, they were videotaped while answering anxiety-provoking questions (e.g., "Count backwards from 117 to zero in intervals of 13"). These videos were then coded by raters for how anxious the participants appeared. Results showed a replication of the main conditioning effect—participants in the experimental condition showed higher scores on the self-esteem IAT compared to those in the control condition. Furthermore, participants in the experimental condition were rated as less anxious compared to their counterparts in the control condition. While these results are preliminary, they suggest that not only does creating a cognitive *self–acceptance* association lead to enhanced implicit self-esteem, it also helps people cope with ego-threatening situations.

We are excited by the prospect of employing conditioning paradigms to delve more deeply into the nature of implicit self-esteem. There is much work to be done here. Consider that implicit self-esteem is typically thought of as a unidimensional, good/bad response. Explicit self-attitudes, on the other hand, have long been recognized to be composed of at least two dimensions, often revolving around concerns related to communion (e.g., inclusion, attachment) as opposed to concerns related to agency (e.g., dominance, competency). These different dimensions, in turn, have been shown to predict different thoughts, feelings, and behaviors (e.g., Kirkpatrick, Waugh, Valencia, & Webster, 2002; Leary, Cottrell, & Phillips, 2001; Tafarodi & Swann, 1995). Kirkpatrick and colleagues (2002), for example, have shown these two aspects of explicit self-esteem to predict aggression differentially. Whereas the agentic dimension of self-esteem in the form of self-perceived superiority was positively related to aggression against others following an ego-threat, the communal dimension of self-esteem in the form of social inclusion was negatively related to it. These findings mirror those of Baumeister and colleagues, who have found murderers, rapists, wife beaters, violent youth gangs, and even aggressive nations to be characterized by deeply held beliefs of their own superiority (Baumeister, Smart, & Boden, 1996). In a similar vein, Leary and colleagues (2001) have attempted to disentangle the effects of acceptance and dominance on explicit self-esteem. They found that while individuals' perceived level of acceptance tended to be moderately correlated with their perceived level of dominance, each aspect was found to contribute unique variance to explicit self-esteem.

From the perspective of the models just mentioned, it seems reasonable to expect that implicit self-esteem may parallel explicit self-esteem in its complexity and be composed of at least the two dimensions. A recent series of studies supported this multifaceted conceptualization of implicit self-esteem by showing that two versions of the name-letter task in the literature—one version involving rating the *attractiveness* of letters (e.g., Dijksterhuis, 2004) and a second version involving rating the *liking* of letters (e.g., Bosson et al., 2000)—tap into different dimensions of self-attitudes (Sakellaropoulo & Baldwin, 2006). In two studies, a narcissistic frame of mind was activated in some participants by having them either visualize a time when they had impressed others, or read a list of highly positive trait words. Results showed that narcissistic thoughts and feelings, and also aggressive urges on our vignette measure, were associated with a particular pattern of implicit self-evaluation wherein a glowing implicit self-attractiveness was combined with a lack of implicit self-liking. This finding is in line with research showing chronic narcissism to be associated with overly positive self-views on dimensions of agency (e.g., intellectual skills), but negative self-views on dimensions of communion (e.g., agreeableness; Campbell, Rudich, & Sedikides, 2002). The aggression finding also echoes the work on explicit self-esteem of Kirkpatrick and colleagues (2002), in which perceived superiority and perceived inclusion had divergent effects on aggression.

Our findings demonstrating the multifaceted nature of implicit self-esteem also help to explain why our implicit self-esteem conditioning research, in which we bolstered associations between the self-concept and images of acceptance, reduced feelings of aggressiveness while boosting implicit self-esteem as assessed by the *liking* version of the name-letter task, while other implicit self-esteem conditioning research (e.g., Dijksterhuis, 2004) in which associations between the self-concept and positive trait words are conditioned, enhance implicit self-esteem on the *attractiveness* version of the name-letter task. It seems likely that in creating associations, the specific content—and not just the valence—matters. Future research remains to be done to determine whether conditioning the self-concept to agentic themes, such as images of power and dominance, while neglecting or perhaps even undermining the self-concept's association with acceptance and communal themes more generally, might produce more, rather than less, narcissism and aggression, as the work of both Kirkpatrick and colleagues (2002) and Campbell and colleagues (2002) would predict. In other words, conditioning paradigms offer a new tool for examining theoretical assumptions about the specific interpersonal roots of self-esteem.

Procedural Learning

Many of the cognitive-affective processing units that underlie interpersonal cognition fall into the broad category of procedural knowledge (Anderson, 1983): the skills, habits, and rules by which people handle information. This includes focusing attention on specific types of information, drawing spontaneous inferences about ambiguous stimuli, responding to certain events with certain types of behaviors, and so on.

The kinds of skills, strategies, and habits that make up people's processing of interpersonal events are presumably learned largely implicitly, through a lifetime of thousands of interactions with family and close relationship partners. Sometimes these procedures function just fine, but at other times they can exert a distorting influence, creating unbalanced and sometimes unrealistic representations of social life and skewing the person's perceptions of situations and how to react to them.

Selective attention to social threat is one process that has been identified as distorting the perception of social information. When a person disproportionately pays attention to aspects of the environment that represent potential threats to the social self, whether these be angry faces, rejecting comments, or separation cues, this hypervigilance reinforces the perception that the environment is unsupportive and rejecting. This kind of encoding bias has been shown to be related to individual differences in self-esteem, social anxiety, social phobia, depression, anxious attachment, and generalized anxiety disorder, and has been suggested to be a key factor in their development and perpetuation (Bradley, Mogg, Falla, & Hamilton, 1998; Dandeneau & Baldwin, 2004; Mathews, Mackintosh, & Fulcher, 1997; Mikulincer, Birnbaum, Woddis, & Nachmias, 2000; Wells & Matthews, 1994; Williams, Mathews, & MacLeod, 1996).

Selective attention is, in some sense, at the earliest stage of processing information about one's experiences. Negative attentional biases tend to influence later-stage processes, including emotional and behavioral responses, which can make the bias self-sustaining and therefore particularly difficult to modify. In the case of low self-esteem, for example, it is suggested that individuals develop a defensive hypervigilance for social rejection in order to prepare for the worst in ambiguous or threatening social situations (Downey & Feldman, 1996; Leary, Tambor, Terdal, & Downs, 1995). Indeed, in one study individuals with low self-esteem were shown to exhibit more Stroop color-naming interference on rejection words than acceptance words (Dandeneau & Baldwin, 2004), indicating that participants with low self-esteem exhibited a greater attentional bias for rejection than for acceptance. This hypervigilance for rejection information increases the likelihood of perceiving or interpreting ambiguous cues as socially rejecting, thereby increasing individuals' concerns about social threat and perpetuating low self-esteem.

Mikulincer & Shaver's (2003) model of the dynamics of the attachment system likewise has a place for encoding processes, and the self-amplifying cycle they can produce. In particular, hyperactivating strategies, characteristic of individuals high in attachment anxiety, include vigilance for threat signals and attachment-figure unavailability, which exaggerates the potential consequences of threat, and increases the tendency to detect threat in every situation. This is akin to being on constant high alert, making it difficult to differentiate irrelevant from real threat and thereby perpetuating the original fears of attachment unavailability.

Not only do attentional biases contribute to self-perpetuating cycles of emotional distress, they also have downstream physiological consequences. In the stress literature, for example, social-evaluative threat has been found to be one of the most powerful triggers of the stress response, involving a large set of physiological outcomes including release of the stress hormone cortisol (Dickerson & Kemeny, 2004). In a recent study we examined the link between biased attention and cortisol release, using a visual probe task (VPT). In the VPT, pairs of frowning and neutral pictures were briefly shown followed by a probe (: or . .) replacing one of the pictures. An attentional bias for rejection was indicated by faster response times for identifying probes that replaced frowning faces relative to those that replaced neutral faces. Our participants underwent a standard stress induction paradigm involving performing difficult mental tasks under time pressure, then later completed the VPT. The greatest cortisol release under stress was shown by those subjects who later exhibited the greatest selective attention to rejecting faces in the VPT (Dandeneau, Baldwin, Baccus, Sakellaropoulo, & Pruessner, in press). This positive association between hypervigilance for rejection cues and cortisol release while under stress indicates that early-stage attentional processes influence the perception of interpersonal events, which can affect a range of later-stage emotional and physiological consequences.

In short, biased attention can introduce profound distortions into interpersonal cognition, contributing to self-sustaining and self-amplifying cycles with physiological, emotional, and relational consequences. Can this vicious cycle be stopped? We wondered if attentional training could help people reduce hypervigilance to social threat. Relatedly, Pietrzak et al. (2005) reviewed ongoing research of theirs suggesting that some people high in rejection sensitivity seem to be able to avoid some of the downstream consequences of the trait, by self-regulating their attention and interpretations away from the rejecting elements of social situations. Might we be able to help people learn such attention-regulation skills, to reduce or override their chronic bias?

Cognitive skills and habits are learned in much the same way as complex motor skills like playing the piano or swinging a golf club: repetition and practice are key. The process becomes automatic and effortless with enough practice, making social information processing faster, automatic, and more efficient (Rosenbaum, Carlson, & Gilmore, 2001). The challenge, then, is to design a training task that directly targets the attentional bias, and gives people the chance to practice a new cognitive habit.

We developed a simple task to train individuals to inhibit rejection cues, by having them repeatedly identify an accepting face in a 4×4 grid of frowning faces (Dandeneau & Baldwin, 2004). In order to effectively and accurately complete the task, participants must learn to ignore the frowning faces and focus on finding the approving one. We hypothesized that eventually, after dozens of trials, people would learn to automatically direct their attention toward acceptance, while disengaging from and inhibiting rejection. This new cognitive skill could then counteract any selective attention to threat, disrupting the vicious cycle and producing beneficial downstream consequences.

In one early study with this paradigm, individuals with low self-esteem using this task experienced significantly less Stroop interference on rejection words than their counterparts in a control condition who were trained to identify the 5-petaled flower in a grid of 7-petaled flowers (Dandeneau & Baldwin, 2004). Noteworthy is the fact that the attentional training used pictures of faces whereas the Stroop task used words, a cross-modal effect indicating the learning of a generalized skill rather than a more limited attentional response to specific stimuli. The training task did not affect people with high self-esteem, presumably because rejection is not as threatening for them, and because they already tended to inhibit rejection. In a second study, results were replicated using a visual probe task with pictures of smiling and frowning faces (Dandeneau et al., in press). Taken together, these results show that it is indeed possible to modify the earliest stages of attention to acceptance and rejection information.

But what of the late-stage impacts of attentional modifications? Does modifying early-stage attentional processes have any meaningful impact on late-stage responses to social stress? In two field studies we examined the effects attentional training has on late-stage responses to social stress by capitalizing on naturally occurring socially evaluative situations. In our first study we examined levels of exam stress in a group of undergraduate students studying for their final exam. Generally speaking, students respond to the evaluative pressures of the examination period with increases in self-reported perceived stress (Jemmott & Magloire, 1988; Vedhara, Hyde, Gilchrist, Tytherleigh, & Plummer, 2000). As we know from recent interpersonal studies of self-esteem, the possibility of failure is a strong social-evaluative threat that automatically activates an anticipation of criticism and rejection from others (Baldwin et al., 2004; Baldwin & Sinclair, 1996; Leary et al., 1995). Thus worries about social threats can contribute to the experience and expression of stress during the nerve-wracking preparation period leading up to an exam.

Students were asked to play either the experimental or the control version of the attentional training task online for 5 consecutive days leading up to one of their final exams. Daily stress, self-esteem and specific exam-related questions (e.g., "I feel stressed about my exam"), along with state anxiety and school abilities measures, were administered. Results revealed that while the overall perceived level of stress and self-esteem did not differ between groups, specific stress toward the final exam did. Participants in the experimental training condition reported significantly less stress about their final exam on the final day—the day of their exam—compared to those in the control training condition. Following their exam, participants in the experimental condition also reported less state anxiety than control participants (Dandeneau et al., in press). Therefore, practicing an encoding procedure of directing attention away from social threat helped to reduce the evaluative stress of the exam period.

For our second field study, we examined the benefits of attentional training on psychosocial stress in the most stressful workplace context we could think of: a telemarketing call center. For telemarketing representatives, the workplace context is saturated with social and performance evaluation, as well as periodic doses of outright rejection and hostility, leading to high levels of psychosocial stress and burnout. In our study, 23 telemarketers were asked to complete either the experimental or the control version of the attentional training task before their work shifts for five consecutive days. Dependent measures included self-reports of daily self-esteem and perceived stress, cortisol samples on the last day, and sales performances for the period before and during testing. As an objective measure of self-confidence, the telemarketing company's quality control raters, who listen to representatives' conversations with clients, were asked to rate participants' self-confidence.

Results revealed that by the end of the work week, participants in the experimental condition had a significant increase in self-esteem, whereas their control counterparts did not. Participants also reported a significant decrease in perceived stress by the end of the week compared to those in the control group. Results on the cortisol sampling, taken five times across the last workday of the study, indicated that participants who had practiced inhibiting rejection had significantly less overall cortisol release and less reactivity to stress than those in the control condition. As for quality control ratings, participants in the experimental condition were rated as significantly more self-confident following clients' first objection than those in the control group. Therefore, not only did participants report an increase in self-esteem and a reduction in stress, but objective raters also evaluated them as more self-confident in the face of negative social feedback (which, granted, may or may not be a welcome thing if one is at the receiving end of a dinnertime phone call!) Finally, data on sales performance revealed that participants who completed the rejection-inhibition training also had a remarkable 68.9% increase in sales success from the pre-testing period to the period during which they practiced their new cognitive habit on a daily basis.

Taken together these results demonstrate the beneficial impacts cognitive training can have on downstream psychological, physiological, and behavioral out-comes. By modifying a key encoding procedure, in this case the initial deployment of attention toward or away from social threat, it is possible to have powerful effects on self-esteem and stress. Indeed, given the important role social threat plays in the human stress response, these results underscore the benefit of looking at early-stage processes as potential stress prevention strategies rather than "after the fact" response-focused coping strategies (e.g., Gross, 2001).

If attentional training can help telemarketers—who tend to deal with signifi-cant amounts of explicit rejection and hostility on a daily basis—consider the possible benefit for people who are hypersensitive to social negativity in their close relationships. In a powerful analysis of the cognitive processes underlying felt security, Murray et al. (2006) identify a set of *if . . . then . . .* rules that shape the inferences people make, and the behaviors they enact, as they confront the risks of relational dependency. These rules determine appraisals of a partner's acceptance, feelings of hurt in response to a partner's rejection, and the willingness to risk dependence on a partner whose enduring love and caring may not be completely guaranteed. The cognitive dynamics in this model are generally consistent with those that have been identified in other domains of interpersonal cognition, but here the complex patterns of interdependency that exist between individuals in a relationship are emphasized. Murray and Holmes (2000), for example, showed that individuals with low self-esteem underestimated how positively their partners viewed them, whereas individuals with high self-esteem overestimated their part-ner's impression of them. These authors also demonstrated the powerful cognitive biases that lead individuals with low self-esteem to detect rejection in otherwise mundane behaviors and events, inflating the implications of conflicts and inter-preting them as signs that their partner is no longer affectionate and committed toward them. These and similar cognitive biases were shown to "feed the burning fire" of relationship conflicts in a longitudinal study that showed how personality vulnerabilities exhibited by individuals with low self-esteem were exacerbated over time, demonstrating the self-amplifying nature of these cognitive biases (Murray & Derrick, 2005; Murray & Holmes, 2000). We wonder about the impact that attentional training might have in such a close relationship context. Our field studies showed that practicing the procedure of inhibiting attention to social threat helped people feel less stressed and more self-confident. Perhaps this small shift in perspective could also be enough to help relationship partners tolerate the inevitable conflicts and ambiguities that can, if ruminated on, have an undermin-ing effect on relational happiness. Navigating the risks and rewards inherent in close relationships is difficult at the best of times, and selective attention to just the risks is not likely to lead to a balanced perspective.

CONCLUDING THOUGHTS

Social cognitive theory has provided a tremendous framework for advances in understanding interpersonal cognition. When relationships researchers first started to use priming techniques such as activation and reaction-time paradigms, a host of new possibilities for data collection and theory development emerged. The same type of opportunity exists now if we take the next logical step and fully embrace ideas about learning, along with conditioning and training paradigms for studying it.

One source of resistance to this agenda may be the emphasis in the field on stability and continuity, as opposed to variability and change. Some theoretical approaches in particular, such as psychodynamic and attachment approaches, tend to focus on the long-term impact of early interpersonal experiences in defining the personality. Even these models have a place for variability and change, however, whether in response to significant relationship experiences or therapeutic intervention, so there could be much gained from studying change process experimentally. Certainly some aspects of interpersonal cognition (e.g., emotional reactions based on traumatic experiences) may be much less amenable to modify via simple conditioning interventions than the kinds of self–other cognition examined in our studies. Still, experimental research on attachment working models has revealed much about the context-specificity and situational activation of attachment dynamics, and only time will tell whether learning paradigms can offer a similar window into the process of personality change.

One potential payoff of this research agenda is that it may allow us to test propositions about the boundary conditions of interpersonal cognition. Several theorists have suggested that interpersonal cognition is constrained in important ways, both internally and externally. For example, Fiske and Haslam (2005; and Fiske, 1992) argue that there are four fundamental relational models that people use to coordinate interpersonal activity: communal sharing, authority ranking, equality matching, and market pricing. Gilbert (2005), on the other hand, argues that evolution has wired into human psychology a small number of systems that are attuned to specific forms of social relatedness, including care eliciting, care-giving, formation of alliances, social ranking, and sexuality. Work on the attachment system obviously falls within this evolutionary perspective as well. From an interdependence theory perspective, Holmes and Cameron (2005) argue strongly that relational cognition is primarily constrained by the realities of interpersonal situations, and that these realities involve the interdependence of motives and outcomes. All of these models identify some interaction patterns as more relevant to the social perceiver than other interaction patterns. Indeed, ever since Garcia (Garcia & Koelling, 1966) discovered that rats could learn associations between the taste of food and sickness, better than between non-food-related stimuli and sickness, it has been clear that organisms come prepared to learn some kinds of associations and skills better than others. This reasoning suggests a technique for evaluating propositions about fundamental processes: Which ones are learned most easily? In this regard it is perhaps remarkable that our cued activation studies, where a thoroughly non-social cue such as a computer tone can become a signal for interpersonal acceptance or rejection, work as well as they do. Still, one expects that social cues—such as the self-concept, as in our implicit self-esteem studies—are likely to yield better conditioning than others. And, if the theories about fundamental social patterns are correct, some types of associations and procedures should be more easily learned than others.

In addition to these theoretical benefits, there are implications here for applied social psychology as well: We note that this type of research ties in particularly well with recent developments in the field of computer games. With the advent of the Serious Games movement (e.g., Bergeron, 2006), researchers, developers, educators, and health professionals have turned a "serious" eye on computer game technology. From flight training, to learning math, to emulating a safe environment for social phobics to practice novel social skills, serious games are being explored for their usefulness in confronting a host of current concerns: skills training, clinical treatment, education, or the distribution of health information. Using virtual reality, immersive environments can be created in which training, learning, and testing can occur without any substantial risks to patients or research participants (Blascovich, Loomis, Beall, Swinth, Hoyt, & Bailenson, 2002). The training provided by a game is only as good as the theory behind the game's design, of course. Given the richness of the interpersonal cognition literature, including theories of attachment, transference, rejection cognition, and so on, there would seem to be great potential here for applying our knowledge within a gaming environment. In this way, serious games might be used to target such factors in ways that were previously impossible, and to help people modify their ways of looking at self and others in beneficial ways.

All in all, we predict that once interpersonal cognition researchers begin to explore the application of learning paradigms to their domain of interest, it will be as if they have been given a new soldering iron, staple gun, chisel, c-clamp, or ornamental turning lathe. Suddenly all manner of social phenomena will begin to look as if they need shaping, gluing, and wiring together. It is simply amazing what a new set of tools can do, to bring inspiration to a workshop.

REFERENCES

Alden, L. E., Teschuk, M., & Tee, K. (1992). Public self-awareness and withdrawal from social interactions. *Cognitive Therapy and Research, 16* (3), 249–267.

Andersen, S. M., & Chen, S. (2002). The relational self: An interpersonal social-cognitive theory. *Psychological Review, 109* (4), 619–645.

Andersen, S. M., & Cole, S. W. (1990). "Do I know you?": The role of significant others in general social perception. *Journal of Personality and Social Psychology, 59,* 384–399.

Andersen, S. M., Reznik, I., & Manzella, L. M. (1996). Eliciting facial affect, motivation, and expectancies in transference: Significant-other representations in social relations. *Journal of Personality and Social Psychology, 71* (6), 1108–1129.

Andersen, S. M., & Saribay, S. (2005). The relational self and transference: Evoking motives, self-regulation, and emotions through activation of mental representations of significant others. In M. W. Baldwin (Ed.), *Interpersonal cognition* (pp. 1–32). New York: Guilford Press.

Anderson, J. R. (1983). *The architecture of cognition.* Cambridge, MA: Harvard University Press.

Baccus, J. R., Baldwin, M. W., & Milyavskaya, M. (2006). Unpublished research data.

Baccus, J. R., Baldwin, M. W., & Packer, D. J. (2004). Increasing implicit self-esteem through classical conditioning. *Psychological Science, 15* (7), 498–502.

Baccus, J. R., Baldwin, M. W., & Primiano, S. (2006). Unpublished research data.

Baccus, J. R., & Horowitz, M. J. (2005). Role-relationship models: Addressing maladaptive interpersonal patterns and emotional distress. In M. W. Baldwin (Ed.), *Interpersonal cognition* (pp. 334–358). New York: Guilford Press.

Baldwin, M. W. (1992). Relational schemas and the processing of social information. *Psychological Bulletin, 112* (3), 461–484.

Baldwin, M. W., Baccus, J. R., & Fitzsimons, G. M. (2004). Self-esteem and the dual processes of interpersonal contingencies. *Self and Identity, 3* (2), 81–93.

Baldwin, M. W., Carrell, S. E., & Lopez, D. F. (1990). Priming relationship schemas: My advisor and the Pope are watching me from the back of my mind. *Journal of Experimental Social Psychology, 26* (5), 435–454.

Baldwin, M. W., & Fehr, B. (1995). On the instability of attachment style ratings. *Personal Relationships, 2* (3), 247–261.

Baldwin, M. W., Fehr, B., Keedian, E., Seidel, M., & Thompson, D. W. (1993). An exploration of the relational schemata underlying attachment styles: Self-report and lexical decision approaches. *Personality and Social Psychology Bulletin, 19* (6), 746–754.

Baldwin, M. W., Granzberg, A., Pippus, L., & Pritchard, E. T. (2003). Cued activation of relational schemas: Self-evaluation and gender effects. *Canadian Journal of Behavioural Science, 35* (2), 153–163.

Baldwin, M. W., & Holmes, J. G. (1987). Salient private audiences and awareness of the self. *Journal of Personality and Social Psychology, 52* (6), 1087–1098.

Baldwin, M. W., & Kay, A. C. (2003). Adult attachment and the inhibition of rejection. *Journal of Social and Clinical Psychology, 22* (3), 275–293.

Baldwin, M. W., Keelan, J. P. R., Fehr, B., Enns, V., & Koh-Rangarajoo, E. (1996). Social-cognitive conceptualization of attachment working models: Availability and accessibility effects. *Journal of Personality and Social Psychology, 71* (1), 94–109.

Baldwin, M. W., & Main, K. J. (2001). Social anxiety and the cued activation of relational knowledge. *Personality and Social Psychology Bulletin, 27* (12), 1637–1647.

Baldwin, M. W., & Meunier, J. (1999). The cued activation of attachment relational schemas. *Social Cognition, 17*, 209–227.

Baldwin, M. W., & Sinclair, L. (1996). Self-esteem and "if . . . then" contingencies of inter-personal acceptance. *Journal of Personality and Social Psychology, 71*, 1130–1141.

Bargh, J. A., & Ferguson, M. J. (2000). Beyond behaviorism: On the automaticity of higher mental processes. *Psychological Bulletin, 126* (6), 925–945.

Bargh, J. A., Raymond, P., Pryor, J. B., & Strack, F. (1995). Attractiveness of the underling: An automatic powerrightwards-arrow sex association and its consequences for sexual harassment and aggression. *Journal of Personality and Social Psychology, 68* (5), 768–781.

Baumeister, R. F., Smart, L., & Boden, J. M. (1996). Relation of threatened egotism to violence and aggression: The dark side of high self-esteem. *Psychological Review, 103* (1), 5–33.

Bergeron, B. (2006). *Developing serious games*. Hingham, MA: Charles River Media, Inc.

Berk, M. S., & Andersen, S. M. (2000). The impact of past relationships on interpersonal behavior: Behavioral confirmation in the social-cognitive process of transference. *Journal of Personality and Social Psychology, 79* (4), 546–562.

Blascovich, J., Loomis, J., Beall, A. C., Swinth, K. R., Hoyt, C. L., & Bailenson, J. N. (2002). Immersive virtual environment technology as a methodological tool for social psychology. *Psychological Inquiry, 13* (2), 103–124.

Bolles, R. C. (1972). Reinforcement, expectancy and learning. *Psychological Review, 95,* 394–409.

Bosson, J. K., Swann, W. B., Jr., & Pennebaker, J. W. (2000). Stalking the perfect measure of implicit self-esteem: The blind men and the elephant revisited? *Journal of Personality and Social Psychology, 79* (4), 631–643.

Bower, G. H. (1986). Prime time in cognitive psychology. In P. Eelen (Ed.), *Cognitive research and behavior therapy: Beyond the conditioning paradigm* (pp. 13–26). Amsterdam: North Holland Publishers.

Bowlby, J. (1973). *Attachment and Loss: Vol. 2. Separation: Anxiety and anger.* New York: Basic Books.

Bradley, B. P., Mogg, K., Falla, S. J., & Hamilton, L. (1998). Attentional bias for threatening facial expressions in anxiety: Manipulation of stimulus duration. *Cognition and Emotion, 12* (6), 737–753.

Bretherton, I. (1990). Communication patterns, internal working models, and the intergenerational transmission of attachment relationships. *Infant Mental Health Journal, 11* (3), 237–252.

Campbell, W. K., Rudich, E. A., & Sedikides, C. (2002). Narcissism, self-esteem, and the positivity of self-views: Two portraits of self-love. *Personality and Social Psychology Bulletin, 28* (3), 358–368.

Cantor, N., & Kihlstrom, J. F. (1985). Social intelligence: The cognitive basis of personality. In P. R. Shaver (Ed.), *Review of personality and social psychology* (Vol. 6). Beverly Hills, CA: Sage.

Dandeneau, S. D., & Baldwin, M. W. (2004). The inhibition of socially rejecting information among people with high versus low self-esteem: The role of attentional bias and the effects of bias reduction training. *Journal of Social and Clinical Psychology, 23* (4), 584–602.

Dandeneau, S. D., Baldwin, M. W., Baccus, J. R., Sakellaropoulo, M., & Pruessner, J. C. (in press). Cutting stress off at the pass: Reducing stress and hypervigilance to social threat by manipulating attention. *Journal of Personality and Social Psychology.*

Davila, J., Burge, D., & Hammen, C. (1997). Why does attachment style change? *Journal of Personality and Social Psychology, 73* (4), 826–838.

De Houwer, J., Thomas, S., & Baeyens, F. (2001). Association learning of likes and dislikes: A review of 25 years of research on human evaluative conditioning. *Psychological Bulletin, 127* (6), 853–869.

Dickerson, S. S., & Kemeny, M. E. (2004). Acute stressors and cortisol responses: A theoretical integration and synthesis of laboratory research. *Psychological Bulletin, 130* (3), 355–391.

Dickinson, A. (1989). Expectancy theory in animal conditioning. In S. B. Klein (Ed.), *Contemporary learning theories: Pavlovian conditioning and the status of traditional learning theory* (pp. 279–308). Hillsdale, NJ: Lawrence Erlbaum Associates, Inc.

Dijksterhuis, A. (2004). I like myself but I don't know why: Enhancing implicit self-esteem by subliminal evaluative conditioning. *Journal of Personality and Social Psychology, 86* (2), 345–355.

Downey, G., & Feldman, S. I. (1996). Implications of rejection sensitivity for intimate relationships. *Journal of Personality and Social Psychology, 70* (6), 1327–1343.

Downey, G., Freitas, A. L., Michaelis, B., & Khouri, H. (1998). The self-fulfilling prophecy in close relationships: Rejection sensitivity and rejection by romantic partners. *Journal of Personality and Social Psychology, 75* (2), 545–560.

Farnham, S. D., Greenwald, A. G., & Banaji, M. R. (1999). Implicit self-esteem. In

D. Abrams & M. A. Hogg (Eds.), *Social identity and social cognition* (pp. 230–248). Malden, MA: Blackwell Publishing.

Fehr, B. (2005). The role of prototypes in interpersonal cognition. In M. W. Baldwin (Ed.), *Interpersonal cognition* (pp. 180–205). New York: Guilford Press.

Fiske, A. P. (1992). The four elementary forms of sociality: Framework for a unified theory of social relations. *Psychological Review*, 99 (4), 689–723.

Fiske, A. P., & Haslam, N. (2005). The four basic social bonds: Structures for coordinating interaction. In M. W. Baldwin (Ed.), *Interpersonal cognition* (pp. 267–298). New York: Guilford Press.

Fitzsimons, G. M., & Bargh, J. A. (2003). Thinking of you: Nonconscious pursuit of interpersonal goals associated with relationship partners. *Journal of Personality and Social Psychology*, 84 (1), 148–163.

Fitzsimons, G. M., Shah, J., Chartrand, T. L., & Bargh, J. A. (2005). Goals and labors, friends and neighbors: Self-regulation and interpersonal relationships. In M. W. Baldwin (Ed.), *Interpersonal cognition* (pp. 103–125). New York: Guilford Press.

Garcia, J., & Koelling, R. A. (1966). Relation of cue to consequence in avoidance learning. *Animal Learning and Behavior*, 4 (3), 123–124.

Gilbert, P. (2005). Social mentalities: A biopsychosocial and evolutionary approach to social relationships. In M. W. Baldwin (Ed.), *Interpersonal cognition* (pp. 299–333). New York: Guilford Press.

Greenwald, A., & Farnham, S. (2000). Using the implicit association test to measure self-esteem and self-concept. *Journal of Personality and Social Psychology*, 79 (6), 1022–1038.

Gross, J. J. (2001). Emotion regulation in adulthood: Timing is everything. *Current Directions in Psychological Science*, 10 (6), 214–219.

Hermans, H. J. (2005). Self as a society: The dynamics of interchange and power. In M. W. Baldwin (Ed.), *Interpersonal cognition* (pp. 388–414). New York: Guilford Press.

Holmes, J. G., & Cameron, J. (2005). An integrative review of theories of interpersonal cognition: An interdependence theory perspective. In M. W. Baldwin (Ed.), *Interpersonal cognition* (pp. 415–447). New York: Guilford Press.

Jemmott, J. B., & Magloire, K. (1988). Academic stress, social support, and secretory immunoglobin A. *Journal of Personality and Social Psychology*, 55 (5), 803–810.

Kirkpatrick, L. A., Waugh, C. E., Valencia, A., & Webster, G. D. (2002). The functional domain specificity of self-esteem and differential prediction of aggression. *Journal of Personality and Social Psychology*, 82 (5), 756–767.

Leary, M. R. (2005). Interpersonal cognition and the quest for social acceptance: Inside the sociometer. In M. W. Baldwin (Ed.), *Interpersonal cognition* (pp. 85–102). New York: Guilford Press.

Leary, M. R., & Baumeister, R. F. (2000). The nature and function of self-esteem: Sociometer theory. In M. P. Zanna (Ed.), *Advances in experimental social psychology* (Vol. 32, pp. 1–62). San Diego, CA: Academic Press.

Leary, M. R., Cottrell, C. A., & Phillips, M. (2001). Deconfounding the effects of dominance and social acceptance on self-esteem. *Journal of Personality and Social Psychology*, 81 (5), 898–909.

Leary, M. R., Tambor, E. S., Terdal, S. K., & Downs, D. L. (1995). Self-esteem as an interpersonal monitor: The sociometer hypothesis. *Journal of Personality and Social Psychology*, 68 (3), 518–530.

Lewicki, P. (1985). Nonconscious biasing effects of single instances on subsequent judgments. *Journal of Personality and Social Psychology*, 48 (3), 563–574.

Lydon, J. E., Burton, K., & Menzies-Toman, D. (2005). Commitment calibration with the relationship cognition toolbox. In M. W. Baldwin (Ed.), *Interpersonal cognition* (pp. 126–152). New York: Guilford Press.

Mathews, A., Mackintosh, B., & Fulcher, E. (1997). Cognitive biases in anxiety and attention to threat. *Trends in Cognitive Sciences, 1* (9), 340–345.

Mikulincer, M. (1998). Attachment working models and the sense of trust: An exploration of interaction goals and affect regulation. *Journal of Personality and Social Psychology, 74* (5), 1209–1224.

Mikulincer, M., & Arad, D. (1999). Attachment working models and cognitive openness in close relationships: A test of chronic and temporary accessibility effects. *Journal of Personality and Social Psychology, 77* (4), 710–725.

Mikulincer, M., Birnbaum, G., Woddis, D., & Nachmias, O. (2000). Stress and accessibility of proximity-related thoughts: Exploring the normative and intraindividual components of attachment theory. *Journal of Personality and Social Psychology, 78* (3), 509–523.

Mikulincer, M., Hirschberger, G., Nachmias, O., & Gillath, O. (2001). The affective component of the secure base schema: Affective priming with representations of attachment security. *Journal of Personality and Social Psychology, 81* (2), 305–321.

Mikulincer, M., & Shaver, P. R. (2003). The attachment behavioral system in adulthood: Activation, psychodynamics, and interpersonal processes. In M. P. Zanna (Ed.), *Advances in experimental social psychology* (Vol. 35, pp. 53–152). San Diego, CA: Elsevier Academic Press.

Mikulincer, M., & Shaver, P. R. (2005). Mental representations of attachment security: Theoretical foundation for a positive social psychology. In M. W. Baldwin (Ed.), *Interpersonal cognition* (pp. 233–266). New York: Guilford Press.

Mischel, W. (1973). Toward a cognitive social learning reconceptualization of personality. *Psychological Review, 80,* 252–283.

Mischel, W., & Shoda, Y. (1995). A cognitive-affective system theory of personality: Reconceptualizing situations, dispositions, dynamics, and invariance in personality structure. *Psychological Review, 102,* 246–268.

Mogg, K., & Bradley, B. P. (2002). Selective orienting of attention to masked threat faces in social anxiety. *Behaviour Research and Therapy, 40* (12), 1403–1414.

Mongrain, M. (1998). Parental representations and support-seeking behaviors related to dependency and self-criticism. *Journal of Personality, 66* (2), 151–173.

Murray, S. L., & Derrick, J. (2005). A relationship-specific sense of felt security: How perceived regard regulates relationship-enhancement processes. In M. W. Baldwin (Ed.), *Interpersonal cognition* (pp. 153–179). New York: Guilford Press.

Murray, S. L., & Holmes, J. G. (2000). Self-esteem and the quest for felt security: How perceived regard regulates attachment processes. *Journal of Personality and Social Psychology, 78* (3), 478–498.

Murray, S. L., Holmes, J. G., & Collins, N. L. (2006). Optimizing assurance: The risk regulation system in relationships. *Psychological Bulletin, 132* (5), 641–666.

Pearce, J. M., & Bouton, M. E. (2001). Theories of associative learning in animals. *Annual Review of Psychology, 52,* 111–139.

Pierce, T., & Lydon, J. (1998). Priming relational schemas: Effects of contextually activated and chronically accessible interpersonal expectations on responses to a stressful event. *Journal of Personality and Social Psychology, 75* (6), 1441–1448.

Pietrzak, J., Downey, G., & Ayduk, O. (2005). Rejection sensitivity as an interpersonal vulnerability. In M. W. Baldwin (Ed.), *Interpersonal cognition* (pp. 62–84). New York: Guilford Press.

Ratelle, C. F., Baldwin, M. W., & Vallerand, R. J. (2005). On the cued activation of situational motivation. *Journal of Experimental Social Psychology*, *41* (5), 482–487.

Rosenbaum, D. A., Carlson, R. A., & Gilmore, R. O. (2001). Acquisition of intellectual and perceptual-motor skills. *Annual Review of Psychology*, 52, 453–470.

Rusbult, C. E., Lange, P. A., Wildschut, T., Yovetich, N. A., & Verette, J. (2000). Perceived superiority in close relationships: Why it exists and persists. *Journal of Personality and Social Psychology*, 79 (4), 521–545.

Sakellaropoulo, M., & Baldwin, M. W. (2006). The hidden sides of self-esteem: Two dimensions of implicit self-esteem and their relation to narcissistic reactions. *Journal of Experimental Social Psychology* (in press).

Scarvalone, P., Fox, M., & Safran, J. D. (2005). Interpersonal schemas: Clinical theory, research, and implications. In M. W. Baldwin (Ed.), *Interpersonal cognition* (pp. 359–387). New York: Guilford Press.

Shah, J. (2003). The motivational looking glass: How significant others implicitly affect goal appraisals. *Journal of Personality and Social Psychology*, 85 (3), 424–439.

Shoda, Y., & Smith, R. E. (2004). Conceptualizing personality as a cognitive-affective processing system: A framework for models of maladaptive behavior patterns and change. *Behavior Therapy*, 35 (1), 147–165.

Tafarodi, R. W., & Swann, W. B., Jr. (1995). Self-liking and self-competence as dimensions of global self-esteem: Initial validation of a measure. *Journal of Personality Assessment*, 65 (2), 322–342.

Vedhara, K., Hyde, J., Gilchrist, I. D., Tytherleigh, M., & Plummer, S. (2000). Acute stress, memory, attention and cortisol. *Psychoneuroendocrinology*, 25, 535–549.

Wells, A., & Matthews, G. (1994). *Attention and emotion: A clinical perspective*. Hove, UK: Lawrence Erlbaum Associates Ltd.

Williams, M. G., Mathews, A., & MacLeod, C. (1996). The emotional Stroop task and psychopathology. *Psychological Bulletin*, *120* (1), 3–24.

Zayas, V., & Shoda, Y. (2005). Do automatic reactions elicited by thoughts of romantic partner, mother, and self relate to adult romantic attachment? *Personality and Social Psychology Bulletin*, *31* (8), 1011–1025.

Author Index

Subject Index

Page entries for headings with subheadings refer to general aspects of that topic.
Page entries referring to figures and tables appear in **bold**.

Printed in Great Britain
by Amazon

87879429R00192